Vincent Cronin

LOUIS AND ANTOINETTE

THE HARVILL PRESS

LONDON

First published in Great Britain 1974 by Collins Harvill

This paperback edition first published 1996
by The Harvill Press,
84 Thornhill Road,
London NI IRD

1 3 5 7 9 10 8 6 4 2

© Vincent Cronin 1974

Vincent Cronin asserts the moral right to be
identified as the author of this work.

A CIP catalogue record for this book
is available from the British Library.

ISBN 1 86046 102 6

Printed and bound in Great Britain by Butler & Tanner
at Selwood Printing, Burgess Hill

FOR
CHANTAL

Illustrations

Contents

LOUIS AND ANTOINETTE

VINCENT CRONIN is well known for his historical biographies and for his two-volume history of the Renaissance ("Probably the best book that has ever been written on the Renaissance" *Times Educational Supplement*). His other historical biographies include *Louis and Antoinette*, *Catherine, Empress of All the Russias* and *Napoleon*, the last of which has been translated into eight languages and is a standard biography both in Britain and in France ("To present Napoleon plausibly . . . takes nerve, originality, prodigious powers of research and a true historical imagination" Michael Foot, *Standard*). His most recent book is *Paris on the Eve 1900–1914*, a collective portrait of the key figures in art, literature, science and politics in the cultural capital of Europe on the eve of the First World War. His dual biography of *Louis XIV* ("The most sympathetic account of Louis XIV as a man we have" A. L. Rowse), and his biography of *Catherine, Empress of all the Russias* ("A quite overpowering portrait of a great and admirable woman", *Spectator*) are also available as Harvill Paperbacks.

White marble sculptures for the Rambouillet diary, by Pierre Julien. Private collection (*Wildenstein*)

Plates belonging to the Sèvres dinner service commissioned by Lopuis XVI. Windsor Castle (*Reproduced by gracious permission of H.M. the Queen*)

Gold louis d'or issued in 1785 by the Strasbourg mint. Bibliothèque de Strasbourg.

Louis XVI. An unsigned portrait given by the King to Comte de Moussy Lacontour in 1787. Private collection (*Giraudon*)

Honoré de Mirabeau, by Boze. Musée Granet, Aix-en-Provence (*Giraudon*)

The storming of the Bastille. Contemporary drawing (*Mansell Collection*)

The crowd invading the Assembly on 10 August 1792, drawing by Gérard. Louvre (*Archives photographiques*)

Medal commemorating 6 October 1789. Bibliothèque Nationale, cabinet de médailles (*Bibliothèque Nationale*)

Parisian women marching on Versailles. Coloured etching in the Bibliothèque Nationale (*Bibliothèque Nationale*)

Louis XVI, by Ducreux. Musée Carnavalet (*Bulloz*)

The Queen in 1791, by Kucharsky. Château de Versailles (*Bulloz*)

The Execution of Louis XVI. Contemporary mezzotint (*Mansell Collection*)

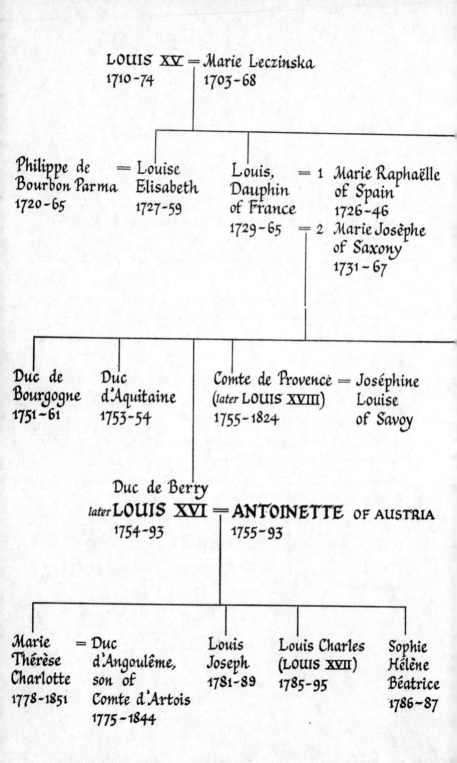

LOUIS **XV** = Marie Leczinska
1710–74   1703–68

Philippe de   = Louise   Louis,   = 1 Marie Raphaëlle
Bourbon Parma   Elisabeth   Dauphin   of Spain
1720–65   1727–59   of France   1726–46
                                1729–65   = 2 Marie Josèphe
                                                 of Saxony
                                                 1731–67

Duc de   Duc   Comte de Provence = Joséphine
Bourgogne   d'Aquitaine   (later LOUIS **XVIII**)   Louise
1751–61   1753–54   1755–1824   of Savoy

                Duc de Berry
            later **LOUIS XVI** = **ANTOINETTE** OF AUSTRIA
                1754–93   1755–93

Marie   = Duc   Louis   Louis Charles   Sophie
Thérèse   d'Angoulême,   Joseph   (LOUIS **XVII**)   Hélène
Charlotte   son of   1781–89   1785–95   Béatrice
1778–1851   Comte d'Artois   1786–87
              1775–1844

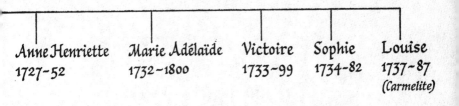

Anne Henriette
1727–52

Marie Adélaïde
1732–1800

Victoire
1733–99

Sophie
1734–82

Louise
1737–87
(Carmelite)

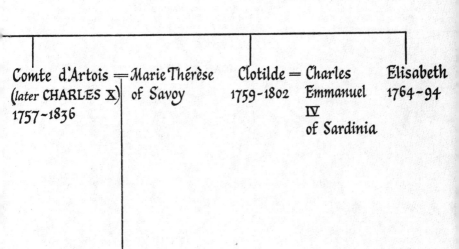

Comte d'Artois = Marie Thérèse
(later CHARLES X) of Savoy
1757–1836

Clotilde = Charles
1759–1802 Emmanuel
IV
of Sardinia

Elisabeth
1764–94

Louis Antoine
Duc d'Angoulême
1775–1844

Charles Ferdinand
Duc de Berry
1778–1820

Preface

THIS is a biography of King Louis XVI and his Queen. I have aimed at a balanced double portrait based on reliable, sometimes unpublished sources, and taking account of latest scholarship.

The Queen is usually referred to as Marie Antoinette. That was her State name, used in official documents, but it was used less during her lifetime than later, under the Restoration, which liked the connotations of Marie. The name by which her family and friends knew the Queen was Antoinette: she signed her letters Antoinette, she was referred to by ordinary Frenchmen as Antoinette and, if Court writings are to be believed, she was called by her husband Antoinette. Almost certainly, too, the Queen thought of herself as Antoinette, and that is why I have chosen to call her that in these pages.

Louis XVI has generally been portrayed as a nonentity or, in the many Lives of the Queen, as an inadequate husband, almost a butt. For reasons that will emerge in the book, he has not had justice done to him. He is too often known simply as the King who wrote 'Rien' in his diary on the day the Bastille fell. He did indeed write 'Rien' and with reason, because it was primarily a hunting diary, and there happened to be no hunt that day.

Antoinette too has been tagged with a bad line: 'If they have no bread, let them eat cake.' She never spoke it: indeed such words are almost inconceivable on anyone's lips in the humanitarian late eighteenth century. They were spoken a century earlier by another Queen, Marie Thérèse, Spanish-born wife of Louis XIV, and were familiar to young Jean Jacques Rousseau in 1737, eighteen years before Antoinette's birth.

The lives of Louis and Antoinette were exceptionally closely linked, and one of the main reasons, paradoxically, is that their union was so improbable. France and the Holy Roman Empire, both claiming the heritage of Rome, had been enemies for 900 years, and during that time no French king had ever taken an Austrian wife (Louis XIII's wife, Anne, was Spanish, 'Anne of

Austria' being a courtesy title). So in marrying Antoinette Louis brought his wife to a country where hatred of Austria was almost as old as France. Louis tried to protect her from it, she sought protection with him, and this made for such a degree of involvement that their lives can hardly be treated apart.

The first writings against Antoinette appeared shortly after her marriage and towards the end of the reign became extraordinarily obscene. In the Bibliothèque Nationale these pamphlets, some illustrated, are hidden away in 'L'Enfer' – Hell; the British Museum, passing no judgment, keeps them in the Private Case. Their effect on the Queen's life was great, and the lies they contain are the source of many later false interpretations. I consider them in due place and, more fully, in Appendix A.

Louis also has suffered from partisan writing, chiefly during and immediately after the Revolution. Most damage was done by an edition of Letters of Louis XVI, published in 1803. The majority are not by Louis at all; they are forgeries by the two editors, Imbert and Babié, and although Babié later confessed to the fraud, they are cited to this day by those who wish to portray Louis under the Revolution as a whimperer.

The marriage too has suffered from being written about on hearsay or partial evidence. Rather than interrupt the narrative, I discuss earlier interpretations of the marriage in Appendix B.

Given the untrustworthy nature of many French sources before and during the Revolution, it becomes imperative to check events or so-called events against the reports of foreign ambassadors. The letters of the Austrian ambassador, Mercy, to Maria Theresa were published, with significant cuts, in 1875 and because they are extremely detailed they have been drawn on heavily by all biographers. But we now know that Mercy was by no means impartial and that, for reasons which will appear in the text, he was biased against Louis. In the Vienna archives there is an unpublished note in Mercy's hand asking the Queen's reader, Vermond, to send false information to Vienna in order to back up Mercy's own false report that the King had yielded to his Ministers, whereas we have documentary proof that on this occasion it was Louis who took the decision and made his Ministers yield.

Mercy's reports, therefore, have to be treated with caution, and I have preferred wherever possible to rely on the dispatches of the English ambassadors, who had no cause to be biased for or against the King. The most important is David Murray, Lord Stormont, ambassador during the first four years of the reign, a man of integrity and perceptiveness.

The most important sources for the reign are the writings of the King and Queen themselves: Louis's boyhood essays, diary, accounts, minutes, speeches and some one hundred authentic letters; Antoinette's letters to her mother and her brother Joseph. Among other first-hand sources is the diary of the abbé de Véri, who lived at Versailles from 1774. A refugee during the Revolution, he hid his 277 notebooks behind a chimney. Forty-seven were gnawed to pieces by rats but the remainder provide a valuable behind-the-scenes record of Louis's government.

England was the vogue under Louis XVI and many English people came to Versailles. Again because they have no political axe to grind, I have drawn on the letters, diaries and other writings of Horace Walpole, David Hume, the Duchess of Northumberland, Countess Spencer and her daughter Duchess Georgiana of Devonshire, Dr Johnson's friend Mrs Thrale, the agricultural expert Arthur Young, Dr John Moore, Dr Edward Rigby and many others, including Thomas Blaikie, gardener to the Comte d'Artois.

I have used manuscript material from the following archives: Hof und Hausstaatsarchiv, Vienna, for Antoinette's letters to her mother, including two key passages from letters in 1773 which were omitted from the so-called complete edition of that correspondence published in 1933 and which set the marriage in a new light; the Archives Nationales for Louis's diary, letters and minutes for the Dauphin's education, also for details about the aftermath of Varennes; the Archives départementales de la Drôme for unpublished parts of Véri's diary, notably for the years 1787–8; the Archivo Histórico Nacional, Madrid, for unpublished letters of Fuentes, Spanish ambassador in France; the Public Record Office for reports of the British ambassadors in Paris; the Chatsworth archives for letters relating to Antoinette, including rare letters from Jules and Gabrielle de Polignac; and the British Museum for the Auckland Papers. My friend, M. Tarbé de Saint-Hardouin, kindly lent me the unpublished memoirs of Théophile Vauchelet, whose father was with Louis in the stenographers' box on 10 August 1792.

A word about the value of money. Inflation had begun under Louis XV and continued into his grandson's reign. Philip Thicknesse wrote in 1777: 'I found no greater alteration in Paris, after ten years' absence from it, than the prodigious difference of expense; most articles, I think, are one third dearer, and many double.' In France generally purchasing power between 1735 and 1789 fell by 20%.

The unit of currency was the livre: 20 sols or sous = 1 livre; 3 livres = 1 écu; 24 livres = 1 louis d'or. A 4 lb. loaf of bread cost around 8 sols while the paperbound plays Antoinette bought for her Trianon library, and which after 1784 she could not afford to bind, each cost about 1 livre 4 sols. The best seat at the Opera cost 10 livres. Linguet estimated that a man needed 300 livres a year to satisfy his material needs. Dr Portal, a fashionable physician, earned 34,000 livres annually, while in 1789 State revenue totalled 475 million livres. Though no exact equivalent is possible, it would be roughly true to say that with one livre you could buy in 1780 what £1, or U.S. $1.65, would buy in 1989.

Finally I wish to thank the following: the Duke of Devonshire for permission to quote from the Chatsworth Family papers, the Duc de Castries, the late Comte Wladimir d'Ormesson, Madame P. Girault de Coursac, whose valuable book, *L'éducation d'un roi*, I read after I had completed most of my own research: she has helped me on several points of detail; Monsieur Jean Egret, Monsieur Delafosse, director of the Archives des Yvelines, Madame Simone Poignant for etiquette under Louis XV, Mr P. Trevor-Roper for information about myopia, the staff of the London Library, and Mrs Barbara Lowe for her careful typing of the book.

Versailles and its Master

THE Château of Versailles, in the middle of the eighteenth century, was an unusually large country house of brick and pale grey stone belonging to the King of France, Louis XV. The main block, a third of a mile long, was flanked by numerous other buildings, the whole forming a many-faceted complex with varied functions.

The house had begun as a hunting lodge, and one of its functions still was to provide the King and his friends with good hunting. Four or five times a week the King would ride to hounds; the trees echoed to the wail and whoop of *trompes de chasse*, as he and his suite galloped after the stag or wild boar. His ancestors in the dense oak forests of Gaul had kept the land clear of dangerous animals; now those actions were ritualized, but the King's shedding of wild blood still possessed symbolic importance.

No less important than stables and kennels was the chapel. Here the King had been christened and married, here he heard Mass and, alone among laymen, received Communion under the forms of both bread and wine. Versailles was the seat of a divine-right monarch and, aware of it or not, the King derived his title to rule from the supreme royalty of Christ. The mighty hunter was also the anointed of the Lord.

Versailles was also a billet for officers in the seventeen squadrons of the King's Household Troops, Gendarmes, Swiss Guards, Bodyguards, Musketeers – Grey or Black according to the colour of their horses – each wearing a distinctive uniform of blue, white and red in different combinations. Their function was to defend the King from his enemies, and every month he passed one or more squadrons in review.

When they retired, army officers filled many of the important posts at Court, such as marshal of the diplomatic corps and governor of the royal princes. Altogether there were about a thousand courtiers at Versailles, attended by as many servants. But there were too many officers chasing too few jobs, and this made for frustration and faction.

The courtiers were noblemen, but it should not be thought that the nobility was a closed caste. Any Frenchman whatever his birth might be ennobled by purchasing one of some four thousand offices. However, there was no great rush to obtain the privilege of wearing a sword, for once ennobled, a man might not engage in the lucrative professions of manufacturing or trade, which the commoners insisted were their preserve.

Because their traditional role was service in the army or navy, which were poorly paid professions, noblemen were exempt from the *taille*, one of three direct taxes paid by Frenchmen. This was an esteemed honour, but of very little financial worth. Many of the nobility were poor, and the real income of nearly all was declining, for while commoners could increase their wealth quickly through manufacturing and business, the nobles were debarred from doing so. This fact is basic to Versailles, hence the point of Talleyrand's quip: 'A Court is an assembly of noble and distinguished beggars.'

The King and his courtiers being cultivated men, Versailles was a centre for the arts. Here new plays and operas received their first performance, including the comedies of Goldoni of Venice, resident writer and Italian master to the King's daughters. The chapel had one of the best orchestras and choirs in France. Paintings by Claude Lorraine, Poussin, Watteau, Nattier and a hundred masters were displayed in the State apartments, a new lot every year. In answer to fashion, skilled craftsmen turned out a profusion of marquetry tables and delicately curved chairs, of cabinets and bookcases; for an exacting clientele dressmakers and jewellers, silversmiths and enamellers, pyrotechnicians and pâtissiers expended their artistry.

Versailles was a garden. Le Nôtre's living geometry – circular pools set off by lines of box bushes and quincunxes of trees – had to be kept trim; each spring the flower-beds patterned like brocade were replanted, each winter the orange trees taken in to the warmth; there were vegetables and fruit to be grown for the great house, there were ponds to be kept stocked with goldfish, there were gondolas on the lake to be gilded every season, and a whole Olympus of statuary to be kept immortal.

Versailles was a wild-life reserve. Among the animals in its park were lions, tigers, camels, dromedaries, a rhinoceros and a she-elephant – a particular favourite of the King, who even on winter days would trudge through the snow to pat her wrinkled head.

Versailles was a shopping centre. Near the main staircase shop-keepers from the town had set up wooden stalls, and though many complained that they were unsightly and really must be removed, from year to year they remained, selling trinkets, millinery, the *Gazette de France* and – for not all courtiers were young – trusses. Here under the counter you could buy Voltaire's latest satire – though it had been condemned by Parlement and copies burned by the King's executioner.

Versailles was a warren of underground presses. At least a dozen important courtiers owned a press and enough type to print their own invitations, the facile verses they wrote for their mistresses, and short political tracts. These presses were also arsenals which could turn out wounding libels and scurrilous satires.

Versailles was a kind of theatre, where King and courtiers performed a small repertoire of traditional plays entitled *Le Lever*, *La Réception des Ambassadeurs* and so on – indeed, when he appeared in public the King was said to be *en représentation*; yet Versailles equally was a kind of prison, where the King and his courtiers were shut off from the ordinary free life of Frenchmen.

Versailles was a stud, where the stallion King, pampered and fussed over, produced progeny. Versailles was the seat of government, the administrative centre of the world's most powerful state. Here the King ruled with the help of Ministers who lived and worked in the same house as he and his courtiers. The Council Chamber was only half a minute from boudoirs and ballroom, and if he wished to stay in office a Minister must excel not only at writing dispatches but at turning a neat compliment.

Versailles was also in many ways an illusion. Its god-like master, who simple Frenchmen supposed had only to lift a finger to secure justice, only to sign his name to make them happy, was a man like them, who before he could do good must first master himself and then act with and through others. Versailles indeed exemplified Aristotle's perennial mystery of the one and the many. It housed a thousand sophisticated Frenchmen of varied views and one King who, in a sense, embodied all. How could one man speak for many? Yet, if he did not speak, how could the many act in unison?

For all its complexity, there was a definite mood at Versailles in mid-eighteenth century, as unmistakable as a house's smell. What it was can be seen from one small detail and one short incident.

During the reign of Louis XIV there had been plenty of hunting dogs at Versailles, but no cats. The King would not permit cats, which were then associated with the devil and with witches. Since then Versailles had changed. Cold marble halls had been divided into small panelled rooms, the stiff furniture was now curved and softly upholstered, each apartment had its own kitchen, and behind the wainscoting there scurried mice. 'Gothic' prejudices against cats were smiled at in this enlightened age, and cats were admitted not only to catch the mice but to share in the happiness everyone was bent on finding.

The present King, Louis XV, was very fond of cats. As a boy while sitting silent at Council meetings he would play with a cat called Charlotte, and now he owned a particularly beautiful favourite. If one asked what lay behind the high, pedimented, velvet-curtained windows in the middle of the first floor, what in fact was the centre, the ultimate secret of Versailles at this time, one might find an answer in front of the fireplace of the Council Chamber. There, on a crimson damask cushion, lay the King's cat, a white Persian, very plump, with long silky fur, contentedly purring.

On a certain evening in the middle of the reign two courtiers happened to be in the Council Chamber, looking for some distraction. One of them bet the other that he could make the King's cat dance and, his bet accepted, fetched from his room a bottle of strong scent called 'A Thousand Flowers'. Uncorking the bottle, he poured a few drops of the stinging scent on to the paws of the sleeping cat. It was a cruel thing to do, but courtiers at Versailles would rather be cruel than bored. Pained by the spirits in the scent, the cat bounded from its cushion, jumped on to the table, miaowing piteously. There it began to dance up and down, to caper and turn somersaults, while the two courtiers laughed delightedly. Suddenly the door opened and in came the King. He demanded an explanation, then said coldly: 'Gentlemen, you may remain here. But if you wish to amuse yourselves, don't do so at the expense of my cat.'

A beautiful stranger, peaceful and contented, is tormented by bored courtiers: it was to happen again, but the second time without a happy ending.

The cat's owner was a tall, handsome man, regal, graceful in his movements and with lazy cat eyes. He had lost both parents at the age of two and grown up without affection or discipline into a shy person, less at ease with men than with women and animals. One of his pleasures was feeding the hens, pigeons and rabbits he kept on the palace roof, another roasting, grinding and preparing his own coffee. Public affairs, except for foreign policy, bored him. He was a boudoir King, happier choosing a dress for his mistress than drafting an edict for his people.

In law the French monarchy was an absolute monarchy; the monarchy and the state were one and the King's will was ultimately the supreme law. Consequently the nobility and the Parlements, more or less subordinated and excluded from effective participation in real political power, were inevitably in perpetual opposition to the monarchy.

The fundamental evil of the day was an old-fashioned system of taxation that hit the poor harder than the rich. The nobility and Parlements persistently attacked the monarchy on this point, although at heart they did not want changes made in a system that favoured them, and their attacks kept the Government dangerously weak. When he began ruling personally, Louis had a prime duty to reform taxation by shifting some of the burden from the people to the clergy, who were untaxed, and to the rich nobility, who could have borne a greater share. Louis kept delaying this reform. In 1748 he came close to it when his Minister, Machault, announced a 5% tax on all incomes without exception. It would have required only reasonable firmness on Louis's part to see the measure through, but when the bishops, as well as the rich nobles, opposed it, and the Queen, his daughters and all the Court dévots pleaded with him to leave the clergy immune, Louis yielded weakly and dropped the reform.

This was a serious failure, and Louis made it worse by spending heavily. In 1741, yielding to the military men at Versailles and his mistress, Madame de Châteauroux, who wished him to play Mars to her Venus, Louis plunged France into the long War of the Austrian Succession, which had to be paid for with higher taxation. When finally an unadvantageous peace was signed, instead of economizing, Louis built, for a new mistress, the Petit Trianon and other expensive houses. The French people, who had once given him the name Well-Beloved, were beginning now to associate Louis with favourites, extravagance and indecision, while the Parlements profited from his lack of interest in public affairs to increase their pretensions. 'The Government is no longer esteemed or respected,' wrote a former Minister in mid-century, 'and what is worse, it is digging its own grave.'

Louis's wife was Marie Leczinska, daughter of Stanislas, a Polish nobleman elected King of Poland in 1704 and subsequently deposed. She had no royal blood in her veins and was socially much inferior to Louis. She was also six and a half years older than he. She was a good woman but dressed badly in queer-looking furs and peacock plumes, and she declined to put on rouge. She did her duty by rearing a son as well as six daughters, but she could not – no one expected her to – win the King's love.

The Queen, however, adored her husband and suffered when he began spending long hours in the company of Madame de Pompadour. The Pompadour was much more amusing than the Queen and among the means she found for distracting Louis from state affairs was a parrot named Vert-Vert who, jealous of the King's cat, would screech gutter names at the proud purring creature, while the Pompadour and Louis went into gales of laughter.

What was the Queen to do? She was by nature fearful, particularly of mice and of ghosts. When the King's earlier mistress, Madame de Châteauroux, died suddenly, the Queen lay awake half the night, thinking each sound was the ghost of Madame de Châteauroux, until finally her maid said, 'Even if she did come back, would it be *your* room she'd come to?' at which the Queen laughed so much that for a little while she forgot her fright. Such a woman plainly lacked the courage and wit to prevent Madame de Pompadour becoming mistress of Versailles; this indeed eventually happened while the Queen declined into a Polish gloom, than which there is none deeper. She took to wearing a black mantilla and embroidering altar cloths while Joinville's biography of an earlier Louis – the one who had been a saint – was read to her by Moncrif, her Reader and author of an early, delightful book about cats. She created a fashion for *belles mignonnes*: skulls that one gazed at to convince oneself of the vanity of worldly things. Hers was ornamented with tresses of hair and lit with candles, and it was said to be the skull of a famous courtesan, Ninon de Lenclos.

The King and Queen had one son: a tall, dark young man, fat in early life not from overeating but from some metabolic imbalance. Like his mother, he was high-principled and religious; he had his father's intelligence and had received a good education. But he was inclined to Polish glooms and to go to extremes; the King judged him correctly in saying 'His temper is Polish – hasty and changeable.' One day, out hunting, he had the misfortune to cause the death of his squire, Chambors. The death was an accident, no one was to blame, but the Dauphin reacted characteristically. He never again rode to hounds, and even years afterwards would say, 'I can still see poor Chambors' body running with blood.'

The Dauphin decided instead to take violin lessons from Mondonville, one of the King's violinists and a good composer. But Guignon, first violinist of the Chamber and of the Chapel, known as 'the king of violinists', protested on the grounds that he was senior to Mondonville and was already violin master to the Dauphin's sisters. It was a typical Versailles situation, with protocol omnipotent, and the Dauphin, although he had a strong will, was obliged to learn the violin from Guignon, whom he liked much less than Mondonville.

The Dauphin also performed well on the clavichord and had a good *basso profondo* voice. He commissioned Royer, his clavichord master, to set Jean Baptiste Rousseau's pious 'ode to Fortune' to music, and made quite a name at private concerts by singing this difficult forty-minute piece.

The musical moody Dauphin was rather scorned by the hard-riding courtiers of Versailles, but on Tuesday, 9 February 1747 he became the centre of interest, for that evening he was to escort his bride to his wedding ball. In preparation for this, as darkness fell, servants went along the main façade of Versailles lighting rows of earthenware pots containing tallow and wax, candles in triangular frames, fairy lights in coloured paper lanterns, even concealed bonfires in the garden grottoes; and Versailles became a palace of light.

This light came to a dazzling focus in the nearly new ballroom. Its crystal chandeliers held hundreds of candles, their flickering flames reflected in the gilded woodwork and row upon row of looking-glasses. Here, at six, the guests began to arrive, showing their invitation cards decorated with garlands and cupids, signed by Monsieur de Bonneval, administrator of the King's Little Pleasures. Men wore powdered wigs, embroidered silk or velvet suits, silk stockings and buckled shoes, with a sword at their hip. Ladies wore low-cut silk or brocade dresses stretched wide over panniers, with a train according to rank. Every lady – it was a feature of Versailles – wore on each cheek a perfectly round patch of bright rouge, precisely three inches across, quite stark, not shaded with the colouring of the face, as odd in its way as Mohawk war paint.

Once gathered, the guests waited expectantly for the Dauphin. His first wife, red-headed Marie Raphaëlle, daughter of the King of Spain, had died in childbirth seven months ago, and the Dauphin, who loved her deeply, had vowed he would never re-marry. The courtiers, murmuring sympathetically, exchanged knowing looks and sought an eligible princess. It was Maréchal Maurice de Saxe, France's best soldier, who suggested the daughter of his half-brother, Augustus III, Elector of Saxony and King of Poland. Augustus was only a moderately good King, being more interested in music and painting than in decrees, and his wife, daughter of the Emperor of Austria, spent an undue amount of time at her prie-dieu, but what was wanted was health and fertility. Augustus and his Queen were robust and had ten children, while Augustus's father had knocked up a half-century of bastards.

At six-thirty the King arrived, followed by the Queen, happy as always to be with her husband. Then came the Dauphin in a gold-embroidered suit and his fifteen-year-old bride in a long white and silver gown. The guests found fault with Marie Josèphe's nose, not sufficiently thin, her lips, which were judged too full, and the way she leaned slightly forward when she walked, but they liked her pretty chestnut hair, and her lively blue eyes and her smile. 'She is not beautiful,' Madame de Pompadour noted, 'but she is graceful and has a certain something that pleases more than beauty.'

Because of a chilblain on her foot, Marie Josèphe could not dance, so the Dauphin opened the ball with his sister Anne Henriette. They danced in the centre of the seated guests to music provided by an orchestra of 150 players, and were followed on to the floor by the princes and princesses, each in turn according to rank. Then the King from his armchair named gentlemen and ladies, including the Pompadour, to dance minuets. In all, twenty were danced, then came an interval for refreshments, and finally two contredanses, or English country dances, which were becoming very popular although, as Horace Walpole noted, at the French Court they were 'encumbered by the long trains, longer tresses and hoops.'

These balls were the most beautiful events to take place at Versailles, the ladies' diamonds flashing as they turned in the stately measures of the minuet, so that the figures too seemed composed of light; people talked of them for weeks afterwards and they became the subjects of engravings.

The ball ended early, at nine, and was followed by a small dinner for the bridegroom and bride at a horseshoe table in the Queen's stiflingly hot ante-room. After dinner the King and Queen led the young couple to the Dauphin's apartments, on the ground floor overlooking the Parterre du Midi. Watched by the King and Queen and over a hundred courtiers, her ladies removed the Dauphine's jewellery, shoes and ball dress. At this point, leaving the Queen to hand her her nightdress when the moment came, Louis led the male courtiers into the Dauphin's dressing-room, where he watched his son undress, and handed him his nightshirt. That his Majesty should deign to attend on his son underlined the importance of this wedding night.

The Dauphin and his bride then went to the Dauphine's bedroom and got into the curtained four-poster that had earlier been blessed and sprinkled with holy water by a bishop, with prayers that it might prove bountiful. Then the curtains were pulled back, as in a theatre, and the King and Queen and courtiers scrutinized the young couple seated between the sheets. 'She looked quite attractive in her nightcap,' one courtier noticed, 'and rather embarrassed, but less so than the Dauphin.' At the King's suggestion, Maurice de Saxe passed through the ruelle and whispered a reassuring phrase in the bride's ear. Then all the courtiers withdrew, and last of all the King.

The Dauphin found himself in the same room, with the same furniture, where his first wife had died. It was of red-haired Marie Raphaëlle he was thinking and their happiness together, whereas the Saxon girl beside him was a stranger, first met two days ago. A tougher man might have dismissed the past, but the Dauphin was inclined to take things to heart and, besides, he was young for his seventeen years. Overwrought by the festivities, by dinner in a stifling room, and by the heartlessness of a system which coupled princes and princesses like livestock, he began to cry. It was an awkward moment for Marie Josèphe, but instead of being offended she encouraged the Dauphin to give vent to his feelings. 'Your tears,' she told him, 'show me the kind of affection I can hope one day to win.' The certain something noticed by the Pompadour was a loving heart.

With a soldier's bluntness Saxe wrote to the bride's father: 'In spite of the Dauphin's efforts nothing happened last night; the net result was a lot of fuss and neither of them slept a wink.'

For a long time to come nothing happened. Courtiers whispered that the Dauphin had been sexually excited by his first wife's red hair, which was believed to have aphrodisiac qualities, and could find nothing to rouse him in this piece of Dresden china, but the truth was more complicated. The Dauphin had fallen under his mother's puritan influence. Whenever he passed a theatre, he would make the sign of the cross; when he first saw the Pompadour he put out his tongue at her and even when travelling in the same carriage refused to speak a word to her; he had also inherited Marie Leczinska's Polish awe of, and respect for, the dead. As a result the Dauphin seems to have thought that by making love to Marie Josèphe he would be betraying his adored Marie Raphaëlle, just as his father, in making love to the Pompadour, was betraying his adored mother.

The Dauphine suffered quietly, signing a letter to her brother '*Marie Josèphe la triste.*' It looked as though this marriage, like Louis XV's, would prove a failure. And then, unexpectedly, the Dauphin matured; the positive side of his character came uppermost. Three years after the wedding he and Marie Josèphe had their first child, a daughter, followed in 1751 by a son. But it was only in the fifth year of their marriage that Marie Josèphe truly won her husband's heart.

The Dauphin then contracted the dread disease of smallpox and Marie Josèphe decided that she would nurse her husband herself: an innovation at Versailles. In a plain dress she organized the sickroom in a practical manner and when the doctor called, a certain Pousse new to Court, he told the attendants, 'Do as this little woman says, for she understands perfectly what is required.' Then he turned to her. 'What's your name, my good woman?'

The Dauphin kept calling, 'Pépa! Pépa!' Dr Pousse thought he was delirious until told that this was Marie Josèphe's pet name. On three hours' sleep a night she nursed him safely through his dangerous illness and won his entire affection.

The Dauphin and Dauphine lived quietly in a backwater of Versailles, away from the Pompadour's flashy main stream. A courtier recalls visiting them in their simple one-windowed living-room, the Dauphine stitching embroidery, the Dauphin at his desk, 'stacked with the best books, new ones every week', both so open and unceremonious they were 'just like a bourgeois couple'. The Dauphin was barred by the King from speaking in Council or leading an army; whence more Polish gloom, which might have led to bitterness and a rift but for Pépa's sweet influence. Although her father had driven the Queen's father from the throne of Poland, she won over Marie Leczinska, and was treated as a daughter both by her and Louis. She managed also to keep peace with the Pompadour.

The Dauphin's and Dauphine's son born in 1751, called the Duc de Bourgogne, enjoyed good health, but a second son, born in 1753, died in infancy of whooping cough, and in an age when only one in two children reached maturity, the line was as yet far from secure. When in the summer of 1754 Marie Josèphe was again expecting a child, great interest attached to the coming birth.

The Duc de Bourgogne's governess, Madame de Marsan, would also be governess of the new baby. She was a most important person, with the right to sit on a chair in the presence of royalty and to use an oval, not just a round, silver chamber-pot. It was she who chose the layette, including eight pairs of sheets, and a silver set for making the baby's gruel, comprising two milk pots, a box for flour and a box for salt, the whole when not in use kept shut with a lock, for security reasons.

'At four in the morning of 23 August the Dauphine, thinking she had colic, got up quickly, without waking her husband or calling anyone . . . Afterwards, as she returned to bed, the Dauphin woke; he rang for servants and, as the pains increased, called the obstetrician.' At a quarter to seven, in the palace of Versailles, Marie Josèphe gave birth to a boy.

The King, who was hunting at Choisy, hurried to see this second surviving grandson, and was pleased to find him bigger and plumper than Pépa's previous children. He decided the boy should have the honorary title of Duc de Berry, and by this name he would be known until, in boyhood, he came to be christened publicly. Meanwhile he was baptized privately – *ondoyé* – invested with the blue sash of the Order of the Holy Spirit and carried to his own apartment by Madame de Marsan. When darkness fell a firework display was given, for which the King lit the fuse, a little pleasure of which he was very fond.

Every day for a fortnight representatives of one of the guilds of Paris came to perform a festive dance in the Marble Courtyard, to shout 'Long live the King, the Dauphin and our new prince,' and to present the swaddled Duc de Berry with one of their products: a loaf of bread, a barrel, a hat, a broom and so on; afterwards they received a sum of gold from the King. Yet despite all the celebrations, being a baby at Versailles was not much fun. According to the Duc de Berry's aunt, 'The wet-nurse's only function is to suckle the child when brought to her; she may not touch it. There are cradle-rockers and other ladies whose job that is, but they may not take orders from the wet-nurse. There are set hours for giving the child exercise, three or four times a day. When the hour strikes, even if the child is sleeping, it is woken up for exercise.'

It soon became clear that the Duc de Berry was getting insufficient milk. He was a big child with a hefty appetite, and the wet-nurse had had her baby only three weeks before: too soon, it was believed, for her to provide abundant milk. On 5 September the Duc de Luynes confided to his diary: 'The wet-nurse has great trouble in giving the child milk; Madame de Marsan is doing everything possible to have her changed [there were six wet-nurses in reserve]; she several times informed the King; the Queen is very annoyed that no change has been made; the Dauphin too finds it disgraceful, yet nothing is done.'

It was an all too familiar cry at Versailles: 'nothing is done,' because of protocol. Slowly the dark truth emerged. The extremely well-paid post of wet-nurse fell within the responsibility of the Minister of the Household, the Comte de Saint-Florentin, a member of the King's pleasure-seeking set, and he had given it to one of his numerous girl-friends. Not until mid-September was this unsatisfactory person packed home. For the first three weeks of his life, in the richest palace in the world, the King's grandson went hungry.

The Duc de Berry was weaned at eighteen months. Again he gave cause for anxiety. He would not eat, he cried, he lost weight. This time his mother took things firmly in hand. She called in a Swiss doctor, Tronchin, scorned by Court physicians on account of his unorthodox methods, for Tronchin believed not in bleeding but in perspiration, and he had actually told a duchess who complained of the vapours to get out of bed and *do* something, such as sweep her room. Tronchin examined Berry, found that he was cutting four big teeth, and packed him off for the summer to the bracing fresh air of Meudon. His mother visited him there every afternoon: he returned in September eating well and brimming with health.

When Berry was one year old, his mother gave birth to another son, the Comte de Provence; when he was three to her last surviving son, the Comte d'Artois; and when he was four to a daughter. Meanwhile his elder sister died, and although another sister was to be born in 1764, throughout his childhood Berry was the second in a family of four boys and one girl.

Everyone's attention was focused on the eldest son, the Duc de Bourgogne, a small child with fine features and lively black eyes. He was extremely precocious – at seven he presented to the King a little book of Geometry Problems compiled by himself – and also extremely self-assured. One New Year's Day the ambassador of the Order of Malta offered him homage, adding, 'My Lord, we hope that the diplomatic corps will be presenting you its good wishes in the same way eighty years from now.' Bourgogne gave him a stern look. 'Why not a hundred?' Another time he was handed a petition which contained a eulogy of his gifts of mind and character. He let the paper drop on the main stairway, telling his tutor to leave it there. 'Someone will find it and read it. The contents will get about.'

In April 1760 this paragon of princehood developed an abscess of the thigh, which caused him to limp. Surgeons performed a painful operation, which Bourgogne bore bravely, but his thigh did not heal. The unfortunate boy had tuberculosis of the bones and lymphatic glands: the disease known as king's evil because the King's touch could sometimes – but not in this case – cure it. He was obliged to give up his lessons, and to remain in bed or in a wheelchair.

Berry was then turning six. Normally he would have remained with soft, reassuring Madame de Marsan until the age of seven, when royal children left the nursery and were handed over to the gentlemen charged with their education. But his parents decided that Berry should make this transition immediately so that he could be a companion to poor Bourgogne.

So Berry was wakened one morning and, instead of putting on his swansdown dress, made to stand naked in front of the royal doctors and surgeons, who tapped, measured, knocked and peered at every part of his body. They found him normal and healthy, and wrote this down in a long report. Then he was dressed for the first time in boy's clothes, with breeches and buckled diamond shoes; Madame de Marsan led him to the King's apartment, and formally handed him over to the King. With equal formality the King then entrusted Berry to his Governor, a Breton duke named La Vauguyon, who led the boy to the Prince's apartments, much grander than the nursery, one room having a dais where the boys could receive ambassadors.

Berry may have suffered from this early move to the world of men. He was certainly to suffer from the next eight months. Most of that time he spent in Bourgogne's sick-room, wholly subordinated to the needs and wishes of his brilliant brother. Sometimes the two played soldiers, sometimes cards. Bourgogne invariably won and if Berry happened to look downcast, delivered a stiff little lecture on how to be a good loser.

As his illness grew worse, Bourgogne developed an ostentatious piety. Every week he read aloud to Berry a list of his recent sins, being careful also to mention those failings he had corrected.

Another embarrassing moment occurred when a courtier asked Bourgogne whether, like Esau, he would sell his birthright for a mess of pottage: in other words, whether he would let Berry inherit the throne in exchange for Berry's good health. 'Never,' he replied. 'Even if I had to spend all my life in this sick-bed.'

All the while Bourgogne was getting paler and thinner, eaten away by the disease. Presently it infected Berry too, though only his lungs. In Lent 1761 he had to go to bed with a high fever, racking cough and spitting of blood. His robust little body carried him through, but on the eve of Easter 1761 Bourgogne died. For his parents and the King, who had thought very highly of him, it was a terrible blow.

As the shock receded, people at Versailles began for the first time to look with interest at Berry. They saw a boy with a white skin, fair hair and big blue eyes, the lashes of which were thick and dark. He was very tall for his six and a half years, and rather reserved. Though his brown-eyed brothers, Provence and Artois, were chatterboxes, Berry spoke little. But he seemed to feel things. When the time came for a dear visiting aunt to return home, Provence told her how very, very sorry he was; Berry said nothing, but there were tears in his eyes.

He was now a future King of France. But he had been brought up without the adulation usually given to future Kings. He had received no flattery, no petitions eulogizing his qualities. On the contrary, all through his formative years he had been put in the shade, treated as a foil for brilliant Bourgogne. As a result, he was that rare creature, a prince with a poor opinion of himself.

When Berry was seven, another gala event took place, as important in its way as the Dauphin's wedding ball. This was the christening of the Dauphin's four children: and to save money – for there was a new war on – the Dauphin made it a single ceremony. Dressed in a silver brocade suit trimmed with Spanish lace, Berry was escorted by his father to the King's study, and from there, in procession, to the white and gilded chapel. Under Coypel's ceiling of *God in Glory* they were joined by the Queen, no longer young but still a-flutter to be with her husband. The King and Queen seated themselves in armchairs, while the Dauphin, the Dauphine and their children took elbow-chairs beside them. At a distance were the princes and princesses on folding stools, and in the balcony ambassadors and their wives.

His parents had decided to call Berry after St Louis, famous for

CHAPTER 2

The Boy

AT the time of Berry's christening the most influential lady at Versailles was still the Pompadour; and the most influential man, after the King, was her protégé the Duc de Choiseul, Minister of Foreign Affairs. Choiseul came of an old Lorraine family, which considered itself quite the equal of the Bourbons. He was short, round-faced, with baby blue eyes and a turned-up nose, but he carried himself like a prince, held his head in the air, wore red trousers and spoke with total assurance. He was immensely rich and his place at Chanteloup virtually a palace, with its own orchestra and troupe of actors. In the park stood a seven-storey pagoda on which were carved the names of 210 princes, dukes and other dignitaries whom Choiseul had entertained. For pressing the table linen there was a special cylindrical ironing machine – the first in France. There was a piggery of fifty prize pigs, and when Choiseul enquired how they were his pigman would reply: 'My lord does them a great honour; they are all in splendid health.'

'Splendid' was the key to Choiseul. He had followed a splendid career in the army with an equally splendid one as ambassador. His love-affairs were as splendid as they were numerous. He had a beautiful little wife who adored him and a beautiful tall mistress, Madame de Brionne, by birth a Rohan, the family which considered itself second only to God. He was a connoisseur of art and spent on a snuff-box what lesser men spent on a mural. He was witty: 'The watches of Ministers are always six months slow.' He was everything a King's servant should be except prudent.

Choiseul spent heavily. When two thousand villagers on the shore of Lake Geneva, peeved by an ordinance of the Swiss Government, asked permission to cross into France and settle in a spot called Versoix, Choiseul announced a characteristically reckless plan: Versoix would rise as a great commercial port, a monument to French genius, and it would be called Port Pompadour. The scheme proved a flop, and Voltaire quipped:

his justice and compassion, and also much admired by the Queen. But instead of calling him plain Louis – which now had other connotations – they were going to make the link especially close by giving Berry the same two names as the saint: Louis Auguste.

The christening began. Holding a lighted candle encircled with silver moiré, Berry knelt in the sanctuary to be blessed and anointed by the mitred Grand Almoner, to hear the words 'Ludovicus Augustus' and to rise as Louis Auguste. Provence was christened next, receiving the names of Louis Stanislas Xavier; then Artois, who was named Charles; and last their sister, who became Marie Adélaïde Clotilde Xavière.

It seems to have been a happy occasion. The King was pleased because he liked small children; the Queen because she enjoyed religious services, the longer the better; the Dauphine was pleased at seeing the family united if only for an afternoon; the Dauphin because he found an occasion for moralizing: when signing the parish register he pointed out the last entry, the child of a Versailles workman: 'In the eyes of men,' he told his sons, 'you will one day be greater than this child; but if he is better morally then in the eyes of God he will be greater.'

As for Louis Auguste, it seems likely that he too in his reserved little way was pleased. Having renounced the devil, he and hi brothers were immediately faced with delectable temptation in th form of fruit drinks, ices, platefuls of cake and taffeta-lined baske beflowered and beribboned, containing caskets of sweets a sugared almonds. Each child received four dozen boxes of suga almonds for members of his household, and of course there plenty of the delicious pink and white ovals left over for the chi themselves as they trooped upstairs, proud of their bran names, to the highlight of the day: a marionette show in thei little theatre.

Envoyez-nous des Amphions
Ou vos peines seront perdues.
A Versoix nous avons des rues
Mais nous n'avons pas de maisons.[1]

Far more disastrous for France was Choiseul's recklessness in foreign affairs. France's overseas interests had long clashed with those of her traditional enemy, England, and in 1756 a probably unavoidable war broke out between the two rivals. At the same time France lost her traditional ally, Prussia, which, under Frederick the Great, had begun to pursue an independent line. The sensible thing would have been to disengage from Continental affairs until the war with England ended. Instead, on Choiseul's advice, abetted by the Pompadour, Louis signed an alliance with another traditional enemy, Austria, and thus had to fight simultaneously an overseas and a Continental war. France was not equal to such a contest, and the Seven Years' War proved an unprecedented disaster. In 1757 when news came of the battle of Rossbach, the most ignominious defeat ever sustained by France, the Pompadour murmured to Louis, 'After us the deluge.' But the deluge came in their lifetime, when by the peace of 1763 France lost Canada and India, was obliged to dismantle the fortifications of Dunkirk and – a terrible humiliation – to allow an English commissioner to live permanently in Dunkirk to see that they were never rebuilt.

The effects on France were profound. Trade declined and prices rose, while taxes remained high. Opposition hardened and the name of Antoinette de Pompadour became hated. At Versailles morale fell among the courtier officers, many of whom lapsed into frivolity or cynicism. The King tried to forget. Hiding his identity under the name of a Polish count, and fortified by a mixture known as 'General Lamotte's drops', he would slink off to his private brothel, the Parc aux Cerfs. Returning at dawn, he would grind and prepare himself a cup of strong coffee. 'What would the world be without coffee?' And then, sadly, 'After all, what *is* the world – with coffee?'

Increasingly Versailles became polarized: at one pole the King, his mistress and the fast set – Choiseul, who attended Mass with the latest saucy novel hidden in his missal, and Richelieu, procurer-in-chief who took milk baths and shod his horses with silver. At the

[1]Amphion played his lyre with such magic skill that stones moved of their own accord to form the wall of Thebes. 'Send us some Amphions or all your efforts will be in vain. At Versoix we have streets, but not a single house.'

other pole were the Dauphin, his sisters, the Queen, certain steady courtiers, and the priests.

The Dauphin was still barred by his father from speaking in Council. He was deeply upset about the state of France and opposed Choiseul, particularly his suppression of the Jesuits in 1764, but he lacked the power and qualities of leadership to be more than an armchair politician. 'Repulsed, fettered, humiliated,' he wrote in 1762 to his friend the Bishop of Verdun, 'I live for my children, who are my sole consolation.'

The world in which Berry spent his boyhood was therefore peculiarly complex. Beyond Versailles, from the great land of France, ominous rumblings were heard, particularly from Paris, where the King did not dare set foot, even for a day. In Versailles court life continued its dazzling round of balls, operas, hunts and receptions. But in the Dauphin's apartments, a house within a house, all was sober and serious: books, music, early to bed, and the Dauphin's personal supervision of his sons' schooling.

Berry did his lessons in a ground-floor room facing south, upholstered in crimson damask. He worked seven hours a day. In Latin he began with Cornelius Nepos and went on to Tacitus, whom he admired and whose concise, powerful style was to influence his own. In History, which fell into three parts – Biblical, classical and French – he showed a retentive memory, especially for dates, and this became one of his best subjects. In Physics he had a first-rate teacher, the abbé Nollet, and at twelve and a half had mastered the properties of gases. Mathematics was made interesting by problems from real life such as this one, set for Berry when he was eleven: 'On 10 February 1766 three princes have a combined age of 30 years, 11 days; the second is 1 year, 2 months and 24 days younger than the first; and the third 1 year, 10 months and 22 days younger than the second. Calculate the age of each of the princes.' The correct answer corresponded with the ages of Berry, Provence and Artois.

Berry's favourite subject was Geography. At eight, he specially asked for and was given an atlas of the world; at ten he was able to fill in 29 out of 30 place names on a blank map of Italy and Savoy, the only one he forgot being Lake Annecy – then part of Savoy. His teacher was the great Philippe Buache, an expert on marine charts, and under Buache's guidance at the age of eleven Berry wrote a 58-page *Description of the Forest of Compiègne*. The first part consists of a list of the main geographical features of the forest, while the second part is a guide to the forest with the distance of each place in it from the château of Compiègne. Both are the result of practical work with chain and sextant. At fifteen he compiled a coloured scale map of the Environs of Versailles, a model of neatness and precision, decorated with small landscape paintings, all in his own hand, which would do credit to an experienced cartographer.

For Religion Berry had no less than three teachers: a fervent Breton named Coëtlosquet, former bishop of Limoges, an Italian-born priest named Soldini, and a Jesuit, Guillaume Berthier, well known as an adversary of Voltaire. From them and his parents Berry derived a firm belief in the truth and principles of Christianity, and a special devotion to the Sacred Heart of Jesus, which priests of the Eudist order had popularized as a symbol both of Christ's overflowing love for man – denied by the Jansenists – and of loyalty to the Holy See. Whereas his brothers wore their faith lightly, even as a boy, according to his mother, Berry appeared 'penetrated with religion in all its aspects'.

Lessons in Political Theory took place against the background of Louis XV's struggle with an increasingly assertive Parlement, so much stress was laid on the need for firmness, as well as on the more obvious points that a King must be just and make his people happy. Berry summed up his lessons in two sentences of his own: 'For the happiness of the world it is desirable that Kings should be good without however being too indulgent, in order that kindness on their part should always be a virtue and never a weakness'; 'From the weakness of Kings stem factions, civil war, the tremors which shake and ruin the State and end by completely overthrowing it. Were I to doubt the truth of this, I have only to look at the history of any and every nation.'

Firmness, however, must never be harsh. Berry had to study certain passages in Fénelon's *Aventures de Télémaque* and re-write them in his own words. One passage concerns the esteem a King should have for farmers. Fénelon begins: 'Clamp taxes, fines and even if necessary other rigorous penalties on those who neglect their fields . . .' but Berry, in re-writing it, strikes a more positive note: 'The condition of farm workers must be honoured as one of the most useful to the State . . .' Only later and incidentally does he mention taxes and fines: Fénelon's 'rigorous penalties' he omits altogether.

One of Berry's exercises was to choose twenty-six maxims from *Télémaque* and to print them himself in book form. Helped by his brothers, and using his aunt's press, in a fortnight he set up the type and printed twenty-five copies of his *Moral and Political Maxims derived from 'Telemachus' concerning the Science of Kingship and the Happiness of the People*. It is a neat piece of work. Berry had a copy bound and took it proudly to 'Papa Roi.' The King's eye fell on certain passages: 'at the court of corrupt princes, favours and passions run in the same channel,' and 'the prince should withhold his confidence and give signs of displeasure and scorn to those who, stifling the voice of religion, shame and decency, make a parade of vice, and glory in what should be veiled in shame.' Instead of making the expected compliment Papa Roi turned to his grandson. 'Monsieur, your work is finished. Break up the type.'

Berry possessed only an average intelligence. He was never to be quick and brilliant. All his life this was to be a serious limitation. On the other hand he was studious and persevering. He liked books and learning things. Even after his formal education had come to an end, he taught himself English, Italian and Spanish well enough to read at sight in all three languages.

A close comparison of Berry's written exercises and the lessons on which they were based is revealing of the boy's character. Berry liked to condense an idea to the limit and to cut unnecessary adjectives: a sign of a precise mind; wherever possible he changed a passive to an active verb: a sign of manliness; he had a predilection for the categorical imperative and made great play with the verb 'ought': a sign of a sense of duty; he often used the word 'continual' – for example, 'the exercise of continual beneficence' and expressions like 'all my life' and 'for the rest of my life': a sign of tenaciousness; wherever a lesson tended to divide care for the people's happiness between a King and his Ministers, he altered it to make clear that this task fell to the King and the King alone: a sign of his willingness to accept responsibility.

Physically Berry was slim and very strong. As a boy he suffered from short-sightedness. This failing had entered the Bourbon family through Jeanne d'Albret, whose son, Henri IV, had to wear spectacles in later life, while the Regent, Philippe d'Orléans, was very short-sighted and always wore spectacles. Evidently Berry's short-sightedness was not serious, otherwise spectacles would have been prescribed for him, and as he grew older he seems to have conquered it altogether. When the time came for him to take up shooting, he taught himself to gain pretty clear distance sight by half-shutting his eyes.

Morally Berry inherited the rather scrupulous nature of both parents. This, coupled with self-distrust and sensitized by a strict upbringing, made him slow at taking decisions, for he easily became distressed that he might be making a wrong choice. In regard to sex, he seems to have been taught to view with excessive alarm sins of the flesh, Madame de Pompadour being cited as the prime dreadful example of what happened when a prince yielded to passion.

What were Berry's boyhood recreations? Riding, exercises on the parallel bars, whist and chess. He and his brothers also indulged in a good deal of horseplay, and a favourite diversion of Berry was to romp with one of the valets named Grau, who was 'as big as a giant and ticklish as a kitten.' He also had to take part in certain symbolic occupations of propaganda value: for example 'to encourage agriculture' he was taught to use a plough and drive a straight furrow. A print which circulated in 1768 shows Berry ploughing a field.

When he was eleven and a half Berry began to keep a diary. Many children do this and soon lose interest, but the tenacious Berry was to keep up his diary all his life. Early entries reflect three main interests: religion, riding and travel. Berry put a cross against those days when he attended Mass, and entered Easter Duties, Sermons, Vespers, Benediction. On 21 August 1766 he noted: 'I rode for the first time, at Puy dauphin,' and on 9 December the following year: 'First lesson in dressage. Went for a ride.' Berry loved riding and was to become an excellent horseman, but he had the honesty to note in his diary the three occasions on which he fell. Finally, he entered all the different moves to the various royal castles, the most important being to Compiègne in summer and to Fontainebleau in autumn. It would seem that Berry enjoyed the excitement and new impressions of travel, even travel limited to the Ile de France, and his favourite book was *Robinson Crusoe*.

The three brothers make an interesting contrast. Berry fair, strong, broad-shouldered, reserved, unassertive, not brilliant; Provence dark, delicate, very clever, with a phenomenal memory and of a literary turn of mind; Artois also dark, very agile, good at all sports, casual and with a gift for repartee that made him the talk of the Court. For example, he had the habit of saying 'Diable!' and having been warned by his teacher Defougères that if he continued to do so the devil would end by appearing to him, Artois went to a corner of his room, joined his hands and said: 'Little devil, do appear, do come and take away tiresome Monsieur Defougères.'

His young brothers were inclined to play up Berry. One day he happened to say '*Il pleuva*' instead of the correct '*Il plut*'. 'What barbarism!' sneered Provence, 'A prince ought to know his own language.' Another time the three boys went out for a walk. One of the younger – probably Artois – forgot his hat and was going to turn back to fetch it. Berry, who was near the door, said: 'You go on, I'll fetch it.' As he was returning with the missing hat, La Vauguyon saw him, and since obligingness towards his brothers had evidently become something of a habit, took Berry to his study and lectured him never to forget his dignity and pre-eminence. Berry, however, sometimes did forget. A provincial orator having complimented him on his precocity, Berry interrupted. 'You are mistaken, sir, it is not I who am clever, it is my brother of Provence.'

Berry saw less of his sisters than of his brothers. He was idolized by the younger of them, Elisabeth, who seems to have sensed in him an underlying strength and protectiveness not noticed by others. Once, during open house at Saint-Cloud, Berry wandered off among the public and little Elisabeth followed him, clinging to his coat tail. The crowds, anxious to witness this unusual sight, pushed so close around them that finally Berry had to lift Elisabeth in his arms: 'Gentlemen, please take care you don't crush my little sister, or she won't come and see you again.'

Among Berry's distractions were foreign visitors. Horace Walpole came: 'Yesterday I went through all my presentations at Versailles. 'Tis very convenient to gobble up a whole royal family in an hour's time.' Another to cross the Channel was David Hume. His *History of England* had appeared in French, and the fifty-two-year-old Scotsman received a warm welcome: 'I am convinced that Louis XIV never, in any three weeks of his life, suffered so much flattery.' Slight as a young man, Hume had now grown portly, which caused Diderot, ever one for irreverence, to remark, 'The word has been made flesh.' Hume was roped into playing charades, and one evening dressed up as a sultan, while two of the prettiest ladies sat on either side of him as his slaves, hoping for compliments from the great man. It was a far cry from his Edinburgh club, and Hume merely sat there for a quarter of an hour, patting his ample belly, slapping his knees, and saying, 'Well now, mesdemoiselles, here we all are!' Finally one of the ladies went off in a huff: 'That man's good only for munching veal.'

Hume's sympathetic treatment of the Stuarts made him *persona grata* to the royal family, and in late November 1763 he was invited to Court. 'What happened last week,' Hume wrote to a friend, 'when I had the honour of being presented to the Dauphin's children at Versailles, is one of the most curious scenes I have yet passed through. The Duc de Berry . . . stepped forth, and told me how many friends and admirers I had in this country, and that he reckoned himself in the number, from the pleasure he had received from the reading of many passages in my works. When he had finished, his brother, the Count de Provence who is two years younger [in fact, one year], began his discourse, and informed me that I had been long and impatiently expected in France; and that he himself expected soon to have great satisfaction from reading my fine History.' Hume adds that the incident will surprise his friends the *philosophes*, who held that princes were brought up on bigoted, out-of-date books and ideas.

All the while his father was watching Berry's education. He personally supervised his Latin, while Marie Josèphe, a cultivated lady who could read Virgil and Tasso at sight, supervised History and Religion. The Dauphin once penalized Berry for slack work by forbidding him to follow in a carriage the famous St Hubert's Day hunt, a punishment which the King judged excessive.

Berry spent his boyhood, then, in a happy family within an unhappy palace. From loving parents he derived a positive, open attitude to life, and from his teachers an excellent education. The point has to be emphasized, for already gibes were put out by Choiseul's set, who hated the Dauphin. One – quite untrue – insinuated that La Vauguyon was a backwoods bigot, who had got his job by bribing one of the Dauphin's valets to tell him daily the name of the book his master was reading. He then studied the book and impressed the Dauphin by talking about it with casual profundity.

Every summer Berry watched his father, as Colonel of the Dragoons, put on his green uniform with red facings, his helmet trimmed with tigerskin, and ride off to Compiègne for manœuvres. In the summer when Berry was eleven his father got soaked to the skin, caught a bad cold, and by early October was in bed with tuberculosis, spitting blood. He was visited by his mother the Queen and, possessing like her a morbid streak, he asked with relish whether she liked mummies. No, she replied. 'Soon you are going to have one,' said the Dauphin. 'The hot medicines they're giving me are drying me up.'

He had his black hair cut off and given to his sisters, a gesture which Diderot found 'touching and reminiscent of antiquity'. To save the nation expense he directed that his body should lie not at Saint-Denis but at nearby Sens. He had never forgotten his first wife and asked that his heart should be buried beside hers. On the morning of 20 December 1765 he died. According to Horace Walpole, 'It was one of the few deaths (I mean of those who die in public) void of pedantry, affectation or bigotry.'

Berry took this loss very much to heart. According to La Vauguyon, he felt the death more than his brothers. The King, who loved his family after his fashion, came to comfort and embrace them: both of them, as they clung together, were in tears, and the King said, 'Poor France! A King of fifty-five and a Dauphin of eleven.'

For Marie Josèphe her husband's death was the last in a series of calamities. She had been unsuccessful in persuading France to secure the throne of Poland for her adored brother Xavier, she had seen her native land invaded and her mother die a prisoner of King Frederick II of Prussia. She cut off her lovely blonde hair, gave up wearing rouge, and would not open her clavichord. Even after the long period of mourning she hung her apartment with black crape and lit it with yellow candles.

On her table Marie Josèphe placed a relief model of the vault in Sens cathedral where her husband was buried, and she marked the place where, she said, she would soon lie. She ate almost nothing and rushed through her meals in seven minutes, until her doctor made her extend them to fifteen. She grew very thin and soon it became clear that while nursing her husband she had caught his disease. On 9 March 1767 she called her sons, tried to speak to them but was too weak, and gave them her blessing. On 13 March Berry, now known as the Dauphin, entered in his diary – and the writing, usually neat, was jerky and uneven – 'Death of my mother at eight in the evening.'

According to eyewitnesses, the little Dauphin was deeply affected by this second loss. He grew pale and very thin, and some courtiers thought it would not be long before he joined his parents in the vault of Sens cathedral. Even five months later his uncle was informed that the Dauphin was in very delicate health. But as on the earlier occasion, a basic physical robustness carried him through.

The Dauphin was now twelve. The loss of his parents had left him very lonely, and he was still too young to stand by himself. He needed affection and guidance, but where could he find them? The King was engulfed in pleasure, the Queen in piety. Happily, the King's unmarried daughters were living in Versailles, and when he lost his parents, the Dauphin turned to them.

'The four Mesdames, who are clumsy plump old wenches, with a bad likeness to their father, stand in a bedchamber in a row, with black cloaks and knotting-bags, looking good-humoured, not knowing what to say, and wriggling as if they wanted to make water.' So the malicious Horace Walpole. In fact, they were delightful if somewhat eccentric ladies. The eldest, Adélaïde, was gay and full of gumption. When war broke out with England, she was found one evening, eleven years old, leaving Versailles on a donkey, clutching a little bag in which were thirteen louis won from her mother at cards: 'I am going to make the English lords sleep with me in turn, which they will be honoured to do, and bring their heads to Papa.' Adélaïde was not only patriotic but also extremely haughty, and became outraged if anyone called her Royal Highness: she was Madame, eldest of the Daughters of France, and when the King dined in public, she sat immediately on his right. No foreign prince had been deemed worthy of her hand.

The second sister, Victoire, was tall and fat – Louis XV called her Coche, meaning Sow – and she played the bagpipes. She also played the guitar and viola. It was to her that Mozart père dedicated his young son's piano sonatas, Koechel 6 and 7. The third sister, Sophie, was very plain and abnormally timid; 'she walked extremely quickly, and so as to recognize the people she passed without looking at them she had formed the habit of glancing sideways, as hares do.' Only during a thunderstorm did Sophie overcome her timidity: then, because she was frightened, she gave her hand to whoever happened to be near. The youngest sister – at this time aged thirty – was Louise: pretty, small, stoop-shouldered and fond of reading history.

When the King came each morning to take his breakfast coffee with his sisters, Adélaïde would pull a bell to alert Victoire, Victoire pulled a bell to alert timid Sophie, and Sophie pulled a bell to alert Louise, who lived right at the end of their vast suite of apartments. By the time Louise arrived the King had finished his coffee and she had time only to give him a quick kiss before he left for the hunt.

The four spinster aunts were very fond of their food, but they were also very scrupulous. Lent became a time of heart-searching. The great question was whether one could eat water-fowl, which they adored. One day Victoire, the greediest, invited a bishop to dinner at which she served a water-fowl, perhaps swan or woodcock.

She then asked the bishop whether the bird could lawfully be eaten during Lent: in other words, whether it was *maigre* or *gras*. The bishop made a show of giving the matter grave consideration, then replied that according to canon law the bird should be taken out of the oven and placed on a very cold silver platter: if the juice congealed within a quarter of an hour, the bird must be deemed *gras*; if the juice remained liquid it could be eaten. Victoire was delighted with this reply. She at once applied the test, the juice remained liquid, and a delicious meal was had by all.

The aunts gave a warm welcome to their orphaned nephews and nieces. 'You are in your own place here,' Adélaïde told the young Dauphin, who was her godchild. 'Have fun, make a din, knock things over, break anything you want.' He found an atmosphere of easy good cheer in the aunts' apartments, their window-boxes gay with flowers.

During three years of close relationship with his aunts, the Dauphin was most influenced by Adélaïde. His father had taken a gloomy, almost hopeless view of France; his mother, being Saxon, had seen her adopted country as merely one in the concert of Europe. But Adelaïde, eldest Daughter of France, took an unquestioningly confident pride in her native land, and she hated France's enemies, England and especially Austria, with all the strength of her passionate, somewhat virile nature. From his aunt Adélaïde the Dauphin imbibed a new confidence in France, and the beginning of confidence in himself.

The aunts were more indulgent to the King than their brother had been, but in 1769, when he took an unspeakable new mistress whose name, never mentioned by the aunts, was Madame Du Barry, they added their spinster voices to the general condemnation of royal favourites. Once more, from a new source, it was drummed into the Dauphin that pretty women were an occasion of sin.

The lesson was driven home in an unexpected way. Some time after the Dauphin's adoption by the aunts, Louise began to keep very much apart. She had her lady-in-waiting read history to her for five hours on end, as though in a hurry to learn as much as possible; she received long mysterious visits from the King; she seemed distant and tense. Her sisters wondered whether a marriage was going to break up their quartet. Certainly some secret plan was being hatched. Then, at seven in the morning of 11 April 1770 Louise put on a plain dress and a hat with a pink ribbon, slipped out of the palace without saying goodbye, and drove to the

Carmelite house in Saint-Denis, one of the poorest and austerest convents. She had wanted to enter it for two years; only after much pleading had the King given his permission.

Louise's departure caused a sensation. Not since the Middle Ages had a daughter of the King taken the veil. There were many who disliked the turning of Versailles into a brothel, its evil influence spreading out to infect all France, but here was someone who had dared to do something about it. It became known that Louise had shut herself up in order to pray for the conversion of the King.

Louis and his brothers sent their aunt letters that reflect their character. Provence, who was showing signs of a weak constitution, feared she would be unable to stand the rigours of the cloister; Artois, aware of the gallery, spoke of the great example she was giving the world. Louis showed most feeling – 'I am in despair at being parted from you' – and what struck him was Louise's courage in leaving the world. Evidently Louis felt himself lacking in the kind of courage that hurts those near and dear – as Louise had hurt the King – and that braves established norms.

Louise's spectacular departure coincides with the end of the future King's boyhood. He was now well educated, with certain fixed principles and his own particular bent. He had suffered more than most boys of his age. For long he had lived in the shadows, first of Bourgogne, then of the rather morbid, indrawn family life which culminated in the loss of his father and mother. Then he had lacked confidence; he still did, but from Adélaïde he had learned the beginnings of self-assurance. He was steady not brilliant, reserved not assertive. This was unusual at Versailles, which liked its princes flashy, and as the time approached for him to marry, word circulated among the courtiers of Choiseul's set that the future King was a dull, boorish creature.

CHAPTER 3

The Impossible Marriage

IN a rococo bedroom of the Hofburg, furnished with black and gold lacquerware and heated by a faïence stove, the Empress Maria Theresa reclined on a low armchair reading and signing State papers. She was a good-looking, plump lady of thirty-eight, with long golden hair, pale blue eyes and strong white teeth. The date was 2 November 1755, but her windows as usual were open wide: she closed them only for her chancellor, Kaunitz, a fussy man who could not bear draughts.

Maria Theresa was the best queen Europe had known since Elizabeth of England. Extremely energetic – in summer she rose at five – possessed of stalwart power of mind and great common sense, she carried her people bravely through two long wars and gave them prosperity symbolized in a strong currency, the gold thaler bearing her image. Morally she was perhaps over-strict and she tried, without success, to make prominent men in Vienna stop keeping mistresses. Among those she charmed was the British ambassador, who described her face as 'filled with sense, spirit and sweetness'.

From time to time her husband Francis came into the bedroom to ask how she was. The former Duke of Lorraine, he was a handsome soft-eyed German with French blood, a grand-nephew of Louis XIV. He had shown courage leading rescue teams during the Danube floods of 1744, but lacked the toughness to be an effective general. He was not bookish either, and could not spell the simplest words: *à cette heure* became *asteur*. But he possessed a gift for making money, successfully handled his wife's finances and was known as 'the Court banker'. The rest of the time he hunted the stag, listened to Haydn and let his wife rule.

As evening fell and candles were lit, Maria Theresa felt the pains of labour. She laid down her pen but remained in the low armchair – no nonsense for her about going to bed – and at half past seven gave birth to her fifteenth child. Having ascertained its sex, she entrusted it to a nurse, picked up her pen and resumed her job of ruling.

The child was christened Maria Antonia Josepha Joanna. Maria was a tribute to the Blessed Virgin, and formed part of the official names of eight of the Empress's other daughters, but it was not used. The new child was called Antonia or more often, since French was spoken in the Hofburg, Antoinette.

She was a fair, blue-eyed, very lively girl, and although the youngest but one, not indulged. 'I insist on their eating everything,' Maria Theresa instructed the nanny, 'with no fault-finding and no picking and choosing. Further, they must not be allowed to criticize their food. On Fridays, Saturdays, and all other fast-days they will eat fish . . . See that they eat sugar as little as possible.'

Antoinette was taught Italian by Metastasio, Court librettist and famous author of classical tragedies. She learned Austrian history and the Austrian version of French history, notably different from the French version, for it failed to mention that France was God's gift to the planet Earth and taught that Louis XV's parents had been poisoned by the Regent. She learned to draw, and at ten made quite a good red chalk likeness of her father. She learned to play the harp and, with Gluck as her teacher, the spinet and the clavichord. But just as her birth had been informal, so was her education. Antoinette was not given the rigorous training Louis received, and this shows in her handwriting, carelessly formed and sprawling.

Her home would have fitted into one wing of Versailles and its atmosphere was more spontaneous, more 'natural'. Her mother slept in a double bed with her father and often, to avoid disputes about precedence, everyone sat down at table pell-mell. 'You cannot possibly conceive with what familiarity her Majesty the Empress conversed with my wife,' wrote Leopold Mozart when Antoinette was twelve, 'talking to her partly of my children's smallpox and partly of the events on our grand tour; nor can you imagine how she stroked my wife's cheeks and pressed her hands.'

Antoinette's childhood was happier than Louis's. She never felt lonely, for there was always someone to play with – Ferdinand, a year older than she, Maximilian, a year younger, or one of her many sisters, whose friendship meant much to her. Especially happy were the family musical evenings, when Ferdinand played the kettle-drums, her eldest brother Joseph the 'cello, Christina the clavichord, and Antoinette, who had a pleasing voice, sang French songs and Italian arias.

The children combined in different degrees their mother's strength and their father's sensibility. Joseph was strong, so was Maria Amalia, later Duchess of Parma. Antoinette was more sensitive. Aged eight we hear of her having a bout of nervous convulsions and lying on her bed for an hour unconscious, while the other nervous member of the family was her favourite sister, Caroline, later Queen of Naples. Her mother she loved deeply, but also feared. Maria Theresa took rather too much pleasure in discovering, and pulling out, small weeds from her children's spiritual garden. The governess in her could be at times oppressive.

While Antoinette was growing up, Louis XV and his Foreign Minister Choiseul were considering how best to salvage French foreign policy from the ruins of the Seven Years' War. They decided that France must offset Prussian power by making a permanent ally of Austria, so they instructed the French ambassador in Vienna to begin tentative negotiations for a marriage between the Dauphin and the Empress's youngest daughter. To many it seemed unnatural, even impossible, that France and Austria, enemies for hundreds of years, should be linked by marriage, but Choiseul assured his master that it would bring France new splendour, while Maria Theresa was big enough to see that the extraordinary proposal would strengthen Austria. After long diplomacy in 1768 she formally accepted.

Choiseul, wishing to ease Antoinette's transition to France, sent her as tutor the abbé de Vermond, a lowly college librarian who would do exactly as Choiseul said. Vermond noticed Antoinette's 'vivacity' and said her education had been neglected. Too much should not be made of Vermond's report: a more flattering one would have been tantamount to declaring himself superfluous; moreover, Vermond was judging by French standards, witness his further remark: 'I am sure that after her marriage she will know the names of all the colonels and recognize their regiments by the colour of their uniform and the number on it.'

At Maria Theresa's request, Choiseul also sent a Paris dentist – the Empress wished Antoinette's teeth to be as strong and white as her own – and a Paris hairdresser. Antoinette had a high prominent brow, which was not the fashion, and Maria Theresa got the hairdresser to arrange Antoinette's frizzy fair hair with its red glints so as to lessen this imperfection.

What were Antoinette's feelings about her engagement? She realized that in worldly terms it was splendid, but she was certainly dismayed when Vermond, repeating the gossip of Choiseul's circle, depicted the Dauphin as far from brilliant and passed her the dim engraving of him ploughing.

Antoinette was groomed for marriage by her mother. Twice a week she sat at the Court gaming-table, where stakes were higher than at Versailles and her father once lost 30,000 ducats in a night; on other evenings she learned poise by presiding over her own games of cavagnole or lotteries. She went to operas, ballets and balls, and received streams of advice from her mother. She was going to France as a living pledge of the new alliance. She must make herself loved by the people of France. She must keep out of politics. Above all, she must make a success of her marriage. 'The only true happiness in this world is a happy marriage. And that depends on the woman being obliging, gentle and amusing.'

In the spring of 1770 Antoinette kissed her mother, brothers and sisters goodbye, gave a last pat to her beloved boxer dog, and was swept away in a cavalcade of forty-eight six-horse carriages to an island in the Rhine near Kehl. Here the ceremony of handing-over took place. In a tent not unlike a bathing tent divided down the centre, the French made Antoinette undergo a symbolic ritual in order to demonstrate that she was wholly ceasing to be Austrian. All her Austrian clothing was removed, even her stockings and vest, and, quite naked, she was handed over to the punctilious Comtesse de Noailles. For a sensitive fourteen-year-old the experience proved unnerving and, as she left her Austrian ladies and stepped into the French side of the tent, Antoinette burst into tears.

In Strasbourg she received a warm welcome: bells pealed, poems were read, speeches made, dances performed. She was entertained by the Cardinal Archbishop, who presented to her a woman aged 105 who had never known a day's illness.

'Princess, I pray heaven you may live as long as I, and as free from infirmities.'

'So be it,' said Antoinette. 'if it is for the happiness of France.'

On the afternoon of 14 May Louis XV and the Dauphin, attended by the princes of the blood and Court dignitaries, waited for Antoinette on the edge of the forest of Compiègne. Choiseul, by special permission, had gone ahead to be the first to welcome her. The King asked Bouret, an official who had seen her at Strasbourg, how he found the Dauphine, and whether her breasts were fully formed. Bouret replied that she had a charming face, beautiful eyes and so on.

'That's not what I mean. I'm talking about her breasts.'

'Sire, I did not take the liberty of looking at them.'

'Then you're a ninny. It's the first thing one should look at in a woman.'

The Dauphine arrived at three o'clock. She sprang lightly from her carriage, almost ran towards the King, and sank to her knees before him. He raised her, embraced her, and presented Louis, who in accordance with etiquette kissed her on the cheek.

Antoinette's first reaction to Louis we do not know. But we do have the view of the Duchess of Northumberland, who was staying with Choiseul's friend, the Maréchale de Mirepoix, and like Antoinette had been given an unfavourable report of Louis.

'I expected to have found him horrid,' she noted in her diary, 'but on the contrary his figure pleas'd me very well. He is tall and slender with a countenance *très intéressant* and a look of good sense, his complexion is rather pale and his eyes are large. He has a great quantity of fair hair which grows very well to his face.'

Louis's first reaction to Antoinette was probably also one of agreeable surprise, for all those close to him were predisposed against Austria and had seized on any points against her. She was certainly a very pretty girl, slim with not very full breasts, beautiful arms and hands, eyes blue as his own and a rose and white complexion. She was less tall than he: 'very little and slender', according to the Duchess of Northumberland. 'I should not have taken her to be above twelve years old. She is fair and a little marked with smallpox.'

Two days later, on a bright sunny afternoon, Louis and Antoinette knelt side by side in the packed gilt and white chapel of Versailles. Louis wore a suit of cloth of gold spangled with diamonds; Antoinette white brocade: 'the corps of her robe was too small and left quite a broad stripe of lacing and shift quite visible, which had a bad effect between two broader strips of diamonds.'

'The Dauphin appeared to have more timidity than his little wife. He trembled excessively during the service and blush'd up to his eyes when he gave the ring – [twelve had been made, so that one would be sure to fit]. When Mass began and they presented him with a book, he looked quite relieved to have an excuse for not looking about him.'

So Louis and Antoinette promised to be faithful to each other unto death and were pronounced man and wife by Archbishop de La Roche Aymon. Antoinette was a little nervous too and when signing the register made a blot with her pen.

At supper Clotilde, 'round as a ball', 'gobbled down the meat on her plate, her eyes seemed to devour all the rest that was on the table. The Dauphin ate very little, seem'd quite pensive and busy over his plate playing with his knife.'

After supper the weather clouded, rain fell and the firework display had to be postponed. The couple were escorted by the King and Queen to the Dauphine's bedroom on the ground floor. There they went through the same formalities as the Dauphin's parents had gone through, the King handing the nightshirt to his grandson. At last the ritual was complete, and all withdrew. The King was well pleased, so was Choiseul. They had pulled off a tricky political marriage, and believed they now could relax. But the reality was not quite so simple.

The Dauphin, with his esteem for order, was not one to let feeling run ahead of reason and the self-distrust that had shown itself in the chapel acted as a further check on feeling. He had never met girls of his own age, for at Versailles children were conspicuous by their absence, and so he had been denied a normal sexual awakening. Nor had he had a chance of courting this bride whom he had seen for six hours at the most, or of responding to her charms.

Louis had been brought up puritanically. From his father he had learned that chastity is a prime virtue; from La Vauguyon that women are a peril to kings. Against the background of Louis XV's excesses, bed was almost a bad word. In a very real sense the shadows of the Pompadour, the Du Barry and the Parc aux Cerfs fell across young Louis.

More serious still, Louis felt checks with regard to this girl in particular. She had been given him by Choiseul, his father's enemy, whom Louis disliked. His mother had wanted him to take a Saxon, not a Hapsburg, bride. Aunt Adélaïde had filled his mind with stories against Austria. 'Before his marriage,' Antoinette was later to recall, 'M. de La Vauguyon had alarmed him about the domination his wife would try to exercise over him. This black-souled man took pleasure in frightening his pupil with all the bogies invented against the House of Austria.'

Over against these checks was the enormous importance attached to the wedding night. The bed was the centre of the royal stud, the breeding-ground of kings, the stadium where the Sun King and his grandfather had so magnificently gone through their paces. Tomorrow, Louis knew, the sheets would be looked at with seeming casualness, in fact with the utmost care: not only the French Court but, through their ambassadors, Madrid, London, Turin would know whether he had proved himself a man.

In some youths this knowledge would have overridden the checks, but Louis was still very self-distrustful about his public image, and so it served to intensify them. Like his father in the same room twenty-three years earlier, Louis seems to have suffered a deep inner conflict, though of a different kind. He wished to fulfil his obligations, but for a number of reasons felt unable to. Something, at the deepest level, locked.

What were Antoinette's reactions? She had probably been told about the early frustrations of arranged marriages, and sister Caroline, in Naples, wrote that she pitied Antoinette: 'One suffers martyrdom, all the greater because one must pretend outwardly to be happy.' There is no reason to think Antoinette suffered martyrdom. Possessed, as her doctors noted, of 'a sanguine temperament', she saw the bright side of things, and to her mother, whom she informed of all her joys and sadnesses, she did not at this time even mention the matter. The King and his family, the courtiers, the wonder of Versailles, balls and other festivities: these were more than enough to occupy her.

When the weather improved, the postponed firework display took place, but no corresponding event occurred in the Dauphine's bed. During the fortnight following the wedding Louis came to know Antoinette and to feel her charm, as did the King and most of his family. Certain restraints, certain areas of the log-jam cleared. Had Antoinette been left to herself, Louis would almost certainly have soon overcome his remaining inhibitions. Unfortunately Antoinette was not left to herself. Day and night, Louis discovered, this girl of fourteen was being watched.

The first person watching her was her tutor and spiritual adviser, the abbé de Vermond. A severe-looking man of thirty-five, with thin lips and sombre, piercing eyes, he spent several hours daily with Antoinette, giving her lessons, reading to her and helping her with her letters to her mother. Soon he began to give himself airs, and the jumped-up librarian was receiving Ministers and bishops lolling in his bath. Louis might have overlooked this, and the fact that his wife's tutor was a tool of Choiseul. What he could not overlook was that Vermond spied for the Austrian Government both on Antoinette and himself. Of this he was very soon to have positive proof.

The second person watching Antoinette was the Austrian ambassador to Versailles. Outwardly Comte Florimond Claude de Mercy was the perfect polished courtier: tall, lean, handsome, cool-eyed, suave, rich. He seemed to have every reason for strength; in fact, as his portrait and a taste for scent suggest, he was weak. He had been born in Liége forty-three years previously. At two he had lost his mother and was left by his father, an army officer, to be brought up by an uncle. That early loss, coupled with delicate health, had made him cold and timid. He declined to take on the responsibilities of marriage; instead he chose as his mistress a plain little opera singer, Rosalie Levasseur, a social inferior who would make few demands, and his one aim in life was to continue his comfortable existence in the Petit Luxembourg with Rosalie and his 15,000 bottles of vintage wine. One thing threatened this idyll: he was next in line as Chancellor. That demanding post he did not want, so if he were to avoid being recalled to take it up, he must make himself indispensable at Versailles. He must become Antoinette's Doppelgänger. This is how he set about it.

'I have made sure of three persons in the service of the Archduchess,' Mercy wrote to Maria Theresa, 'one of her women and two of her manservants, who give me full reports of what goes on. Then, from day to day, I am told of the conversations she has with abbé de Vermond, from whom she hides nothing. Beside this, the Marquise de Durfort passes on to me everything she says to her aunts. I have also sources of information as to what goes on whenever the Dauphine sees the King. Superadded are my personal observations, so that there really is not an hour of the day as to which I am not instructed concerning what the Archduchess may have said or done or heard.'

At least once a week Mercy wrote a long secret letter to Vienna based on his spy reports, notably those of Vermond. These letters not only described incidents in the private life of Louis and Antoinette but reported actual overheard conversations.

At this point appears the third person who dominated Antoinette, the Empress Maria Theresa herself. The energy of this remarkable woman was such that she conducted a regular detailed correspondence with each of her married children over a period of ten years or more, and since Antoinette had made the most important match, her letters to the Dauphine were the ones which received most care.

When she received Mercy's secret reports, Maria Theresa wrote to Antoinette saying that she had 'read in the newspapers' about such and such behaviour at a ball, say, or the gaming-table; sometimes she criticized it, often she suggested a different course. Her advice was nearly always sensible and Antoinette followed it.

Antoinette did not know that Mercy's reports, not the newspapers, were behind her mother's letters, but Louis did. Like any man worth his salt, he resented the key-hole peeping by paid agents, and the ordering of his wife's life by this very powerful woman in Vienna. But what really angered Louis was his discovery that Mercy, in his letters to Maria Theresa, did not tell the truth.

Mercy, aware of his own weakness, knew that he would be indispensable to the Empress only by appearing strong. The best way of appearing strong was to suggest that the Dauphin was weak, and would do as Antoinette wished. Since he, Mercy, controlled Antoinette, he would appear in Vienna as a man of quite exceptional power, one who controlled the future King of France, and his indispensability was then assured.

Louis's youngest sister Elisabeth seldom in her life used a harsh word about anyone, but she did describe Mercy as an 'old fox'. The image is apt. Mercy was too astute to lie, but he did twist every possible incident so as to discredit Louis. He started by retailing to Maria Theresa the Choiseul set's opinion: 'Nature seems to have refused everything to the Dauphin,' and followed that up with illustrations. Here is one from this early period.

Antoinette was continually urged by Maria Theresa to do some solid reading: 'You need it more than other girls, because you are not accomplished in music or drawing,' hard words that caused Antoinette to murmur, 'She makes me out an animal.' The Dauphine did in fact read Sully's *Memoirs*, the chronicles of L'Etoile, a historical novel about King Philippe Auguste, and Hume's *History of England*: 'very interesting, although one has to remember he is a Protestant' – in all, four books in four years. Louis, who continued his education after his marriage, and even spent part of his allowance on buying books and paying teachers, was already an assiduous reader and keen bibliophile. But Mercy repeatedly reports that Antoinette is trying, by her good example, to make the boorish Dauphin do some solid reading. On 20 April 1773 he writes:

Her Royal Highness has spent Lent very quietly; I hope she will send your Majesty details of what she has read; I know from the Abbé de Vermond that she has read more and reflected on her reading more than at other times of the year. Monsieur le Dauphin is gradually becoming accustomed to reading too: he shows curiosity about the latest news; he has the newspapers and certain periodicals read to him, and he gives an odd moment to reading history. This beginning of industriousness is, without contradiction, the effect of insinuations by Madame the Archduchess, and she is justly proud of it.

What could Louis do about this network of intrigue? Dismiss Vermond? But the abbé was Choiseul's appointee and was well liked by Maria Theresa; he had done nothing specifically wrong, and he would be terribly hurt. At Versailles one tried not to hurt people's feelings. But even if he were prepared to hurt Vermond, would it be possible to remove him any more than it had been possible for his father to take violin lessons from the agreeable Monsieur Mondonville rather than horrid Guignon? Almost certainly not.

All his life Louis had seen the King of France enslaved by a woman, and it had been drummed into his head how bad that was for France. In his modest way it was his ambition in life to become a good King. Was the girl Antoinette a party to an Austrian plot? Or just an innocent decoy? As yet he could not tell. But he did possess proof that his bride was dominated by two men he detested and by a powerful Empress who in her youth had waged war on France.

Antoinette, on her side, discovered that she was sometimes being spied on. Six weeks after the wedding 'a curious thing happened. I was alone with my husband when M. de La Vauguyon comes hastily to the door to listen. A footman who is either a fool or a very honest man opens the door and M. le Duc is found planted there like a pikestaff, unable to retreat. Then I pointed out to my husband the inconvenience of allowing people to listen at doors, and he took it very well.' Plainly the hostility between France and Austria was being used by unscrupulous men on both sides to further their own ends.

'Madame la Dauphine,' writes Vermond, 'believes that none of her private papers are safe. She is afraid of skeleton keys, and of people rifling her pockets while she is asleep. This fear, real or imagined, has a hold on her. She wished to re-read your Majesty's last letter and, believing it would be stolen anywhere else, kept it all night in her bed.'

The insecurity Antoinette felt in her early days at Versailles expressed itself in a constrained attitude to her husband, so that Louis began to experience a double check: his own suspicion of Austria playing on his wish not to jeopardize his future role as King, and the constraint shown by Antoinette which played on his psychological inhibitions to sex.

Now at Versailles husband and wife slept in separate rooms. Except on his wedding night, if he wished to sleep with Antoinette, Louis must get up, leave his apartment and feel his way down a corridor to his wife's room. For a long time to come he did not go down that corridor.

His grandfather had an eye for such things, and early in July he asked Louis when he intended to consummate the marriage. Louis replied, 'When the Court moves to Compiègne,' evidently because then Mercy would be out of the picture. But when the moment came Louis caught a feverish cold, plainly brought on by anxiety, which demanded that he remain a fortnight at Versailles, where Antoinette looked after him. When they did join the Court at Compiègne, Louis still kept his wife at a distance, and on the return to Versailles again fell ill. His behaviour was partly nerves, but to the extent that he willed it, he seems to have decided not to get deeply involved with Antoinette until he discovered what political role if any she was playing.

In one sense this was a ridiculous situation, in another an ordeal. However, the lingam had not yet become Europe's idol, and the young couple's life continued with a fair measure of happiness. Both were developing and finding new interests, which before long were to lead them to self-fulfilment.

CHAPTER 4

Husband and Wife

Louis and Antoinette developed considerably as persons in the four years following their wedding. From immature boy and girl they became young adults, each with a marked character. The stresses within their marriage hastened that development, intensified as they were by an unexpected conflict over the King's mistress, but the development itself was to lead in due course to harmony.

Many eighteenth-century gentlemen practised a manual craft, partly for pleasure, partly in order to share an experience with the so much idealized artisan class. Louis XV modelled ivory on a rosewood-handled lathe; the Dauphin with his strong physique preferred more exacting work. He learned how to mix mortar, handle a trowel and lay a straight course of stone. If he happened to see masons building a new wall or paving one of the palace yards, he would remove his jacket and join them. He liked carving wood and had a carpenter's shop installed in his attic. He liked metalwork and had his own forge, where he hammered out bronze ornaments for a fireplace and a fine, strong table of steel and ormolu copper, both decorated with golden-rod, lilac and sunflowers.

In one of his plays Sedaine praises a gentleman for knowing 'all the arts and sciences from painting to locksmithing': a craft then at an exciting phase of development that would culminate in the invention by Robert Barron in 1778 of the double-action tumbler lock. Louis learned locksmithing from a Versailles artisan and became proficient. From a recreation it became a real interest, and he designed and constructed locks for his own use.

Locksmithing demands strength and neatness – two characteristics we have already met in Louis – but his concern to have things safely under a lock and key of his own invention suggests exceptional caution, going beyond a normal wish to keep his private papers out of reach of Vermond and Mercy's other spies.

That caution showed itself also in a very unFrench reserve. 'On the first of [June],' writes the Duchess of Northumberland, 'the King of France sent to the Dauphin his usual allowance for his

menus plaisirs, a thousand crowns. The Dauphin bid his valet de
chambre lock it up in his drawer and bring him the key, which he
did, and then the Dauphin calling another servant, ordered him to
go and buy him a little wooden box of ye price of 12 sols. Having
got it he put into it the whole sum the King had sent him and wrote
the following letter to Monsieur Sartine, Lieutenant of the Police:

' "I have heard about the disaster in Paris [more than a hundred
killed when crowds stampeded] and am deeply saddened. The only
money I have is my monthly allowance from the King. I am sending
you that; please give help to those who need it most. I hold you in
esteem."

'He sealed this up with the box and, calling one of his pages, bid
him carry it to the Lieutenant of Police, not either hinting to ye
page what he carried, nor to what intent. The Lieutenant of Police
was so charmed with the letter that he read it aloud to the boy, who
mentioned it at his return. The Dauphin was quite unhappy at its
being known and strictly charged all his people not to mention it.'

Given this reserve, it is not surprising that Louis was happiest
when out in the open air. After his marriage he spent many after-
noons with his gun dogs drawing game from the thickets of the
park, and sometimes returned home with fifty brace of partridge or
woodcock. He occasionally shot swallows on the wing, which was
then considered sport, and on one day bagged two hundred.

Louis's favourite occupation was hunting the stag. He never lost
an occasion of putting on the blue and crimson velvet-cuffed jacket
of the King's hunt, and he found intense enjoyment in the clean
smell of horses, leather and autumn leaves, the barking of the
English hounds, the finding of hoof-prints, the special language of
the *trompes de chasse* spelling out the movements of the quarry, the
growing excitement as the stag was overtaken, and then the kill.
Sometimes Louis arrived alone on the scene; then he jumped down
and, avoiding the antlers that could easily maim, himself plunged a
hunting knife into the stag's neck.

Once in the saddle Louis threw aside the caution he showed at
his desk. According to the Spanish ambassador, 'He rides so well
that it is hard to follow him – indeed, it is thought that he exposes
himself to dangerous falls.' Physical courage in the open air came
easily to Louis; moral courage towards people he was to find more
difficult.

Louis entered in his diary the result of each day's hunt, and if it was
particularly eventful, wrote a detailed account of it: purely factual

with no ripple of emotion. He noted the parts of the forest where stags abounded, and those where they were scarce. At the end of each year he summarized the number of stags, deer, roebuck and wild boar that had been taken. Similarly he totted up, by month and year, the number of game-birds he shot. Louis seems to have felt a need to reduce any disorder in daily life to the order of statistics. The trouble is that he made of this commendable practice a fetish. For example, at the end of each year he calculated the number of days he had spent away from Versailles, and even, when he married, the total time he had so far spent away from Versailles: 852 days. Such laboriously compiled statistics seem to have been quite useless: they suggest a tendency in Louis, at this age, to retreat from central realities to reassuring details.

Louis's special friend since the death of his parents had been Aunt Adélaïde, but from a motive to be considered later his aunt took Antoinette under her wing, and the two became inseparable. Still cautious of his new wife, Louis cooled towards Aunt Adélaïde; at the same time, feeling threatened by the trio dominating Antoinette, he looked about for an ally.

Louis turned, cautiously at first, in the direction of his grandfather. He had been taught to see only the weak roué; he found an enthusiast for the chase whose prowess he could admire. In June 1770 Louis asked and was given permission to attend the King's private hunting suppers: on average once a week. These were occasions of camaraderie where stories were exchanged and the excitement of the gallops relived in the glow of a wood fire and red wine.

Louis and his grandfather quickly became close friends. The King wrote to the Duke of Parma saying that in Louis he had found a new son: 'I love him with all my heart, for he returns my love.' He gave him a leather gold-fitted hunter's tool-kit to which Louis all his life attached great sentimental value.

Louis attended more and more of the private hunting suppers, and he enjoyed them. But he did not say so in his diary. Instead he marked the days on which he attended them with an *s*, the only other sign, a small cross, being set against days on which he heard Mass. He seems to have felt that there was something specially secret and important about his relationship with the King, which gave him an ally just when he needed one most.

Meanwhile, Antoinette was settling in to Versailles and getting to know her husband's family. She got on well with Provence, who had fine black eyes and told stories that made her laugh, and with Artois, who shared her fondness for dancing. But of the three brothers, she told her mother, she preferred her husband. She did not much care for plump ten-year-old Clotilde, who was goody-goody – but she liked Elisabeth, aged six, who had a sense of fun. The King, susceptible to pretty young girls, she quickly charmed and soon he was doing her favours: ordering comedies twice a week because she liked the theatre, and letting her hold a private dance every Wednesday. It was the King not her husband who dominated her day, as she described it to Maria Theresa on 12 July 1770.

'I get up between nine and ten, dress, say my prayers and break-fast. Then I go to my aunts, where I usually find the King. At eleven I have my hair done. Towards noon my household assembles and anyone not of the populace may enter my room. I put on my rouge and wash my hands; then the men leave and the women stay, while I put on formal dress. Mass is at noon. If the King is at Versailles, I attend Mass with him, my husband and my aunts; if he is absent, I go alone with the Dauphin. We dine in public and by half past one have finished, for we are both very quick eaters. Then I go to the Dauphin's apartment and, if he is busy, return to my own. I read, write or work with my hands. I am making an embroidered jacket for the King. It hardly advances but with God's help I hope it will be finished a few years from now. At three I again go to my aunts, and the King comes there too.

'At four the abbé de Vermond comes to my rooms; from five to six every day I have a clavichord or singing lesson. At half past six, unless I have a walk, I nearly always go to my aunts, usually accompanied by my husband. From seven to nine we play at cards, but when the weather is fine I go for a walk, and the game is held in my aunts' apartment. Supper is at nine, and when the King is absent, my aunts join us; when the King is in residence, we sup with them and then wait for the King, who usually arrives at a quarter to eleven. While waiting, I stretch out on a canapé and sleep until he arrives; but when he is absent, we go to bed at eleven.'

To this unexacting age-old curriculum Antoinette brought her special tastes. She had a fondness for flowers, and filled her apart-ments with hyacinths, tulips and roses. She had her boxer sent to her and acquired two other dogs. She had what Mercy calls 'a passion for children'; at garden parties she made straight for the children and had them presented to her, and she engaged as maid a certain Madame Thierry because the woman brought with her her little boy of four.

Antoinette found Versailles's stiff ceremonial silly and laughed at it in the timid person of Madame de Noailles, whom she nicknamed 'Madame Etiquette'. One day she was being taught to ride a donkey – her mother vetoed horse riding because 'it will spoil your complexion and figure' – and she fell off. To friends who hurried to help Antoinette said, 'Leave me on the ground. We must wait for Madame Etiquette. She will show us the right way to pick up a Dauphine who has tumbled off a donkey.'

Antoinette had been brought up to feel a ready concern for the people and this reveals itself in two incidents that caused favourable comment. One day at Compiègne she was following the hunt in her calèche when the stag sought refuge in a river. The only way to the river lay across a field of ripening wheat, but she would not let her driver turn into the field, much to his surprise. She preferred to miss the kill, she said, rather than cause loss to the peasants, who never received adequate compensation.

During another hunt a peasant was badly gored in the thigh by the stag; the King shouted for him to be cared for but it was Antoinette who stopped, got out, had the injured man placed in her calèche, revived the man's wife, who had fainted, with smelling salts, and brought them both back to Fontainebleau.

Strong-mindedness such as this Antoinette showed even towards the King. Both he and Louis had promised La Vauguyon that his daughter-in-law Madame de Saint-Mégrin should have the place of mistress of the Dauphine's wardrobe. Antoinette, who knew La Vauguyon was working against her marriage, flatly refused to let her have it, and she got her way.

Antoinette was quick to stand up for her rights: sometimes over-quick, and this is a symptom of her early insecurity. At fifteen Provence married a Piedmontese princess, very plain with dark down on her upper lip, in no sense a rival. But when the newcomer had a library made in her apartments, Antoinette demanded one too. She was fobbed off by Madame de Noailles with a few plain wooden shelves, and at this she lost her temper. She immediately had the shelves unscrewed, waited until they were carried away and then superintended the installation of proper glass-enclosed carved cupboards.

Such was the position in the early days of marriage: Louis in his workshop or out hunting, Antoinette with her flowers, her dogs, and other people's children, each for different reasons unsure and constrained. And now yet another shadow fell between them.

Jeanne Bécu was the illegitimate daughter of a woman from the Champagne region who had become a cook in Paris. After starting life as an assistant in a milliner's shop Jeanne attached herself to a Gascon pimp and cardsharper, Comte Jean Du Barry, known from his large female entourage as 'Mahomet'. She spent four years working for Mahomet as a high-class expensive prostitute. Then she came to the notice of the King, lonely since the death of Madame de Pompadour. She had no conversation, nothing to recommend her but the bloom of youth and sexual expertise. The King ordered her to marry Du Barry, so that she could come to Court, and installed her in the late Queen's apartments.

'What do you see in her?' Richelieu asked.

'Only this. She makes me forget I will soon be sixty.'

'Her eyes are of a lively light blue and she has the most wanton look in them that I ever saw,' writes an English lady. 'Her eyebrows are well formed, and so is her nose; her mouth is pretty, her lips very red and her teeth fine, but she has a kind of artificial smirk which also savours strongly of her old trade.' On visiting her in her apartment, the same lady found her surrounded by 'four *femmes de chambre*, two on their feet and two on their knees. She seemed in a very bad humour and called them a great many *bêtes* and scolding one of them in particular, she said she believed never did sow produce such a stupid pig. The Comte de Saint-Florentin said to her, "Don't be impatient, Madame;" she replied with great fierceness, "Shut up. I tell you she's a real pig." '

The new favourite threw money about, filling her rooms with porcelain- or ebony-encrusted furniture, with costly ivories and leather-bound volumes of erotica. The markers on her quadrille game were encrusted with solid gold; she rode in the most sumptuous carriage yet seen, painted by Vallée with cupids, hearts and beds of roses, and decorated with the arms and motto of the Barrymores of Ireland, to whom, she claimed, the Du Barrys of Gascony were related. She had herself painted over and over: often as Flora, in a light silk dress with love knots of myrtle, roses on her brow, and pearls on her shapely arms, but also, to pique the King's jaded appetite, as a curly-haired boy playing the guitar.

Madame Du Barry received the King every afternoon at her *pavillon* of Lucienues, a gift from her royal lover, and over fruit and a glass of Spanish wine discussed new ways of asserting herself.

The King allowed her to decide which plays and operas should be given at Court. At Bordeaux a ship was launched called *The Comtesse Du Barry*. She had her Bengali slave, Zamore, baptized and the Prince de Conti's son – a prince of the blood – stood godfather. 'This street-walker has just received the homage of Europe,' wrote Walpole. 'The holy Nuncio, and every Ambassador but he of Spain, have waited on her, and brought gold, frankincense and myrrh.'

How did Louis react to this powerful woman? As a boy he had watched his father snub and cut the Pompadour, and he had been taught to abhor royal mistresses. He certainly felt no respect for Madame Du Barry. But in making a friend of the King, he had had to accept her, and it was she who received him at the hunting suppers. Louis was polite to her for the King's sake. In true Versailles fashion he compromised.

Antoinette's first reaction to the favourite is expressed in a letter to her mother: 'It is pitiable to see the weakness he [the King] has for Madame Du Barry, who is the silliest and most impertinent creature imaginable.' Antoinette is concerned chiefly about the King, not the favourite; she likes her men to be strong and is disturbed at his subjection.

Antoinette had been entrusted by the King to Aunt Adélaïde and this Daughter of France loathed Madame Du Barry. Aunt Adélaïde's hatred of the upstart exceeded even her hatred of Austria and she set herself to make an ally of Antoinette. In this she succeeded, for the two had much in common, including gumption and a fondness for dogs and music. Aunt Adélaïde then convinced Antoinette that Madame Du Barry had the King in her clutches and that it was the duty of all right-minded princesses to show disapproval.

Madame Du Barry quickly made a warning sign. That summer she prevented one of Antoinette's ladies pushing past her in the stalls of the Court theatre, and when the other persisted, made a scene. She got the King to send the lady away from Court, and Antoinette, crying secretly in her room, could obtain no redress.

Antoinette had only one political ally at Court, the splendid Duc de Choiseul. As Minister of Foreign Affairs he had arranged her marriage and he championed the Austrian alliance. She felt a severe shock therefore when on 14 December 1770 Madame Du Barry secured Choiseul's dismissal, and an even greater shock when Madame Du Barry gave his job to the Duc d'Aiguillon, one of her lovers and opposed to Austria. Antoinette now saw the Du Barry not just as a threat to the King but as a threat to herself and to her marriage. The fact that Louis continued to see the favourite socially heightened her alarm.

One day, says Mercy, Antoinette gave her husband 'a lecture on this excessive liking for the hunt which spoiled his health, and on the unkempt and rough appearance resulting from this exercise'. What she was really objecting to were the after-hunt suppers with Madame Du Barry. Louis retreated to his apartments, but Antoinette pursued him, and 'continued to point out, somewhat strongly, all the drawbacks of his way of life'. The scene ended with both Louis and Antoinette in tears.

Another incident is described by Mercy. 'The prince had some days earlier brought on an attack of indigestion by eating too much pastry; at supper Madame the Dauphine had all the dishes containing pastry removed from his table and forbade any more pastry to be served until further order.' From motives already explained Mercy again suggests that the Dauphine has her husband well under control, and for long the passage has been cited as proof that Louis was a glutton who guzzled himself sick. Louis's eating habits will emerge later. For the moment it is enough to notice that the King served richly spiced food at his suppers in order to stimulate his sexual powers, and that Louis's rare attacks of indigestion – four in four years – always occurred after supper with the King, one being the occasion described by Mercy. The real motive for Antoinette's displeasure was that Louis had again supped with the King and Madame Du Barry.

The weapon of disapproval at European courts was silence. Louis's father had used it against the Pompadour, Louis used it against Vermond, and Antoinette now used it against the Du Barry. Whenever the favourite appeared, Antoinette spoke not a word to her.

Louis took a poor view of this. He wanted peace at Court. When Madame Du Barry complained to the King, and he through Madame de Noailles hinted that the Dauphine should appear less distant to Madame Du Barry, Louis urged Antoinette to comply. As Maria Theresa gave the same advice, Antoinette yielded, though to do so, she felt, was not 'honest'.

On New Year's Day 1772 the Court ladies came to pay their respects to the royal family. Madame Du Barry arrived with the new Foreign Minister's wife, the Duchesse d'Aiguillon, a respectable lady who had been a friend of the late Queen, and the Maréchale de

Mirepoix, known as 'the little cat', who treated life as a big joke and to whom the Pompadour had left her diamond watch. Antoinette spoke first to the Duchesse d'Aiguillon, then turned to the Du Barry. Looking the favourite straight in the eye, she said, 'There are a lot of people at Versailles today.' No more than that, but it sufficed. The King, her husband and Madame Du Barry were delighted.

The year that had opened with signs of reconciliation turned out to be the worst so far for Louis and Antoinette. Frederick of Prussia proposed to Catherine of Russia and Maria Theresa a three-fold partition of Poland, which had long been under French influence. Maria Theresa hesitated to act against the spirit of the new alliance, writing to her son, 'What a bad example we shall be giving if we prostitute our honour for a miserable morsel of Poland.' But she was outmanœuvred by Frederick and finally in self-defence occupied Polish Galicia.

The King was furious; so was Louis. The French ambassador, Louis de Rohan, having failed to give Versailles due warning of the partition, tried to win back favour by sending d'Aiguillon a witty dispatch vilifying Maria Theresa. D'Aiguillon passed it to Madame Du Barry, who at her next party read to the guests Rohan's droll account of Antoinette's mother shedding crocodile tears over Poland. There began to be talk in her circle of disowning the alliance, and d'Aiguillon insinuated to the King that Maria Theresa's letters to Antoinette, which Antoinette kept hidden or burned, contained anti-French advice. Madame Du Barry then followed up her victory by letting it be known that she would call at the Dauphine's apartments one day in October.

Antoinette now thoroughly detested Madame Du Barry, but again she was advised by Louis and the King to speak to her. On the morning of the appointed day she prayed, 'O God, if it is Thy will I should speak, make me speak. I shall act as Thou shalt deign to inspire me.'

The ladies arrived and Antoinette, as before, spoke first to the Duchesse d'Aiguillon. Then, glancing at Madame Du Barry but not addressing her directly, she added in a cold tone: 'What weather! All day it's been impossible to go out.'

This time Madame Du Barry was not pleased. Antoinette's tone and expression amounted almost to a snub. She decided to step up her attacks on 'the redhead': a scornful allusion to the red tints in Antoinette's hair, which were considered unattractive.

One day Antoinette and the Comtesse de Provence, returning from a visit to Aunt Victoire, stopped to look at a sundial on the palace wall. Above were the royal apartments, where the favourite lived, and suddenly from that direction came hurtling down a pailful of slops. Antoinette's dress was bespattered, and angrily she went to show it to the King. 'Papa, just see what happens when one walks under your windows! You ought to get your household in better order.' Louis asked which window the slops had come from. 'From one of yours.' The King understood, said he would scold the culprit but did nothing.

Such incidents were at most galling; much more serious was a full-scale attempt to wreck Louis's and Antoinette's marriage. On the day after his wedding Provence informed the King, who liked such details, that he had been 'four times happy' and that his bride had enjoyed it 'marvellously'. It was known, by contrast, that Louis had not yet consummated his marriage. The anti-Austrian party, grouped around Madame Du Barry and now allied with Provence's circle, sought to keep Louis and Antoinette apart, and eventually to secure a dissolution of their marriage on grounds of nullity.

In the autumn, when the Court moved to the honey-stoned Renaissance château of Fontainebleau, they bribed the Inspector of Buildings to stop work on Louis's apartments, which were to have been redecorated in time for his arrival. Instead of being next to Antoinette, Louis found himself at the far end of the castle.

Louis said nothing; Antoinette went to her bedroom and wept. But then she acted with great energy. She went straight to the King, explained what had happened and asked him to put things right. This time she got her way. The painting and gilding were speeded up, and a week later the young couple's temporary separation ended.

Louis meanwhile had had ample occasion to observe Antoinette's behaviour. Over Madame Du Barry she had followed his advice, though falteringly; over the Polish business, though much provoked, she had shown restraint. She was certainly influenced, through Mercy, by her mother, but Maria Theresa's advice, Louis deduced, was 'Keep out of politics.' At Fontainebleau she had shown a touching readiness to save the marriage. All in all he considered she had acted 'honestly' – a word often on her lips – and he felt satisfied that she had no intention of working against him politically.

A major obstacle to consummation of the marriage was now removed. Louis, moreover, had matured physically. At eighteen he was a young man of exceptional strength. He could grip a spade in his right hand, seat a teen-age boy on the blade and, without bending his arm, slowly lift spade and boy to shoulder-height. This strength gave him a certain assurance, as did his friendship with the King. What he still lacked was confidence in himself as heir to the throne, and this, shortly after his eighteenth birthday, he acquired.

The first official visit of Louis and his wife to Paris, long delayed by Court jealousies, took place on 8 June 1773. They drove to Notre Dame through flower-strewn streets and triumphal arches, and dined publicly in the concert-hall of the Tuileries. They then walked in the gardens, tumultuously cheered for their many acts of kindness towards poor people. 'There was such a great crowd,' says Antoinette, 'that we remained for three-quarters of an hour without being able to go forward or back. The Dauphin and I several times ordered the guards not to strike anyone, which made a very good impression.' Then they appeared on the Tuileries balcony, while handkerchiefs were waved and hats thrown in the air. The Duc de Brissac turned to Antoinette: 'Madame, two hundred thousand people have fallen in love with you.'

'M. le Dauphin behaved admirably:' even Mercy admitted it, while Antoinette wrote: 'He answered all the speeches wonderfully well, he noticed everything that was done for him, and above all he saw the zeal and happiness of the people, for whom he showed a great deal of kindness.' At the Opéra a week later, and at the Comédie Française on the 23rd Louis again had the satisfaction of being warmly cheered, and this at a time when the King was so unpopular he dared not set foot in Paris. It gave him the confidence he needed.

Louis was now a changed man from the insecure youth of three years before. He had cleared up his suspicions of his Austrian wife, and his doubts about himself. In July he and the rest of the Court left Versailles for Compiègne, a modern country house with a portico and small, intimate rooms. Here, in the garden or in the quiet of her apartment, a young man was able to be alone with his pretty wife. Louis that summer fell in love with Antoinette; he kissed her, even in public, every evening he arranged for plays to be performed for her privately in his apartment, jolly plays which, as one observer noted, took people's minds off Court intrigue. Afterwards he went to her bedroom; two letters hitherto unpublished in any biography of Louis or Antoinette, suggest that consummation of the marriage then took place.

'I can tell my dear Maman, and her alone,' writes Antoinette on

17 July 1773, 'that since our arrival here my relations with him have much progressed and I think our marriage has been consummated, although I am not yet pregnant; for that very reason the Dauphin does not want it made known yet; how happy I should be if I had a child next May. My menstruation is abundant and normal; during those periods you can be sure I do not ride.'

In her next letter, dated 13 August, Antoinette continues the story. 'Two days after writing to you the Dauphin and I thought we ought to tell the King what had happened. He embraced me with great tenderness and called me his dear daughter. It was decided to reveal our secret; everyone is very pleased about it. Since then there is no decisive news as to whether I am pregnant. On the last day of the month I had my period, as usual a few days early. I still haven't given up hope of having a child in May.'

Other evidence tends to confirm the view that during this summer at Compiègne, when Louis was eighteen and Antoinette seventeen, they became man and wife in the full sense. They walked about arm in arm, and this unusual practice became the fashion: courtiers and their wives who rarely exchanged a word now wished to be seen arm in arm for a whole evening and, we are told, they found the time drag. Louis held up his head before the King and his brothers, while now it was Madame Du Barry who made advances to Antoinette. In January 1774 she arranged for the Comte de Noailles to show Antoinette a pair of ear-rings belonging to a Paris jeweller, each set with four diamonds and worth 700,000 livres. If Antoinette liked them – and the Du Barry knew she was fond of jewellery – why, she could keep them: she, Madame Du Barry, would arrange for the King to make her a present of them. Antoinette took much pleasure in saying she was satisfied with the diamonds she already possessed: a reply that for once won her mother's complete approval.

Louis, we know, felt personal relations deeply, and although he kept quiet about it, we may guess that he now experienced happiness, all the more intense after three years of turmoil. He was in love, and to Louis as to any young man that meant a great deal. But also his marriage was now in order, things were regular, and to someone like Louis that meant quite as much.

The King meanwhile was ageing prematurely, sucked dry by Madame Du Barry. When he rode to hounds it was noticed that he sat hunched in the saddle.

'I must rein in the horses,' he told his doctor.

'You'd do better to unharness them.'

On Wednesday 27 April 1774 the King dined with Madame Du Barry and Louis at Trianon, and that evening complained of a headache and shivering. He was hurried back to Versailles and in on him closed the doctors he was accustomed to talk about so often because he feared them. They twice drew from his body four big vials of blood; they probed, weighed, talked Latin and at last issued a bulletin gravely informing the world that his Majesty's urine was 'praiseworthy both in quantity and quality'. But they knew that his disease was smallpox and that the reign of fifty-nine years was drawing to a close.

It had begun well enough, but the second half had been disastrous, with its lost wars and heavy spending on kept women. Asked to pray for the stricken King, Parisians quipped: 'Our father who art in Versailles, hallowed be thy name; thy will is done neither on earth nor in heaven . . .'

Louis and Antoinette were forbidden the sick-room for fear of infection, so they waited in their own apartments, apprehensive for one they regarded with affection and even more on their own account, should they be called to rule so young. Brave Aunt Adélaïde nursed her father, helped by the other aunts. They were torn between wishing to see the King prepare his soul and anxiety lest by telling him the nature of his disease they might precipitate a shock, what was technically called a *révolution*, that would kill him instantly. Finally, they did tell him, and on the afternoon of 4 May, as a condition of absolution, the King sent Madame Du Barry away.

On 7 May the King made his confession to the almost blind, saintly abbé Maudoux, enumerating his sins since his last confession thirty-eight years before, while the courtiers, watch in hand, timed the sacrament at a full sixteen minutes. Two days later he received extreme unction. 'He was motionless, his mouth open, his face neither deformed nor showing any sign of agitation, but towards the end swollen and copper-coloured, like a Moor or negro.'

It had been arranged that a candle should burn in the window of the sick-room and be blown out when the King drew his last breath. From their own windows Louis and Antoinette anxiously watched the candle, while the hours ticked away. At 3.15 in the morning of 10 May the flame was blown out. The doors of the Œil de Bœuf antechamber were then flung open and the Lord Chamberlain, the Duc de Bouillon, advanced to the railing. 'Gentlemen,' he said, 'the King is dead.'

CHAPTER 5

The Young King

THEIR trunks had been packed, their coach stood waiting, and as soon as the candle went out Louis and Antoinette left the infected palace. As shouts went up of *'Vive le Roi!'* Louis's eyes filled with tears and he hid his face. They drove to Choisy, the small house where the late King had received news of his grandson's birth. There they would remain for nine days, Louis not even able to see his possibly contagious Ministers. A reign usually began in a flurry of excitement, meetings and pressure; this one began, characteristically, with Louis alone in his study.

'I feel the universe is going to fall on me,' Louis said on becoming King, and the image is revealing from his usually reserved lips. He was thinking first of his kingdom.

France was very big: the biggest state in Europe save Russia, inhabited by 25 million people, all but a million of whom drew a living from the soil. Frenchmen produced wheat, oats, barley and olive oil, raised cows, sheep, goats, pigs and horses; however, thanks to better hygiene and medicine, there had been in the eighteenth century such a population explosion that it was a hard job – and it would be Louis's job – to feed so many mouths.

Only half a million Frenchmen produced goods in workshops, for manufacturing in this conservative country had developed more slowly than in England and Holland. So there were few exports to cover imports of wheat. Then again, many of the colonies that had provided wealth under Louis XIV had been lost in Louis XV's wars. These had greatly aggravated the chronic insolvency of the state, the inevitable consequence of the ever-increasing costs of government in a country where most of those who possessed wealth had managed to secure either partial or total exemption from taxation. Inheriting an enormous accumulated debt, Louis XVI and Antoinette were confronted also with an annual deficit of 22 millions. Deficit was a word often to be thrown in their faces; it was in fact something they inherited.

France's army and navy were in a poor state of morale, partly as the result of defeats, partly because the late King had lost his people's affection. Reports spoke of lax discipline and embezzlement. The English commissioner in Dunkirk was like a pistol pointed at France's head.

France, above all, was administratively a much divided land. Region was walled apart from region by immensely complicated customs barriers, local taxation systems, different weights and measures, conflicting codes of justice. These divisions overlapped, rather like superimposed, quite different jigsaw puzzles. Even at the comparatively simple level of legislation, Louis found himself in some respects King of thirteen Frances rather than of a single state. Their names were Normandy, Brittany and newly acquired Lorraine, Dauphiné in the Alps, Béarn in the Pyrenees, and eight more: like lumps of iron on Louis's workshop forge, not yet properly welded. Voltaire could quip that with each change of horses one found a change of laws, but for a King it was no joke. Almost everything he did would have to be done thirteen times.

Louis XIV had said in effect, '*L'état c'est moi*,' and his words had found an echo among Frenchmen, since he came to the throne after a disruptive civil war and they saw the need of a unifying hand. The new King could not truly use the same phrase. Each of the thirteen former provinces had recently become much more conscious of ancient rights; a regional independence had grown up clustered around the local Parlement; lawyers poring over dusty scrolls were claiming this prerogative, that tax exemption; France was now undoubtedly a more difficult country to rule than the France of Louis XIV.

France was divided politically too. 'Whatever dreams the levity of the country may form of halcyon days and a golden reign,' wrote Stormont, 'every instrument of faction, every Court engine is constantly at work, and the whole is such a scene of jealousy, cabal and intrigue that no enemy need wish it more.' In law and in theory the King's will was final and his power supreme, but each faction wanted a different kind of cut-down King. The princely families wanted one who would restore their alleged ancient rights of participation in the work of government; the ordinary nobles a King who would maintain their local privileges and perhaps lead them to victory on the battlefield; the Paris Parlement wanted a King who would consult them deferentially on all decisions; the encyclopædists one who would initiate major reforms. When Aunt Louise gave young Louis her portrait inscribed: 'For the eldest son of the Church . . . His reign, already determined by his uncommon virtue, will be that of Faith,' she was speaking for a hierarchy that wanted a King to burn books and suppress Protestant services. And what of the mass of Frenchmen? They wanted a kindly father-figure, a new Henri IV, mixing easily with them, bantering and drinking wine in their taverns, easing their lot, ensuring, as Henri put it, 'a chicken in their pot on Sundays'.

'I feel the universe is going to fall on me': Louis's words applied equally to himself. In a boyhood essay he had written, 'The power of the throne is absolute, nothing can check it, but it must be based on justice and reason; and people must always be allowed to advise and enlighten it.' Balancing this very high conception of his new role, Louis had a very low opinion of himself. He knew himself to be inexperienced, ignorant and, especially, alone. His isolation at Choisy symbolized a larger isolation. Whereas the great families, the Rohans of Brittany, the Condés of the Ile de France, were knit together by a web of intermarriage, Louis had wed a foreign princess, as had his brothers, and so he lacked these powerful family alliances. At the top of the pyramid he was peculiarly vulnerable.

The first thing Louis did when he arrived at Choisy was to write to the Minister of the Household, saying he wished to be known simply as Louis, not Louis Auguste. The second thing was to decide on an adviser.

An obvious choice, and the one suggested by Antoinette, was the Duc de Choiseul. But Louis remembered Choiseul's hostility to his father and disliked his costly policy of splendour: as he pithily put it, '*Tout ce qui est Choiseul est mangeur.*' A list of possible advisers had been left him by his father; high on it he found the name of Comte Jean Frédéric de Maurepas: 'A former Minister, now in disfavour . . . has retained the true principles of politics.'

Maurepas started as an infant prodigy, succeeding his father as Secretary for the Navy at the age of fourteen and a half. He had risen to be Minister of the Navy and at thirty-nine was reckoned by the Prussian ambassador to be the best Minister in the land. From his mother, a La Rochefoucauld, he had inherited a ready wit that served him well at Versailles. For example, young Louis XV had had the tiresome habit of tearing his courtiers' lace cuffs, and Maurepas determined to check it. One day he arrived wearing exceptionally beautiful lace. The King sauntered up and ripped one of the cuffs to pieces. Maurepas coolly ripped the other, saying,

'That gave me no pleasure at all,' but in such a way that the King reddened and tore no further lace.

Another time Maurepas entered the apartments of the Queen. Finding everyone looking miserable, he asked why. 'The Queen has lost a kinsman,' someone explained, 'today is the first day of mourning. No one dares start a game and her Majesty is bored.' Maurepas knew the Queen's fondness for a flutter. Putting on a very grave expression, he said, 'Not even piquet? Piquet is sheer mournfulness.' Even the Queen smiled.

Wit, however, led to a fall. Maurepas disapproved of the Pompadour's interference in politics and began to write clever verses against her. She complained to Maurepas, then Minister of the Household, and told him to discover who had written the verses, strongly suspecting that he was their author. Maurepas gave a vague, off-hand reply.

'You are not very respectful, Monsieur, to the King's mistresses.'

'On the contrary, Madame, I have always respected them, whoever they may be.'

That evening at a party somebody said to Maurepas that he seemed to have had an interesting visitor. 'Yes,' he replied, 'the Marquise. It won't do her any good. I'm not lucky to the mistresses. I seem to remember that Madame de Mailly came to see me two days before her sister took her place, and of course everyone knows that I poisoned Madame de Châteauroux. I bring them all bad luck.'

The Pompadour told Louis, said she feared for her life and demanded Maurepas's dismissal. Two days later she had the satisfaction of seeing the King write a note to Maurepas: 'I request you herewith to resign your Ministry . . . and retire to Bourges within the week.'

That had been twenty-five years ago. Maurepas, adaptable, settled down to the life of a country gentleman, happily married but childless, caring for his estate, in the evening acting in amateur theatricals. He was forgotten at Versailles save by a few who recalled, under the veneer of wit, a man of integrity; the Dauphin, Aunt Adélaïde, who had spoken well of him to Louis, and the Duc de La Vauguyon, who before his recent death had also recommended one who had been a trusted friend.

Louis sat down at his desk in Choisy and wrote to Maurepas: 'I am the King, and many, many obligations are contained in that one word: but I am only in my twentieth year. I do not think I have acquired all the necessary knowledge . . . I have always heard your integrity spoken of, as well as the reputation that your deep knowledge of affairs has so rightly won you. It is this that induces me to beg you to be so kind as to help me with your advice and understanding.'

Louis had never seen Maurepas face to face, only once from a window. He found a plainly dressed dignified figure, slightly below middle height, grey-haired, with a rosy face, intelligent eyes and a wide, humorous mouth. He spoke in the precise way Louis liked and showed an astonishing memory for a man of seventy-three.

The two talked in general terms about the country which, as Antoinette wrote to her mother, 'the late King left in a very bad state.' Among his questions, Louis asked, 'What is the best way of correcting the morals of my people and restoring them to a due sense of virtue and religion?'

'There is only one way, Sire: show them a good example.'

Louis formed a favourable first impression. He liked Maurepas's common sense – 'extremely agreeable and *sensible*' was Horace Walpole's summing-up – his gaiety and the immense experience from which he could hope to learn. At the same time Louis was determined not to be dominated, and he probably sensed, as Stormont did, that Maurepas had 'a timid, irresolute mind'. Maurepas seemed the man Louis was looking for: someone who knew the ropes and could train him to govern.

Maurepas could remember the day when young Louis XV had appointed a prime minister, and now, at the end of their interview, he said to the new King, 'Your Majesty then makes me Prime Minister?'

'No,' said Louis. 'That was not at all my intention.'

'I understand. Your Majesty wishes that I should show him how to do without one.'

Whereas a prime minister would have worked alone with the King, and afterwards in the light of those meetings taken decisions with other Ministers, Louis appointed Maurepas a principal Minister without portfolio. He would sit in the Cabinet to advise the King but not share power with him; hence his Court nickname, 'the Mentor'.

As regards day to day business, Louis at once made an important innovation. His grandfather had not himself opened letters and dispatches. He let Ministers do that and gave them directives how to answer. Louis, however, was determined really to rule, so he began each day by opening all letters and distributing them to the appropriate Ministers. In this way Louis was the first to have cognizance of any important business. When it came to answering the letters, Louis either replied himself or read, and sometimes modified, the final text of a Minister's reply. In the first weeks of his reign Louis wrote more than sixty letters to his Foreign Minister, and letters of instructions to ambassadors abroad nearly all carry the word 'Approved' in the King's neat hand.

On 20 May, as soon as Ministers came out of quarantine, Louis called a Cabinet, and now the difficult part of his reign began. The three most powerful Ministers, Chancellor de Maupeou, Terray the Finance Minister, and the Duc d'Aiguillon, Foreign Minister, owed their appointment to Madame Du Barry. Known from their bilious complexions as the three yellow men, they seemed to him to symbolize the dissoluteness of the late reign; and were also very unpopular because they had pursued policies that clashed with strong vested interests.

Louis had been brought up to believe that 'War should be decided on only after the most measured deliberation, and only when it is unavoidable,' but that was certainly not the view of the Duc d'Aiguillon, a man of aggressive character and military tastes, Colonel of the crack Light Horse, and also Madame Du Barry's lover – to his estate at Ruel she had gone on leaving Louis XV's sick-bed. On 2 June Louis asked Maurepas, who was d'Aiguillon's uncle, to invite d'Aiguillon to resign. D'Aiguillon did so, but took it hard and at once began intriguing to regain power.

Louis appointed to the vacant post Charles Gravier, Comte de Vergennes, a tall, unostentatious man of fifty-seven with the mask-like face of a career diplomat. Louis's instructions to him were brief: 'Honesty and restraint must be our policy.' In other words, an end to ruinous wars.

While ambassador in Constantinople Vergennes had married the widow of a Greek surgeon, Anna Testa, with two children. The snobs of Versailles had circulated gossip about Anna, simply because she was Greek, and had so far prevented her from being received. Louis, knowing that Vergennes wished it, at once arranged for Anna to be presented at Court, a friendly act which brought tears to the eyes of the usually reserved Vergennes.

Louis's Cabinet reshuffle was now unexpectedly interrupted. Fifty persons at Court, including Louis's aunts, went down with smallpox, and ten died. Though inoculation was then in its infancy and had recently resulted in several fatalities, Louis decided to be inoculated. Not only that, but his brothers should be inoculated too – Antoinette had had a mild form of the disease. Despite the pleas of his doctors and of Archbishop de Beaumont, who frowned on inoculation as 'unnatural', Louis was inoculated at Marly on 17 June, and for the second time found himself in isolation. According to Stormont, 'no one was to attend him who had not had smallpox and he has had the humanity to extend this order to his lowest servants.' He ran a temperature and felt an urge to vomit, Antoinette telling her mother gaily that 'he has very spectacular spots on his nose, wrist and chest,' the Duc de Croy confiding to his diary alarm for the King 'working unceasingly instead of hunting, in the full heat of summer, his bloodstream in a state of revolution.'

In early July Louis recovered from inoculation and resumed normal life. His fondness for travel, geography and scientific instruments led him to take keen interest in the navy. The Minister he had inherited was Bourgeois de Boynes, a fat beer-drinking lawyer who couldn't tell a mizzen-mast from a bobstay and had 'mislaid' three million livres. Louis wished to remove him, provided he could find a suitable successor.

Among those with whom Louis discussed the matter was Maurepas's close friend and confessor, abbé Joseph Alphonse de Véri, formerly Auditor in the Rota, a papal tribunal that decides whether certain marriages may or may not be dissolved; an intelligent man of moderate views and, at fifty, more in touch with the rising generation that Maurepas. Véri in fact was Maurepas's *éminence grise*, as was noted by young Lieutenant Buonaparte: 'Madame de Maurepas, who ruled Monsieur de Maurepas, was ruled by Monsieur de Véri . . . an economist and a friend of Turgot. It was Véri who selected Turgot to occupy a place in the Government.'

Louis as a rule had little fondness for priests but he liked Véri and was later to employ him. It is quite probable that he did first hear from the abbé about Anne Robert Turgot, who had shown exceptional ability as the King's intendant in Limoges, and Maurepas agreed with Véri that Turgot was the right man for the Navy.

Louis began to reflect on the proposed change. Boynes, unlike d'Aiguillon, was not obnoxious to him. He had done his job reasonably well. Like many physically strong men, Louis recoiled from hurting people; above all to their face. It was Maurepas who had dropped the hint to d'Aiguillon; Boynes he would have to dismiss himself. 'The indecision in the King's character begins to obtrude,' Véri noted. 'He wished to dismiss M. de Boynes yet so far has not succeeded in doing it.'

On Tuesday 19 July Louis was prodded by Maurepas. 'Affairs of state,' Maurepas said, 'require decision. You do not want to keep M. de Boynes. You have spoken to me well of M. Turgot; take him for the Navy since you have not decided to part with abbé Terray.'

'The King gave no reply, but in the evening upon returning from his stroll he wrote asking M. de La Vrillière [Minister of the Household] to summon Turgot immediately to his presence.' First Louis dismissed Boynes, then he appointed Turgot Minister of the Navy, confiding to Maurepas that if he thought well of Turgot he might give him a higher post.

Louis next turned his attention to the two strongest men in the old Government. Chancellor René Nicolas de Maupeou, a stocky lawyer with thick black eyebrows, had initiated major structural changes in French government by suspending the Parlement of Paris in 1771, ostensibly for its refusal to obey a royal command but in reality in order to end its perpetual obstruction of royal policy. According to Walpole, Maupeou 'does as much hurt *against* all law as any of his profession ever did *by* law.' He was arrogant and, said Louis, 'he hardly deigns to look at me, let alone speak me a word.' As Chancellor he could not be dismissed, but he would have to be asked to resign.

The other Minister, abbé Terray, was a tall, stooping, forbidding figure known as 'the great buzzard'. He had cut State spending, which Louis approved of, but his hands were not clean, he had squandered heavily among Madame Du Barry's friends and was generally detested.

Louis worked with Terray every week, and this increased his anxiety. 'I should like to be able to keep him,' Louis told Maurepas, 'but he's too much of a rogue. It's annoying, very annoying.' When Maurepas suggested Turgot for Terray's post, Louis raised objections: 'He is very much a man of theory; and he has associations with the encyclopædists' – Turgot had actually contributed to the *Encyclopédie*, the book which by arranging all things alphabetically did so much to erode hierarchies, and where 'Roi' was just another word between 'Rohandrians', a Madagascar tribe, and 'Roide' meaning 'stiff'.

On 24 August Louis had a long talk with Turgot about the economy and afterwards was pressed by Maurepas. Louis admitted that he still wished to dismiss Maupeou and Terray, but spoke of postponing nominations till the following Saturday.

'Certainly not!' retorted Maurepas. 'That is not the way to govern a State. Time, I repeat, is not a thing that you can waste at your caprice! You must give your decision before I leave.'

Louis protested that he was only just twenty and overwhelmed with business.

'You've always told me you wanted an honest Minister. Is Terray honest? If not, change him. That is your function. The last few days, the abbé Terray has given you openings. At the end of the day's work he's asked you if you were pleased with his administration.'

'I didn't dare,' Louis admitted. 'I was brought up to feel afraid when speaking to a Minister.'

That same day Louis overcame his fear of 'the great buzzard' and also, in his person, of the corrupt Court that had weighed on his boyhood. He dismissed Terray, and obliged Maupeou to resign. The date was 24 August, the feast of St Bartholomew, so courtiers quipped that the young King had perpetrated a new Massacre.

It had been customary to exile dismissed Ministers – a ritual peculiar to France and Turkey, said Maria Theresa – but Louis softened the blow by allowing Terray and Maupeou to live in the Versailles region. Terray narrowly escaped being thrown into the Seine by angry Parisians, then retired to his estate at La Mothe, where he was consoled by the Baronne de La Garde. 'Terray has been downgraded from Minister to private soldier,' said the wits, 'since in future his only occupation will be to mount guard.' As for Louis, 'I am assured,' writes Stormont, 'that the first time the King went a-hunting after the Chancellor's disgrace, the Compiègne fishwives followed him with acclamations of "Vive le Roi!" and said, "*Votre Grand Père a bien chassé mais il n'a jamais fait une aussi belle chasse que celle que vous venez de faire!*" '[1]

So far Louis had been living at Choisy, La Muette, Marly and Compiègne. But on the first day of September he installed himself in the King's splendid gilt and white apartments on the first floor of Versailles, and this marks the start of personal rule with his own Government. He gave Antoinette adjoining apartments; to Maurepas and his charming wife, known from their closeness as Philemon and Baucis, he gave apartments immediately above his own, formerly occupied by Madame Du Barry. Véri received rooms too:

[1]'Your grandfather was a good huntsman but he never hunted to half such good effect as you've just done.'

he was so well-off he kept a coach-and-six, his own chef and his own pastry-cook.

Louis had a wholly new Cabinet save for the Minister of the Household. It comprised Maurepas, Vergennes, Turgot and three new members: Gabriel de Sartine, Maréchal de Muy, War Minister, and a Norman lawyer friend of Maurepas, Armand de Miromesnil, who became simply Keeper of the Seals, for Louis discontinued the powerful post of Chancellor. It was a Cabinet notable for the modest origin of its members. Louis presided over it on Sundays and Wednesdays; it took decisions by majority vote and these were published over the King's signature as edicts or decrees. On Tuesdays Louis worked with his Council of Finances, on Saturdays with the Council of Dispatches, which dealt with provincial admin-istration. Louis's attitude at this stage is summed up in his phrase at the first Cabinet meeting: 'I wish to acquire a thorough knowledge of all that concerns the prosperity of my kingdom. Above all, gentlemen, do not forget St Louis's maxim: "Everything unjust is impossible." '

Louis found learning a full-time occupation, and it was noticed that when Papillon de La Ferté, comptroller of the King's Menus Plaisirs – the department devoted to his minor amusements – came to ask for orders, Louis said, 'My Menus Plaisirs are to walk about in the park. I do not need you.'

Louis worked alone with his Mentor on Tuesdays and Fridays, and together they tackled by far their biggest problem: what attitude to adopt to the Parlements. These bore no resemblance to English Parliament. They were law courts of the highest rank com-posed of magistrates and lawyers who bought their seats at a high price. Whereas an English member of Parliament was an elected representative of the people, on whose behalf, theoretically at least, he spoke, the men of the French Parlements spoke for themselves and their quite small class, the *noblesse de robe*: that is, lawyers who had acquired the rank and privileges of noblemen.

The most important of the thirteen Parlements was that of Paris, whose jurisdiction extended over ten million people in northern France, and which was known simply as Parlement. By tradition rather than legal force it had arrogated to itself the right of registering certain royal edicts, notably taxation measures, before they could become law. If it raised objections, the King could go in full state to the magistrates and hold a *lit de justice*: that is, seated on his throne – originally a bed of cushions – under a dais, he formally stated his will, and Parlement was then bound to register the edict.

Parlement, however, by continuing to utter 'remonstrances' could encourage its sister Parlements in the provinces to refuse to register the same edict. To this the King might reply by exiling Parlement and so depriving magistrates of their well-paid jobs in Paris: in this way he could usually bring them to heel. Throughout the reign of Louis XV conflicts of this sort had simultaneously checked royal power and stultified Ministers' efforts to modernize France.

In 1771 Parlement capped long and vociferous opposition to the King's heavy spending by going on strike, whereupon Chancellor de Maupeou exiled all its members to Troyes, and in order that justice could continue to flow went a stage further: he created new courts and new judges, but without compensating members of Parlement. Maupeou had in effect suppressed the Parlement of Paris, and he also suppressed two provincial Parlements, those in Rouen and Douai. This gave the Crown more power, but rendered it unpopular, for the Parlements, past masters of the art of propaganda, had succeeded in identifying their cause with that of the populace. The question facing Louis was, Should he or should he not continue to rule without Parlement?

Louis's father had hated Parlement for its anti-clericalism, and once said that you could rule France without magistrates, but not without bishops. Maria Theresa believed that Louis should rule without the obstructive lawyers, and so did Louis's brother Provence: 'If you restore the exiled Parlements,' he warned, 'France will soon see republican senators, like those in Geneva, Venice or Berne, and the King will become hardly more than a doge.'

Maurepas disagreed. He told Louis, 'Without Parlement, no monarchy. That is the principle I learned from my grandfather, Chancellor de Pontchartrain.' Pontchartrain had been Louis XIV's Chancellor, and Maurepas was saying in effect that even so absolute a monarch as the Sun King had tolerated Parlement.

Louis, we know, wanted to rule personally, and was jealous of his authority. But he was sufficiently a child of his age to have great trust in the people. He wanted to take account of public opinion and so win that popularity his grandfather in later life had lost. Knowing this, Maurepas told Louis, 'You must listen to public opinion and follow it. A monarch who recalls Parlement will be considered a friend of the people.'

Louis saw that such a decision would make his task as King more difficult. But the manner of Parlement's suppression had been unjust; whenever the obedient judges appointed by Maupeou appeared in the streets they were shouted at and booed; and informed opinion generally favoured a return to the traditional system. For these reasons Louis decided to restore Parlement in November. To those, like Provence, who threw up their hands, Louis replied, 'It is the people's wish, and I want to be popular.'

Louis would have to make a speech. On such occasions Louis XV had been so shy he could hardly read four sentences without faltering. Maurepas kept impressing the need to speak firmly, and he got the young King to rehearse while one of the Ministers beat time with his hand.

'Too quick,' said the Minister. 'We can't hear you.'

'If only,' sighed Louis, 'I had Provence's grace and measured speech! *He* would do it well. But I mumble.'

On 12 November Louis, wearing an ermine mantle embroidered with fleurs de lis, drove to Paris and entered the great hall of the Palais de Justice, bordering the Seine. Here were assembled the princes and peers, whose hereditary right it was to sit in a full session of Parlement. Louis went to his throne and announced that it was his will to re-establish the former magistrates. The exiled Parlement, who had been recalled from Troyes, then filed in: slightly over one hundred lawyers in scarlet robes. They knelt until receiving a signal to rise.

'The King my grandfather,' Louis told them, 'challenged by your resistance to his orders, took what measures were necessary to maintain his authority and administer justice. Today I am calling you back to functions that you should never have laid aside. This is a favour I am doing you; never forget it.' 'His Majesty,' says Stormont, 'spoke with great dignity, and with as much readiness as if he had been accustomed to speak in publick.' When Parlement had registered edicts controlling its future activities, Louis made a second speech, telling the lawyers they could count on his protection so long as they did not exceed the due limit of their powers. Afterwards Louis was congratulated by Maurepas on an excellent performance.

Louis's apprenticeship was now complete, but his true character had not yet emerged. He had shown weakness about dismissing Ministers, strength in his way of speaking. 'The King,' says Stormont, 'seems to be very unwilling to be governed or to have the appearance of being so. Whether this comes from a mind that feels its own strength or from one that wishes to conceal its weakness, a little time will tell.'

Antoinette, meanwhile, was also emerging from the chrysalis. On coming to the throne she had felt first a flush of exultation. 'I cannot but marvel,' she wrote to her mother, 'at the dispensation of Providence thanks to which I, the youngest of your children, have been chosen to be queen over the finest realm of Europe.' She was especially pleased at the departure of 'the creature'. From Ruel Madame Du Barry had gone to the convent of Pont aux dames, with instructions from Louis to see no one, since she knew State secrets.

Antoinette now found herself free to behave in her own style. Partly by temperament, partly by upbringing, she liked naturalness. When she felt something strongly, she liked to show it, not to bottle it up, as the French so often did. For example, out of respect for the King it was not 'done' to clap during royal performances. One evening, when she was seventeen, Antoinette had so much enjoyed the dancing of Mademoiselle Heinel that she clapped – and went on clapping. A precedent was set, and soon all the spectators made it a habit to show their approval of a good performance by clapping, even in the presence of the King.

As soon as she became mistress in her own house, Antoinette bought a cabriolet, a little two-wheeled one-horse carriage, and drove it herself. It went fast and required considerable skill to handle. That a Queen of France should travel about so informally was absolutely unprecedented; Mercy called it dangerous and common, and he begged his ward to choose some more stable vehicle. But Antoinette was Queen now, and nobody was going to stop her little cabriolet.

The next thing she relaxed was table etiquette. It was forbidden for her, as either Dauphine or Queen, to eat at the same table as any man save a member of the royal family. On the days when Louis supped with his hunting friends, Antoinette could not share his supper. She had to eat alone with twenty-five or thirty women. As Véri admits, this was a stupid and ridiculous custom, which did not exist at German courts. Antoinette had petitioned Louis XV to relax the rule but without success. Now, as Queen, she got her way. On 22 October for the first time since Versailles was built a Queen of France supped with men other than royalty to share her table.

Louis meanwhile was so busy! Each time she lingered in the

cabinet where he was working on State papers, he said gently, 'Madame, I have business to attend to.' Antoinette would have liked to play a political role but Louis would not allow it. Sometimes she even found it difficult to see him during working hours.

One day, according to a well-informed observer, a 'Grey Sister', that is, a nun of the order of St Vincent de Paul wearing a winged cornet, came to ask for an interview with the King. 'Impossible,' said a secretary. Half an hour later the Grey Sister returned, saying she had something extremely important to tell the King. The captain of the guard ushered her into the cabinet. 'Sire, my convent wishes me to congratulate you on the success of your inoculation, and to ask your help for our impoverished house.' She gave details; the King seemed interested and promised to do something. As she was ushered out, the Grey Sister burst into peals of laughter. Everyone thought she was mad, including the King, who ordered her to be detained but treated gently. This made the Grey Sister laugh even more. 'What! No one recognizes me!' It was the Queen.

Louis was too busy to go to the theatre in Paris but Antoinette went regularly, and to the opera. Her liking for naturalness and simplicity here coincided with the Parisians' taste. They wanted an informal King, like Henri IV, and though they had a less clear concept of their ideal Queen, they were more than delighted when Antoinette came to their city informally, dressed simply *en petite robe*, and accompanied not by an awesome suite or mounted guard, but just by a few friends. A Paris bookseller named Hardy wrote admiringly in his diary of the friendly way Antoinette mixed with ordinary Parisians. It was such a complete break with custom he called it 'a revolution'.

Together, as apart, the King and Queen sought to win the people's good will. When they stayed at the hunting lodge of La Muette near Paris, instead of keeping the gates closed as Louis XV had done, they opened them wide so that all could walk freely in the park. On their accession they had the right to a large present of money – *le droit de joyeux avènement* – which the Parisians would have raised by a tax on wine and coal. The King and Queen waived the present, amounting to 24 million livres.

They had made a good beginning to a reign which, as Véri saw, must bring either reform or revolution. Louis's recall of Parlement and appointment of honest Ministers delighted Parisians, who hung on the statue of Henri IV a notice: 'Resurrexit'. As Henri had reconciled Catholics and Protestants, so they hoped Louis would reconcile the very rich and very poor. Louis too was thinking along these lines, for he opened a fancy-dress New Year's ball dressed as Henri IV. Paris shopkeepers placed in their windows portraits of the young King and Queen; song-writers hailed a new Golden Age. Only Antoinette was wary: 'I am worried by so much popular enthusiasm . . . for it will be impossible to content everyone in a country where their vivacity makes them wish everything done in a minute.'

CHAPTER 6

The Reformer

LOUIS XVI grew up in a gilded slum, in the sense that money was nearly always short at Versailles. His grandfather spent so heavily on his mistresses that salaries of servants, including Louis's tutors, remained unpaid for years. When he was five, Louis saw the royal plate melted down for coinage, and a Minister named Silhouette launched an austerity programme: trousers without pockets, dresses without flounces were called à la Silhouette. The Minister did not last, but silhouette has remained the word for a mere outline of vacant black. As for Versailles, Benjamin Franklin noted: 'The waterworks are out of repair, and so is great part of the front next the town, looking with its shabby half brick walls and broken windows not much better than the houses in Durham Yard [a poor street in London].' In 1770, after the beautiful wedding fireworks, Louis XV asked Terray what he thought of them; Terray replied '*Impayables!*', meaning 'superb', but also 'unpayable'.

Against such a background Louis was naturally taught the importance of thrift. It was drummed into his head that only if the rich were careful with money would they have enough over to help the poor. By nature, as we have seen, Louis was neat and orderly, so it comes as no surprise to find him, at eighteen, starting to keep accounts, and that in these he noted each expenditure, however small. 'For a watch-glass, 12 sous; to Bastard for postage of a letter, 9 sous; for paper, 4 sous; for thread, 10 sous.' Every month he totted up what he had spent. Once he wrote: 'I cannot make out what error has glided into my accounts for some time past, but on the 9th of this month I could not find at the bottom of my privy purse some money that I had forgotten there a few years ago. I am therefore obliged to go over the general account once more.'

Before becoming King, Louis had an annual allowance of 108,000 livres. In a typical year, 1773, he spent it like this: 23,448 livres to servants whose wages had been left unpaid by the State, 2,000 livres to the curés of Versailles, 61,404 livres in old-age pensions to former servants, 14,650 livres to the poor, and only 6,498 livres on himself.

The money Louis spent on himself went on clocks, watch repairs – his watch was constantly going wrong, perhaps because he worked with his hands, perhaps because his nervous disposition affected the movement – a telescope, mathematical instruments, drawing paper and pencils, two pairs of guns, which he paid for in twelve instalments, flowers and fruit, especially peaches, grapes and melons. At the end of every month save one he had a credit balance. In October 1773 he overspent his allowance and had to borrow 537 livres from his valet de chambre, paying the loan back in twelve monthly instalments.

When he became King, Louis continued to spend thriftily. In February 1777 he wished to acquire the 31-volume *Encyclopédie*; finding a new set beyond his means, the King of France bought this essential reference work second-hand.

In 1775 Louis spent 384,343 livres 7 sous 5 deniers, a surplus over income of 81,836 livres 10 sous 4 deniers. These accounts continue until 1784 and at the end of each year save 1775 Louis had a credit balance. Louis also kept another group of accounts, covering expenses in the Petits Appartements, that is, for suppers, private entertainments and the like. At first he noted in his own hand every single item: for example a bottle of red wine, 15 sous, cauliflowers and spinach, 1 livre 16 sous. From 1776 he had too much other work to be able to itemize each purchase and he gave only a monthly total. This he compared with the same month the previous year, adding an explanatory note of the difference. Louis's accounts for the Petits Appartements continue until July 1790 and, allowance made for the rise in costs, show a remarkable stability. The annual total in 1776 was 237,973 livres; in 1789 283,372.

Louis's economic policy stems directly from his character and the fact that when he came to the throne France was living beyond her means. This was particularly true of Versailles. Many noblemen, finding that the fixed income from their estates did not keep pace with the rising cost of living, ran their establishments on credit. Louis XV had not minded; the new King did mind. He knew that many shopkeepers went needy because courtiers left their bills unpaid. He also knew that these courtiers were powerful, and that one curbed them at one's peril.

Two months after his accession, Louis was asked to grant a stay of proceedings on behalf of the Prince of Nassau against his creditors.

The Prince was important, the request usual, and everyone expected the King to say yes. But Louis refused. 'When a man can keep mistresses,' he said, 'he can pay his debts; the Prince won't have a stay of proceedings while I'm on the throne.' Another nobleman who enjoyed an income of 50,000 livres was heavily in debt; he proposed to pay off his creditors at the rate of 15,000 livres a year. Louis insisted he pay 35,000 to his creditors, retaining only 15,000 for himself, and forbade the dunned man to appear in Paris or Versailles until he had wiped out his debt.

By demanding financial integrity from those who lived in his house, Louis was doing a service to France. But he immediately made enemies, not only the indebted men themselves, but their uncles and aunts, their grandfathers and countless cousins.

Louis simultaneously set about the task of applying his personal principles to the country at large. He wished to reduce expenditure, balance the budget and eventually to ease the burden of taxation on the poor. For this he needed a Finance Minister who thought as he did, and as soon as he had settled into his new routine he began scrutinizing possible candidates, among them his new Minister of the Navy.

The Turgot family originated in Scotland – a Turgot had been bishop of St Andrews – and for generations had provided public servants. Turgot's father had been chief administrator of Paris and built the city's first proper sewer. Young Turgot was shy as a child, and when his mother received friends, he would hide behind a screen or sofa. Later he studied for the Church. While reading theology at the Sorbonne he met a charming girl, Minette de Ligniville. He played badminton with her, wearing his soutane, fell in love with her, and although she was miles above him socially, proposed. It was rather a vain thing to do, even for a brilliant student, and it seems to have been this vanity in Turgot's character that caused Minette to turn him down. Minette married a millionaire tax farmer, Claude Adrien Helvétius, but Turgot preferred to rest on the brilliant proposal rather than choose a girl of his own class and he never married.

At twenty-four Turgot lost his faith in Christianity. Countless of his contemporaries had the same experience but went on to become parasite abbés. Turgot said, 'I cannot possibly resign myself to wear, all my life, a mask over my face.' He abandoned the Church for the service of the Crown.

A physician at the court of Versailles, François Quesnay, whom

Louis XV called 'the Thinker', was teaching a new economic theory, whose roots lay in Rousseauism. Land, said Quesnay, is the source of wealth, and the only productive class are farmers. Industry makes its profits at the expense of farmers, and its products have plunged France into 'dissolute luxury'. Quesnay proposed that the State should spend less, should reduce taxes on farmers, and should do everything possible to stimulate agricultural production.

Turgot adopted Quesnay's views and when he became intendant of Limoges in 1761, sought to put them into practice. He encouraged the local Society of Agriculture to discover adequate methods of storing buckwheat and maize, tons of which were being lost to the corn weevil and grain moth. In his thirteen years as intendant, he built 450 miles of roads. During the famine years of 1769-72 he mortgaged his own estates to give relief.

Aged forty-seven, in appearance Turgot was tall and well-proportioned, with a full face, piercing brown eyes and shoulder-length hair. He had many of the same qualities as Louis: he was orderly, hard-working and concerned about the poor; but he had certain marked defects. He had an annoying habit of answering arguments in advance; he had a condescending turn of phrase; he was dogmatic, always serious, and sometimes ponderous. As a wit remarked, Turgot did good things badly. Also, he could be very touchy and the slightest criticism made him blush.

Louis liked Turgot's principles and though he was clearly not an easy person to work with decided to promote him. On 24 August 1774 he appointed Turgot Controller General of Finances.

'Let us turn to first principles,' Turgot was fond of saying. He and Louis did so now. The King's principle was the happiness of his people. For the Greeks happiness had been well-being of the spirit – *eudaimonia*; in the New Testament it was something man attained only in Heaven. But for Frenchmen now, according to the *Encyclopédie*, 'The possession of material goods is the foundation of our happiness.' People were much more concerned than ever before to become better off financially, and it was up to the State to help them do so.

Direct taxes, which composed the bulk of France's revenue, were of three kinds: the *taille*, a tax on property in southern France and on personal wealth as an index of property in the rest of France, from which clergy and nobles were exempt; *capitation*, a poll-tax which in theory everyone paid; and the *vingtième*, a tax on income, originally 5%, now 10%, paid by nobles and commoners alike.

In direct taxes and indirect taxes on salt and wine the average family paid about 50 to 60 livres a year. Louis wished to reduce some of the taxes, but Turgot showed that until the annual deficit had been wiped out, this could not be done. For the moment they would have to be content with not increasing taxes.

'No bankruptcy, no increase of taxes, no borrowing . . .' Turgot summed up their programme. 'There is only one way of fulfilling these three aims: that of reducing expenditure below receipts, and sufficiently below to ensure each year a saving of 20 million livres with a view to the redemption of long-standing debts. Failing this, the first gun-shot will drive the State to bankruptcy.'

Louis offered to make cuts at Versailles and agreed to look for a Minister of the Household brave enough to effect them. For the moment Louis decreed that writs permitting expenditure of public money should never be issued without his knowledge, and that in future his brothers and their wives, instead of having separate kitchens and tables, should eat with him and Antoinette, an annual saving on staff and food of 2 million livres.

The King and Turgot next turned to the long 4 lb. loaf of crusty bread, the basis of life for most Frenchmen. In a normal year the grain harvest was just sufficient to provide bread for everyone at a price of 8 sous for a 4 lb. loaf. In a bad year grain had to be imported. There were two schools of thought about the grain trade. Some believed that it should be controlled, each region keeping and consuming the grain it grew. Others believed that grain should circulate freely, subject to the law of supply and demand. Some measure of freedom had been tried from 1764 to 1771. In good years it worked well, in bad years less well, for in some regions people became alarmed that all their local stocks would be bought up and sent away, and this led to inflated prices.

In 1771 Terray had reimposed control of the grain trade and organized a grain administration headed by two financiers, Sorin de Bonne and Doumerck, who were to receive 2% on all transactions plus interest on money they loaned. Working first in one locality, then in another, the two financiers caused a rapid fluctuation of prices, which resulted in speculation. Véri, touring the provinces in 1773, found that everyone believed a monopoly existed and that enormous profits went to enrich the King, Madame Du Barry and Terray.

In September 1774, with Louis's approval Turgot re-established freedom of the grain trade: that is, knocked down the barriers separating the thirteen Frances, and began dismantling the machine operated by Sorin de Bonne and Doumerck, whose dismissal he obtained in 1775. Unfortunately, the harvest of 1774 was only fair. In the spring of 1775 Turgot was obliged to import grain, but he paid a subsidy of 18 sous on every quintal of wheat, 12 sous on rye, so that the price of bread rose only a little.

People became alarmed when they saw their grain being shipped off to the towns; they thought the Government was leaving them to starve. In fact there was no shortage of grain, but there was a surplus of fear. On 18 April 400 peasants crowded into Dijon, plundered houses, tore up streets and demolished a mill. Elsewhere there were sporadic protests, the very people who had called for an end to monopoly now reviling freedom.

On 2 May Louis was starting for the hunt when he met a crowd of people armed with sticks arriving at Versailles by the road from Saint-Germain, where there had been riots the day before, and making for the town market. Louis returned to the palace, ordered the gates shut and sent orders to the Prince de Beauvau, military commander at Versailles, to call out troops, but with the express sitpulation not to allow them to use arms. Turgot and Maurepas had gone to Paris, where further riots were feared.

At 11 a.m. Louis wrote to Turgot:

Versailles is attacked and they are the same men of Saint-Germain ... You can count on my firmness. I have just ordered the guards to march on the market. I am very much pleased with the pre-cautions you have taken on behalf of Paris, it was for there I was most afraid. You will do well to arrest the people of whom you speak but, above all, when you have got them – no haste and many questions. I have just given orders for what is to be done here and for the markets and mills in the neighbourhood.

The crowd, 8,000 strong from twenty villages around, found the town market shut and pillaged it. Then they forced the gates and entered the palace courtyard. Louis went on to the balcony and tried to speak. But he was shouted down. Then the Prince de Poix, an inexperienced youth of twenty-three who was nevertheless a colonel, entered the courtyard at the head of the royal bodyguard. The crowd pelted him with flour. The Prince got flurried and shouted: 'How much do you want to pay for your bread?'

'Two sous the pound.'

'Very well. Two sous let it be.' He gave the necessary orders, and promised the bakers compensation. The crowd marched back to the town and demanded bread at that price. If it was refused, they seized it.

At 2 p.m. Louis wrote to Turgot: 'We are absolutely peaceful . . . I am not going out today, not because I'm afraid, but to give things time to settle. PS. M. de Beauvau interrupts me to tell me of a foolish manœuvre that was made, to let them have bread at two sous.' When Turgot returned, Louis discussed the situation with him. 'We have a clear conscience,' he said, 'and with that we are very strong.' They agreed that Poix's order must be disregarded and bread sold at the current price of $3\frac{1}{2}$ sous a pound.

Next day rioters began pillaging in Paris. Some carried placards: 'If the price of bread isn't lowered, we shall exterminate the King and all the race of Bourbons.' In Versailles only one man had been injured, but here the disturbances were more serious, and the police had to arrest 162 people. Parlement, seeing a chance of asserting itself, claimed the right to try the rioters, but on the 5th Louis summoned Parlement to Versailles and warned them not to meddle. Again, says a diarist, he spoke 'with a force and a firmness infinitely beyond his years'. 'The fact is,' Louis explained afterwards to Turgot, 'I feel much more embarrassed with one man alone than with fifty.'

This was an age when in England a poacher of deer was sent to the gallows and a youth could be deported for stealing a pie at a fair. The courts tried the 162 people arrested and sentenced two of them to death for theft and pillage: a master wig-maker and a gauze-maker. On 9 May bread fell a sou and by the 16th the disturbances were over.

Louis and Turgot were puzzled by the bread riots. Bakeries and granaries were well stocked, prices had been higher a few years back without precipitating disturbances, and the mouldy barley bread the rioters carried had been specially prepared. Véri noted that the Versailles crowd was gentle, even jovial, and concluded that the dearness of bread was only a pretext. It looked as though someone had organized the disturbances. Some accused Terray, others the leader of the princely opposition, the Prince de Conti – that would explain the anti-Bourbon placards. There was no conclusive proof, but Louis had already made powerful enemies, and both he and Turgot were left with the uncomfortable feeling that certain men would stop at nothing to oppose their new policies.

In fact, the problem lay deeper than personal rancour. In France as in many other European countries prices had been rising throughout the century. Although it had not yet been given that name, inflation was at work, and this was Louis's real enemy. Slow but fairly steady inflation affected not only the price of basic foodstuffs but government expenditure too, and would make it difficult for Louis to run the administration without taxing more.

Louis and Turgot were impatient to introduce further economic reforms, but for several reasons had to delay them. In January 1775 Turgot suffered a painful attack of gout and for four months had to be carried in a chair to Louis's apartments for their three-hour working sessions. At the same time Louis and Turgot had to deal with a disastrous outbreak of murrain. While Turgot imposed *cordons sanitaires*, Louis in February decreed that all infected cattle must be slaughtered and buried in deep graves. He paid a third of the animal's value and the cost of disposing of it. In the one province of Béarn this cost him 700,000 livres; altogether he paid out several millions – a hard blow to his savings plan.

Finally, Louis's coronation approached, or rather his *sacre*, for it was the anointing with oil supposedly brought from Heaven by a dove that gave a French King his divine right to rule. Even here Louis wished to economize. 'We must, if possible, reduce the expenses of my coronation . . .' Louis instructed his Minister of the Household. 'You will also express my wish to the Provost of the Guilds of Paris that there should be no festivities in that town, and that the money allocated for them should be employed for the benefit and relief of the inhabitants.'

At seven in the morning on Trinity Sunday 1775 Louis arrived at the door of Reims cathedral wearing a white satin suit, violet cloak embroidered with fleurs de lis, and violet satin red-heeled boots. He was met by Archbishop de La Roche Aymon, who had christened and married him, now old and doddering, and in a short speech congratulated on having all the virtues, especially a love of order – which is not strictly a virtue. To the sound of fanfares Louis walked up the aisle and took his seat on the dais in the middle of the sanctuary.

Turgot had suggested dropping the promise 'to exterminate heretics' from the coronation oath, but Maurepas feared that would irritate the bishops, and Louis stuck to the traditional wording. The Archbishop wished Louis a long just reign and 'the strength of a rhinoceros' to scatter his enemies; he administered the five anointings, and placed on his head Charlemagne's crown.

Louis was escorted to his throne, where he received ceremonial kisses from his two brothers; this brought applause from the spectators, among them a sixteen-year-old schoolboy, Georges Jacques Danton, who had walked sixty miles from Troyes to be present. 'Such enthusiasm,' the Duc de Croy noted, 'I have never seen before . . . The Queen was so stirred with joy that she shed a flood of tears; she was obliged to wipe her eyes with her hand-kerchief.' Louis noticed Antoinette's emotion and was deeply touched. Afterwards he spoke about it repeatedly to his courtiers and, according to Mercy, gazed at his wife adoringly.

As part of their policy of mingling with the people, Louis and Antoinette spent more than an hour that evening, unescorted, in the big wooden gallery between the archbishop's house and the cathedral, walking about and speaking to the citizens of Reims. 'It is astonishing,' Antoinette wrote to her mother, 'and at the same time very pleasing to be so well received two months after the grain riots and despite the fact that bread continues unfortunately to be dear . . . Even if I live two hundred years, I shall never forget the day of the *sacre*.'

To Maurepas, who had been detained at Versailles, Louis wrote: 'It has been tiring but now it is over . . . I wish you could have been here to share my satisfaction. It is only right that I should work for the happiness of a people who contribute to my happiness. I am now going to attend to that. The need is urgent, but with courage and your advice I shall succeed. Goodbye until Monday evening. Louis.' After reading the letter Maurepas said to Véri: 'I'm beginning to love him, as a father loves a willing child.'

Back in Versailles a crowned King, Louis dismissed the Minister of the Household, La Vrillière, who was old and dominated by his voracious Irish mistress. In his place Louis appointed Chrétien Lamoignon de Malesherbes, aged fifty-four, a bluff, dumpy, pipe-smoking countryman who lived in a cottage, being too poor to keep up his big Louis XIII château. His favourite occupation was botany, and he liked practical jokes, such as holding a piece of burning paper under the nose of someone asleep. Malesherbes held a high post in Parlement – First President of the Cour des Aides, a body which pronounced on all edicts relating to taxation – but he was that rare being, a Parlementaire with liberal opinions and opposed to privilege. During his twenty years as Chief Censor, 'he rendered,' said Voltaire, 'infinite services to human genius by giving a greater liberty to the press than it has ever known before – we are already more than half Englishmen.'

Malesherbes surprised Versailles by continuing to wear his magistrate's costume, dark brown suit with muslin cuffs, jabot speckled with tobacco or snuff, his round periwig, not always carefully combed, set any old how on his square head. The courtiers, laughing up their sleeves, clustered round the kindly man who was now the channel of royal bounty. One wanted an embassy, another a dukedom, a third the office of First Squire. It has to be remembered that most of these men were driven not by greed but by need, and many lacked the money to repair the leaking roofs on their châteaux.

On the King's instructions, Malesherbes refused these petitions, one and all. He explained that the nine hundred officials and servants of the Household were costing the State 36 millions a year. That was too much; they simply had to be cut down. Malesherbes even refused one of the almighty Rohans, the Princesse de Guéménée, a continuation of her pension, saying in his bluff way, 'You must know, Madame, that the rule of females is over.'

The Princess drew herself up. 'Yes, Monsieur, but not that of impertinents.'

Malesherbes next turned his attention to *lettres de cachet*. Unless caught *in flagrante delicto*, no Frenchman could be arrested without a writ, which was conditional on witnesses, and by the time the writ was prepared, the culprit had often fled. The *lettre de cachet*, bearing the royal signature and seal, had originally been designed to arrest a man presumed guilty and forestall his flight. Though only about four in a thousand were used against political pamphleteers, the letters were regarded by enlightened opinion as tyrannical, and indeed they had occasionally been used by unscrupulous Ministers to settle private scores. On Malesherbes's advice Louis made an important reform designed to reduce the chances of a miscarriage of justice: each letter in future had to be countersigned not only by the Minister responsible but also by a council of magistrates.

The Minister of the Household was answerable for State institutions in Paris and Malesherbes astonished everyone but Louis by taking this part of his job seriously. He began by inspecting the prisons. French prisons generally were among the best in Europe: no prisoners wore irons and all had at least straw to sleep on, which was not so in England. However, some Paris prisons were appalling, notably the Bicêtre, which held 4000 men, half prisoners, half paupers, madmen and men with venereal disease. John Foster, visiting it in 1776, wrote: 'This prison seems not so well managed as those in the city; it is very dirty: no fireplace in any of the rooms: and in the severe cold last winter, several hundreds perished.'

Malesherbes was so distressed by what he saw that he wanted to take Louis round the Bicêtre, but Maurepas advised against it: 'If the King sees the prisons, there will be no more prisoners.'

Louis told Malesherbes to make a report on improving conditions, to review possible miscarriages of justice and to liberate anyone who had been unjustly confined. With Louis's approval Malesherbes eventually freed more than one hundred prisoners, some from the Bastille. A leading *philosophe*, d'Alembert, wrote to Frederick the Great: 'All the nation shouts in chorus "A better day dawns upon us" . . . The priests alone make sound apart, murmuring softly.'

Louis's reforms so far had been minor: economies, the breaking down of provincial barriers, improvements in justice. But he and Turgot realized that, if France was to become a less unequal and more prosperous society, structural reforms must be made. These they now listed.

The first concerned artisans. As things stood, the guilds, known as *jurandes* and *maîtrises*, had a monopoly of artisan work and what would now be called light industry. No one outside a guild might practise a trade and no one might join a guild until he met the guild's extremely high standards. As a result France possessed comparatively few skilled workmen, and these few turned out luxury goods at prices for the very rich. Turgot, on economic principle, opposed luxury. He wanted a new law abolishing most of the guilds, and permitting anyone to work at whatever trade he pleased. He thought the public quite capable of protecting itself from any attempt by the free artisans to foist upon it inferior goods.

The second major reform was designed to free peasants from the *corvée*, a system whereby they had to put in a number of days' labour each year, without payment, on repairing the roads of France. Turgot proposed to suppress the *corvée* altogether and to levy a tax of 12 million livres on property-owners, for they, he argued, were the ones who chiefly benefited from the roads. This reform was bound to excite intense opposition because, although the tax was small, exemption from it symbolized social status; and many property-owners were noblemen, traditionally exempt from the *taille* or any tax like it. If the edict could be made law, then it would create a precedent and make it possible later to shift the burden of taxation away from the peasants, thus reducing the glaring gap between rich and poor which affronted all feeling men.

To make the edicts less offensive to Parlement, they were to be submitted with four other minor reforms which Parlement could only welcome: one reduced the tax on suet, another abolished the Caisse de Poissy, a Gothic institution which loaned money to Paris butchers and recouped itself handsomely with levies amounting to 15 livres on the price of each animal sold for meat.

For much of the autumn and winter of 1775 Louis studied the Six Edicts and the best way of making them law. In November he was alone at Fontainebleau, for first Maurepas, then Turgot fell ill of gout and had to leave, which prompted an opposition quip: 'The King's Ministers are trickling away, *goutte par goutte*.' When they returned, it became clear that the Cabinet was divided. Armand de Miromesnil, the hard-headed Norman lawyer who was Keeper of the Seals, strongly opposed them; Maurepas, becoming jealous of Turgot's influence, was non-committal; while even Malesherbes seemed worried about his friend's reforms. When Mercy asked him news of the Government, Malesherbes joked: 'Maurepas does nothing, Turgot does everything, and I doubt everything.'

Foreseeing the strength of the opposition, Malesherbes advised Turgot to go slowly and first to enter into negotiation with certain influential Parlementaires. But Turgot believed in the power of truth and justice. He refused to compromise. When Malesherbes suggested that the Six Edicts should be spread over a number of years, Turgot, who was forty-eight, replied, 'In my family we die at fifty.'

Louis still supported Turgot, but with reservations about his high-handed tone, as is shown by an entry in Véri's diary for 2 July 1775. Véri says he gave Turgot the following warning: 'Yesterday morning . . . you recounted to me with the greatest elation what you had said in Monsieur de Maurepas's presence about the claims of Monsieur Francès to the Navy. Hardly had you left than the King remarked, "You heard that. Only his friends have merit and only his own ideas are good." . . . I wanted to tell you this in order to acquaint you with the King's opinion which you imagine to be entirely in your favour.'

After studying a critique by Miromesnil and an answer to it by Turgot, both of which he caused to be read aloud to him twice, Louis said, 'In making my decision I intend to follow my conscience.' What his conscience pictured was France's poorest class obliged to leave their fields in order to cart, break and shovel stones for up to fourteen days every year without payment. On 9 February 1776 Louis sent the Six Edicts to Parlement.

A full session of Parlement included princes and peers as well as magistrates. The acrimonious Prince de Conti had a financial stake in the guilds and if they were abolished stood to lose 50,000 livres annually; peers scented an infringement of the nobleman's status, while magistrates, as men of law, distrusted any interference with the *status quo*. They combined to draft a series of remonstrances to the King on the theme 'The first rule of justice is to conserve for each individual that which belongs to him.'

Two days later Louis replied, 'My Parlement must respect my wishes,' and followed this up with a full answer written by Miromesnil and corrected by Louis in his own hand. 'There is no question of a humiliating tax,' he explained, 'but merely of a small imposition to which everyone ought to be honoured to contribute, for I am setting an example by paying it myself on my domains.'

On 8 March Parlement sent to Versailles a second set of remonstrances. This was unusual and implied extremely serious opposition. Louis was advised by all his Ministers save Turgot and Malesherbes to yield. But where the people's good was concerned Louis could be firm, and he announced that he would hold a *lit de justice*.

On 12 March Louis seated himself on a canopied throne in a corner of the Bodyguards' Hall at Versailles. On his right sat the princes of the blood and lay peers, on his left the ecclesiastical peers and marshals of France, at his feet the High Court presidents, the scarlet-robed councillors of Parlement, and various other officials.

Louis ordered the edicts to be read aloud. Then the Advocate General, Séguier, made a speech defending the guilds: 'It is constraints, hindrances and prohibitions that make for the glory, reliability and immensity of French trade' – a defence of luxury goods which the Court ladies in the gallery applauded. As for the *corvée*, Séguier said road repairs should be carried out by soldiers; a tax of this kind on the second estate would disorder the whole intricate mechanism of French society. He called on Louis to listen to the advice of the eminent men of the realm, his august brothers who, to Louis's disappointment, both opposed the edicts, the princes of the blood, the Ministers of his Council, and the peers of the realm, for it was through them that the nation proclaimed its wishes.

Louis listened attentively to Séguier, then watched Miromesnil go round the Parlement, starting with Monsieur, as the Comte de

Provence was now called. Each member expressed his opinion to Miromesnil in a low voice, and Louis could guess from their faces that most of the opinions were unfavourable. But, as Stormont said, 'His Majesty shews an uncommon desire of easing the lower class of his subjects, and of lessening the burthens under which they groan;' as for Parlement, it would not be sitting at all but for him. When Miromesnil returned and bowed, Louis said: 'You have heard the edicts which my love for my subjects has led me to promulgate. I expect them to be obeyed.'

France was a monarchy; by long tradition Parlement might not resist the wishes of the monarch present in person. Grudgingly and muttering under their breath, the magistrates registered the Six Edicts.

CHAPTER 7

More Reforms and a Reverse

EVERY morning at eight-thirty and every evening at seven, either
in his simply furnished study or in the gilded, frescoed Council
Chamber, Louis worked with his Ministers at the task of government
and reform. Almost every week he published some new decree
designed to alleviate suffering or to improve the welfare of his
people. Many were suggested by Turgot, but it was the King who
decided which should be adopted, he who often modified the texts,
he who lent them the weight of his authority, and ensured that they
were carried out. Here are some of them.

In March 1775 Louis issued a decree granting free treatment to
anyone suffering from venereal disease; in the same year he increased
the number of cases of medicine distributed free to the needy from
742 to 2,268. He abolished a medieval privilege whereby only the
main Paris hospital, the Hôtel Dieu, might sell meat during Lent,
and this had the effect of lowering prices. He appointed d'Alembert,
Condorcet and the abbé Bossut to report on river and canal
navigation, and assigned 800,000 livres for improvements. Since
rabbits were multiplying in the royal forests and causing damage to
crops, he arranged for the destruction of these animals on Crown
land, jokingly sending the decree to Turgot with a marginal note:
'As you see, I too am doing my bit.'

More sweeping was the reform of the carrying trade proposed
and effected, with the King's active encouragement, by Turgot.
Formerly individual companies had received concessions for
carrying passengers and parcels under 50 lbs. Services were in-
frequent, timetables uncoordinated, charges varied, heavy old-
fashioned vehicles, either berlins or stage-coaches, made the journeys
incredibly slow: on average 22 miles a day.

Turgot nationalized the carrying trade. He introduced a new
type of light coach, with four, six or nine seats, which the public
called a *turgotine*, and arranged for it to be drawn by post-horses.
Prices remained the same but passengers saved on accommodation,

for journeys were now much quicker. Paris to Bordeaux, which formerly took 14 days, now took only 5½. France, in a sense, became three times more united. The Controller General dispensed with the old Sunday-morning halts, producing predictable complaints from the clergy that 'Travellers in turgotines have learned to skip Mass, like Turgot himself.'

Encouraged by Parlement's registering of the Six Edicts, Louis and Turgot moved on to other reforms designed to unify the thirteen Frances. In April 1776 they published a reform of the wine trade. Here, as in the grain trade and the carrying trade, a log-jam situation existed. Monopolies dating from the fifteenth century forbade the people of Bordeaux to drink wines other than those produced in the seneschalsy of Bordeaux, and no vintner could sell retail unless a burgess of the town. To protect Bordeaux wines, wines of Languedoc were forbidden to descend the Garonne for sale elsewhere in France or abroad until St Martin's Day, and those of Périgord, Quercy and Haute Guienne until Christmas. Other towns imposed similar restrictions. Louis and Turgot drafted an edict to give the wine trade complete freedom and, like many of Louis's other edicts, its preamble specified the King's intention in issuing it: 'to concern himself unceasingly with the happiness of his peoples'.

This edict had to go before the provincial Parlements. Those of Toulouse and Dauphiné registered it at once, but the Parlement of Bordeaux rejected it and only later accepted a much modified version. Even so, the reform stimulated demand and production of wine grapes, reduced the price of wine in the shops and eventually led to an export trade worth 60 million livres a year.

Both Maurepas and Turgot, in different ways, were 'outsiders', and Louis chose a third outsider to be his Minister of War. Charles Louis, Comte de Saint-Germain, was born of a family of poor nobles in the mountainous Jura region. After studying in a Jesuit seminary, at seventeen he exchanged the Church for the army. He served under the French and the Prussian flags, and ended, curiously, as a Field Marshal in the Danish Army. Now aged sixty-eight, he learned of his appointment while pruning his trees on his small estate in Alsace. Though he possessed neither wardrobe nor carriage he hurried to Fontainebleau and presented himself before the King: a humble man, a strong disciplinarian and, according to Stormont, with 'the good of the service much at heart . . . His great aim is to abolish . . . the *corps privilégiés* . . . and to put the whole army upon a footing of equality, as it is in the Prussian and still more in the Austrian service.'

Louis and Saint-Germain together set about these reforms. Acting on the new Minister's first maxim: 'Self-interest in the army has replaced honour. This must stop. No one should get rich by soldiering,' they decided that in future promotion must be by merit, not seniority; posts must not be sold; there must be no sinecures; every rank must have definite duties. To reduce the plethora of colonels – 900 for 163 regiments – no one in future could become a colonel without fourteen years' service, six as colonel *en second*. In future officers must serve with their regiments at least six months a year.

The King's Household troops cost too much. A lieutenant in the Bodyguard got 10,000 livres a year, a lieutenant on the frontier 400 livres. Both Louis and Turgot wanted cuts. But since many of these privileged posts had been bought and paid for in good coin, their holders would have to be reimbursed. Saint-Germain made a start. He disbanded two companies of Musketeers and retired a number of junior officers, including a certain Captain de La Fayette.

Saint-Germain also decentralized the Ecole Militaire, so that boys of eight, instead of coming to the demoralizing world of Paris and the Court, attended one of twelve new military academies in the country. He also tried to reform the Invalides. Built by Louis XIV for wounded and aged soldiers, this institution had degenerated into a place where any ex-soldier after 24 years' service felt entitled to live comfortably at the State's expense. It was crowded with ne'er-do-wells in their forties and cost France 2 million livres a year. Saint-Germain limited numbers to 1500, only sick and wounded. The healthy remainder – more than a thousand – he sent to their home villages. There five-sixths of them took to begging and living on alms, and their so-called plight caused an outcry. Before the year was over they were back again in the comfortable Invalides. This was the century of humanitarianism but, as Saint-Germain discovered, humanitarianism can prove very costly.

Saint-Germain forbade forced recruiting and ended the death penalty for deserters, who were henceforth to be employed on building fortifications. These were humane measures in tune with the mood of the age. On the other hand, the new Minister was struck by the poor discipline of French troops. Attributing this to the absence of corporal punishment, he issued a ruling that in bad cases of insubordination a soldier might be beaten with the flat of a sword, though in no case was he to receive more than fifty blows.

Some tightening of discipline was certainly necessary, but this particular ruling caused an outcry. It offended liberal thinkers and many officers. All Saint-Germain's excellent reforms were forgotten and he was branded as a monster, importing to *la douce France* the rigorous practices of the Prussian army. One officer declared he would willingly be beaten with the edge of a sword, but with the flat never. As a result, though the new ruling remained while Saint-Germain was in office, it was rarely applied.

Despite this one little set-back, Louis in the spring of 1776 had reasonable grounds for optimism. He had five excellent Ministers. He had instituted a number of important reforms. He had cleared Versailles of the Du Barry's favourites. He had cut expenses in the Royal Household. He had re-established Parlement, but let it see that he was master. He had ended the *corvée*, which was a kind of servitude. He had plans for relieving the excessive pressure of taxation on the lower and middle classes. The way seemed clear ahead. But precisely at this juncture he ran into a storm of opposition.

The abolition of the *corvée* in March 1776 came under particularly heavy attack because, as Séguier had said in Parlement, the road-levy put an additional burden on small landowners, and this class was already taxed to the bone. René de Chateaubriand, the writer's father, had to run away to sea because their Brittany estate could not feed the family; in the neighbourhood of Auch the nobles ploughed their own fields, while in the Boulonnais Smollett noticed that country gentlemen had given up shooting from lack of money to buy themselves a gun. Why, it was argued, should landowners alone bear the new tax, since roads were used by travellers, the Post, and merchandise from abroad? It would be bound to increase their costs in producing wheat and therefore the cost of bread.

The abolition of guilds with their exacting standards of artisan-ship was also attacked, on the grounds that low-quality work would flood the market, and the 'little man' would suffer. With the guild of couturières abolished, one writer foresaw evil days when men would be making ladies' dresses: 'A man's coarse hands will press a lady's delicate waist; his roving eye, under the pretext of taking exact measurements, will linger on certain parts of her body.'

As well as such ridiculous fears, there were many genuine arguments against the abolition of guilds. France, it was held, could stay prosperous only through *dirigisme*, and happiness was equated with a high degree of differentiation, not with a free-for-all where anyone could turn his hand to anything. But the loudest attacks on Turgot's edicts did not come from the theorists; they came from Parlement.

Parlement had a vested interest in the guilds, since they provided fertile ground for lawsuits. One between the guild of old clothes dealers and the guild of tailors had dragged on for 250 years, giving rise to 400 adjudications and Heaven knows how many thousand livres in fees to lawyers who sat in Parlement. So, although in 1582 Parlement had consistently opposed the creation of guilds, the red-robed lawyers now found excellent reasons for bringing them back anew.

The leader here was Prince Louis François de Conti, good-looking, eccentric, full of himself and opposed to almost everything, including God. When the abbé Prévost, libertine author of *Manon Lescaut*, applied to him for the post of chaplain, Conti said, 'Are you joking? I never hear Mass.' 'Exactly, my lord; I never say it' – and Prévost got the post. Conti's Paris residence, the Temple, had been one of the rare places where men might practise a trade and sell their goods without belonging to a guild, and since the passing of Turgot's edict he stood to lose 50,000 livres a year in shop rents. Now aged fifty-nine, stricken by gout and a fistula, Conti was a dying man and knew it – he had even stretched out in his coffin and, characteristically, complained that it was too tight – but before dying he intended to get Turgot's edict repealed.

Thin, barely able to walk, wrapped in cloaks, Conti dragged himself to every session of Parlement and when a pamphlet favourable to Turgot appeared, *The Inconveniences of Feudal Rights*, by one Monsieur Boncerf, Conti launched such a bitter attack upon it that Parlement condemned the pamphlet to be burned. Turgot was so upset that he asked Louis to intervene. Louis did. He wrote to the First President of Parlement ordering that no action should be taken against the pamphlet. Conti growled, said nothing, and quietly made plans for a counter-attack.

If Conti's aims were selfish, many both within and without Parlement were genuinely alarmed that Turgot aimed to end all hierarchies. A pamphlet entitled *Turgot's Prophecy* announced that the Minister intended to abolish all class distinctions:

Du même pas marcheront
Noblesse et roture.
Les Français retourneront
Au droit de nature . . .[1]

Turgot had no such aim in mind, but the fears voiced by Parlement gradually permeated society, so that one group after another turned against the Controller General. The first group to do so was the financiers. In 1775 Turgot had begun negotiations for a 60 million livre loan from Dutch bankers who, being more experienced and efficient than their French counterparts, lent at $3\frac{1}{2}$%. Turgot had been able to use the prospect of his Dutch loan to bring down French interest rates from their usual 5%, thereby cutting France's deficit. Annoyed by the Dutch loan and foreseeing reduced profits if Turgot remained in power, early in 1776 the French financiers adopted a definite plan of withholding the advance of capital upon which the Government largely depended. They said Treasury revenue was falling and that this resulted from Turgot's failure to give them adequate support. Meanwhile the opposition in Parlement had frightened the smaller capitalists, who began to withdraw their deposits. Money grew scarce; Turgot, embarrassed, had to pay the financiers a higher rate of interest, and saw his hopes of reducing the deficit disappear.

The next body to oppose Turgot was the Church, all the more surprising since, on Maurepas's advice, Turgot had exempted the Church from his new road levy. It was enough that the Controller General had contributed the article on 'Existence' to the *Encyclopédie*, knew by heart Voltaire's occasional poems, and did not go to Mass, while his turgotines, racing across France on the day of rest, prevented travellers too from going to Mass. He had tried to persuade the King to omit from the coronation oath the promise to exterminate heretics. Like Malesherbes, another contributor to the *Encyclopédie*, he preached religious toleration. Indeed, he was known to favour a large-scale immigration of Protestant craftsmen, descendants of those Huguenots whom Louis XIV of sacred memory had so wisely dragooned to foreign lands.

If the Church opposed Turgot from fear, the Court did so on solider grounds. The Court, it has to be remembered, lived by

[1]Nobles and commons
Will march as one,
Every Frenchman
Nature's son.

niceties. When ending a letter, Louis wrote: 'I pray that God may keep you in His worthy custody,' but if he was writing to a duke or to a Spanish grandee, he must remember to put 'His holy and worthy custody'. When he received cardinals, he must remember to see that three silver pots were kept hot on the brazier, one containing milk, one coffee, and one chocolate: no one any longer knew why, but if one of the pots was missing it would be considered an insult. Again, when the Court moved to the small palace of Fontainebleau, many courtiers had to be billeted in the town, where their names were chalked on the allotted front doors – just as their forebears' names had been chalked on Italian doors when Charles VIII invaded Italy 300 years before, such was the continuity in French life. Ordinary courtiers' names were written in white chalk, but princes, and princes alone, had the privilege of yellow chalk. Should one of Louis's officials forget the yellow chalk, he and the King would make a lifelong enemy.

Now Turgot had no time for these niceties. By nature curt and gauche, he put the ladies off, as he had once put off Madame Helvétius, and many of the men also. He possessed, according to Stormont, 'a coldness of manner which is naturally construed into haughtiness . . . He does not know how to soften or qualify a refusal.' At Versailles this would have been disastrous even if Turgot had been following a popular policy. But when in conjunction with Saint-Germain Turgot suppressed, axed and totally did away with a thousand Household Troops, selected from the best families of the kingdom, and did not even have the grace to be gentle about it, then the Court decided they had had enough of Monsieur Turgot.

How did the Court get their own back on Turgot? Here is one small but revealing example. Early in 1776 a workman who helped Louis turn wood on his lathe said: 'Sire, I see here only two men who are friends of the people, yourself and Monsieur Turgot.' Louis was touched and repeated the tribute to Antoinette, who in turn told her friends. However, according to Véri, the Court soon got to work and 'insinuated to the King and Queen that the workman had been bribed to make the remark by Turgot'.

Louis found even his own brother opposed to Turgot. Monsieur had put up the idea of a colonial trading company, only to have it rejected by Turgot, who believed – and hoped – all colonies would soon become independent. But it was less from pique and more as a champion of the *status quo* that Monsieur wrote and circulated an anonymous brochure, *The Dummies*: 'Once upon a time, in Persia, there lived a man who was gauche, heavy, dense, shy out of vanity, timid out of pride . . . His name was Togur, and his mania was that he had to be right about everything.' The dupes of this man are Ali Bey (Maurepas), the Mullah (Véri) and the Sophy (Louis). 'The Sophy is an honest man who is ill informed and so does greater political harm than a perverse man who is well informed.' Togur intends to make a clean sweep of French society; he is nothing less than a despot and the Sophy has become 'the leading dummy in his kingdom'.

Louis became aware of the growing opposition to Turgot's two controversial edicts in the spring of 1776. Normally when the King had registered edicts in a *lit de justice* the matter was considered closed, but now hostility to the edicts actually increased after they had been made law. Louis had upheld Turgot for eighteen months; he now considered they were at the point where Turgot himself must respond, adapt and disarm opposition.

Now Turgot was touchy. At the slightest criticism he went red. According to Stormont, he was 'impatient of the least contradiction'. Louis himself the previous summer had found that 'only his friends have merit and only his own ideas are good.' As opposition grew, instead of adapting himself, Turgot became even more overbearing until finally he did himself grave damage by what is known as the affair of ambassador de Guines.

Comte Adrien de Guines, aged forty-one, was a jolly fat man who, in order to appear slimmer, wore extremely tight breeches. He had two pairs to go with each of his coats, one for sitting and one for standing, and his valet would ask him solemnly: 'Will Monsieur le Comte be sitting down today?' If he expected only to be standing, he would climb on to a chair and descend into the tighter pair of breeches held out to him by two of his men.

Guines had served as a colonel in the Seven Years' War and through his friend Choiseul had been appointed ambassador in London. He was an excellent flautist and commissioned Mozart's flute and harp concerto K 299, which he liked to play with his harpist daughter. His fondness for music and genial good humour had made him a friend of Antoinette.

At the end of 1775 Turgot sent three abbés on a secret mission to England. They were to try to persuade certain wealthy Huguenot industrialists to return to France and build up the French economy. If only from courtesy, Turgot should of course have informed

Guines, but in fact he failed to do so. Guines, knowing nothing of Turgot's instructions, reproved the abbés and shipped them back to France. Turgot wrote Guines a sharp letter and complained to Louis.

At a meeting of the King's Council on 22 January 1776 Turgot placed before the other Ministers an intercepted letter to the Court of Spain which suggested that Guines, contrary to instructions, had informed the English Court that France would give neither direct nor indirect aid to the English colonies in America. Turgot made a great fuss about the letter and insisted that Guines be recalled. Guines being her friend, the Queen was informed. Her relations with Turgot had so far been good; she approved of his economy programme and the previous summer had collaborated with him in postponing indefinitely a costly fête at Marly. It seemed to Antoinette that Guines had indeed acted imprudently and that Turgot did right to recall him.

Guines returned from London on 25 February and was warmly welcomed by the Choiseul clique, who clamoured for a public enquiry, in the hope of embarrassing the Government. Guines spoke to the Queen and convinced her that he was innocent of Turgot's charge. And what was Turgot doing anyway, meddling in foreign affairs? Choiseul's friends put the same question to the Queen.

Turgot suggested that Guines's dispatches should be read in the hearing of the King, Vergennes, Malesherbes, himself and – unheard-of innovation – of the Queen. Turgot then made a tactless remark to Véri: 'If a woman has to exert an influence on the King's decisions, isn't it better that it should be she rather than a Pompadour or a Du Barry?' Almost certainly this came to Louis's ears and it would have displeased him greatly, for it assumed that the Queen exerted a political influence, whereas in truth from the very beginning of his reign he had taken scrupulous care to keep her out of politics, and all the evidence suggests that he succeeded. Turgot's remark would also have displeased the Queen, for it put her on a par with the hated Madame Du Barry, made of her a mere intriguer for selfish ends.

Louis and his Council decided that Vergennes should investigate the charges, since they concerned a man in his department. There, for the moment, the matter rested. But Turgot had damaged himself in two ways: by his high-handed attitude in a sphere not strictly his, and by causing the Queen to lose her initial satisfaction with him. Antoinette's political role was almost nil, but her opinion naturally counted at Court.

Turgot's next piece of tactlessness related to the Board of Excise, a sovereign law-court composed of Parlementaires which had a right to examine and approve edicts affecting taxation. The president, Barentin, asked for two months to study the Six Edicts; Turgot allowed him barely a week. On 19 March, when the Board met, Barentin approved the Edicts but complained bitterly that the Board had had no time to study them: 'laws are being published of which we remain ignorant.'

Malesherbes, the bluff kindly botanizer who was such an able Minister of the Household, was shocked by Turgot's haste in this matter, all the more so since he himself had once been president of the Board of Excise. Malesherbes did want reform but equally he wanted respect for the rights of the Board of which for so many years he had been a leading member. Malesherbes had accepted Louis's offer to enter the Government only with great reluctance, and now he felt that in continuing to support Turgot's uncompromising line he really was being untrue to his Parlementaire origins. At the end of April 1776, on the grounds that he needed a rest, he handed Louis his resignation – which Louis accepted only in May – and under the name of plain Monsieur Guillaume set off on a walking and flower-collecting tour of the Alps and Pyrenees.

Louis, who liked him as a man and esteemed him as a Minister, was very sorry to lose Malesherbes and even sorrier to find himself with a weakened Cabinet facing the gravest crisis of his reign. For in April Conti, launching his counter-attack, persuaded Parlement to make further remonstrances to the King, ostensibly about the protection he had afforded Boncerf's pamphlet, *The Inconveniences of Feudal Rights*, in fact in protest against the two controversial edicts.

Louis believed the two edicts were good for France and he was angry with Parlement for continuing to oppose them. 'One notices on the King's face,' says Véri, 'the same look every time Parlement behaves contrary to his wishes. His expression alters and one sees that he has had to make an effort to contain himself.' He could silence Parlement by sending it into exile, as his grandfather had twice done. This would give him temporary victory, but in the larger sense Louis saw that it would be a defeat, since, on Maurepas's advice, he had decided to rule in co-operation with Parlement.

Louis saw very well that although he might be able to rule in opposition to Parlement, he could never do so in opposition to public opinion. Now Turgot, not just by his edicts but by his high-handed attitude, had alienated, and was continuing to alienate, public opinion, in the shape of the bankers, the Church, the Court and even ordinary Parisians. Louis had notice of this one day in April 1776 when he happened to meet Antoinette returning from the Opéra. He asked her what sort of reception she had had and, judging from her silence that it had been cold, he said teasingly:

'Apparently you weren't wearing enough plumes in your hair.'

To which Antoinette replied, 'I'd like to see you, Sire, with your Saint-Germain and your Turgot. I think you'd be well and truly hissed.'

It was in April that Louis began to consider dropping Turgot, not because he was a reformer but because his personality was proving an obstacle to the very reforms they both wanted.

Turgot, meanwhile, hurt by Malesherbes's resignation and, as a consequence of that, a cooling towards him of Maurepas, was growing still more inflexible. Each time Parlement submitted a remonstrance against him or his edicts, he threatened to resign unless Louis supported him on every point. His tone became so overbearing that his friend Véri advised him in his own interests not to speak to the King in person, but to write him a letter, since he created a more favourable impression on paper.

Following this advice, between 12 and 28 April 1776 Turgot wrote two letters no longer extant to the King, intimating that he could not carry on unless given full support, including the right to choose Malesherbes's successor. Louis did not reply. On 30 April Turgot wrote the King a third letter, seven pages long, and this has survived.

Turgot first complains of the 'cruel silence' with which Louis had received him on the previous Sunday, and also of Louis's failure to reply to his two earlier letters. He then lashes out. The Keeper of the Seals, Miromesnil, is an intriguer. Maurepas is weak – he cannot hold a course, he is ruled by his wife, subject to petty fears and murmurs at Court. Louis XV had been another weak man, hence the evils of his reign and the lessening of royal authority. As for the present King, Turgot criticizes even him; 'You are too young to be able to judge men . . . You have said yourself, Sire, that you lack experience and need a guide.' Who is that guide to be?

'My own character, which is firmer than his [Maurepas's], must naturally place his in the shade. My shyness perhaps gave him, especially at first, some consolation; but I have reason to believe that quite soon he came to fear that I would obtain your Majesty's confidence independently of him . . . You have been told that I am hot-headed and flighty; it hardly seems to me that all I tell you resembles the words of a fool; to me it seems that the measures I have introduced, in spite of the outcries and resistance to which they have led, have succeeded precisely as I announced ... Monsieur de Guines would still perhaps be ambassador in London had I not taken on myself to let your Majesty know certain facts which it was the duty of other Ministers to let you know.'

After more beating of his own drum Turgot comes to the point. 'Some people think you are weak, Sire, and indeed on occasions I have been afraid that your character has this defect. On the other hand, on more difficult occasions, I have seen you show real courage.' It is for the King now to choose courageously between Maurepas and himself, between a weak or a strong guide.

Louis was very displeased by this essay in self-justification and its statement of a complex problem in black-and-white terms of weakness and strength. He was being asked, in effect, to get rid of Maurepas and let Turgot have a hand in all departments of the Government. Louis summed it up by saying, 'Monsieur Turgot wants to be me, and I'm not having it.'

Because he had alienated public opinion and because he was now making intolerable demands, Louis decided to dismiss Turgot. He was not thereby abandoning his plans for reform. He would continue to work for justice and prosperity but, in deference to the opposition, more tactfully than Turgot could ever do.

Louis dismissed Turgot on 12 May. According to Véri, it was Louis's own decision, seconded but not prompted by Maurepas. Two days later Louis put Maurepas in temporary charge of the Finances; and in August he modified the two edicts. In future each parish could choose between repairing its roads by *corvée* or paying a lump sum; the guilds were re-established, though reduced in number and with mastership fees cut by half.

Conti was not there to exult, having returned the week before, permanently this time, to his coffin, but the rest of Parlement jubilantly claimed they had inflicted a great defeat on 'the innovators'. In fact it was only a reverse. Louis, at twenty-one, could expect a long reign; there would be time yet to re-enact this legislation.

Had Louis behaved weakly? According to Véri, no. 'The King finds it difficult to refuse someone to his face; on the other hand he shows not the slightest fear in all the plans which seem to him to demand courage and resolution.' For twenty months he had upheld, in the public interest, a Minister detested by bankers, the Church, the Court and Parlement. As Turgot's secretary, Du Pont, told the margrave of Baden, Louis encountered more opposition in an attempt to relieve the people than his grandfather in oppressing them. Politics is the art of the acceptable and for the moment Louis had found a particular pair of changes unacceptable.

In summarizing the complicated events of the first two years of his reign, we may say that Louis carried through important reforms and suffered one reverse. But this reverse carried a venomous sting in its tail.

Vergennes, having investigated the behaviour of Guines in London, reported to the Council that he saw no grounds for action against him. The name of an innocent man had been besmirched and Antoinette wished her friend to receive amends. She suggested to Louis that he should write Guines a letter expressing satisfaction with his conduct and create him a duke. This was only justice. Louis wrote the letter and on 11 May gave Guines a dukedom.

Choiseul and his friends seized on Guines's dukedom to circulate a false report that the Queen had brought about Turgot's disgrace. They added that she had lost faith in Maurepas too and wanted Choiseul to form a new Government. Now Mercy was constantly on the watch for incidents that would show the political power of the Queen, and therefore of himself, the Queen's mentor. He therefore wrote to Maria Theresa: 'The Controller General, learning that the Queen hates him, largely for that reason decided to resign; the Queen's plan was to demand that the King should dismiss Turgot, and even send him to the Bastille, on the same day as the Comte de Guines was created a duke ... she was angry with Turgot for having recalled the Comte de Guines.'

Mercy's letter is a travesty of the facts. The Queen played no direct part in Turgot's fall. According to Véri, 'the Queen opposed him only mildly', and the truth is expressed by Antoinette herself in a letter of 15 May: 'I admit to my dear Maman that I am not displeased by these departures [of Turgot and Malesherbes] but I had nothing to do with them.' However, the damage was done. As senior ambassador at the Court of Versailles, Mercy had influence and his views, echoed as usual by other ambassadors less close to the Queen, found their way abroad and from there back to Paris. A decision taken freely by Louis in the light of public opinion was attributed to the intrigues of his meddlesome wife.

CHAPTER 8

The King at Home

EVERY morning the first candles to appear at Versailles, always behind the same windows, were those of the King's apartments at the centre of the first floor. Here the valet de chambre dressed and folded away his camp bed; then drew back the curtains of the King's four-poster, saying, 'Sire, it is six o'clock.'

Louis got up and put on a dressing-gown. When he first became King he was shaved by his valet de chambre. He had four valets, each on duty for a quarter of the year, but he found that only one of them gave him a smooth shave. At first Louis wished to have this valet shave him every morning, but the others made such a terrible fuss that now Louis shaved himself.

At the beginning of the reign the Duc d'Estissac, Master of the Wardrobe, had come to take the King's orders for suits.

'How many are usually provided each quarter?'

'Six, sire.'

'Then make me six in ratteen.' That was the plainest m....... to be found.

Louis put on whatever clothes his valet handed him, without a glance: on weekdays a brown ratteen suit, on Sundays an embroidered white or gaily coloured velvet. The only sign t... distinguished him from mere courtiers was the diamond st... t... Order of the Holy Spirit, which he wore on his left br..... to have his hair curled and powdered, then breakfaste...... juice and a very unroyal slice of toast without butter. A.... put on his hat and went out to face the world.

Louis was five foot seven inches in height, a coup.... above the average for his time; he had a strong body tha. eai.y inclined to stoutness. His best features were his aquiline Bourbon nose and the blue eyes inherited from his mother; his brow receded, his lips were too full, and his chin was rather fat. He lacked the striking good looks of Louis XV; but his gaze was straight and he held his head high.

The first item on Louis's daily programme was an hour and a

half's walk accompanied only by the young Prince de Poix, Captain
of the Guard. Louis never missed this walk, even in the severe cold
of January 1776, when he put on a thick overcoat and went well
into the country. On that occasion he paid poor men to break the
ice on the ponds and to clear the streets of snow, and he personally
pardoned men who had been arrested for stealing firewood in the
forest of Ville d'Avray.

As a schoolgirl his mother had been careful of time and if one of
her teachers arrived late, she would look at her watch and say, 'So
many minutes lost.' Her son inherited this trait. According to one
of his courtiers, 'Louis XVI was perhaps the most punctual and
exact man I have known; he never made anyone wait, and did not
like to wait himself . . . I once heard him scold the Chapel music-
master because a motet had run on a few minutes after Mass had
ended.'

So Louis was invariably back in time for his *petit lever* at eight
o'clock sharp, when he received the First Gentleman of the Chamber,
accompanied by other household officials, and with them planned
his day. Then he left the formal high-ceilinged public rooms and
climbed a staircase decorated with antlers and heads of wild boar
to his private apartments. These reflected his character and interests:
his study, dominated by Holbein's portrait of the scholar-humanist
 asmus, with papers covered in his neat, regular, medium-sized
 iting carefully filed and locked away; his geography room,
 perhaps a map he was roughing out lying on the table amid
glo es, armillary spheres and other instruments, including a scales.
One day, finding his friend the Duc de Croy looking very thin after
an ess, Louis made him stand on the scales, where he found the
D ndeed thin, since he weighed one pound under seven stone.
  top of his apartments, beside his workshop, Louis had
  s turned into a library, decorated in pale blue and gold.
  put together the best collection of books ever assembled
b   h King. His liking for precise fact is reflected in the titles,
n a n-fiction. Of the almost 8000 volumes 586 were English,
nearly all books published during his reign and which Louis bought
because he wanted to read them. Among his historians he had
Burke, Dalrymple, Gibbon, Hamilton, Ramsay, Robinson; he had
Caver's *North America* and Watkain's *Botany Bay*, Shakespeare's
plays, Fielding's *Tom Jones* and of course his favourite *Robinson
Cruso*: the castaway who survives by using his hands.

Louis spent much time in this library, reading not only books but newspapers. He subscribed to the chief European newspapers, including the Dutch *Gazette de Leyden* and the London *Morning Chronicle*, and by reading them regularly Louis got a truer and fuller picture of events in Europe than did his courtiers, reading only the chauvinistic *Gazette de France*.

When he left his private apartments for the stately public rooms filled with courtiers, Louis cut an undistinguished figure. To start with, he had no small talk. He was more interested in facts, figures and the work of government than in people, and he could never make those little personal compliments or allusions that win courtiers' hearts. Moreover his voice, without being hard, was not agreeable, and if he got worked up it became shrill.

Louis's turn of speech was precise, not witty. Only a couple of witty phrases have been recorded. After listening to a course of long Lenten sermons which had ranged from finance to international politics, Louis said, 'A pity! If the abbé Maury had touched on religion, he would have covered everything.' On another occasion Louis appointed bishops to Clermont-Ferrand and to Saint-Flour, one a holy man, the other intelligent, and afterwards he remarked, 'I have just sent the *Saint Esprit* to Auvergne: the *saint* to Clermont and the *esprit* to Saint-Flour.'

Louis, according to one of his Ministers, was 'quite incapable of saying anything apposite to distinguished generals, leading ambassadors, commanders of provinces or to magistrates who had done him good service in assembly or tribunal.' This is a great shortcoming in a king. Louis, moreover, could often be brusque. When Choiseul returned to Court after four years' exile, Louis greeted him curtly: 'You have grown fatter, Monsieur de Choiseul, and you have lost your hair . . . you are getting quite bald.'

Louis had the strong man's hearty attitude towards illness. 'Ah, Monsieur de Croy! You've been sick, I hear. The trouble is you take too many medicines.' It was true, but Croy felt hurt.

Sometimes Louis could be downright callous. One day a Minister arrived late, explaining that he had come from the bedside of his dying son; all Louis could murmur was 'Ah . . . it's a bore,' and at once began work with the Minister.

Louis's interest in working with his hands, in clockwork, in order and in punctuality to the exclusion of human feeling was attributed by some courtiers to insensibility, but this is incorrect. According to Stormont, Louis was 'naturally of a warm violent temper' and we have seen his strong feelings when his parents died, his tears at the death of his grandfather. In his schoolboy essays he habitually replaced La Vauguyon's *'esprit'* and *'âme'* by *'cœur'*. The truth seems to be not that Louis was insensitive but that he felt things very deeply and distrusted his ability to cope publicly with his feelings. Perhaps as a boy he had been wounded by the cynicism of Versailles; perhaps he felt insufficiently intelligent or sure of himself as King to be able to control them. At all events he adopted a pattern of life aimed, so to speak, at earthing emotion.

Louis had almost no dignity or sense of dignity. He would go for walks alone on the roof of Versailles simply because, as he put it, 'Where else can I get a breath of fresh air without putting someone to trouble?' His sword was a continual embarrassment to him and he never knew what to do with his hat. Ceremonies bored him and he would hand newly promoted marshals their prized batons like a quartermaster dishing out sausages.

Louis had no presence, either. At a ball one evening in the Salon d'Hercule he had difficulty in passing through the crowd and, once in the room, could find no armchair. He was offered one side of her folding stool by an obliging lady and there, on half a stool, sat down the King of France.

Louis was scolded afterwards by Maurepas: 'Eight hundred guests, and you walk in without being announced, without your Captain of the Guard! . . . The ambassadors were scandalized.' Louis, according to Véri, blushed, lowered his head and made no reply.

The Court admired a man according to three criteria: good looks, wit and sexual audacity. Louis possessed none of these characteristics, and so they did not admire him. They esteemed him, never anything more. The actions of earlier kings had been recorded in minute detail by diarists, but after the Duc de Croy's death in 1783 no one bothered to note the day-to-day doings of the King, Véri being more interested in behind-the-scenes intrigue. The new mood at Court was summed up by that colourful roué Maréchal de Richelieu. As a boy he had known the court of Louis XIV, where Madame de Maintenon used to slip him sweets, and he had procured sweets of a different kind for Louis XV; in 1776 he said to Louis XVI: 'Under the first King [Louis XIV] people did not dare say a word, under the second they spoke in hushed tones, now they speak out loud.'

Louis, then, lacked a King's usual awe-inspiring aura; he was punctilious, matter-of-fact and unforthcoming. But he had other facets to his character. To start with, he possessed a sense of humour. In his youth it was schoolboyish and took the form of roistering. He and his brothers loved running round the private apartments, tussling and throwing one another on to the sofa. In the last year of his grandfather's reign Louis was seen with his brothers to run 'with great glee to tickle one of the King's valets de chambre, as he was carrying out the King's dirty clothes.'

Louis liked practical jokes too. On hot summer days he had an awning erected over his balcony, and jets of water sprayed on to it, to keep the balcony cool. Sometimes he would gravely lead one of his more dandified friends on to the balcony and delightedly watch the bewigged figure splutter under the spray of water.

This love of horseplay, which Louis perhaps inherited from his Saxon ancestors and which makes his sense of humour closer to the English than to the French style, occurred also at the *coucher*. Louis would then rag with his pages and try to lasso them with his cordon bleu. The chief butt was Captain de La Roche, keeper of the palace zoo, a gentleman with no liking for soap and water who carried to the royal bedroom 'the stench of a wild boar in its lair', yet wore a prodigious number of rings and jewels. Louis would tease La Roche, and the pages would steal his wig, hide it and finally throw it on top of the King's bed. La Roche grew very cross but at last with the good nature often found in animal lovers forgave them all with a favourite phrase, 'N'*en parlons plus*, say no more about it.' This, which they had been waiting for, would send everyone into peals of laughter, and, as the candles were extinguished at eleven sharp, Louis would repeat deliberately 'N'*en parlons plus.*'

Louis loved his horses – he once listed the names of 120 horses he had ridden – but had a strong dislike of cats. Perhaps he associated them subconsciously with his grandfather's mistresses, or perhaps he recalled an unfortunate incident. One day a fat Persian cat curled up in the royal close-stool and went to sleep. The time came for Louis to sit on the close-stool; at a certain moment the cat woke, tried desperately to get out and in so doing scratched the royal bottom. Louis jumped up in pain and rang all the bells within reach. The incident, noted by one of the King's pages, happily did not recur, perhaps because it was Louis who installed at Versailles the water-closets invented during his reign by Joseph Bramah and known in courtly language as *lieux à l'anglaise*.

Whatever the reason, Louis certainly disliked cats. There were now far too many cats at Versailles, they were to be heard at night in the gutters miaowing, hissing, squalling. When he went for his walk on the roof Louis sometimes watched the arrival of visitors through a telescope mounted there, at other times he would carry a gun and take pot shots at the cats. One day he shot a pet cat belonging to Madame de Maurepas. She was naturally very upset, the King apologized and gave her another, and Maurepas smoothed over the incident with a little joke. But it was one more story in the hands of Louis's critics: a King of France shooting cats on the palace roof!

When alone with his friends, Louis dropped his hard, brusque public manner and was generally gay, often joking. His friends were mostly Normans, who are quiet and logical, like the Duc de Coigny and the Duc d'Harcourt, or shy men like the Comte d'Angiviller, his hard-working Superintendent of Buildings. He won the affection of his servants, and was idolized by his favourite valet, Thierry. But basically Louis, like his father before him, was a family man, and he reserved his chief affection for his brothers, sisters and wife.

Monsieur had the same rather stout build as Louis but not the strong body. He suffered from weak hips and could not even sit a horse. He possessed a quick intelligence, a sense of humour and ready wit that delighted the Court. Louis was the punctual brother, but it was Monsieur who coined the aphorism, 'Punctuality is the politeness of Kings.'

Monsieur had a literary turn of mind. He swamped his letters in classical allusions and in quotations ranging from Virgil to Charles XII, and he helped to write the libretti for two *opéras comiques*, *Panurge dans l'Ile des Lanternes* and *La Caravane du Caire*. But underneath the glitter Monsieur was a curiously negative person. This comes out in his translation of Walpole's *Doubts concerning Richard III*, which he fills with privatives not found in the English such as *improbable*, *impossible* and – a word rare at the time – *inexistant*. Moreover, for all his boasting on the day after his wedding, Monsieur produced no children, and he was not in love with his plain Italian wife, Josèphe, whose chief pleasure in life was to catch little birds in a net and have them made into a soup in her private apartments.

Monsieur spent heavily. Although unable to ride them, he kept a string of thoroughbred horses, he dressed in expensive diamond-spangled suits, kept a horde of literary retainers and travelled about France with an imposing suite.

Monsieur believed in a strong absolute monarchy, supported by the Church. He wanted Louis to suppress those books by the *philosophes* which the bishops pronounced dangerous. He had none of Louis's feeling for the common people, and he voted against the Six Edicts.

Louis's youngest brother, Artois, was totally different. He possessed a slim, athletic body; he rode, shot and danced with easy grace. He could even dance on a tight-rope. He was not intelligent, but he had charm, and flirted with every pretty woman he met.

Unlike Louis and Monsieur, Artois was wild. Against the King's express wish he fought a duel with the Duc de Bourbon, whose wife he had been rude to at a masked ball, sustaining a few slight cuts. He gambled for high stakes. When war broke out, he insisted on rushing off to take part in the siege of Gibraltar, where, however, he showed no military gifts whatsoever.

Artois, as a good ladies' man, thought it necessary to dress with the utmost chic. His wardrobe contained the finest embroidered suits in France and 365 pairs of shoes. He threw money about on paintings, sculptures, clocks, snuff-boxes, vases – all the arts save books. His biggest single expense was the Bagatelle. One day he bet Antoinette 100,000 livres that he could construct and furnish a house in the Bois de Boulogne within nine weeks. He engaged 900 builders and craftsmen, requisitioned loads of stone, paying compensation, however, and within the stated time put up an Etruscan style house, furnished down to curtains and carpets.

Louis and his brothers were extremely close, probably because of their early orphaning. Louis saw that his brothers were much more successful at Court than he was, but he felt no jealousy on that score. On the contrary, he was proud of Monsieur's ready wit and Artois's easy grace. He considered them his closest friends and his allies in ruling France.

They, for their part, recognized Louis's good qualities but distrusted his feelings for the people. They probably considered him rather odd because he liked to open the kitchen door and chat with whoever was there, even the scullery boy, and Artois too voted against the Six Edicts. But fraternal feeling was stronger than any particular differences of opinion, and they certainly possessed a basic loyalty to their brother the King.

When he came to the throne Louis asked Monsieur and Artois to call him not 'Your Majesty' but 'Brother'; he wished in fact that their old friendly relationship should continue, and so it did. Almost every day Louis had supper in Monsieur's apartments, and when, as often happened, he was too busy to take Antoinette to a Paris ball, he deputed Artois to escort her, and also to keep an eye on her. When Artois fell in love with an actress named Mademoiselle Duthé – he had married a princess of Savoy so the Court quipped that after his dry *gâteau de Savoie* he was taking *du thé* – Louis overlooked the scandal and allowed the relationship to continue, though he did once order the Governor of the Invalides to watch out for his brother's carriage as Artois hurried incognito to his actress's arms and to fire the salute due to princes. Louis forgave him the requisitioning of materials for the Bagatelle, even for the duel he fought against his orders. 'The Comte d'Artois,' writes Walpole, 'forgetting that his brother is King, treats him with all the familiarity of their nursery. It was thought necessary to correct this; and M. de Maurepas was commissioned to give the hint. Being urged, he said the King would grow offended.

' "Well," said the Prince, "and if he is, what can he do to me?"

' "Pardon you, my lord," replied the Minister.'

Louis carried fraternal indulgence to the point where it became a very serious failing. Both brothers, as we have seen, spent heavily, in particular Artois. Whenever they ran into debt, they came cap in hand to Louis and asked him to pay. Partly from affection, partly perhaps from a wish not to hurt, Louis could refuse his brothers nothing. He did pay, and paid over and over again. He paid gambling debts, tailors' bills, travelling expenses, pensions for worthless hangers-on; he paid the bills for ballet costumes, snuffboxes, paintings, gardens, for Monsieur and Artois, driven the one by a feeling of physical inadequacy, the other by high spirits, spent far beyond their means. The full enormity of their extravagance can be seen from these figures: between 1774 and 1789 Louis and Antoinette spent on their own households 11.4 million livres; in the same period Louis approved payments to Monsieur and Artois from State funds of 28.3 millions. This means that the personal economies Louis with such difficulty pushed through at Versailles were more than offset by his brothers' reckless spending. According to Miromesnil, a Minister who saw him daily for many years, 'once in his study, feelings of fear and alarm have no influence on the King's decisions,' yet once outside that study Louis could not refuse his brothers anything.

Louis's relationship with his sisters was equally close. His elder sister Clotilde, still as round as a butter-ball, left home in 1775 to marry a son of the King of Sardinia and Piedmont; she was to lead a life of such exceptional unselfishness in adverse circumstances that after her death her cause of beatification was introduced, though never carried through, and to the Church she is known as the Venerable Clotilde.

Louis's other sister, Elisabeth, was now a young lady entering her teens. She had a fresh rose-and-lily complexion, an affectionate nature and the King's sense of humour – she addressed her closest friend Madame de Bombelles as 'Dearest Bomb'. Elisabeth was so fond of Louis that she turned down two offers of marriage, saying 'I prefer to remain at the foot of my brother's throne than to ascend any other.' She wished for a time to join her Aunt Louise in the Carmelites, but Louis, who valued her friendship, opposed the idea; instead she took a nursing course and was to devote her life to helping the sick poor.

When Louis became King, his aunts, in accordance with Court etiquette, left Versailles and went to live in the nearby houses of Bellevue and Brimborin. While Antoinette was only Dauphine Adélaïde had been a friend to her, but when she became Queen, Adélaïde's old suspicions of Austria returned. A few weeks after the accession she wrote to Louis in concert with the Prince de Condé, warning him against 'suffering himself to be too much influenced by the Queen'. Louis, who disliked being told what to do, especially by a woman, began to treat Aunt Adélaïde with considerable coolness.

Louis's relations with Antoinette entered a new phase as soon as he became King. At the moment when he shouldered heavy political responsibilities he perceived that his wife wished to share them. Antoinette had spent most of her life at a Court where her mother exercised absolute power, and it was natural for her on becoming Queen to wish to do as much. She began by asking Louis to recall Choiseul from exile. Louis declined. Antoinette however insisted, saying that it was humiliating for her not to obtain pardon for the man who had arranged her marriage.

'If you put it like that,' said Louis, touched, 'I can refuse you nothing.' And he allowed Choiseul to come to Paris.

Antoinette then wished to get Choiseul back into the Council. In Reims for the coronation she cleverly contrived that Louis himself should fix a time when she might speak alone to Choiseul; she and the splendid Duke had a long talk; the news got about and people began to whisper that Maurepas's days were numbered. Louis, however, saw through Antoinette's little scheme and told her plainly that in no circumstances would he recall Choiseul. He also made clear to her that he would on no account allow her to meddle in politics. He had the satisfaction of seeing Antoinette obey him to the letter, with all the more alacrity since Maria Theresa too wished her to keep out of politics.

Having consummated his marriage in 1773, Louis naturally hoped to produce an heir. But the months passed without sign of a child. In 1775 he consulted several doctors, including Moreau of the Hôtel Dieu, who told him that he saw no physiological reason why Louis should not father a child. Louis continued to hope, but he felt a certain inadequacy towards his wife during these early years, particularly as she was so fond of children, and he tried to make it up to her in other ways. For example, he allowed her to choose the friends she wished, to go to all-night balls in Paris, carefully chaperoned by Artois, and to indulge in the pleasures she had enjoyed as a child, although they were no part of French tradition, such as sleigh-rides through the winter snow.

Louis was now so occupied that he saw his wife only at certain moments of the day. One such moment was going to the hunt. Here is a description by Artois's Scots gardener, Thomas Blaikie: 'The King was dressed almost like a country farmer, a good rough stout man about twenty-five . . . the Queen which is a very handsome beautiful woman sat opposite . . . the whole company seemed exceeding free and gay with an open cheerfulness which is not common to be seen amongst the higher ranks in England . . . they still continue to ride with large jackboots with funnel-shaped tops; certainly if a shower happens those boots will be full of water in a few minutes.'

The Queen, wearing a shovel hat with three big feathers, rode side-saddle on a light grey horse richly caparisoned with blue velvet and silver embroidery. Sharp-eyed Mrs Thrale noticed that most of the hunting horses were stallions 'and vicious, of course', also that the youngest and prettiest Court ladies had no qualms about hawking and spitting. Louis allowed distinguished visitors to accompany his hunt: one was the special English envoy, Nathaniel Parker Forth, who had the unusual distinction of killing a wild boar with a single blow of his whip.

After hunting Louis took a bath. At his own expense he had two tubs installed in his bathroom, one for soaping, one for rinsing, and he made frequent use of them. Contrary to popular belief, the courtiers were particularly fastidious about personal cleanliness.

Most took a daily bath, and the ladies had a choice of forty different deodorants. When the young Comtesse de Provence arrived from less civilized parts, Louis XV tried to enlist the help of her parents to explain to her that teeth are made to be brushed, and the body to be washed. The Piedmontese ambassador could not understand why the King raised such a fuss about 'things that would be considered as details of no consequence whatever at any other Court'.

Another occasion when Louis had an opportunity of being with his wife was at dinner. In the main salon a small rectangular table was laid with two places, and two large green armchairs were placed side by side so close that they touched. Louis sat with Antoinette on his left. They had their backs to the fireplace, and about ten feet in front of them was arranged a semi-circle of stools for the duchesses, princesses and other privileged ladies, behind whom stood the other ladies and any visitors.

'They had a damask tablecloth neither coarse nor fine,' writes Mrs Thrale in 1775, 'without anything under, or any napkin over. Their dishes were silver, not clean and bright like silver in England – but they were silver: pepper and salt standing by them as it is the custom here and their dinner consisted of five dishes at a course [carried to the table from charcoal braziers nearby]. The Queen eat heartily of a pye which the King helped her to, they did not speak at all to each other, as I remember, but both sometimes turned and talked to the Lord in waiting.' 'The Queen,' adds Dr Johnson, 'was so impressed by Miss [Queenie, Mrs Thrale's eleven-year-old daughter] that she sent one of the gentlemen to enquire who she was.'

The food was delicious, largely thanks to Louis XV, who had encouraged his ladies to invent new dishes. Marie Leczinska gave him, and the world, *bouchées à la Reine*, Madame de Pompadour *filets de sole Pompadour*, the fish being cooked in champagne, with truffles and mushrooms, and served garnished with shrimps, Madame Du Barry *perdrix en chartreuse*, a much heavier concoction than the Pompadour's, consisting of partridge stewed in white wine with a small cabbage, pickled pork and sausages. Even military men contributed recipes: Maréchal de Mirepoix the classic sauce which bears his name, Maréchal de Richelieu a sauce made of eggs and oil, given the name of *la mahonnaise* – mayonnaise – after his capture of Port Mahon in Minorca.

Louis XVI's reign saw the introduction of soya and curry, while garlic became popular against the vapours. From Strasbourg a chef named Jean Joseph Close gave France *pâté de foie aux truffes*. Ice was much used and a favourite dessert was *bombe glacée*. Monsieur, a gourmet, invented a costly recipe for cooking an ortolan inside a partridge, stuffed with foie gras and truffles.

Louis liked his food and, especially after hunting, had a hearty appetite. He usually began with pâté, went on to cutlets and vegetables – among which green beans and fried artichokes were favoured at Versailles – a salad seasoned only with lemons, and ended with fruit and a glass of Malaga. Throughout Lent he fasted, eating nothing from breakfast to supper. Antoinette, who breakfasted off hot chocolate with whipped cream and a brioche, ate sparsely at midday – the large helping of pie noticed by Mrs Thrale seems to have been exceptional. Her favourite dish was roast duck. Complicated dishes did not suit her and she once suffered painful indigestion after eating iced cheese. She drank only water, preferring that from Ville d'Avray.

In the late afternoon Louis liked to go to the theatre with his wife. He particularly enjoyed Molière, and ordered his comedies to be performed twice a week during the season. Afterwards there would be games and here Louis's tastes differed from those of his family. Monsieur preferred whist, Artois billiards, and Louis backgammon, which he played for never more than an écu a point. Antoinette liked gambling games such as cavagnole – a kind of lotto played with dice, or reversi, and, true to her heredity and upbringing, she staked high. Just how much she spent on gambling we shall see later. Louis himself rarely gambled and tried to discourage the practice.

Louis was urged by Maurepas to enforce his own good example by making Antoinette stop gambling, but he had his private reasons for not wishing to be a spoilsport and he said nothing, though urged three times by his Mentor. Finally Maurepas got quite cross.

'You belie the Latin proverb, *regis ad examplar totus componitur orbis*, an adage particularly applicable to France. Everyone knows you don't like games of chance and yet, for lack of a word from you, everyone gambles in your presence.'

Louis felt the force of this remonstrance for, according to Véri, he lowered his head, blushed and said nothing. 'What more can I do?' said Maurepas to Véri afterwards.

Louis's indulgence of Antoinette's gambling was to have no such serious consequences as his indulgence of his brothers' heavy spending, but it arose from the same mixture of warm affection and personal inferiority, as though he were saying to himself: Who am I to inhibit the pleasures of these charming people?

Louis's affection for his wife and his wish to take her part on all but State affairs appeared very clearly in February 1775. During that month Antoinette's eighteen-year-old brother Maximilian arrived in France. Like most members of royal houses at this period, Maximilian wished to avoid the expense of a large suite and the time-consuming municipal receptions traditionally accorded to visiting royalty, and he travelled incognito, taking the name of Comte de Bourgaw. Once in Paris, he waited for the visit which an Emperor's son had the right to expect from princes of the blood. These were the Prince of Condé, who had already joined Aunt Adélaïde in warning Louis against his wife; the Prince de Conti, so acrimonious that Louis XV had never wished to employ him, and leader of opposition to the Six Edicts; the Duc d'Orléans and his dark small-featured son, Philippe, Duc de Chartres, the best dressed man in Paris. These haughty princes declared that it was for Maximilian to pay them the first visit, since he was travelling merely as a Comte. What they were really concerned to do was assert themselves and snub Austria.

Antoinette was deeply hurt and complained to Louis. He, for his part, was faced with a difficult choice. There was no precedent in the matter, since an Emperor's son had never before come to France incognito. The princes liked cocking snooks at the Crown and traditionally had to be humoured. But Maximilian was his wife's brother, and Louis felt bound no less by affection for her than by common courtesy to support him. He, Monsieur and Artois clubbed together to give an opera and sumptuous fancy dress ball at Versailles in honour of Maximilian. The young man enjoyed himself but the princes pointedly stayed away and spread the story that Austria had been given precedence over France.

Antoinette did what she could to put things right, welcoming the princes warmly a few days later when they condescended to come to Court, but the damage was done. Henceforth the princes, notably Orléans and his son, Philippe, Duc de Chartres, were to talk against Louis and his wife.

Louis made a number of other enemies in his first two years: former Ministers, like Terray, whom he had dismissed, Choiseul, whom he recalled from exile – a serious error of judgment due to the Queen – but would not employ, the Parlementaires, whose wishes in regard to the Six Edicts he had overridden, and courtiers whose claims to pensions Malesherbes declined to allow. There existed then, from the very earliest period, a strong underground opposition to the King in and around Versailles, and one of its earliest productions, probably by Choiseul's set, was this verse:

> *Maurepas était impuissant,*
> *Le Roi l'a rendu plus puissant,*
> *Le Ministre reconnaissant,*
> *Dit: Pour vous, Sire,*
> > *Que je désire*
> *D'en faire autant.*[1]

The implication was that Louis was incapable of producing a child, and that Monsieur, the heir to the throne, was the man courtiers should cultivate.

Most of his day Louis spent at his papers and dispatches in his study or Council Chamber, and this practice of working, so to speak, at home meant that he was surrounded by family and courtly pressures. Louis knew how to distinguish public and domestic issues, and on the whole he resisted these pressures, for he possessed a tough core and is described by Véri as 'hard rather than indulgent'. This inner toughness struck Miromesnil also: 'I have never known anyone,' he writes, 'whose character was more contradicted by outward appearances than the King . . . He is good and tender-hearted; you can never speak to him of disasters or accidents to people without seeing a look of compassion come over his face, yet his tone is brusque, his replies are often hard, his manner unfeeling and in taking decisions he is firm and courageous.'

This estimate of the King's character is confirmed by the Duc de Croy, the courtier Louis put on the scales, who also emphasizes Louis's discretion: the King, he says, was reserved towards courtiers, especially the Queen's friends; 'he took great care not to reveal his intentions to them or even to discuss State affairs, especially money matters. He saw clearly and true, and although he had no original ideas, on the whole few Kings of France have ruled personally as much as he did.'

[1]Maurepas was impotent,
The King made him omnipotent,
The grateful Minister said, Sire,
All I can possibly desire
Is to do the same for you.

CHAPTER 9

The Queen's Happiness

WHEN she became Queen at eighteen, the main lines of Antoinette's physique and temperament were laid. She had a slightly built, small-boned body of medium height with the distinctive marks of the thoroughbred: fine aquiline nose, narrow wrists and ankles, slender hands. She had perfectly made shoulders, lively blue eyes and a smooth, fair complexion. She was considered beautiful, but hers was the beauty of youth and high spirits, not that of a Bellini Madonna: her brow was a shade too prominent, the underlip in anger a shade too protruding, the reddish blonde hair inclined to be frizzy.

Her health was not robust. She had a weak chest, for which she had to drink ass's milk, and even in summer easily caught cold and sore throats. She was deficient in iron but could not stomach the iron-rich foods prescribed for her, nor could she fast during Lent as her mother did. By temperament she was highly strung and felt things deeply. Her letters are full of what she feels, mostly pleasure but also alarm, especially when she senses she has displeased her mother, and it is a sign of her emotional temperament that her menstrual periods often occurred several days before they were due.

Quick to feel, Antoinette was quick also to show her feelings, especially in the expression of her eyes, and her page, Tilly, says he had never met anyone whose face so markedly registered tenderness or displeasure. In short, although not robust, Antoinette possessed great nervous energy and gave the impression of being extremely alive: for Stormont her chief characteristic was 'great quickness and vivacity'.

Antoinette's instincts, her tone, her way of feeling and thinking were Austrian, not French. She valued feeling and spontaneity more than reason. She tended to go to extremes. She was not suave, not discreet. As a stranger she naturally saw through the conventions of French Court life; what others took for granted she found funny and, being Austrian, when she found something funny she laughed outright. Although she soon lost the ability to speak German, she possessed to a marked degree what her mother approvingly termed 'German frankness'.

It is not surprising therefore that the quality in her husband Antoinette most respected was his *droiture* or straightforwardness. In the autumn after the consummation of their marriage, Louis was seen by Mercy's spies to kiss his wife.

'Do you love me?' he asked her.

'Yes, sincerely,' Antoinette replied. 'You can be sure of that. And I respect you still more.'

There is no call to doubt the honesty of that declaration. Despite their contrasting temperaments, she so quick, he so steady, and their different interests, Antoinette during this period was in love with her husband. The marriage that had begun so unpromisingly was now a source of happiness to her. *Bonheur, plaisir, tendre, joie, contente* – in her letters to her mother these are the words that glimmer like sunlight on a lake.

Antoinette wished to be not only a wife to Louis but in a full sense Queen of France. Having failed to get Choiseul into the Council, she quickly understood that henceforth she was barred from politics. She could never emulate the great Empress, a lock of whose hair she wore next to her skin. Young, beautiful and popular she might be, but she would never be a ruler like her mother, the adored and feared.

What courses were open to her? She could retire into her apartments, those same rooms where Marie Leczinska had moped and prayed and lost at piquet. She could emulate her two Piedmontese sisters-in-law: cook and sew and exchange spiteful gossip, while their husbands dallied with amusing French mistresses. Antoinette had too much spirit for that, and also too much public spirit, for she really meant it when she said that she wished to work for the happiness of France. She decided finally to take the lead wherever she sensed that she had something useful to give.

The first opportunity to present itself was opera. Charles Burney wrote in 1771, 'The French . . . have stood still in music for thirty or forty years', and Antoinette, arriving from the most advanced musical city of Europe, found Paris applauding revivals of Lully's stiff works and bad productions of declamatory Italian operas.

Among German composers Antoinette particularly liked Christoph Willibald Gluck, because his music was spontaneous and full of feeling. Gluck's latest opera, *Iphigénie en Aulide*, had been turned down by the Académie Royale de Musique, but Antoinette used her influence behind the scenes and finally got it accepted. Then she invited Gluck to Paris to supervise the production.

Gluck, who came of a long line of Danube foresters, was a difficult man of fifty-nine with revolutionary ideas about opera and opera production. What he wanted was naturalness, so he almost threw a fit when he saw how French singers rolled their eyes and sawed the air, while the chorus stood like dummies on either side of the stage throughout the performance – the men, with arms folded, separated from the women, who all held fans.

He had a good Iphigenia in Sophie Arnould, but Larrivée as Agamemnon seemed to have no comprehension of the part. When Gluck chivvied him, he would reply: 'Wait till I get into my costume, you won't recognize me then.' At a later rehearsal Larrivée reappeared in his costume, but his interpretation remained the same. 'Oh Larrivée, Larrivée!' cried Gluck. 'I recognize you!'

Although there were a great many ballet interludes, the very vain dancer Vestris wanted yet another, in which his son should star. Gluck peremptorily refused. '*Quoi!*' stammered Vestris. '*Moi – le dieu de la danse!*' 'If you are the god of the dance, Monsieur, dance in heaven, not in my opera.'

Gluck kept threatening to return to Vienna and for five anxious months Antoinette had to soothe him, as well as the opera company. It was thanks to her that the production took place at all.

On 19 April 1774 Antoinette, Louis, Ministers and all the Court took their seats in the Paris opera house. They were familiar with the plot, from Racine's play: how the goddess Diana produces a calm, which prevents the Greek fleet in Aulis from sailing against Troy, how Agamemnon is advised by a seer to sacrifice his daughter Iphigenia, and how at the last moment Diana is appeased without bloodshed, and Iphigenia is restored to her parents and to Achilles, who loves her. But the austere power of the music, fifty years ahead of its time, puzzled an audience habituated to facile tunes and superfluous ornaments. Though Antoinette applauded, the first night was not a success.

Antoinette arranged a second performance, which went better, and took the lead in championing Gluck against the majority, who preferred Italian opera in the person of Piccini. In August she arranged a performance of *Orphée et Eurydice*, which scored a success, and she brought Gluck back to Paris each year until 1778. In a letter to Antoinette, Gluck said that he owed his success to her protection and it was to her – 'sensitive and enlightened Princess, who loves and protects all the arts' – that he dedicated his master-piece, *Iphigénie en Tauride*.

By championing Gluck Antoinette did a great deal to change the course of French opera and to improve standards of production. The company themselves saw this, for when *Iphigénie en Aulide* was given in Paris on 13 January 1775, at the climax of the second act Achilles, instead of turning to his followers with the opening words of the Chorus, '*Chantez, célébrez votre reine*,' came forward and sang:

Chantons, célébrons notre reine.

Tumultuous applause then broke out in all parts of the house, the chorus was encored and cries of '*Vive la Reine!*' continued so long that the performance was held up for eight minutes.

Antoinette liked music that expresses deep feelings simply: the reverse of the pompous and artificial. She found this quality in Antonio Sacchini and him too she invited to Versailles, where he dedicated to Antoinette his fine opera *Renaud*, which won him the name of 'the Racine of music'.

Antoinette also had a particular fondness for ballet. As a girl of eleven she had danced with her sisters in *Il Parnasso Confuso*, text by her Italian teacher Metastasio, music by Gluck, and it evidently remained a happy memory, for she brought to Versailles a painting of the performance. In ballet as in opera she liked naturalness; she particularly encouraged Mademoiselle Heinel, the first dancer to pirouette, and this new movement meant dispensing with the heavy trappings inherited from the Sun King's reign. Antoinette made suggestions to Bacquer, the designer, for lighter and more graceful costumes, and she arranged the Hungarian and Flemish country dances performed at the reception for her brother Maximilian. But her changes did not involve increased expenditure. When Rameau's *Castor and Pollux* was produced in 1777, the budget was half that of a production under Louis XV, moth-eaten woollen stockings used by soldiers seven years before being darned and worn by Greek gods.

Antoinette wished also to take the lead in fashion. Here again she found an over-formalized situation. French ladies wore brocade, satin, moiré, hand-painted taffeta, sheared Florentine velvet of variegated colours, excessively complicated patterns, and adorned all over with fringes, laces and ribbons, which could be worn in any one of two hundred and fifty ways.

Antoinette, rejecting these fussy fashions, decided to dress simply and naturally. She usually wore materials of a single gold colour known as *cheveux de la Reine*. The following year she received a taffeta in a new shade of purplish brown, to which the couturier had given the affected name of 'Honest Compromise', and this prompted Louis, who took an interest in Antoinette's clothes, to say laughingly, 'It's the colour of a flea (*puce*)!' Under the name of puce, purplish brown taffeta became the fashion that season, with various sub-shades such as flea's belly, flea's back, and flea's thigh.

In the autumn of 1777, at the races, Antoinette appeared in a dress with a close-fitting bodice and slashed skirt, made of flesh-coloured gros de Tours embroidered with garlands of blue flowers having brown stems and green leaves, a white mantlet and a white hat; 'the whole ensemble,' says the Countess Spencer, 'was perfectly beautiful and in the best taste.' On another day at the races the Queen was again judged by an Englishwoman, Mrs Thrale, 'to be dressed with the utmost simplicity'.

One advantage of wearing simple clothes in a single colour was that Antoinette saved money, and since Maurepas was constantly on to her about economies, she took pleasure one spring day in 1776 in pointing out to him that she was dressed simply in green.

'Look, even my slippers are of satin *vert uni*.'

'Madame,' replied Maurepas, with a nice turn of phrase, 'I am not in the least surprised to see the *univers* at your feet.'

In 1775 the English fashion for wearing hair extremely high invaded France. Hair was pinned up, padded out by artificial hair, and held in place by gauze and pins. The edifice was then decorated with plumes to represent, say, a ship tossing on the waves, or a mountain with silvery waterfalls. Ladies with hair piled three feet high had to travel to a ball with heads poked out of their carriage windows.

Antoinette followed this fashion and got a small neat serious man named Léonard, who called himself not a hairdresser but a Physiognomist, to drive out from Paris to heap her beautiful hair high. Her hairstyles, however, never became as extravagant as those, say, of the Duchesse de Chartres, who had a scale model of her son's nursery in her hair, complete with nanny, Negro servant and a parrot pecking at a cherry.

In 1776 Antoinette fell ill – more of this illness will be said later – and according to Lady Clermont 'her hair since her illness has fallen almost all off.' It was soon to grow abundant again, but that autumn Antoinette had an extra reason for wearing chignons and lots of feathers. 'The heads are full as high as last year,' Lady Clermont continues, 'but not *near so high* as in England.'

Antoinette's love of music and beautiful dress came into their own at the balls she loved to give and attend. Here again she preferred simplicity. Her favourite dances were country dances, and in 1775 she asked her friend Countess Spencer kindly to send her three or four books of English country dances from London, particularly 'Over the hills and far away'. She also enjoyed masked balls at the Paris Opéra. These she attended informally, making her coachmen wear grey overcoats over their royal blue livery. 'She thought no one recognized her,' says Madame Campan, 'but the moment she entered the building everyone did. However, they pretended not to, so that she might keep her illusion of being incognito.'

Again, the absence of luxury and lavishness in the evenings surprised Mrs Thrale: 'There were no diamonds at all at Court but the Queen's ear-rings, and she had no other jewels on her head – a pair of pearl bracelets with a picture on each were all that looked like ornaments of expense; her gown was a gauze adorned with flowers.'

It was not only in the arts, fashion and dances that Antoinette took the lead. As soon as there was some new activity she wanted to take part in it. When Artois bought an open two-wheeled carriage called a *diable*, faster than her cabriolet, she went driving with him in it. A craze started for tilting at the ring; Antoinette went to watch and presented prizes to the winners. In winter she went with her friends for rides in sleighs with jingle-bells.

The most important of these innovations occurred in the autumn of 1775 when she attended one of the first horse-races to be held in France. A course was marked out near Paris; there were three runners, belonging to Artois, the Duc de Chartres and the Duc de Lauzun, all ridden by English jockeys. Among the spectators was Dr Johnson, who grumbled that he could not see who was in the lead, since all three jockeys wore green, the colour of Artois, who organized the race.

Parisians of all classes swirled around the Queen, assessing the horses, making bets, and here for the first time we glimpse the Paris fishwives, smelling strongly of herring, who from time immemorial had the right of saying what they liked to the royal family, and were to weave in and out of Antoinette's life like a Greek chorus. They called on her now to give France an heir. It is Mrs Thrale who noted 'the riot raised at ye course today by forty-three fisherwomen who surround the Queen, and with the loudest voices and frantic gestures uttered a thousand gross obscenities in her ears till she was forced to give 'em money to be rid of them.'

Finally Antoinette 'was placed in a booth in which there was no chair to sit on till one had been fetched from Paris, four miles away.' From there she watched the horses line up and finally they were off. The race lasted six minutes; during that time Antoinette and her ladies 'clapped their hands, and almost shouted when the winner came in [belonging to Lauzun]. She praised the jockey who won, and stroked the horse.'

Under Antoinette's patronage, horse-racing became popular and soon races were held almost every week. Although she did not attend every race, she continued to show a marked interest in the sport. Louis, who had time to attend only one race, found it very odd that Antoinette, a Queen of France, should display her feelings by cheering and shouting at racehorses in full view of the public; and on the next visit of the Comédie Italienne he got the leading actors to give him an imitation of the Queen and his brother at the races, laughing delightedly at their performance.

In the evenings, as we have seen, Antoinette liked to play cards for money. After some months of losses she was told by Louis to stop. However, she pleaded with him and obtained the right to one last session. She played all through the night and far into the morning. At 4 a.m., 1800 livres down, she went to bed. But that evening she continued the same game at a private house. She left at 3 a.m. but her friends continued well into daylight, and it happened to be All Saints' Day, when it was not done to play cards. Louis found out and scolded Antoinette.

'You allowed one last session,' she replied, 'without stipulating how long, so we had a perfect right to go on for thirty-six hours.'

'Really!' exclaimed Louis, unable to repress a smile. 'You are all a worthless lot!'

In January 1777 Mercy went through Antoinette's accounts and found she had incurred debts, mainly from gambling, during the past year amounting to 487,272 livres, which she had no means of paying. Louis, however, came to the rescue and since he refused to draw on the Treasury, decided to pay the sum by instalments out of his privy purse, which then amounted to 1.2 million livres a year. 'As he is naturally very thrifty,' sayd Mercy, 'this generosity astonished the Queen.'

Louis indulged his wife as he did his brothers. At the end of 1779 he again came to her rescue, giving her 100,000 livres to pay gambling debts. But now Louis began to gamble at cards too. At his first attempt he lost 1700 louis and having given all his spare cash to Antoinette had no means of paying. It was now Antoinette's turn to come to the rescue; she gave her husband 1200 louis and the rest he borrowed elsewhere.

The Queen's wardrobe allowance had been fixed in 1725 at 120,000 livres; adequate then but not fifty years later. Antoinette was expected every day to wear a morning dress, an afternoon dress and an evening dress of sufficient distinction to demonstrate France's leadership in fashion. Her chief dressmaker was Rose Bertin of the Faubourg Saint-Honoré, a round-faced, snub-nosed, small-eyed Norman, with the Norman's traditional closeness to money. She charged her clients, including Antoinette, very high prices indeed, and to one customer who protested she retorted, 'Eh! Do you pay Vernet only for his paints and canvas?' She had a point there, for she possessed true artistry. Antoinette bought about 170 dresses a year, most of them from Rose Bertin. During the early years of the reign they cost her around 160,000 livres, so she was over-spending her wardrobe allowance by 40,000 livres. That sum is included in the debts paid by Louis in 1777.

Because Louis was careful with his own money and therefore able to pay his wife's debts, Antoinette proved less of a charge on the State than Louis's brothers or even than his aunts, who liked to travel across France to take the waters at Vichy, a ruinously expensive distraction, since etiquette decreed they should be accompanied by 250 persons and 160 horses. Louis was indulgent to his wife over her gambling and to some extent over her wardrobe, but there is no question at all of him conniving in criminal extravagance. As for the ballets Antoinette helped to arrange for the Court, Turgot, in approving the budget for them in 1775, said that he considered it quite reasonable.

The most important thing in life for Antoinette was friendship. It is a word that recurs in her conversation and her letters from the very earliest years. In coming to Versailles she lost the intimacy of her sisters and brothers, which had meant so much to her, and she began to look for new friends.

Antoinette found that the important people at Versailles were ex-army officers and their wives, whose ancestors under Louis XIV and Louis XV had given their lives on the battlefields of Austria. She naturally found herself treated by them with suspicion, even as an enemy alien. Moreover, they were mostly much older than she and some were quite fossilized: when it was mentioned that a certain lady had had a baby, old Maréchale de Termes, aged eighty, was heard to murmur, 'Do they still make love nowadays?'

Antoinette invented her own name for these old fogies. She called them 'Centuries'. She could not get through to them. She saw people as sealed envelopes and what she liked to do, in her own phrase, was 'to open envelopes'. By that she meant being natural and informal, telling them what she liked, what made her laugh, what made her cross, and the heartfelt, perhaps absurd, inanities which are sometimes the solidest basis of friendship.

Antoinette succeeded in finding such friends, but outside the narrow circle of the palace. The first was Marie Thérèse Louise de Savoie Carignan, Princesse de Lamballe, a pale, slim, sad-eyed lady with big hands, a prominent nose and long curly fair hair, six years older than Antoinette and like her a stranger, having been born in Turin. Marie Thérèse was a childless widow, who spent most of her time with her immensely rich father-in-law, the Duc de Penthièvre, seeking out cases of distress and relieving them. The Duke was known as 'father of the poor', Marie Thérèse as 'the good angel'.

Marie Thérèse de Lamballe was abnormally sensitive. The slightest shock and she would fall into a faint lasting up to two hours. The smell of a bouquet of violets made her ill; the sight of a lobster or a crayfish, even in a painting, caused her a nervous fit. To this misfortune was added another: since there was no prince of suitable age available, she would never be able to remarry.

Antoinette liked sensitive people and also people she could help. She took quickly to Marie Thérèse and wished to have her at Court. Madame de Noailles having resigned, in 1775 Antoinette had Marie Thérèse appointed Lady-in-Waiting in her household, a position where they would see each other daily. 'Picture my happiness,' Antoinette wrote to the Comte de Rosenberg, 'I shall make my dearest friend happy and in so doing gain even more than she.'

Antoinette and Marie Thérèse went for long walks arm in arm, exchanged secrets and established close ties of sympathy. Everything the one felt, the other felt too, and because Marie Thérèse was so sensitive this sometimes led to unusual happenings. One day, while boating on the canal, Antoinette said she felt unwell, whereupon Marie Thérèse immediately fainted. Another time a window-pane happened to break near the two friends: Antoinette received a few scratches, but Marie Thérèse was so alarmed for the Queen that she lost consciousness for several hours, had to be bled, and then to take the waters at Plombières.

Antoinette's second close friend was also an outsider, an impoverished noble lady from the provinces. Gabrielle de Polastron belonged to an old Gascon family and at seventeen had married another Gascon, Comte Jules de Polignac. She first appeared at a Court ball in 1775; a petite Raphaelesque beauty with swan neck and dark velvety eyes. Antoinette asked her why she appeared so seldom at Court. 'I'm not well enough off,' replied Gabrielle. Her husband, an Army colonel, had a salary of only 4000 livres a year.

Gabrielle was rather delicate and often had to take the waters. She was a very sensible person with a warm heart and she believed, like Antoinette, that 'the greatest happiness is to be with friends'. She disliked as much as the Queen did formality and fussy clothes: often her only ornament was a freshly-picked rose in her hair. She was gay and unpretentious. One day her well-educated sister-in-law, Diane de Polignac, a lady-in-waiting to the Comtesse d'Artois, suggested she cultivate her mind by reading the *Iliad* and the *Odyssey*. Gabrielle smilingly answered that she knew all about the Greek poet and, in proof, burlesqued a well-known line of verse:

Homer was blind and played the oboe!

Antoinette, says Madame Campan, the Queen's personal maid, found this turn of mind very much to her taste.

So the second friendship began, just as close as the first. In order that Gabrielle could appear at Court, Jules de Polignac would have to have an official position, so Antoinette appointed him successor to the Comte de Tessé, her First Equerry, at a salary of 12,000 livres, and with an apartment close to her own, at the head of the great marble staircase. When Gabrielle left to take the waters, Antoinette counted the days till her return and once committed the unheard-of sin of missing a hunting supper to which Louis had invited her in order to hurry to Paris, without escort or bodyguard, and embrace dearest Gabrielle on her return.

Feeling, naturalness, informality – these were the qualities esteemed in the Queen's circle, and they are to be found in another of Antoinette's friends. Duchess Georgiana of Devonshire was two years younger than Antoinette whom, according to Lady Clermont, she resembled a little physically and in occasionally lapsing into a far-away look. A very emotional person, who could rarely get through a letter to her mother without dropping into poetry, Georgiana met Antoinette first in 1772 and again in 1774, the year she married Devonshire. The two became very fond of each other. Georgiana translated for Antoinette her first poem on Hope and taught her and the Polignacs how to dance the Lockhart.

Georgiana kept in touch with her French friends by letter. She was particularly fond of Gabrielle, whom Lady Jersey and the Duke of Dorset also esteemed. True to her 'natural' feelings, Georgiana wished to suckle her second child herself, which was then very unusual for a lady accustomed to the fatigue of high society, and she wrote to Gabrielle for advice. Gabrielle's reply shows the sound common sense underlying her light-hearted manner: 'It is for you, my dear Georgiana, to see whether you have enough self-control to resist keeping late hours. There – you wanted my advice, and I have given you it frankly.'

Antoinette brought to her circle the downright humour of the Hofburg. If she saw something funny, she laughed openly, where a French lady would repress a smile. On at least one occasion at a formal dinner she laughingly flicked bread pellets across the table at Louis, and it was not unknown for her and her friends to throw each others' hats in the canal. Once she saw a friend, Madame de Gouvernet, in the corner of a doorway shaking hands with the English ambassador. She had not seen this form of greeting before, found it very funny, and on the many occasions when the Ambassador and her friend were present, she never failed to tease him: 'Have you shaken hands with Madame de Gouvernet?'

'It is impossible,' writes Lady Jersey, 'to conceive anything so pleasant as the Queen's manner, she improves upon acquaintance astonishingly, and has a way of obliging in trifles that is charming.' One such trifle occurred when young Germaine de Staël was presented at Court. Impetuous and gauche, she jumped from her carriage, weakening the seams of her satin and lace dress, so that when she came to perform the third of the three traditional low curtseys before the King and Queen, the trimmings of her train parted company with her. While the courtiers drew in their breath at this shocking occurrence, Antoinette took Germaine into her boudoir, asked her chambermaid to sew up the train, and engaged Germaine in conversation until the damage was righted. Louis too was considerate to Germaine, remarking gently, 'If you cannot feel at ease with us, you cannot feel at ease anywhere.'

On his accession Louis had at his disposal two charming houses in the grounds of Versailles. 'The Trianons have always belonged to the King's favourite,' he told Antoinette, 'so it is right that I should give them to you.'

Antoinette accepted only the Petit Trianon, a seven-roomed *pavillon* designed by Gabriel for Madame de Pompadour. There she liked to gather her friends for informal living, far from Court fussiness; here she liked to wear light clothes instead of the formal dresses with panniers five feet across and a train up to ten and a half yards long. Etiquette was relaxed so that when she entered, her friends need not interrupt their needlework or game of billiards. At the Trianon, she said, she could be herself: '*Là, je suis moi.*'

It was quite usual for a Queen of France to spend much of her free time at one of the Trianons. Between 1741 and 1750, neglected by her husband, Marie Leczinska had retired from Court life to the Grand Trianon, usually with one or more of her young daughters – Louis's aunts – for days on end.

Antoinette saw that her husband hardly ever had time to attend the Opéra or Comédie Française in Paris, and these companies performed for only a short season at the palace. She thought it would be a good idea if plays could be given at the Trianon, to which Louis could walk across after his day's work. At first she got actors in, but they were sometimes difficult, wishing to choose the plays and to perform only to large houses. Finally Antoinette decided that she and her friends would do the acting.

This was an innovation. To please Louis XV Madame de Pompadour had acted in light comedies, but never until Antoinette did so had a Queen of France trodden the boards. The only young man Louis allowed to take part in the plays was Artois. Other male parts were given to courtiers in their fifties, with the exception of the Comte de Vaudreuil, a friend of Artois, who was in his thirties. Women's parts were taken by the King's sister, Madame Elisabeth, and Diane de Polignac. They were taught how to deliver their lines and to sing recitative by a retired actor named Caillot. The audience comprised the King, Monsieur, the wives of Monsieur and Artois, and some ladies of Antoinette's household, never more than forty in all.

Antoinette herself sometimes played the lead, as in the musical comedy, *Le Devin du Village*, but usually she took the role of a servant. A typical Trianon play was Sedaine's *La Gageure Imprévue*. A scheming lady, Madame de Clainville, becoming jealous of her husband's friendship for a young woman, pretends to fall in love with a visiting army officer, only to discover that the young woman is really her husband's impoverished niece, for whom he is arranging a marriage. The plot is helped along by a manservant, Lafleur, and Madame de Clainville's maid, Gotte: they of course are wiser than their employers: 'A servant is an ass if at the end of seven years he doesn't control his master.' Antoinette played the maid Gotte and ended the gay little drama on a note of hope: 'If only this adventure can cure my mistress of her scheming!'

A Queen playing a simple serving-girl: there was something in this situation which appealed to Antoinette. It was slightly fantastic, a little ridiculous, and for that reason the sober French, with their classical sense of order, frowned on it or thought it 'singular'. But the Viennese girl laughed and laughed. And it made such a pleasant change from that other part she had to act, across in the palace. As she wrote to her sister in 1777: 'People think it very easy to play the queen – they are wrong. The constraints are endless, it seems that to be natural is a crime . . .'

At the Trianon Antoinette could be natural. After the play, in summer, she liked to walk on the terraces of Versailles. In the cool of the evening, arm-in-arm with Marie Thérèse or Gabrielle or one of her sisters-in-law, she would stroll along trim sanded paths while in the moonlight the statues of gods and goddesses cast shadows on the lawn. Soon, at the suggestion of Artois, the musicians from the chapel were summoned and installed on a rostrum, where they played far into the night. Attracted by the violins, people from the town of Versailles came to listen and stroll. Antoinette would wander quite freely among them, as King Henri IV used to do in the Paris streets. Once, thinking herself unrecognized, she sat on a bench with a clerk from a Ministry and a private belonging to Monsieur's bodyguard, and struck up a conversation with them – as though Sedaine's play had a fourth act and she were still the servant Gotte.

Many of the handsome young courtiers sought to win the Queen's heart, the most assiduous being an army officer, ten years her senior, who belonged to one of the oldest families in France. Armand Louis de Gontaut Biron, Duc de Lauzun, was all nose and nerves. He had abandoned his wife, a timid little bird, a week after their marriage, and gone for a while to Warsaw, where he mingled love and free-lance diplomacy. His good looks appealed to the Queen and in the summer of 1775 she allowed him to accompany her almost every time she rode to hounds. One day she admired a white heron's plume on his colonel's tricorne. Lauzun gallantly handed her the plume, and she wore it one evening in public. Encouraged by this, and not over-bright, Lauzun asked for an audience. Antoinette granted it but, according to her personal maid Madame Campan, she soon reopened her doors, saying in a loud, angry voice: 'Leave, Monsieur.' Lauzun bowed deeply and disappeared. Antoinette was very upset, and told Madame Campan: 'That man will never darken my doors again.'

Lauzun, by now head over heels in love, bought a suit of the Queen's blue and gold livery. Clad in this, he followed her about all day as a lackey, and even slept at the outer entrance of her apartments. The Queen made no sign of recognition, and Lauzun was in despair, when a good opportunity arose of making himself more conspicuous. Her Majesty was to drive from Trianon, and at the moment she approached her carriage Lauzun knelt, that she might tread on his knee instead of the carriage step. The Queen called a page. 'I desire that that man be dismissed; he is very awkward; he does not even know how to open a carriage door.'

Antoinette had no more trouble with Lauzun. Artois was the only young man she saw a lot of and he, the King made sure, treated her with the utmost correctness. For the moment she did not want things otherwise. She enjoyed a little mild flirting, but no more. Like her mother, she was chaste. When she took a bath, she wore a long flannel shift buttoned up to the neck, and when she got out, she signalled to two maids to hold up a sheet to screen her from her ladies.

What of the familiar concept of Antoinette the scatterbrain? It is a charge sometimes made in Mercy's letters, but Mercy was quite capable of exaggerating a tiny oversight into a crime, so that he could be the necessary rectifier of disorder. When one turns to Antoinette's more than three hundred letters, only once does she do a scatterbrained thing. That is in 1785 when she mislays the itinerary of her sister, who was visiting France, and so cross was Antoinette with herself that she said to Mercy: 'I'm a scatterbrain.' A real scatterbrain would probably not have made that admission.

During her first years as Queen, Antoinette achieved what she had set out to do. She freed herself from the 'Centuries'. She succeeded in leading her own life according to her own values. She acquired close, loyal friends. She behaved frankly and naturally. She took part in a wide variety of activities. All this combined to convey to observers a deep impression of joy.

Antoinette's joy spread joy among her friends, but not everyone fell into that category. She alienated the high nobility by taking in outsiders like Marie Thérèse de Lamballe and Gabrielle de Polignac. She, no less than the King, was blamed by the Princes for siding with Maximilian. She alienated unscrupulous politicians like the Duc d'Aiguillon, who longed to return to power and whose attempts to win her favour she consistently repelled.

Antoinette during these early years became a target for calumny. According to the most intelligent woman observer of the time, Germaine de Staël, she whose train had split during her presentation: 'For this there is one sad and simple reason: it is because she was the happiest of women.' The explanation is broadly correct, but needs to be developed. Antoinette was happy in her married life; unlike the courtiers she did not take lovers, and to many at Versailles this clean-living happiness seemed a criticism.

The calumnies fall into three main groups. First are the criticisms of her achievements. Walpole picked one up: 'They say she does not dance in time,' adding, 'but then it is wrong to dance in time.' The lead she took in fashion was criticized also. 'The continual changes in her style or dress,' says Véri, 'are the real cause of the people's ill-feeling towards the Queen. The petit bourgeois claims he is being ruined by the fantasies of his wife and daughters who want to imitate the diversity of the Queen's wardrobe. The shopkeeper and manufacturer no longer have a sure basis for estimating what will sell.' Some even claimed that the Queen's preference for plain materials had a political motive: luxurious silks were produced in Lyon, linen in the Austrian Netherlands.

The second group of calumnies credited Antoinette with lovers. As early as July 1774 she was said to sleep with Lamballe, her friend's brother-in-law, and the beautifully dressed, small-featured rake, Philippe de Chartres. On her moonlight walks she was said to indulge in saturnalia with Lauzun and others. The letters M.A.C.L., meaning *maison assurée contre l'incendie*, were painted on those Paris houses insured against fire; disgruntled courtiers whispered that they had another meaning: *Marie Antoinette cocufie Louis.*

The third and most wounding group were directed at her friends. The circle of the Duchesse de Chartres, who had wanted that lady to get the post of Superintendent of her Household, attacked Marie Thérèse de Lamballe, when the post was given to her: how demeaning, they said, for them to have to take an oath of loyalty to this foreign-born widow of a man descended merely from Louis XIV's bastard son.

Gabrielle de Polignac came under attack because she and her family received money in order that they could keep up the standard of living expected of the Queen's friends. She was called an intriguing little climber, and her family parasites, though the total spent on the Polignacs in fourteen years was less than Madame de Pompadour had spent in one.

Antoinette put into her friendships much of the emotion that could not yet go into her marriage. It was emotion, nothing more. But the underground presses at Court began to turn out songs which while scoffing at Antoinette's childlessness, put her friendships in a revoltingly vicious light. One making the rounds in 1776 is quoted in bookseller Hardy's diary:

> . . . *Pour avoir posterité,*
> *Il faut à cet amour botté*
> *Grandir la porte de Cythère;*
> *Antoinette qui sait cela,*
> *Pour grandir cette porte-là*
> *Fatigue plus d'une ouvrière.*
> *Que de talents sont employés!*
> *La surintendante a beau faire;*
> *Les ris, les jeux, les petits doigts,*
> *Y signalaient de vains exploits . . .*[1]

Louis succeeded in impounding some of these scurrilous songs put out by disaffected courtiers, but others were passed around and believed by many, since it so happened that the French name at that time for Lesbianism was *le vice allemand*.

It was probably these sneers at what Antoinette considered her 'sacred friendships' that caused the Queen to fall ill in 1776 with a high fever, for which she took quinine. Little is known about that three-weeks' illness – Mercy tried to hush it up – but it was probably of a nervous, perhaps hysterical nature, since much of her hair fell out.

The illness was something of a crisis in Antoinette's life, and everything depended on her husband. Would he stand by her, or side with the Court? Louis at once made quite clear that he supported Antoinette in her friendships, just as he did with her debts. He gave

[1] In order to have children booted Cupid must widen Aphrodite's door; this Antoinette knows, and she tires out more than one worklady widening that door. What talents are employed! The Superintendent works away; laughter, games, little fingers, all her exploits proved in vain.

unmistakable signs to the Court that he liked Gabrielle de Polignac and Marie Thérèse de Lamballe personally, and approved of his wife's intimacy with them. It meant a great deal to Antoinette. She was able to ride the crisis and by late autumn was again her happy self. The attacks in fact helped to mature her. The evidence lies not only in the more assured and very serene tone of her letters but in her handwriting. Formerly a childish sprawl, in 1776 quite suddenly it becomes neater, better formed and much more confident, with a strong backward flourish to the d's. It was a sign that Antoinette believed herself able, with Louis's help, to triumph over the calumnies and sneers.

CHAPTER 10

The Neckers

'A FACE showing youth and joy; fair hair, and a fair complexion, animated by blue, bright, soft and sparkling eyes; a small but well-shaped nose; lips curved in a graceful smile; a large and well-proportioned figure' – so a Swiss girl named Suzanne Curchod described herself. She might have added that she belonged to the poor petty nobility, was the daughter of a Protestant pastor, could read and write Latin, solve quadratic equations, play the harpsichord and violin and, as her self-portrait suggests, saw life through a haze of romantic fiction. At Lausanne she founded a literary circle, the Académie des Eaux, and here she liked to be known not as Suzanne but as Thémire, the heroine of a tender novel by Mademoiselle de Scudéry.

Suzanne alias Thémire fell in love with Edward Gibbon, who was on the Grand Tour, and he with her. But Gibbon's father would not hear of them marrying: as Gibbon put it: 'The romantic hopes of youth and passion were crushed . . . by the prejudice and prudence of an English parent. I sighed as a lover, I obeyed as a son.' Gibbon, in fact, was only too glad to obey, not being the marrying sort. He continued to see Suzanne as a friend, for he liked her talk, even if she rather overdid the emotion. At Voltaire's *Zaïre*, a dry tragedy if ever there was one, he noticed Suzanne sobbing ostentatiously: 'however, when she removed her handkerchief, all that could be seen was a fresh and rosy face, without a trace of tears . . . How that girl plays at sensibility!'

Gibbon is too hard on her. Literature apart, Suzanne Curchod was a young lady of strong and generous emotions. She rather frightened most men and at twenty-five had not yet found a husband. In that year Germaine de Vermenoux, the widow of a Swiss army officer resident in Paris, came to Geneva for a consultation with the now fashionable nature-doctor, Tronchin. When she returned home in 1764 Germaine took Suzanne with her, in the lowly role of companion and governess to her eight-year-old son.

Among Madame de Vermenoux's friends was a Genevese named

Jacques Necker. At fifteen he had left school to enter the bank of Isaac Vernet as a clerk. At eighteen he was sent to the Paris branch. During the peace negotiations of 1762-3 he made a fortune by the judicious purchase and sale of French and English treasury bonds. In 1765 he assumed sole direction of the bank and became a millionaire. He was a big kindly man who talked little and whose half-closed eyes looked over the other person's head.

The governess found the millionaire quite as attractive as any of her story-book heroes, and let her feelings be known. Necker, on his side, was never averse to being hero-worshipped. On this sure basis a marriage was arranged. Suzanne wrote to her bridegroom on the wedding eve: 'O my Jacques, my dear Jacques, never ask me to express my feelings, let me enjoy my happiness without thinking' – but then covered several pages with all she felt and thought. To a friend she confided: 'I am marrying a man whom I should believe to be an angel, if his great love for me did not show his weakness.'

The young couple set up house in the fashionable rue de Cléry. While Necker combined banking with the unexacting diplomatic post of Minister of the Republic of Geneva to the Court of Versailles, Suzanne, like the young Queen, began acquiring French ways and in particular she discovered that 'what is called frankness in Switzerland is known as selfishness in Paris.'

There were then three well-known salons in Paris: Maréchale de Luxembourg maintained the old spirit of French urbanity; Madame Geoffrin protected Diderot and the *philosophes*; while Madame du Deffand, quite blind, and described by Gibbon as 'an agreeable young lady of eighty-two', gathered round her politicians and eccentric Englishmen. Suzanne Necker decided that she too would found a salon, with the emphasis on literature: a more sophisticated Académie des Eaux.

Suzanne opened the drawing-room of her house on Friday evenings. Writers who attended were the Baron de Grimm, Henri Meister, editor of the *Correspondance Littéraire*, the abbé Morellet, the abbé Raynal, and Jean Baptiste Suard, who published the *Journal de Paris* and the only man to attend with his wife: Amélie Panckoucke, a meek creature who had written a novel that belies its promising title, *Letters from a young English lord to an Italian nun*. Also a member of the salon was Ferdinand Galiani, secretary at the Neapolitan embassy, a tiny, self-deprecating, monkey-like man who said, when presented to the King: 'Sire, you see now only a sample of a secretary; the secretary comes later.' Galiani loved cats and confided to Suzanne, whom he called 'My divinity', that he understood cat-language.

After a not very good dinner these and other guests adjourned to the salon, where Suzanne reclined on a *duchesse* and directed the conversation, helped by notes in her little white memorandum book: 'I shall talk to the Chevalier de Chastellux about *La Félicité Publique* and *Agathe* [two of his latest works], to Madame d'Angiviller about love; and I shall promote a literary discussion between M. de Marmontel and M. de Guibert.' Suzanne carried out these duties with sweetness and tact. 'In a conversation,' she said, 'ladies are like those light layers of cotton-wool in a box packed with porcelain; we do not pay them much attention, but if they were taken away everything would be broken.'

Later Mademoiselle Clairon would perform a scene from classical tragedy, an equally famous musician would play clavichord pieces by Scarlatti, Alberti and Mondonville the Court violinist, or, if the company were very lucky, there would be a recital of his latest lines by Suzanne's Great Poet, a catch of whom she was specially proud, since formerly he had attended the salon of her rival, that cold, prosaic Madame Geoffrin.

Antoine Thomas was impoverished, delicate and melancholy: during dinner he sat silent, occasionally groaning to himself. But his poems were the reverse of melancholy, for he specialized in the Eulogy: indeed, it may be said that Thomas made the eulogy and the eulogy made Thomas. Beginning in 1759 with a eulogy of Maréchal de Saxe, he had gone on to eulogies of Chancellor d'Aguesseau, of the great naval captain Duguay-Trouin, of Sully, of Marcus Aurelius, and of Louis XVI's father, capping them all with an essay on the Eulogy as a Literary Form. But these were as nothing to the eulogy Thomas was now writing, a long poem about Peter the Great in the mines of Germany, to be called *La Pétréide*. Suzanne generally encouraged her melancholy friend – one of her memoranda says: 'Praise Thomas again, this time more strongly' – but this eulogy of a Russian she criticized: 'He seems to forget that a savage nation must possess all the faults that exist among civilized nations.' Although seven years her senior, Thomas took a perverse pleasure in such criticism: 'When you have nothing better to do,' he told Suzanne, 'write and scold me. The subject is a good one, and you will find plenty of material.' Indeed yes. Posterity has unanimously scolded Thomas for turning out reams of versified drivel.

Suzanne was on sounder lines in wishing to have Voltaire correspond with her. For a long time she tried in vain, but at last in April 1770 found a way of attracting the sage's attention. 'On the 17th of the month past,' writes Grimm, 'there has been held at Madame Necker's an assembly of seventeen venerable philosophers; in the course of which, after having made the prescribed invocations to the Holy Spirit, eaten a copious dinner and talked nonsense on a number of subjects, it was resolved by unanimous vote to erect a statue in honour of Monsieur de Voltaire.' The sage consented to sit for his statue, and the sculptor Pigalle went to Ferney. 'When the people in my village,' writes Voltaire, who was seventy-six, 'saw Pigalle unpacking the instruments of his trade, "Hey, look at this," they said, "he's going to be dissected; it will be fun." ' Voltaire was not dissected; he was however depicted almost in the nude, for only so would Pigalle undertake the statue. Voltaire did not mind a bit, but Suzanne, with her Swiss provincial grounding, was rather shocked. Never mind, Voltaire wrote her short verses and long letters, and called her Hypatia, after the most brilliant lady philosopher of Alexandria.

So Suzanne established a literary salon. She became famous in Paris, in all France. What of her husband, whose millions paid for the dinners and entertainment? Jacques Necker looked like a kindly St Bernard, and during the literary discussions would make absent-minded entrances and exits, his brown eyes, under arched eyebrows, usually half-closed, his pale yellow complexion, according to the physiognomist Lavater, a sign of 'an integrated peaceful character'. According to one habitué, he 'neither talks nor listens, but amuses himself by sucking his thumbs.'

To Suzanne, however, this quiet man with the massive jaw was 'a pillar of fire'. Perhaps he did not shine in company, but that was because 'my husband's only talent is to possess genius.' According to one observer, 'Madame Necker . . . behaved like an incense-bearer, perpetually swinging a thurible in front of her divine husband.'

This was correct. Suzanne's intention all along in founding her Friday salon was not to make a name for herself, or even for the great melancholy Thomas. She had one purpose only: to win over the most influential writers of Paris so that in sonnet, essay, editorial and gossip-column they could proclaim the genius of the divine husband. Jacques Necker could not do this without her, for, according to Madame du Deffand, 'he puts too much metaphysics into everything that he writes' and was not very good company: 'he does not assist you in developing your thoughts, and you feel more stupid in talking to him than with others, or than when you are quite alone.'

Through twelve years of literary Fridays Suzanne Necker laboured to proclaim the fifth Gospel. Her grateful scribes dragged the name of Jacques Necker into everything they wrote, like stock-jobbers pushing a new and remote gold mine. Necker himself added an occasional work by himself: in 1773, borrowing Thomas's favourite form, a *Eulogy of Colbert*, which the French Academy crowned with its first prize, and in 1775, when Turgot stood most in need of support, a book hostile to the Minister, *On Legislation and the Commerce of Grain*.

By 1776 Suzanne's work was complete. An influential part of French public opinion believed, as she did, that if Necker took charge of the Finances France would enter a new golden age.

Now the French, it has to be remembered, though then a highly sophisticated nation, knew precious little about finance. Saint-Simon hesitates to sully the pages of his *Memoirs* with the name of a financier called Pléneuf, and finance was still almost a dirty word, the reasons being that the nobility originated in the concept of chivalry, and the taking of interest, though always practised on a small scale, still fell under the ban of the Church. France still had no national bank and it is a small but revealing sign that the official reports of the Church Assembly, as well as many State publications, continued to print even very large sums in words, not figures.

Louis and his top civil servants had a regrettable ignorance about such matters as interest rates, national debt and foreign exchange. They knew that inflation and continuing heavy taxes were bad for France, but lacked the technical knowledge for curing them. Nor indeed in an agricultural society were they easily curable. This was the position when a cry went round Paris that the wizard Necker must take over the Treasury.

Louis as King was now firmly in the saddle. This is how he appears in February 1777 to the author of the *Correspondance secrète*, reports prepared for Russia and therefore generally critical of Louis·

We have for King a young prince, good and equitable, who has no vices nor any dominating passion other than that of filling his post with honour, of making his people happy by the triumph of good faith and morals and of deserving the esteem of foreign monarchs . . . Louis XVI spends his time shut up in his library reading what the Ministers place before his eyes, conferring with them and holding councils of state. He loves hunting as much as Louis XV, but, more attached to his daily duties, he often forgoes that pleasure . . . He used to enjoy working with his hands and making locks, he had a workshop for the purpose and succeeded in astonishing people; at present he has not an hour left for this amusement. You might think perhaps from this portrait that this young prince is of a gloomy turn of mind, even unsociable; but no, he has a genuine gaiety, though this is only shown when he is amongst a few friends who enjoy his esteem and confidence.

Louis received from his Ministers (though not from Maurepas) excellent reports of Necker and almost every time he opened a newspaper he would find someone singing the praises of Necker and his charming wife. Necker believed that France's future prosperity lay in manufacturing, not, as Turgot had thought, in agriculture, and this appealed to Louis, with his mechanical interests. After due reflection, he decided Necker merited a trial. There was just one snag however: Necker was a Protestant. Not fourteen years after the Parlement of Toulouse had passed judgment of death on François Rochet for exercising the functions of a Protestant pastor, it required considerable courage to give a Protestant high office.

Louis, however, did just that. In October 1776 he appointed Jacques Necker Director of his Royal Treasury. For nine months he got to know the Swiss banker, finding him genuinely concerned for the poor, inclined perhaps to be over-emotional and maudlin, but by upbringing quite as opposed to luxury as himself, for the good burghers of Geneva dressed in plain black and were forbidden to decorate their horses' harness with silk braid or to have a liveried footman at the back of their carriage.

Louis was satisfied with this period of probation and in June 1777, since foreigners could not sit in the Council of Ministers and Necker could not be naturalized without renouncing his Protestant faith, Louis gave Necker the new title of Director General of Finance, with direct access to him but without membership in the Cabinet.

Necker brought to bear on French finances two guiding principles: Public Confidence and Loans. If people gained sufficient confidence in him and in France they would subscribe to loans, and these coupled with cuts in superfluous spending would balance the budget. Turgot had pinned his faith on the small farmer, Necker pinned his on the rentier.

Necker at once became very popular by withdrawing from his bank his entire fortune and handing it over to his wife to invest in French government stock. He declined to touch a penny of his salary or even accept the usual free box at the Opéra.

Necker floated his first loan, 40 million livres of annuities, in 1777. He had the satisfaction of seeing long queues form outside the Treasury and it was sold out in a day, something that had not happened for sixty years. Necker publicized his loans well and paid interest on the dot, so that altogether in five years he succeeded in borrowing 530 millions, of which Geneva subscribed 100 millions.

Necker's cuts in spending were equally spectacular. He reduced the number of Farmers General, who collected duty on salt and wine, from 60 to 40, and the Receivers General, who collected direct taxes, from 48 to 12. He nationalized the Post Office, cutting the senior staff from ten, each paid 100,000 livres, to six, paid 24,000 livres. He reduced the administrators of the Lottery from twelve to six, saving 60,000 livres.

As a result of these economies Louis at last found himself in the happy position of being able to reduce taxation. The tax he and Necker chose was the *vingtième*, originally a 5%, and now a 10% tax on income from property and workshops. In order to encourage manufacturing, which was the weakest point in France's economy, they abolished the *vingtième* altogether on workshops in country districts and in small towns. They could not abolish it in large towns, for there the tax was levied by municipal bodies with ancient privileges over which the King had no legal power.

Profiting from the lesson of Parlement's recent victory, Louis wished to find some better way of institutionalizing public opinion, and here Necker gave him helpful advice. In Switzerland each canton had its own assembly and conducted its own local affairs. Louis decided to create an assembly in each French province, which would conduct local administration and advise him on reforms.

Louis chose for the first assembly the province of Berry. It produced sheep and cereals, timber and wine; and so was a microcosm of France; then again his early title, Duc de Berry, may have given Louis a sentimental attachment to the province. By decree of his Council on 12 July 1778 Louis instituted at Bourges an assembly of 48 members: 12 clergy, 12 noblemen and 24 commoners. Louis himself chose the first 16 members – Véri was one – who then made their own choice of the remainder. The Archbishop of Bourges was to preside, and each member would have one vote, which meant that commoners carried as much weight as clergy and nobles combined. The assembly would assess direct taxes, carry out road repairs and organize welfare services. It would sit every two years for one month.

The provincial assembly was, for the age, a remarkably advanced experiment. It decentralized, and permitted leading local men to participate in government. It allowed the King to observe a wider spectrum of public opinion than was possible through the red-robed lawyers, and would probably lead to fairer tax assessments. So successful did the assembly prove that, despite the hesitations of his Cabinet, Louis established others in Dauphiné and in Montauban. A plan to establish a fourth, in Moulins, was blocked by Parlement.

The King found Necker a willing helper in his desire to bring order to France. He judged him an honest man though doubtless, like everyone else save Madame Necker, he found him long-winded and with more than his share of conceit. Necker for his part considered Louis 'an excellent prince and the best of men', who entered in detail into every economic question.

The public approved of this collaboration between a reforming King and a financier who, as he frankly admitted, owed so much to his gifted wife. Even Maria Theresa bought Madame Necker's portrait by the Swiss painter Liotard and hung it in her study. When Mercy told her this, Suzanne was so thrilled she asked for a copy of the letter in which Maria Theresa imparted the information, an unorthodox request which Mercy gravely refused. Only Turgot remained sceptical of a financier who trusted loans, not the land. Quietly engaged in translating Virgil's *Eclogues* into French verse, Turgot remarked: 'Only a saint can perform miracles, and for that Necker would have to become a Catholic.'

After two years at the Treasury Necker felt strong enough to begin cuts in the royal Households. He acted as tactfully as Turgot had been brusque, but all the same he needed royal support. Louis gave it willingly. When the ambitious Comtesse de Brionne protested to him against cuts affecting her son the Prince de Lambesc, Louis replied, 'Madame, why are you meddling? This has nothing to do with you.' Again, in September 1780, Louis's friend the Duc de Coigny began intriguing to halt Necker's cuts in the Stables, for which Coigny was responsible. The next time Louis saw Coigny, in his dressing-room, he rounded on him angrily. 'I intend to bring order and economy to every part of my house; those who carp at it I shall break like this glass.' And he let a crystal goblet fall from his hand to shatter on the floor.

Antoinette first met Necker in 1777 and was amused because, unversed in Court ways, he took her hand and kissed it without permission. It was the beginning of a close relationship. Antoinette, like her mother, admired both the Neckers and their kindly principles. 'Of all the King's Ministers,' Mercy writes in 1780, 'M. Necker is the one whom the Queen considers most highly,' and in the same year Antoinette wrote to her mother:

> The King has just published an edict to prepare the way for reform in his Household and mine. If it is carried out, it will benefit the economy, and satisfy public opinion. We must await results in order to count on this, since such reforms were attempted unsuccessfully in the last two reigns. The King has the power and the will to do it, but in this country there is so much difficulty over matters of form that if one does not choose the right one fresh obstacles will arise as in the past.

Necker's cuts effected even more of a saving than Turgot's had done. He abolished 1300 posts in the King's Hunt and 406 posts at Court, including four wine purveyors, eight cellarers, 10 knights of the spit, 16 turnspits and 15 scullions. He even ordered that the candles used to illuminate the palace reception rooms should be lit until finished and not, as before, replaced when only half-burned.

Antoinette co-operated in all economies relating to her own Household save one. She had brought her friend Gabrielle de Polignac to Court; as a result Gabrielle had been obliged to entertain her and her suite on numerous occasions, since this was traditionally inseparable from royal friendship, and in so doing had contracted debts; furthermore Gabrielle had come to mix with people far wealthier than herself, such as the Duc de Guiche, who had asked for the hand of her twelve-year-old daughter. On the advice of her ambitious sister-in-law Diane, Gabrielle requested Antoinette to give her a large estate at Bitch, to pay her debts and to give her daughter a dowry commensurate with her bridegroom's fortune.

Antoinette thought Gabrielle's request excessive. She consulted Louis and Necker, and they agreed. However, having 'taken up' the Polignacs, Antoinette was undoubtedly duty-bound to see that they had sufficient money to meet their new obligations; Louis and Necker thought so too and finally Gabrielle received not the domain of Bitch but 400,000 livres to pay debts incurred in entertaining the Queen and her suite and a dowry of 800,000 livres for her daughter. This gift offended the Court. All the savings and cuts made with Antoinette's co-operation were forgotten and this one justified bounty, because made to a new family, was held against her.

Necker himself, in his characteristically emotional style, was later to sum things up: 'I found some courage when with the King. Young and virtuous, he could and would listen to everything. The Queen also listened to me favourably. But around their Majesties, at the Court and in Paris, to what antagonisms and hatred did I not expose myself! I had all the factions of private interests to combat, and in this continual struggle I risked my frail existence at every moment.'

The Household cuts brought considerable changes to Louis's and Antoinette's way of life. In the summer of 1777, for example, 'the Queen wished the King to spend a week at Trianon. Monsieur Necker pointed out that the visit would cost an extra 50,000 livres, and so it was cancelled.' The annual trip to Compiègne was also cancelled, though to indemnify the townspeople for their loss in provisioning the Court, Louis had to forgo 300,000 livres in taxes. Pensions granted by the King and Queen were now subject to an annual system of accounting, and no new pensions were granted till equivalent old ones had lapsed.

Louis, having for the moment brought some apparent measure of order to France's finances, had time to turn to humanitarian measures. Coming from Switzerland, where hospital conditions were advanced, Necker and his wife found the Paris hospitals appalling and interested Louis in improving them. One day he drove incognito to the Hôtel Dieu and made a tour of the wards. He found patients four to a bed three and a half feet wide; when two wanted to sleep the other two had to get out and lie on the floor. When a patient died, sheets were not changed, even if he had had a contagious disease. Suzanne Necker heard of people hustled to the cemetery before they were dead and conceived a morbid fear of premature burial that was to haunt her all her life. The mortality rate in Paris hospitals was one in four, compared to 1 in 25 in Edinburgh.

Louis issued a decree laying down that at least 300 patients in the Hôtel Dieu should have a bed to themselves; wards were to be established for each category of disease, and separate wards for men and for women. To provide extra beds, Louis, Madame Necker and the Archbishop of Paris put up money for a new hospital in the Saint-Sulpice quarter, where 120 patients were nursed by eleven Sisters of Charity, known to this day as the Necker Hospital. Now that her husband was established in power, Suzanne's salon had become less literary; she called it 'an office of wit and commiseration.'

Louis also improved prison conditions. On land adjoining the Hôtel de La Force he built a house 'for civil prisoners who formerly, in our good town of Paris, were confined pell-mell with criminals'. Again the sexes were separated, which at that time was an innovation. In this model prison Louis paid for the food and clothing of those who had no private means and founded a prison infirmary, run by Sisters of Charity. At the same time he took an interest in Père de l'Epée's training of deaf-mutes, giving this dedicated priest part of the old convent of the Celestins, in Paris, for his school, and later granting him an annual subsidy of 34,000 livres.

Louis's most important reform at this time related to torture. An examining magistrate had the right to use physical force in order to get an accused man to confess his supposed crime. The prisoner, tired, haggard, bearded and vermin-covered after days and perhaps weeks in custody, was seated on a stone stool. His wrists were tied to two iron rings, two and a half feet apart on the wall behind. His feet were attached by long cords to two other rings twelve feet from the wall. The cords were fastened tight, and then made even tighter by placing under them a low trestle. The examining magistrate having seized the prisoner's nose, an assistant forced water down his throat from a drinking horn. Up to four quarts were forced down the wretched man's throat: as his body swelled, so the cords tightened still further, stretching his limbs in an agony of pain. A surgeon knelt beside him, and if the prisoner's pulse began to fail, ordered him to be carried away and the torture resumed later.

A strong body of legal opinion, including Jousse in his treatise on criminal justice, held that torture of accused prisoners was absolutely essential to get at the truth. Louis received from a Councillor in Parlement, Moyart de Vouglans, a Memorandum advocating the retention of 'the question' as it was discreetly called. Louis read it but was not convinced. He was a humane man and he found the practice of torture barbaric. Moreover, as he wrote in his preamble to his edict on the subject, 'I have always wondered whether, when the question is applied, it is not the strength of a man's nerves which usually decides whether he is guilty or innocent.' On 20 August 1780 with a stroke of his pen Louis put an end to torture of accused prisoners. No longer would Frenchmen be racked to the limits of human endurance and beyond. It was one of the most humane acts ever performed by a King of France.

Louis and Necker worked together for four years, winning popularity by their economies and reforms. Theirs proved by and large a highly successful collaboration. But it is one of the characteristics of the reign that every reform engendered, somewhere, hostility.

French princes possessed the immemorial right of appointing their own tax collectors in their own extensive domains. These collectors, beholden to the princes who appointed them, could of course be useful in many ways. When Louis and Necker axed them, the princes were angry. They hardened their political opposition to the King, and moved still closer to Parlement. The most outspoken were the Duc d'Orléans and his son Philippe, but Monsieur and Artois also criticized their brother the King, for although Louis was generous to them, they found they never had enough. Artois even called Louis to his face 'Roi de France et avare' (instead of Navarre).

Maurepas had never been an admirer of Necker. Now nearing eighty, he held the old view that a budget should be balanced with taxes, not propped up with loans. 'Turgomania was bad,' he remarked, 'but Neckeromania is worse.' Maurepas could not understand that Louis, with the openness of youth, should have applied Turgot's methods from 1774 to 1776, and from 1777 onwards switched to Necker's. This caused him to complain to Véri in 1780 that the King lacked consistency, lacked a principle on which to take decisions: 'he acts now in one way, now in another.' Like everything the Mentor said, this got around, with the paradoxical result that during the very period when Louis was being applauded for his reforms by ordinary Frenchmen, he came in for criticism from the Court on the grounds that he was changeable and did not know his own mind.

CHAPTER 11

The First Child

In the spring of 1777 Louis was waiting for an important visitor, Antoinette's brother Joseph, the first Emperor to call on a King of France in his own palace for nine hundred years. Louis particularly wanted the visit to go well. The great expanding powers in Europe were Frederick the Great's Prussia and, to a lesser degree, Catherine the Great's Russia; Louis had become aware of how much France needed Austria, and he said to Vergennes of Joseph's visit: 'Frederick will be furious!' He hoped too that Joseph would efface the bad effects of Maximilian's visit by making a favourable impression on Paris and the Court.

Two men viewed the visit with displeasure. One was the Prussian ambassador, the other the Austrian. Realizing that if he appeared at Versailles he would be seen by Joseph to have none of the influence over Louis of which he had boasted for seven years, Mercy announced that he was ill and retired to bed in the Petit Luxembourg.

Joseph was now aged thirty-five, fourteen years older than Antoinette. In appearance he was lean and austerely handsome, with an aquiline nose, bony cheeks, white teeth and, although he drank only water, a ruddy complexion. To an even more marked degree than Antoinette, the keynote of his life was simplicity. He wore plain clothes, had the elbows of his jacket patched, and habitually dined on a dish of boiled bacon, which became known as Kaiser-Fleisch. His two recreations were the theatre and music. He had a fine bass voice, played the clavichord, the 'cello and the viola, and was particularly good at sight-reading.

Joseph admired Frederick the Great, and wished to modernize Austria as Frederick had modernized Prussia. This for the moment he could not do, since his mother, the dowager Empress, allowed him to control only foreign policy. But Joseph longed for the day when he could abolish the death penalty, proclaim religious tolerance and introduce reforms that were 'useful to humanity', one of his key phrases. Meanwhile, he concentrated on disciplining the Austrian army.

At ten in the morning of 19 April 1777 a hired coach drove through the gates of Versailles, and it is possible that Louis saw it arrive through his telescope on the palace roof. Out of it jumped a man in a black suit and low boots, who gave his name as the Comte de Falkenstein. He was led by the abbé de Vermond to the Queen's apartment, having written in advance: 'So that we shan't have to put on a show for people, I wish the Queen to wait for me in her study and to receive me there alone.'

There brother and sister met and, free from etiquette, gave full reign to their affection. Antoinette, who had been looking forward for months to this moment, was not disappointed: 'I have been so happy,' she later wrote to her mother, 'that it all seemed like a dream.' They talked solidly for two hours, then Antoinette took her brother to meet the royal family.

Louis gave Joseph a warm welcome, embraced him and pressed him to stay to dinner. Three armchairs stood ready in the Queen's bedroom, but Joseph, saying that he was merely the Comte de Falkenstein, insisted on taking a stool, whereupon Louis said he and Antoinette would sit on stools too. Louis called Joseph '*mon frère*', but Joseph insisted on addressing him as '*Sire*'.

Louis was two inches taller than Joseph and better looking, according to the Duc de Croy, who watched the dinner from the doorway. It was Louis who did most of the talking during the half-hour meal, and to Croy and other courtiers at the door he laughingly indicated with gestures their bizarre position, all three perched on stools.

Louis, who liked simplicity, quickly warmed to Joseph. He urged him to stay in the state apartments prepared for him, but Joseph insisted on returning to the two plain rooms he had booked at the Hôtel du Juste in Versailles town, where, like Frederick, he slept on an army camp bed, with a bearskin as a mattress and his overcoat as a blanket.

Louis arranged a full programme of visits and sightseeing designed to suit Joseph's tastes. The Emperor visited Necker and talked finance; he saw Trudaine and learned about France's road- and bridge-building programme; he met France's best soldier, Maréchal de Broglie, and talked war. He visited the deaf and dumb home in Paris and made a note to found a similar home in Vienna. He supped with Stormont and impressed him with his detailed knowledge of military installations at Metz and Verdun, which he had visited en route to Paris.

Joseph won the approval of liberal thinkers with a couple of remarks. Visiting Louise, the King's aunt, in her Carmelite cell, he said with a shudder, 'I'd rather be hanged than live here!' And when the director of one of the Paris libraries expressed regret that the light was poor and therefore he could not show him the works on theology, Joseph replied with a smile, 'My dear sir, where there is theology there is never much light.'

Joseph met Madame Du Barry, and although she was still seductive, he had the tact to describe her as 'plain'. He also met the Duc de Choiseul, but much to Louis's relief made no fuss of him. On the contrary, he remarked, 'If Choiseul had been kept in power, his turbulent spirit would have done France great harm.'

Louis laid on a military review in the plain of Sablons and lent Joseph a chestnut hunting horse, the quietest in his stables. As the two kings watched a body of troops deploy, Louis noticed Joseph's satisfaction.

'Now you're happy,' he said.

'Yes. When I see ten soldiers together, the blood rushes to my head.'

During this review Antoinette's coach happened to pass, drawn by horses decorated with plumes four feet high.

'You must admit those plumes look splendid,' exclaimed the Duc de Croy.

'Especially now they're in fashion,' replied Joseph, with a knowing look at Croy, who was delighted with this allusion to the feathers worn by Court ladies.

Antoinette entertained her brother with a reception at Trianon, by taking him to Gluck's *Iphigenia* at the Paris Opéra, and by singing him arias from Piccini's *Roland*. She had never been so happy since coming to France: all her gay childhood memories were revived in the person of Joseph.

He, for his part, on instructions from his mother, dropped occasional hints to Antoinette about her way of life. He glanced through her library and murmured, 'Hmm. No books on finance and administration, I see.' Another time, watching her dress in her boudoir, he said he thought she was overdoing the three-inch patch of rouge. To Louis's undoubted pleasure, he declared that sovereigns should not gamble for high stakes, since it was their subjects' money.

After years of reading Mercy's censorious reports, Joseph was surprised to find that Antoinette, for all her little failings, was not a dissipated hedonist but a sensible, lovable person, radiating happiness. 'I have become very much attached to my sister,' he wrote to Maria Theresa. 'In her I find a certain spiritedness in life which I gave up long ago, and I see in her that my own desire for life has not forsaken me. Antoinette is delightful. I lived through hours and hours with her without knowing that time was flying.'

Louis enjoyed his brother-in-law's company. He took him hunting and arranged an intimate supper party for him to which he invited his brothers; after the meal, says Mercy disapprovingly, while Joseph talked to Antoinette, Louis and his brothers ran round the room playing games and throwing themselves on to the sofas. Undoubtedly Louis warmed to Joseph's deep concern for his people's welfare, and courtiers remarked how gay and attentive he was to the older man. And Joseph, though usually serious, could be gay too when he wished. Having visited Louis's elephant in the Versailles park, he proposed that it should be mated with a male elephant in the Vienna zoo. He also told amusing stories against his brother Leopold who, he said, was ruining Tuscany with his physiocratic principles, and against his sister Carolina, who, if her husband the King of Naples did anything to displease her, banished him from her bed for a length of time varying with the offence.

Louis was well pleased with Joseph's six-weeks' stay, both politically and domestically. The Emperor won praise from the educated classes in Paris and from the Court. The Duc de Croy went into raptures about his dignified but easy manner, his mixture of reserve and friendliness. 'The people were enthusiastic about him and cheered him loudly; he ought to be flattered by the impression he left behind him. He is the only person about whom only good has been said in a century when good is said about no one.'

The visit then was a big success. But with all his qualities Joseph possessed one distressing weakness, noticed by his mother when he was only a boy: 'the pleasure he is prone to take in seizing on the shortcomings, physical or otherwise, of others and pouring ridicule on them'. Joseph's caustic side had emerged in his criticism of Leopold and Carolina; it was to emerge more forcefully, unknown to Louis and Antoinette, in the comments he made in letters about Versailles and all the royal family except his sister.

Versailles, Joseph informed Leopold, was a futile, dissipated place, where everyone's one aim was to be talked about. 'Aristocrats exercise a despotic power,' each in his own department. 'The King is absolute master only in the sense that he is free to pass from one yoke to another. He can change his ministers, but unless he is a transcendent genius, he can never make himself master of his own affairs.'

Joseph's opinion of Louis will be considered in a moment. Monsieur he described as 'an undefinable being, better-looking than the King but mortally cold. Madame, coarse and ugly, is not a Piedmontese for nothing, and full of intrigues . . . The Comte d'Artois is a fop. His wife, the only one to produce children, is a complete imbecile.'

Joseph's visit occurred at a time when Louis and Antoinette were becoming worried about their childlessness. Indeed, Joseph had been asked by Maria Theresa to ensure that Antoinette was doing everything possible to produce an heir to embody the new alliance. In order to understand Louis and Antoinette's lack of children it is necessary to review their sexual relations since they consummated their marriage in summer 1773.

As we have seen, it was the custom at Versailles for married couples to sleep in separate rooms. If he wanted to make love, Louis had to get up, walk along a corridor, open Antoinette's door and get into her bed. If he happened to be in the mood for love-making, she might not be; and vice versa. Often he could not tell, since they saw each other so little in the day. There was something cold, formal and even inhuman about this arrangement, sanctified by tradition: it rendered impossible that subtle growing together in body and spirit that makes a happily married couple fulfilled and inseparable.

That was one obstacle to children. The second was the fact that when he became King Louis had to shoulder an immense amount of work; even in periods of quiet he had never had much sexual drive, and these new responsibilities absorbed all his energy. Particularly difficult was the year 1776, when he had to get rid of Turgot and modify the two edicts so dear to his heart.

Antoinette gave her mother regular news of the marriage: how they consulted the best doctors, and all finally agreed that there was no physiological obstacle to children; how she did her best to encourage the King to come to her bedroom; where possible she puts the King in a good light, and in January 1776 she tells her mother with naïve pride that 'his body seems to be becoming firmer.' In 1777 she is able to say, 'I don't despair [about having a child], because there is one change for the better: the King shows more keenness in his love-making, and for him that is saying a lot.'

This was the situation when Joseph arrived. Joseph had been married twice, the first time happily, the second time unhappily; he had had one daughter, and both his wives were dead. He intended to stay single, for he confided to Breteuil, French ambassador in Vienna, the curious information that whenever the royal programme called for him to meet an attractive lady, as a safety measure he first went to a prostitute. Plainly his attitude to women and sex was crude.

Joseph probably tried to discover why his sister had produced no children. Louis was not the man to reveal private secrets to a newcomer; as for Antoinette, she had no more to tell Joseph than she had told her mother: namely, that she and Louis slept together from time to time and were still hoping that one day soon they would have a child.

Joseph says nothing of Louis and Antoinette's sexual relations in letters to Maria Theresa. But on 9 June 1777, ten days after leaving Versailles, Joseph wrote a very curious letter to his brother Leopold, Archduke of Tuscany, which must be quoted extensively.

Joseph begins by saying how sorry he is to have parted from Antoinette, 'She is a lovable and honest woman, a little young and inclined to be rash, but with a core of honesty and virtue which deserve respect. I was often astonished by her intelligence and perceptiveness.'

Louis, by contrast, comes in for the damning judgment Joseph passed on nearly everyone he met in France. 'He is a little weak but not an imbecile; he has definite ideas and sound judgment, but in body and spirit he is apathetic. He talks sensibly but has no taste for learning, no curiosity; in short the *fiat lux* has not occurred, matter is still shapeless.'

Joseph then turns to the question of Louis's childlessness. 'In the conjugal bed, here is the secret. He has excellent erections, inserts his organ, remains there without stirring for perhaps two minutes, then withdraws without ever discharging and, still erect, he bids his wife goodnight. It is incomprehensible, all the more so since he sometimes has wet dreams. He is quite satisfied and frankly admits that he performs the act from duty alone and takes no pleasure in it. Ah, if only I could have been there once, I should have put things right. He ought to be whipped, to make him ejaculate, as one whips donkeys. As for my sister, she is not amorously inclined and together they are a couple of awkward duffers.'

What trust, if any, is to be placed in this explanation? First of all, if Joseph had been told these facts by either Louis or Antoinette, he would almost certainly have said so to Leopold; but he does not. Evidently the explanation is his own, or one picked up from Mercy or Vermond. Both were hostile to Louis, both saw how important it was for Austria that Louis, not Antoinette, should be blamed for the childlessness of their marriage. Mercy was quite capable of inventing such an explanation. In fact three years earlier he had thought up quite a different explanation – that Louis suffered from a malformed prepuce – and retailed it to the Spanish ambassador.[1]

Secondly, as Joseph himself admits, the explanation as here given is 'incomprehensible'. To withdraw without having ejaculated is an unnatural, frustrating and eventually very painful experience for any man, and medical science has no instances of such behaviour in an otherwise normal person.

The evidence suggests that Joseph was making up for Leopold's benefit an amusing account of what happened in Louis's conjugal bed. Joseph was writing to his brother, and as one Austrian to another. In such letters he liked where possible to include earthy jokes. It is probable that he had heard several explanations of Antoinette's childlessness in the corridors of Versailles, but he chose to believe, or to invent, this one because it put Louis in a ridiculous light and his sister, whom he loved, in a comparatively good light. Finally the explanation had the great advantage of showing him, Joseph, in his favourite role of 'know-all', the man of the world who could, only given the chance, put matters to rights by indulging a latent cruel streak and whipping the King.

Joseph's opinion of their sexual conduct was, happily, never known to Louis and Antoinette, who continued to lead their own lives after Joseph's departure on 29 May. The summer of 1777 turned out to be a placid period in domestic politics; owing to Necker's cuts, Louis and Antoinette did not have the hustle of moving to Compiègne but remained quietly at Versailles, and Antoinette, following her brother's advice, had fewer late nights. As a result, Louis and Antoinette made love more often.

At the end of August 1777 Antoinette for the first time experienced complete pleasure in sexual relations, and of this too she informed her mother. In September she wrote that though the King did not wish them to make a habit of sharing the same bed, 'he sometimes spends the night with me. I think it would be wrong to badger him into coming more often, because he does come to see me every

[1]There is a fuller discussion of this in Appendix B.

morning in my boudoir. Every day he is more tender and loving.'

In December: 'Since returning from Fontainebleau, the King has made a habit of sleeping with me and has very often fulfilled his marital duties. My period came on yesterday, I am very displeased, but with the way the King is behaving towards me, I am very confident that soon my desire will be fulfilled.'

In March 1778: 'The King spends three or four nights a week in my bed and behaves in a way that fills me with hope.' In April: 'I think I have good grounds for confidence; my period has never been late; on the contrary, it is always a little early; I last had a period on 3rd March, and here we are the 19th April and there is no sign of another period.'

Next day Antoinette said to Louis, 'I'm longing for it to be true, I even imagine I feel morning sickness.' Four days later her doctor, Lassonne, was ready to bet 1000 louis that the Queen was pregnant.

It *was* true. Louis and Antoinette could hardly contain themselves for happiness, and Louis became untiring in his attentions to the mother-to-be. On her return from Marly he ordered a *fête champêtre* and ballet, the theme of which was fecundity and maternal tenderness. Antoinette gave up riding and all occasions that could produce a miscarriage. To please the abbé de Vermond, she chose his brother as her *accoucheur*. This man was good at his job but made inane remarks that sent the Court into fits. As her term approached and Antoinette complained that she had put on weight, Vermond said reassuringly, 'That's because you're big-bellied, Madame,' and when she worried about the ample proportions of her bosom, he again reassured her: 'That's because you're naturally titty.'

On the morning of 19 December 1778 the Keeper of the Seals and the Ministers and Secretaries of State assembled in the large ante-room outside the Queen's bedroom, together with the King's Household and the Queen's Household, including the Princesse de Lamballe and Gabrielle de Polignac. The rest of the Court filled the card-room and gallery. At about eleven o'clock Vermond's voice was heard: 'The Queen is entering labour.'

The waiting dignitaries and the Court immediately rushed forward helter-skelter into the bedroom, followed by many curious on-lookers, for custom ordained that any Frenchman might watch the birth and see with his own eyes that the baby really was the Queen's and not a substitute. Soon the bedroom was packed, with two men actually standing on the furniture to get a better view. Louis had had the foresight to tie to the wall the tapestry screens surrounding the bed, otherwise, says Madame Campan, they would certainly have been knocked over on to the Queen.

Antoinette lay on a special bed without posts near the fireplace. She had been having pains for three hours and was now entering the last stage of labour. At half past eleven Vermond delivered her child. It was not a difficult birth but Antoinette was even more in a state of nerves than Louis had been on his wedding night. She could not hear the child cry and, believing it to be stillborn, began to panic. Then suddenly she did hear its first plaintive wail: this sudden change of emotion, her high-strung temperament and the suffocating atmosphere in the room proved too much for her.

'Help me,' she said. 'I'm dying.' Her body twitched and, as she lost consciousness, became white and cold. Blood trickled from her mouth and nose.

'Air!' shouted Vermond. 'Give her air!'

From All Saints' Day to Easter all the windows at Versailles were hermetically sealed with tapes, to keep out draughts. To open the bedroom windows would be no easy matter but Louis, for once making use of his great physical strength, immediately climbed on to the window-seats, wrenched off the tapes and flung open the windows.

Fresh air swept into the crowded room, but still Antoinette lay unconscious. Vermond told the surgeon to bleed her. Hot water was sent for but in the disorder never arrived. Finally, without hot water, the surgeon bled her on the foot, removing five saucers of blood. This caused the Queen's blood to circulate more normally and she at last came to, having lain unconscious for three-quarters of an hour. A couple of minutes later, according to the Marquise de Bombelles, who was there, and the Queen would have been dead. Meanwhile the Princesse de Lamballe added to the drama by swooning too and had to be carried from the room.

Louis and Antoinette were delighted with their child, even though it was a girl and not the wished-for Dauphin. It was immediately baptized and carried to the royal nursery, not swaddled but, as Maria Theresa advised, dressed 'naturally', that is to say loosely. Its names were Marie Thérèse Charlotte, and its governess one of Antoinette's Rohan friends, the Princesse de Guéménée. In order to avoid a repetition of the accident, Louis laid down that in future the public would not be admitted to the Queen's confinements.

'The King finds it necessary for his health to take a daily walk,' wrote Mercy to the Empress, 'but for a week after the birth he would not leave the palace. When the Queen woke he was the first at her bedside, and stayed there part of the morning; he came again several times in the afternoon and remained there all evening. At other moments he went to see his daughter . . .' Shortly before Christmas, when the baby first clasped his finger, Louis could hardly contain himself for happiness.

Louis's sense of inadequacy was now allayed. The French people considered their King a father: well, he had proved himself a father. As his aunts noticed, 'the King's tone has become firmer and more decisive with the Queen.'

Antoinette was equally happy, her strong maternal instinct at last satisfied. On 8 February she was well enough to go to Paris with Louis and give thanks in Notre Dame. Four hundred caged birds were set free, bread, saveloy and wine were distributed to the Parisians and the fishwives, who had so often shouted obscenely at the Queen to open her legs and get on with it, now cheered her and trooped gaily to the Comédie Française to watch the show free from the royal box. Antoinette even received a letter from Joseph, whose theory had been proved mistaken but who had the grace to show himself pleased.

Louis's and Antoinette's domestic happiness took place against a background of strained relations with Joseph, the origin of which is to be sought in his recent visit. From Versailles Joseph had taken home a view of Louis based less on personal experience than on Mercy's prejudices; Louis, Joseph decided, was 'rather weak' and Antoinette 'forces him to do things he would rather not do'. It was on this basis that Joseph chose to conduct Austrian foreign policy.

On 30 December 1777, after a long illness, Elector Maximilian of Bavaria died, leaving no direct heir. The rightful successor to Maximilian's lands was Charles, the Elector Palatine, a minor prince who lived far away on the other side of the Rhine from Bavaria. Joseph had no trouble in persuading Charles to cede Lower Bavaria to Austria; in return Austria would guarantee Charles's right to the rest of Bavaria. On 15 January, against his mother's advice, Joseph ordered 12,000 Austrian troops to occupy Lower Bavaria.

At once the other German rulers lodged protests at this disturbance of the balance of power. The Elector of Saxony claimed a large chunk of Bavaria and massed troops on Austria's Bohemian frontier; so too did Frederick the Great of Prussia, who had the strongest army in Europe, while the Bavarians themselves protested at coming under Austrian rule. But Joseph was not unduly worried. He felt sure Antoinette would oblige Louis to give him armed support.

Louis was very displeased at Joseph's invasion. 'Your family's ambition is going to throw everything into confusion,' he said to Antoinette. 'They began with Poland; now volume two is Bavaria. I am annoyed for your sake.' Louis meant that France's traditional suspicion of Austria would flare up again, in animosity against Antoinette.

At the political level Louis took immediate action. He instructed his ambassadors to make clear to the Governments concerned that the dismemberment of Bavaria took place contrary to his wishes, and that he viewed it with extreme disapproval.

Joseph was not too dismayed and at once got his mother to put the pressure on Antoinette. Mercy had again got cold feet and taken to his bed, so Antoinette was the only one at Versailles who could intervene with the Government. In a series of pathetic letters Maria Theresa played on Antoinette's feelings, her affection for her mother, her antipathy for Frederick the Great; Maria Theresa added that she was counting on the King's justice and his tenderness for 'his dear little wife' to send armed support promised by the Treaty of Versailles. She even declared 'Any change in our alliance would kill me.'

Antoinette found herself in a dilemma. Her apartments were decorated with her personal coat of arms, the fleurs de lis linked with the double-headed eagle, and every letter she wrote home she sealed with the same coat of arms. She loved her mother and brother; but she also had a solid affection for her husband and France. Moreover, as she kept telling her Austrian family, she possessed virtually no political influence. She did, however, speak to Louis, though not in the passionate terms to which her mother exhorted her. Louis still declined to intervene.

It was Joseph's turn next to make a tragic appeal of his own. 'Since you don't want to prevent war,' he told Antoinette, 'we shall fight bravely and in all circumstances, my dear sister, and you won't have to blush for a brother who will always deserve your esteem.'

Antoinette hid herself in her room and sobbed. Once more she spoke to Louis, only to learn that according to the Treaty of Versailles France was obliged to send troops only if Austria was the victim of aggression, and this was far from being so. According to the Sardinian ambassador's dispatch of 2 May: 'She [the Queen] has again solicited the King to give the Emperor the 24,000 men stipulated in their treaty of alliance; though she was as persistent as possible, even giving the impression that she was ill, this prince has constantly persisted in his refusal.'

'It is only natural,' Louis said to Maurepas, 'that the Queen should be upset by her brother's difficulties and try to get him help.' But he repeated his determination not to meddle in German affairs. Instead of showing himself weak, as Mercy kept saying, Louis calmly held his course. When Frederick the Great invaded Austria in July, and appeals from Vienna became still more pressing, Louis still declined to commit France to war. What he did do was to offer French help in reaching a settlement. He told his ambassador in Vienna, Breteuil, to do everything possible to bring Prussia and Austria to the peace table.

Breteuil's task was not easy. Joseph's vanity was deeply involved, all the more so since his mother had opposed the war, while Frederick the Great, supported secretly by Russia, had won several victories over the Austrian army. Joseph had made a major blunder, based on a mistaken reading of Louis's character, and it is well summed up in a remark made by Joseph to the Comte de La Marck: 'The King's political conduct on this occasion is very far from being what I had a right to expect from an allied Court that professed to be my friend.'

Thanks largely to the efforts of Breteuil, Joseph agreed to withdraw his claims to almost the whole of Lower Bavaria, and peace was signed between Austria and Prussia at Teschen on 13 May 1779. Maria Theresa recognized France's importance in the negotiations by presenting Breteuil with a beautiful table inlaid with precious coloured marble.

So Joseph's attempt to be a second Frederick the Great failed, but thanks to Louis's firmness the peace of Europe was not seriously disrupted. Antoinette had done her best for the alliance at first, but came to realize that Louis's attitude was the right one for France, the country with which, more and more, she was coming to identify herself. She was now mother of a Child of France and hoped before long to be mother of a future King. It was this happiness more than her brother's military activities that preoccupied her in 1779. Letter after letter home exudes the fulfilment of motherhood. After so long playing with children who recognized someone else as their mother, when Marie Thérèse Charlotte was sixteen months old Antoinette was able to write:

She is tall and strong, you would say she was a child of two. She walks by herself, gets up and sits down without being helped, but she hasn't really begun to talk. I want to tell my dear Maman about a happiness I had four days ago. There were several ladies in the nursery and I got one of them to ask her which was her mother. With no prompting the poor little thing smiled at me and came to put her arms round me. It's the first time she has shown she recognizes me; it was a great joy and since then I think I love her much more.

CHAPTER 12

Help to the Insurgents

ONE night in December 1773 some fifty men belonging to a group called Sons of Liberty gathered in the rear room of a printing shop near Old South Church, Boston. Their faces were smeared with war-paint, they had blankets round their shoulders and in their hands hatchets. When Samuel Adams announced in the church, 'This meeting can do nothing more to save the country,' the 'Mohawks' rushed down to the wharf, crying 'Boston harbour a tea-pot this night.' Joined by a hundred others, they boarded the *Dartmouth*, *Eleanor* and *Beaver*, where they worked for three hours with their hatchets, breaking open 342 wooden chests, and throwing the tea into the cold grey waters of Boston harbour.

That dramatic gesture of protest, less against the duty on tea than against British authority, was followed in the spring of 1775 by the first armed resistance to forces of the Crown. On 19 April, at Lexington, Massachusetts, 77 minute-men defied 700 British regulars. Someone opened fire; the British answered with a volley that left eight colonials dead and ten wounded. 'Here once the embattled farmers stood And fired the shot heard round the world.'

In France the shot aroused little attention. The average Frenchman felt scant interest in a mere three million Americans living three thousand miles away. He believed the American climate to be unhealthy, and that it produced an inferior stock. Voltaire was exceptional in saying he would like to end his days there: 'A man can, for a dozen guineas, acquire a hundred acres of very good land; and on these hundred acres he is in truth a King, for he is free and he is a citizen.'

Louis considered the war between England and the 'insurgents' primarily in terms of France's economy. Her West Indian islands, such as Martinique, Guadeloupe, and San Domingo, provided France with sugar, coffee and cocoa. They were her most valuable overseas possessions, and coveted by England. France's ally Spain also had important sugar interests in the Caribbean.

Louis stated his policy in a letter to the King of Spain, four months after the shot at Lexington: 'I know your Majesty's aversion to war and I sincerely share this sentiment . . . England is much occupied with her American colonies and although I do not believe that they will ever come to terms with the mother-country, nevertheless England might try to go to war with us in order to escape her present difficulties. I think, therefore, that we should pay all our attention to preparations . . . in order to avoid war.'

Louis believed he could best avoid war by giving the insurgents the financial help they needed for quick victory. In May 1776 he authorized a loan of 1 million livres, which was presently followed by a further 2 million. He also persuaded Spain to advance 1 million livres. Since it was important that this aid should reach the insurgents without jeopardizing France's neutrality, Louis and Vergennes called in their top, highly improbable secret agent.

Pierre Augustin Caron, born in Paris in 1732, started life as a watchmaker, sold some watches to Louis XV and styled himself 'watchmaker to the King'. Having married a rich widow, he took her name of Beaumarchais, and with the dowry she brought him purchased the office of secretary to the King, which imposed no duties but brought nobility. Tall, slim and handsome, with a ready tongue, he then gave harp lessons to Aunt Adélaïde and became popular at Court. This watchmaker not surprisingly had a passion for wheels within wheels and was soon travelling in England, Germany and Austria in order to negotiate, on the King's behalf, with the authors of libels. His big coup was to hush up a titillating four-volume English libel on Madame Du Barry. He liked his work and, being a born story-teller, regaled his friends with tales of attacks on him by masked agents. He may even have invented some of the libels and libellers he was commissioned to pursue.

Louis and Vergennes appointed Beaumarchais to handle Government money for the insurgents. He at once formed a fictitious agency and, having a taste for Spanish literature and Spanish names, called it Rodriguez Hortalez and Company. Using the money secretly credited to his account by Vergennes, Beaumarchais obtained from French arsenals 200 cannon, 25,000 muskets, 200,000 lbs. of gunpowder, 20 brass mortars, and clothing and tents for 25,000 men. He bought ships and himself went to Le Havre to oversee their loading.

Secrecy was vital. Vergennes had all his letters to the fictitious Spanish company written by his schoolboy son, whose handwriting no one could trace. Beaumarchais travelled to Le Havre as 'Monsieur Durand', but by temperament he was not a secretive person at all: on the contrary, he liked talking about himself and had a flair for publicity. While in Le Havre he could not resist superintending the production of a comedy he had written the previous year, *The Barber of Seville*.

Stormont, the British ambassador, felt pretty sure that Beaumarchais was helping the insurgents with the King's money, and wrote home, 'With the Duplicity of France even Walsingham could not contend.' To Vergennes he protested: 'In the history of the world there is no example of aid given to rebels of a country one professes to be friendly with.'

'We cannot stop smugglers,' said Vergennes.

'Do smugglers go in fleets, sir?'

Louis reaffirmed France's neutrality and ostentatiously ordered that smugglers of arms to America should be arrested and prosecuted. But that winter the King's efforts to help France without becoming involved in war received a set-back with the arrival in Paris of a bluff, bespectacled, elderly gentleman from Philadelphia.

Benjamin Franklin settled in Passy in a house lent by a friend and on which he somewhat showily placed one of the lightning conductors of which he was the inventor. He dined out six days a week, and spoke at meetings of the Academy of Sciences. While his fellow-commissioner, Silas Deane, wrote home for a fine Narragansett horse or two for the Queen, and barrels of such curiosities as cranberries and butternuts, Franklin sought to win public opinion with subtler tactics. In the midst of a game of chess with Madame Brillon or a programme on electricity at the Academy, he would drop some words about his dear country, solemn and sad. He acted up to his chosen role of the thrifty, no-nonsense, 'primitive' republican. Explaining why he kept only one manservant, he joked, 'With two you get only half of one, and with three hardly any at all.' He charmed influential ladies such as Madame Helvétius and received a crabtree stick from the dowager Duchesse de Deux Ponts. With this stick instead of the usual sword and with his tall fur hat, Franklin made himself a familiar figure; portrait painters clamoured for a sitting and, as he wrote to his daughter, 'Your father's face [is] well-known as that of the moon.'

Franklin professed himself as a typical honest American, but he was not quite so honest as he seemed. From his own printing press he produced in both French and English bagatelles, hoaxes and propaganda pieces, including *Supplement to the Boston Independent Chronicle*, a spurious news-sheet which reported wholesale deals between the British and the Red Indians for the scalps of American women and children. In particular, Franklin spread a rumour that the insurgents, unless given military help, might soon be compelled to make peace with England, who would then round on France and seize her West Indian islands. These activities naturally incurred Stormont's anger: 'He will lie, he will promise, and he will flatter, with all the insinuation and subtlety that are natural to him.'

Louis could feel little sympathy with men who rebelled against their lawful King, and felt still less with Franklin personally, whom he received at Court with cold formality. But Diane de Polignac talked about Franklin incessantly, telling her friends and even Louis what a brilliant scientist he was, what a sensible philosopher, what a good family man, since he taught his grandson how to swim by himself swimming the Seine, at Passy, early one morning. Finally Louis could stand it no more. The next time Diane came to Court Louis presented her with an elegant chamber-pot, the bottom of which was adorned with a portrait of Franklin. Round the be-spectacled face was Turgot's motto: 'He wrested lightning from the gods and their sceptre from tyrants.'

Louis was still bent on keeping out of the American war, but once again he had to reckon with public opinion: not Parlement this time, but the nobles, especially the army officers. They wanted to strike at England in the hope of avenging their defeats in the Seven Years' War and also because action was the surest path to promotion. Almost everyone at Versailles was in favour of helping America with men as well as with money. Some of the men volunteered and in November 1776 Silas Deane wrote, 'I am well-nigh harassed to death with applications of officers to go out for America.'

Among these volunteers was a brave and determined young man: Gilbert de La Fayette. He was born in 1757 of the provincial nobility and while still a baby lost his father, cut in two at Minden by an English cannon-ball. He went to school in Paris but he was not clever and won no prizes. However, required to write an essay on the perfect horse, he surprised his teacher by describing one that when threatened with a whip threw his rider and galloped off. He inherited from an uncle a fortune of 140,000 livres a year, married into the powerful Noailles family and took a commission in the Noailles regiment. Pale, lanky, red-haired, with a pointed nose and receding forehead, he looked less like an officer than a wading bird.

Nor was he a shining courtier, being slow to speak and awkward. Having joined the fashionable Society of the Wooden Sword, which burlesqued Parlement and staged ballets, La Fayette was included in one of the quadrilles, but he danced so clumsily that Antoinette could not help laughing at him. That laughter caused an awkwardness between him and the Queen. Many years later, in his letters to his wife Adrienne, he was still speaking of that indiscreet spurt of laughter.

On 11 June 1776, as part of Saint-Germain's economy drive, Captain de La Fayette was placed on the reserve – a nasty blow, for he knew he was a soldier or nothing. Personal humiliation, a sense of being a misfit at Court, patriotism and the desire to avenge his father's death combined to bring La Fayette to Silas Deane's office at the Hôtel d'Hambourg in the rue Jacob. There he contracted to go to America at his own expense, asking in return for the unpaid rank of Major General, for only if he had a high rank could he hope to overcome family opposition.

While arranging to buy a ship, La Fayette lulled suspicions by visiting England, where he met George III. On 19 March 1777 he arrived at Bordeaux, where the *Victoire*, a little merchant vessel armed with two guns, was riding at anchor, ready to take him and a few friends across the Atlantic. He obtained a passport in the name of the Chevalier de Chavaillac, destination the Cape of Good Hope.

Louis was angry that a man of La Fayette's social position should go to the help of the insurgents. He told Maurepas to send a courier to Bordeaux, ordering the nineteen-year-old captain to accompany his father-in-law, the Duc d'Ayen, on a tour of Italy. But everyone in the palace, with the exception of the Noailles, sympathized with La Fayette. According to Maurepas, one of the Court ladies said that if the Duc d'Ayen thwarted so gallant a son-in-law he need not expect to marry off his other daughters. Blind Madame du Deffand wrote to Horace Walpole: 'It's undoubtedly an act of folly, but one which does him no dishonour and which, on the contrary, is characterized by courage and the desire for glory.'

La Fayette received the King's order at San Sebastian. He thought he had better obey it, and returned to Bordeaux. But there he received a letter from his friend the Comte de Broglie, explaining that opinion at Versailles was solidly in his favour, that the hulla-baloo had been raised only the please the Noailles family and advising him to sail. La Fayette did so, on 20 April. Four days later Stormont complained indignantly to Maurepas: 'It would not have happened if, instead of stopping La Fayette alone, the ship and all the officers on board had been required to return to France.'

After a voyage of 54 days, during which he was wretchedly seasick, La Fayette landed in the Bay of Georgetown at the mouth of the 'Great Pedee River. A month's hard journey on foot brought him to Philadelphia, where he was badly received because previous French officers had proved more trouble than they were worth. But La Fayette showed himself a cut above the rest. Serving at his own expense, so obviously eager to win glory and strike at the English, he soon won Washington's friendship. He took up command in August, a nineteen-year-old Major General in an army comprising 11,000 men in hunting shirts or loose linen jackets, armed mainly with French muskets. La Fayette served at Brandywine and got a bullet in his leg. Though he was sometimes to irk Washington with wild plans for attacking the West Indies or Canada, he proved extremely useful. He was well liked, and came to like the Americans. Soon he was writing to Adrienne: 'The happiness of America is linked to the happiness of all humanity.'

The saga of Major General de La Fayette had considerable influence on public opinion in France. Everyone now, it seemed, wanted to win a name by helping the insurgents. The English game of whist was replaced by a new game christened Boston; according to Du Portail, who organized the American army engineers, 'There is a hundred times more enthusiasm for this revolution in any café in Paris than there is in all the United States together.'

Louis was displeased at popular enthusiam for the insurgents and declined to have his hand forced. In July 1777 Maurepas told the special English envoy, Nathaniel Forth: 'The King is naturally steady and pertinacious in his opinions and his natural sentiments are strongly for peace, but it is incredible what pains are taken to shake them . . . His Majesty, Monsieur, Cte Vergennes and myself are perhaps the only persons in this country that sincerely wish peace.' To this number Maurepas might have added the Queen.

The English were particularly anxious that American privateers should not be given asylum in French ports, and Louis gave orders that no such ships were to be allowed in for longer than twenty-four hours. Sartine, the Navy Minister, who wanted war, turned a blind eye to privateers that stayed for lengthy repairs and refitting. Louis reprimanded Sartine in August; according to Stormont, 'he said that his orders had been ill executed because they had been ill conveyed and added that if this happened a second time they should be the last orders M. de Sartine should convey.'

Louis continued this policy of non-provocation until almost the end of 1777. Then an unexpected event occurred. On 4 December a carriage rolled in to the courtyard of the Hôtel Valentinois, in Passy, carrying a young Bostonian, Jonathan Loving Austin, with news from the Massachusetts Council. Franklin and his fellow commissioners hurried out to meet him.

'Sir, is Philadelphia taken?'

'It is, sir. But, sir, I have greater news than that. General Burgoyne and his whole army are prisoners of war!'

The insurgents' overwhelming victory at Saratoga, in which they captured 5,791 men, changed the political picture. There was now a real danger that England might be obliged to come to terms with the Americans. It was for this reason and not, as is often said, because he yielded to popular demands for war, that Louis decided on a more positive policy. On 8 January 1778 he wrote to the King of Spain: 'By various means the English Government will reunite with America and will not forget our ill services; they will fall upon us with as much force as if the civil war had never happened . . . After having taken the advice of my Council . . . I thought it just and necessary . . . to begin to treat with the insurgents and to prevent their reunion with the mother-country.'

On 6 February Vergennes and Franklin signed two treaties: one of friendship and commerce, the other, which they kept secret, binding both countries to a defensive and offensive alliance. Louis, wrote Franklin gratefully, took 'no advantage . . . of our present situation, to obtain terms from us, which otherwise would not be convenient for us to agree to'. The documents were sent across the Atlantic for ratification, but Stormont got wind of them and hurried to Maurepas. 'The news,' he said, 'is admitted in the carriages of the King,' to which Maurepas could not resist replying, 'The news is denied in the carriages of the Queen.'

Louis began to be worried that the English would forestall him in coming to terms with the insurgents, and on 22 February this did seem to be so, for Maurepas arrived in Louis's study saying he had received a secret letter from Nathaniel Forth in which the British envoy revealed the signing of an agreement between the English Government and the Americans. Forth added that he was a dead man if ever his letter were revealed. Maurepas lost his nerve and proposed sending a ship to call back the treaties, which could be used by England as a *casus belli*.

'Perhaps Dr Forth is lying,' said Louis, 'in order to embarrass us. Besides, we should be found out and it would look as though we had taken fright.'

Louis, says Véri, showed more courage than his first Minister. He let the treaties go on their way, and Forth's report turned out to be false.

France and England were now on collision course. On 17 June, off the Brittany coast, a French frigate, the *Belle Poule*, was fired on by an English frigate, the *Arethusa*, and so badly battered it had to be run aground. The Court cried for war, but Louis was waiting for news that Congress had ratified the treaties. This news arrived on 9 July, and the following day Louis instructed his Grand Admiral, the Duc de Penthièvre, 'to begin hostilities against England'.

Louis now had a new role: directing a war, mainly at sea. He was not wholly unprepared. Ships, their instruments and their navigation appealed to his mechanical side, and he had learned from his grandfather the need for a strong navy. He had chosen as Minister of the Navy a former Lieutenant of Police in Paris, Gabriel de Sartine, a cold, modest, reticent man known as 'the street-sweeper' because he had originated the cleaning of Paris streets. Louis and Sartine built up the navy from 30 men-of-war in 1776 to 64 in 1779, when England had only 54. Louis also made two important reforms: he allowed commoners to become officers and he tightened up poor discipline. But a more serious weakness he either could not or did not remedy: the surplus of officers. Five captains for every ship meant that they got too little practice at sea and were old by the time they reached the top. At the outbreak of war Louis's senior admiral, d'Orvilliers, was seventy.

Louis wanted to go to Brest to inspect his ships and talk to the men. Necker would not hear of a formal visit as King, for with all the suite and guard and celebrations, that would cost several millions. Louis then proposed to go incognito as the Comte de Dampierre. But Maurepas and Sartine convinced him that tight security precautions in the Breton port made such a visit at this juncture out of the question. Louis had to be content with a relief map of Brest and models of all his ships, which Sartine rigged up in the gallery of Versailles.

Louis undertook direction of the war with his usual painstaking perseverance, and it was said that 'From the River St Lawrence to the Southern extremity of Florida not a headland, a bay, a river, or almost an inlet, were unknown to him.' But he was a humane person, who disliked suffering and human bloodshed. His heart was not in it. One day the commanding officer at Brest, the Marquis de Langeron, attended a strategic conference at Versailles and said afterwards to Véri: 'The King . . . reasoned well on every subject. But he is very poor at stimulating men to serve him. When I left the study I said to Monsieur de Montbarrey [Saint-Germain's successor at the Ministry of War]: "You should teach your master some of that skill Louis XV possessed in getting men to die." '

One of Louis's cousins, Philippe d'Orléans, Duc de Chartres, hoped to do well in the war, and though he was to fail in that ambition, he now came into the public eye and henceforth was to play an increasingly important part in Louis's life. Philippe was eight years Louis's senior: small-featured, athletic, an excellent horseman, fencer and dancer. So far he had spent his time in trivia. For example, one morning his friend the Comte de Genlis bet him that he could ride to Fontainebleau and back before Philippe could prick 500,000 holes in a sheet of paper with a pin. Philippe took on the bet and lost. But now Philippe hoped to make his name at sea and one day succeed his father-in-law as Grand Admiral.

Philippe took command of his ship, the *Saint Esprit*, at Brest and with 31 other ships of the line sailed to find the enemy. On the forenoon of 27 July, off Ushant in heavy weather, the French fleet engaged 30 English ships of the line under Keppel. Passing each other on opposite tacks, the fleets blasted each other with heavy fire. As the two lines drew clear, the French admiral, d'Orvilliers, signalled to wear in succession, but his signal was not obeyed by Philippe's squadron, so that d'Orvilliers lost his temporary advantage, and the action was not renewed. No ship was sunk or taken on either side, but both the French and British lost more than a hundred and thirty killed.

Back on shore, Philippe hurried to Versailles to give news of the battle to Louis, who was disappointed that the French had not done better, then went on to his house in Paris. Hearing reports that Philippe had engaged seven British ships single-handed, the Parisians staged celebrations in the gardens of his Palais Royal and when Philippe went to the Opéra gave him a standing ovation. Maurepas, who was there, knew that the *Saint Esprit* had held aloof from the battle, and had suffered only one killed and five wounded. When a lady in his box asked why Philippe was being cheered, Maurepas replied with a quotation:

Jason partit, je le sais bien;
Mais que fit-il? Il ne fit rien.[1]

The truth came out with Sartine's official report of the action, which suggested that Philippe had been unduly slow to respond to d'Orvilliers's signal. The Parisians, with typical unfairness, rounded on the prince and made biting jokes about his 'cowardice'. Philippe published letters from his officers defending his conduct, to which d'Orvilliers's friends replied; soon there was such a cannonade of broadsheets that Louis ordered no more published. Philippe then wrote a bitter letter to Louis saying that his hope of becoming Grand Admiral was compromised, and that he wished to transfer to the army: would Louis make him Colonel of the Troupes Légères? Louis did so, whereupon more scoffing: people called the prince Colonel of the Têtes Légères – the Scatterbrains. The upshot was that Philippe, already hostile to Antoinette because of the Maximilian affair, now blamed Louis for not having protected him from Sartine's censure; this unjustified sense of having been cheated out of his naval career was to rankle with Philippe and to have serious consequences.

The battle of Ushant was the first action in a long, mainly naval war, wherein Louis and his Ministers adopted the strategy of striking at England here, there and everywhere. Some ships they sent to the West Indies, some to America, some to India; the remainder during the summer of 1779 they gathered in the ports of Normandy and Brittany for an exceedingly bold operation: a descent on the Isle of Wight and the coast near Portsmouth. With her army and much of her navy in America it posed a grave threat to England.

By early summer 40,000 French soldiers were standing to arms between St Malo and Le Havre, impatient to embark in 400 transports, protected by the French fleet, which had won control of the Channel. D'Orvilliers, the supreme commander, was only awaiting the Spanish fleet, for Louis had persuaded his cousin the King of Spain to join in the war. Seven weeks after the agreed date the Spaniards arrived. By then the winds were unfavourable and for a month, like William the Conqueror, d'Orvilliers paced his foredeck impatiently, while across the channel George III commanded his

---

[1] Jason sailed, I know that well;
But what did he achieve? Damn all.

subjects in the Southern Counties to drive all horses and cattle inland in case of a landing.

At last the wind veered south-east, but by this time a new problem had arisen. Food was never plentiful at this period and its movement across the thirteen Frances woefully slow. The task of feeding 100,000 extra mouths proved too much for the administrative machinery. In particular fruit and vegetables failed to reach the ships and when the right moment came d'Orvilliers found nearly all his crews prostrate with scurvy. He had to abandon the invasion. The Government treated it as a disappointment; no one seems to have foreseen its implications for the provisioning of any growing group, say the city of Paris.

Elsewhere the French fared better. D'Estaing captured St Vincent and Grenada, though he failed to take Savannah. Grasse and Bouillé captured Tobago; Versailles joked about *la prise de tabac*. The Duc de Lauzun conceived and carried out the capture of Senegal, an English colony on the west coast of Africa, though it is true the garrison comprised only four men, of whom three were down sick. Lauzun was presented with an ox and a concubine by the local queen, and in return gave her a drum, 'an instrument of which she is very fond'.

This world-wide naval war proved very expensive. Sartine, moreover, had introduced a new accounting system whereby senior naval officers spent the Navy budget, instead of civil servants as formerly. That budget rose from 34 millions in 1774 to an alarming 169 million in 1778, and it was constantly criticized by Necker, who had to find the money by loans. Finally, in October 1780, Louis was presented with a Turgot-style ultimatum by Necker: 'Either Sartine or me.'

Louis wrote to Maurepas, ill with gout in Paris: 'Shall we dismiss Necker? Or shall we dismiss Sartine? I am not displeased with Sartine . . . but I think we need Necker more.'

If Sartine were dismissed, who would succeed him? The Polignacs wanted it to be a friend of theirs, the Marquis de Castries, a distinguished soldier then Governor General of Flanders. They urged Antoinette to recommend him to the King. Mercy knew that Maurepas disliked Castries and got Vermond to show Antoinette how inadvisable it would be to offend Maurepas by recommending Castries. Antoinette saw the point and decided not to speak to Louis.

Louis worked with Necker a few days later and was shown certain accounts of Boudard de Saint-James, treasurer of the Navy and a close friend of Sartine, from which it emerged that Boudard had robbed the Treasury by putting into circulation no less than 20 million livres of banknotes without Necker's knowledge. Louis was very displeased and told Necker he intended to dismiss Sartine. They discussed a successor and Necker suggested Castries. Because of his fondness for the ladies Louis had once described Castries to Maurepas as an ideal 'Minister of the Boudoir'; on the other hand he knew Castries to be energetic and honest, so he told Necker that he had no objection, provided Maurepas agreed.

Someone in the Polignac set hurried to Maurepas and confided to him, in utmost secrecy, a complete falsehood: that the Queen had gone to see the King and obtained a firm promise that he would dismiss Sartine and appoint Castries. Later, when Louis arrived at his sick-bed, Maurepas believed that Castries's appointment was already decided upon, and acceded to it without demur. But he was secretly hurt that Louis, as he thought, had chosen Castries without consulting him.

Louis appointed Castries Minister of the Navy. It was his doing. But the Polignacs boasted that it was all because of their influence with the Queen. As in the fall of Turgot, Antoinette was charged with bringing about the rise and fall of French ministers.

In this sad business there was one gay touch, the song sung by Parisians about the fallen Sartine:

> J'ai balayé Paris avec un soin extrême;
> Mais, en voulant des mers balayer les Anglais,
> J'ai vendu si cher mes balais
> Que l'on m'a balayé moi-même.[1]

In America, meanwhile, the war was going badly for the insurgents and in 1778 Washington wrote: 'The common interests of America are mouldering and sinking into irretrievable ruin if a remedy is not soon applied.' So France's intervention came just in time.

In April 1779 Louis sent 5,500 French troops under General de Rochambeau to the New World, and more later, the officers including La Fayette's friend Lauzun and a tall Swede, Axel de Fersen. Though eager for immediate action, they had to wait a long time, until autumn 1781.

[1] In Paris I swept with the greatest care, but in trying to sweep the English from the seas I sold my brooms so dear that now my turn has come to be swept away.

General Cornwallis and the redcoats had been driven into a village called Yorktown at the head of Chesapeake Bay. The English navy, under Thomas Graves, was ordered to lend them help. But François de Grasse with 24 French ships sailed in first to Chesapeake Bay, and successfully drove off Graves when he finally arrived with 19 ships. Graves had to withdraw to New York to refit, leaving Grasse in control of the coast.

Washington and Rochambeau were thus able to begin the siege of Yorktown in early October. They had 16,000 troops against Cornwallis's 8000. But Cornwallis showed courage and ingenuity. He blocked the river by sinking ships, and fortified the marshy landward side with redoubts, palisades and abatis.

The Americans and French had superior fire power. Their 41 cannon and mortars pounded Cornwallis, and slowly drove him back until he had only two redoubts. On the night of 14 October an American column under Alexander Hamilton and a French one under the Comte de Deux Ponts launched an all-out attack. By the glare of white and red rockets they stormed the palisades and fought the British hand to hand. In ten minutes they captured the redoubts, Lauzun in particular showing great bravery.

At ten in the morning three days later a red-coated drummer climbed up on the only bit of parapet remaining to the British and beat a parley. Then a British officer came forward; Lauzun, stepping out across the space between the lines, bandaged his eyes with his lace handkerchief and led him to headquarters. He bore a letter from Cornwallis to Washington, asking for a truce. The truce was granted and led to the surrender of Cornwallis with 7073 officers and men. They were forced to march in solemn parade before the Americans and French and to stack their arms, while the bands played 'The World Turned Upside Down'.

The New World certainly had been turned upside down. The war was over bar the shouting, and to this a decisive contribution had been made by the French navy and the 8000 French troops who came to America.

Louis heard the news of Yorktown from Lauzun, who was given this honour as a reward for his bravery. He ordered a *Te Deum* to be sung and told Lauzun to hurry to the bedside of Maurepas. Louis's faithful Minister, aged eighty, was gravely ill; he heard from Lauzun the news of the British defeat and on 21 November he died, his last words a line from Racine's *Mithridate*:

Mes derniers regards ont vu fuir les Romains.[1]

Louis was deeply upset by Maurepas's death. He had been extremely fond of the old man, appreciating in particular his good sense and gaiety. He told Antoinette he would never forget the sacrifices Maurepas had made in leaving his retirement to come and be a father to him. It was with tears in his eyes that he said, 'I shall never again hear my friend in the morning pacing overhead.'

With Maurepas's death Louis, now aged twenty-six, felt experienced enough to dispense with a mentor. He continued to consult his advisers, especially Vergennes, but from November 1781 his rule was to be more personal, in the sense that he himself chose and appointed Ministers instead of having them suggested to him.

Louis had been slow to enter the war and, despite the crushing victory at Yorktown, he was slow to get peace. He wanted France and America to sign a simultaneous peace treaty with England; but a strong body of English opinion favoured peace only with America, followed by an Anglo-American alliance against France. Then came a nasty trick by Franklin. He notified Vergennes that he had signed peace preliminaries with England, and a few days later asked him to lend America 20 million livres, dropping a hint that unless the loan was granted Congress would ratify the peace treaty regardless of France.

Louis had already lent or given to America 18 million livres, as well as sending 8000 French troops. It seemed unchivalrous to say the least that Franklin should now practically blackmail him to pay more. France was running a very heavy deficit and could not afford the full 20 millions. Louis, however, recognizing that Congress was desperately short of money, did lend 6 millions at 5%, which was 2% less than he himself was paying on borrowed money. This had the desired effect. On 30 November 1782 Congress signed preliminary articles of peace with England, and on 20 January 1783 France did the same. The war was officially over; the United States recognized as an independent nation of citizens, each with a right to 'the pursuit of happiness'.

French soldiers returned with stories of how well the ladies of Philadelphia made a cup of tea, and of how American inflation was worse even than French, since a suit of clothes could cost two months' wages. In the other direction French authors sailed out to observe

[1]With my dying look I saw the Romans fleeing.

and write about the new nation. Voltaire, they saw, had been right in saying that toleration created peace and concord, not faction. Of Philadelphia the Comte de Ségur wrote, 'The whole city is itself a temple raised to Tolerance, for one sees there in large numbers Catholics, Presbyterians, Calvinists, Methodists and Quakers, who all practise their religion in complete liberty and who live together in perfect harmony.'

The abbé Robin, a *philosophe*, drew a darker picture. Tombstone researches convinced him that Americans aged early and died young. He was struck by the lack of interest in beauty and graceful living. 'Poetry, which in all other nations preceded science, fails here to utter her sublime and moving harmonies.' Sumptuously furnished mansions and elegant carriages driven by richly liveried slaves persuaded him that moral decay had already set in, a point noticed also by Fersen, who wrote: 'I shouldn't be surprised to see Virginia cede from the other States.'

Louis's first Minister to the United States, Gérard, has a passage in a letter to Vergennes which is of interest in view of the more or less forced loan:

I am sorry to be obliged to add, Your Excellency, that personal disinterestedness and pecuniary probity do not honour the birth of the American Republic with their presence . . . The spirit of mercantile cupidity forms perhaps one of the most distinctive traits of Americans, particularly of those of the North, and this character will no doubt exert an essential influence over the future destinies of the American Republic.

Most French officers returned from America with curiously little interest in the mechanics of democratic government, or even in American guarantees of political liberty. The abbé de Mably spoke for them when he warned that democracy, however good in principle, when unmodified as in America by aristocratic institutions, would lower the quality of life. It was only a small minority who returned convinced that France too needed a less authoritarian style of government; their spokesman was La Fayette. He, like many future revolutionaries, including Danton and Saint-Just, had lost his father young and, never having known authority within the family, resented it all the more within the State; in disregarding Louis's order not to sail he had shown himself a born rebel while still on French soil.

The American war had two main effects on France. It increased the National Debt by close on 1,000 million livres; this was not an insuperable burden, for England successfully carried a proportionately even heavier national debt, but it was to pose grave problems for Louis.

The second effect of the war was to increase French prestige. France did better than in any recent war against England and achieved her objective of seriously weakening her traditional enemy. At last she saw the hated English commissioner leave Dunkirk. In the sense that national morale improved, the war strengthened the monarchy.

Antoinette, according to Monsieur, had 'considered it unjust and politically unwise to protect a people who sought to throw off the yoke of their legitimate sovereign.' But when war did break out, she showed as much patriotism as any born Frenchwoman. She gave La Fayette several audiences on his visit to France in February 1779; she also made and kept a copy of these verses which were being applied to him:

> *Il sait défendre un camp et forcer des murailles,*
> *Comme un jeune soldat il aime les batailles;*
> *Comme un vieux général il sait les éviter,*
> *Je me plais à le suivre et même a l'imiter.*[1]

Antoinette intervened once in American affairs. After Yorktown an eighteen-year-old English prisoner, Captain Charles Asgill of the First Foot Guards, was going to be hanged in reprisal for the supposed killing of an American. Asgill's parents wrote to the King and Queen of France begging them to help. Antoinette took up the matter and with Louis's approval Vergennes made an urgent appeal to George Washington, who forwarded the letter to Congress. Asgill was released and on his return came to Versailles to thank Antoinette.

Finally, what did the War of Independence mean to Louis personally? He was pleased at seeing English power reduced, but he felt little sympathy with the insurgents and one day, finding some turkeys from America had been added to the Versailles menagerie, he crossly told La Roche to remove them. He had gone to war exclusively in the interests of France, but this did not stop many Americans from hailing him as a selfless champion of their freedom.

---

[1] He knows how to defend a camp and to capture walls; like a young soldier he loves battles, like a veteran general he knows how to avoid them: I find him a joy to follow, and even to imitate.

Though later he was to be reviled for imaginary crimes, in 1783 Louis was actually being praised for imaginary goodness to America, and on the eve of his return home Benjamin Franklin wrote to Vergennes words that would have been better spoken, but never were, by some high-placed Frenchman about France:

> May I beg the favour of you, Sir, to express respectfully for me to his Majesty, the deep sense I have of all the inestimable Benefits his Goodness has conferr'd on my country; a sentiment that it will be the business of the little remainder of life now left me, to impress equally on the minds of all my countrymen. My sincere prayers are, that God may shower down his blessings on the King, the Queen, their Children, and all the royal family to the latest generations!

CHAPTER 13

Peace and Prosperity

AT home the years from 1781 to 1785 brought improvements to France, and personal happiness to the King and Queen. Louis's political apprenticeship lay behind him: between his twenty-fifth and thirtieth birthdays he was to rule with a perceptiveness and energy that surprised even his close advisers. As for Antoinette, she was to find a new fulfilment in sharing many of the King's activities.

The period opens with a crisis precipitated by two of the opposition groups, Parlement and the Princes. Ever since Jacques Necker's appointment as Director General of Finances in June 1777, they had writhed in indignation. Parlement was angry with the Swiss banker because he had helped Louis set up three provincial Assemblies and because he raised his loans by decree, not edict, thus allowing them no opportunity to invoke a law from Charlemagne's time against usury. As for the Princes of the blood, they were angry at Necker, as we have seen, for ending their privilege of appointing six collectors of direct taxes.

Jacques Necker believed he could weather this opposition. He enjoyed the firm support of the King, as the recent dismissal of Sartine had shown. He was well liked by the Queen. He was extremely popular with the bourgeois and the ordinary people, who were grateful to him for conducting the war with loans rather than with new taxes. Incense from Suzanne and the initiates of her salon was rising headier than ever.

At the beginning of 1781 Necker conceived the idea of publishing a statement of accounts connected with revenue, taxation and expenditure, which would show the world that France was in a strong financial position. His motive was fourfold: he hoped to discourage England and lead her to make peace; he wished to show the French how little, in proportion to total revenue, was spent on Versailles and the Court; he wished to create an atmosphere of confidence which would enable him to raise further loans; and, not least, he wished to show his opponents in Parlement and among the Princes just how brilliant he was.

Necker published his *Compte Rendu* on 19 February 1781: 116 quarto pages in an azure cover. It contained detailed explanations of sums annually spent on royal lands and forests, upkeep of royal establishments and the salaries paid to those who held appointments at Court, and the pensions of those retired. It gave what appeared adequate proofs to show that if certain reforms were continued the finances could always be maintained on a satisfactory basis, and that despite the enormous cost of the war and the loans, totalling 412 millions, raised to meet it, in 1780 'ordinary State revenues exceeded by 12,200,000 livres ordinary expenses.'

Necker referred to the numerous reforms he had instituted at the Treasury and declared that from the moment he had taken over direction 'he had renounced the pleasantest of private satisfactions, namely, that of serving his friends or of obtaining the gratitude of those who surrounded him.' 'If anyone,' he declared, 'owes employment or place to my favour alone, let him name himself.'

On the last page Necker remembered Suzanne:

In reminding your Majesty of some of the charitable foundations he has created, allow me, Sire, to indicate, without mentioning any names, a person endowed with the rarest virtues who has so greatly helped me to carry out your Majesty's plans; amid the vanities of high rank the name of that person has never been mentioned to you, Sir, but it is only right that your Majesty should know that it is often invoked in the humblest refuges of suffering humanity. It is precious for a Minister of Finance to have found his life companion a real help in a great many details of charity and relief lying beyond his scope and strength.

This extraordinary mixture of statistics and sentiment went down wonderfully well with the public, the more so since the *Compte Rendu* was a 'revelation' of State accounts that had never before seen the light. Thirty thousand copies were sold the first week, the azure-covered book was to be seen in every fashionable drawing-room and its author came to be regarded as a miracle-worker. Such was the cult that a new word entered the language: *Neckeromanie*, and on the strength of renewed public confidence Necker was able to raise a new loan of 108 millions.

Presently the fuss died down, and experts began to take a cold, hard look at the last part of the *Compte Rendu*: figures of receipts and expenses expected in the year 1781. Necker estimated the receipts at 264 millions, and expenses at 254 millions. But he added, almost as an afterthought, that these sums excluded expenses of the war, and money advanced by the tax farmers on taxes due after 1781. The experts calculated that the true figure should have been receipts of 436 millions, expenses of 526 millions, giving a deficit of 90 millions instead of the surplus of 10 millions so proudly predicted.

At first the concealment was noticed only by a few Ministers and financial experts. Asked what he thought of the Azure Book, Maurepas replied drily: 'It's about as true as it is modest.' Then the treasurer of Artois's household, whom Necker had obliged to repay a fraudulently drawn pension, published a brochure pointing out errors and omissions in the *Compte Rendu*. This was followed by criticisms in the newspapers. Writers challenged Necker's view that unlimited credit would lead to unlimited economic activity. They saw rather that it worsened inflation, and it is significant that in England the younger Pitt was soon to establish the sinking fund, a surplus of revenue over expenditure devoted to reduction of the national debt.

The Paris public almost overnight swung against their former hero, as spectacularly as they had swung against Philippe d'Orléans after Ushant. They resented Necker's newly revealed unreliability all the more because of his claim to complete honesty. This sudden loss of popularity hurt Necker, but it need not have proved fatal to him, had not the ill-conceived *Compte Rendu* been followed, in April, by a more damaging publication.

In 1778 Necker had written for the King's eyes only a 'Memorandum on the Provincial Assemblies'. In it he sketched a plan for setting up assemblies everywhere in France to take over from the Parlements all decisions regarding taxation. This would allow Louis to apportion taxes more justly without opposition, since Parlement would be reduced to their original role of magistrates. There were only two copies of the 'Memorandum'; one retained by Necker, the other in Louis's safe.

Louis mentioned the 'Memorandum' to his brother Monsieur, and Monsieur begged Necker to let him see it. Not daring to refuse the heir to the throne, Necker read it aloud to him, and Monsieur, hypocritically professing to have been immensely pleased with it, asked to be allowed to read it for himself. Necker sent the document by a messenger and Monsieur, having tricked him into leaving it with him for a few days, had a copy made.

Shortly afterwards Necker turned down a claim on the Treasury for 1,064,000 livres, which Monsieur insisted was his unpaid share of his parents' heritage. Then came the reduction in the number of tax collectors. Monsieur came to see Necker as a meddlesome republican, whittling away long-established privileges. In April 1781 he decided to strike. He had the 'Memorandum' printed on his own press, and on the morning of 20 April six of the most influential members of Parlement found a copy on their breakfast tables.

There rose a howl of fury not only from Parlement but from writers of almost every shade of political opinion. It soon became known that Necker was the author, and a spate of brochures appeared attacking the financier who dared meddle with venerable institutions. One of the most influential was '*Lettre d'un bon français*', which mercilessly criticized the 'Memorandum'; 'Having begun like John Law, do you plan to end like Cromwell?' The good Frenchman turned out to be no other than Monsieur.

The attacks piled up, coupled now with criticisms of the *Compte Rendu* and Necker's whole policy of reckless borrowing, until they filled three volumes. Necker's vanity was deeply hurt, and in order to salve it he asked the King to give spectacular proof of confidence in himself by making him a member of the Cabinet with unprecedented control of the finances of each Ministry. It was hardly a fair request, Necker being a foreigner, but Louis considered it. He asked Maurepas's advice, then that of Vergennes. Both said they and the whole Cabinet would resign if Necker got his way. Louis explained the position to Necker but the banker stood by his demand, and the King by his refusal. Necker lacked the toughness to face a storm of opposition as fierce as that which had toppled Turgot. He drove on 19 May to Marly, where the Court was staying, and handed the King his resignation.

Louis disliked losing Ministers, and he recognized that Necker had done excellent work. But the Swiss banker's vanity had put everyone's back up, and that habit of not looking an interlocutor straight in the eye was one of several signs that he inhabited a fantasy world. Louis accepted Necker's resignation and began looking for a first-rate new man. Turgot was dead, and anyway the physiocrats' policy of wealth through agriculture no longer matched France's problems. Louis, with his interest in technology and machinery, was beginning to realize that France could become more prosperous only by developing her manufactures.

Now among Louis's top civil servants was a certain Charles Alexandre de Calonne. He came of a Parliamentary family and began his career in the Parlement of Flanders, then switched to the royal service. He had practical experience of working-class needs, as intendant first in Metz, then in Lille, where he gained valuable experience of the textile trade. He believed that manufacturing should be encouraged by subsidies, and France's export trade expanded. Louis decided to give this policy a trial and in November 1783 appointed Calonne Controller General of Finance.

Calonne made a good first impression at Versailles. A tall witty widower of forty-nine, with red hair and dark eyes, he had a smooth, pleasing manner that contrasted with Turgot's ponderousness and Necker's vanity. He was a lover of the arts and owned a first-rate picture collection which included ten Titians and Poussin's *Bacchanalia*.

Calonne understood, as none of his predecessors did, that the surest way to make Frenchmen richer was to increase the Gross National Product, as we now call it. His model was England, his programme Encouragement of Manufacturing. He continued to borrow, as Necker had done, for, as he used to point out, England with a population three times less than France's could support twice as large a national debt. But much of the borrowed money went into helping industry.

To choose a few examples from dozens, Calonne persuaded a gifted English engineer named Milne to instal in the royal hunting-box of La Muette a factory for making mule jennies, and granted a bounty of 1200 livres for each set of machines sold to French industry. He gave Claude Berthollet 6000 livres a year to give up medicine and start research on dyes and bleaching, which eventually led him to discover *eau de Javel*, bleaching water. He subsidized and presented to the King two manufacturers of Lyon, Sarrasin and Jolivet, who had invented a hat-making machine. Of the $5\frac{1}{2}$ millions spent to aid industry in the fifty years before 1789, about one-tenth was granted during the three years of Calonne's ministry.

Louis and Calonne together sought to overcome the nobility's traditional scorn for business and to make it fashionable. The King put up one quarter of the capital in the important crystal-making company at Indret, and bought shares in the Paris Water Company. In the royal palace of Rambouillet, where for so long manufacturing had been deemed an inferior occupation, Louis set up an English machine for making cotton thread. Soon the *grande noblesse* began to follow suit. The Croy family put money into the Anzin mines; the Prince de Conti and Maréchal de Castries invested in the Grand

Combe colliery; the Prince de Poix and the Duc de Mouchy put up money for Martin and Flesselles to start a silk-dyeing works; the Duc de La Rochefoucauld Liancourt for the textile factory of Brives, founded by the English engineer Thomas Leclerc.

Miscellaneous reforms made by the King and Calonne include a decree which ended the exclusion of women from manufacturing and placed them on the same legal footing as men. In Paris they limited the height of buildings and specified that in future streets must be at least thirty feet wide. They cleared the clutter of houses from the Pont Neuf. In order to increase excise revenue, they built a wall round Paris, famous as '*le mur murant Paris rend Paris murmurant*'. They re-established the India Company, abolished in 1769, to trade in cottons, and even sent a merchant ship, at the King's expense, to trade with China.

Louis, meanwhile, carried on with the social reforms that had always interested him. When Dr Doulcet of the Hôtel Dieu discovered a remedy for puerperal fever, the King bought it and published it in 1782, so that everyone, not just Doulcet's patients, could benefit. When Mirabeau's book, *Lettres de cachet*, drew attention to prison abuses, Louis ordered the release of all prisoners detained for family misdemeanours and he shut down the notorious Vincennes, a royal prison for 600 years. By an edict dated January 1784 he freed the Jews from certain tolls dating back to the Middle Ages, explaining that he intended to end all constraints 'which appear to degrade humanity'. The King, who had never resigned himself to the Paris Parlement's opposition on the *corvée*, slowly, perseveringly pressed his reform through the provincial Parlements or Assemblies, and by February 1785 had the satisfaction of knowing that in four-fifths of the provinces of France the hated *corvée* was replaced by a land tax.

One of the ways Calonne stimulated trade was to modernize French ports, and Louis, who had been unable to visit Brest in 1778, in the summer of 1785 fulfilled his ambition of seeing a naval port. He left Rambouillet at 5 a.m. on 2 June, in a scarlet travelling coat, his suite and escort totalling only 56, one sixth of the traditional number. He carried with him a specially prepared map, showing the houses and farms bordering the road, with their owners' names, and on this he traced his route, via Rouen and Caen, to Cherbourg.

There, on 23 June, Louis met the naval officers: as each was presented he pencilled his name in a notebook, saying, 'I hope we shall get to know one another.' He watched manœuvres and firing from a ship of the line, and was rowed out to see a huge conical case filled with stones being lowered to the sea bed, one of eighty to make a new mole. At the crucial moment something went wrong and the cone toppled sideways: several workmen were crushed, one fatally. Louis's first reaction was to hide his face in his hands; then, pulling himself together, he sent his surgeon to help.

Louis started home on 26 June. En route, there were tumultuous shouts of 'Long live the King!' to which Louis replied, 'Long live my people!' At one point, while his carriage lumbered up a steep slope, he was approached by a Norman peasant who sang a song in praise of 'the traveller King'.

'I like your song,' said Louis. 'Who wrote it?'

'I did, my lord.'

'You did! . . . *Bis, bis.*'

'*Bis?*'

'That means, sing it again.'

The Norman did so and, being rewarded with some louis d'or, thrust out his other hand.

'*Bis, Sire, bis.*'

Louis laughed at the Norman's graspingness and gave again.

During his twenty-six day journey Louis found this part of France enjoying prosperity. Food was not expensive: in fact between 1778 and 1789 the price of corn and wine fell. But an increased population was demanding higher standards of welfare from the State and Louis, who made a point of visiting homes for orphans and the aged, found that needs had outstripped funds. In special notes for the King Calonne referred to the Hôpital Général in Cherbourg, 'knowing that your Majesty's first concern is humaneness', and pointed out that its deficit in 1785 was 816 livres. In Rouen the same institution had a deficit of 34,059 livres, while the Hôtel Dieu had a deficit of 44,443 livres. To each of the two latter institutions Louis made a personal gift of 12,000 livres.

Personal generosity could satisfy the Norman peasant who had sung him a song, but it could never of itself cover social welfare or solve France's basic problem, which was the slow growth of national wealth. Louis and Calonne were doing their best to prime manufacturing; but would the new wealth arrive in time to ease the undoubted misery of the poor and weak?

Louis returned to Versailles vastly pleased with his journey: 'My two happiest experiences as King have been the day of my coronation and my time in Cherbourg.' It would have been good for

France and the monarchy too if Louis had been able to make such a journey every year and acquaint himself with urgent problems, but etiquette decreed lavish celebrations and generous gifts; the cost would have been prohibitive and Louis had to content himself with occasional visits to Paris in order to encourage French manufactures.

Closely connected with Louis's encouragement of manufactures was his diplomatic activity to ensure peace, for both were essential to France's prosperity. There is space only to touch on Louis's work in this field, but in the years following the American War he devoted much time to entertaining old friends and trying to make new ones. Among those he invited to Versailles was the Czarevitch Paul of Russia, who looked like a pekinese and tried to bark Louis into a war with Turkey. Louis would have nothing to do with the war but he retained the Czarevitch's friendship, and later sponsored the Convention of Constantinople, which in January 1784 ended the Russo-Turkish hostilities. Louis also mediated in a serious dispute between Austria and Holland over navigation of the Scheldt, and sponsored the Treaty of Fontainebleau, which ended it. In 1784 he declined yet another invitation to join in a war, this time from Sweden against Russia. One result of this pacific policy was that in January 1787 Louis was able to sign a useful trade treaty with Russia: duties were reduced on French wine and soaps, and on Russian iron and tallow.

These were achievements to raise any man's heart and in his private life also Louis had reason to be glad. On 22 October 1781 Antoinette at last gave birth to a son; such was the joy in the streets of Paris that people embraced perfect strangers, and at Court Louis was smiled at for dragging into every conversation 'My son the Dauphin'. In March 1785 a second son was born, the Duc de Normandie; Antoinette felt fulfilled as a mother and the succession seemed secure. When Normandie received the *cordon bleu* old Richelieu could boast that he had seen seven generations of royal children receive that blue ribbon.

Having ensured the line, Louis began to feel surer of himself. He showed more poise, and was more the master of Versailles. One day in 1784, as part of his policy of encouraging manufactures, Louis visited a shop near the Pont Neuf called Le Petit Dunquerque, where he and his suite were shown a range of luxury goods and made some purchases. After they left, the shopkeeper hurried up to Louis and told him a diamond ring was missing. Louis quick-wittedly ordered his suite back, had a tub of bran brought in and, himself leading the way, made each in turn plunge his right hand into the bran, while he watched their faces. The tub was then emptied and in it the ring was found. Back at Versailles a courtier who had shown signs of guilt confessed and Louis, once again showing that he refused to regard nobles as privileged beings, sent him away.

Traces of self-effacement remained, however. 'A certain gentleman,' writes Madame de Bombelles, 'brought an action against the King for more than one million livres. His papers were destroyed when M. Nogaret's house caught fire. When told of the disaster, the King immediately replied, "His papers are burned, I lose my case." ' The sequel is unknown, and perhaps Louis had second thoughts about paying up; but his initial reaction is revealing. And when a son was born to a friend of Antoinette, the bulldog-faced officer Esterhazy, Louis wrote him a note, congratulating him on the birth of his 'little hussar' and signing it simply: 'An Inhabitant of Versailles'.

One result of such signs of self-effacement was that to the public eye the King appeared smaller and his Queen correspondingly larger. This, in turn, raises the question: What was the relationship between Louis and Antoinette after fifteen years of marriage?

In obvious ways they were strikingly different: Louis beginning to put on weight, Antoinette slim; he steady, she quick; he reserved, she open; he with few close friends, she with many; he awkward, she majestic; he seeing the dark side, she the bright; he a keen reader, she bored by books; he unmusical, she happy with harp and clavichord.

But at a deeper level they possessed traits in common. Both had a lot of heart: they felt for those less fortunate than themselves, they loved their children and were happiest when with them. Both had a sense of duty and wanted above everything to do their job well.

Louis was the dominant partner. He was the more intelligent and took the decisions: for example, the appointment of a man outside the Court, the Duc d'Harcourt, as the Dauphin's governor. This suited Antoinette, who was far too strong a character herself to have been happy with a man she could not respect.

Louis certainly found Antoinette attractive; he valued her as a dutiful Queen and – we shall see this later – an outstanding hostess; probably in times of stress he had comfort from her, for she was quick to sympathize, while the fact that he had to protect her against the Court proved an added bond. Was he in love with her? In the early years of marriage he had shown by many signs that he was, and he virtually told her so in 1778, to judge by the following incident. He bet Antoinette that her first child would be a boy, and when it turned out a girl, he spoke to her these lines from her favourite poet, Metastasio:

> *Io perdei: l'augusta figlia*
> *A pagar, m'a condemnato;*
> *Ma s'e ver che a voi somiglia*
> *Tutto il mondo ha guadagnato.*[1]

The following year, when Antoinette caught measles, although hectically busy with the American War, Louis offered to go into isolation with her, and according to Madame Campan, Antoinette's personal maid, during these middle years of the reign Louis was definitely in love with his wife.

Was Antoinette in love with Louis? She had been in 1773, but that seems to have been puppy love. Physically she probably did not find him attractive – she preferred slim men, with dash and charm, like Joseph – and as to character, she was puzzled, and probably disturbed, by his mixture of firmness and effacement, of kingly strength and inability to communicate that strength as a person. Louis lacked the wholly masculine personality Antoinette liked. He was perhaps also too complicated to win the love of a so much more straightforward woman. Anyway, in none of her otherwise revealing letters does Antoinette suggest that she was in love. Probably she had for Louis only a solid affection. But in a royal marriage even solid affection was rare.

Certainly Louis and Antoinette gave the impression of being a united couple. For example, she took to using his language. Louis had a fondness for the phrase '*C'est fâcheux* – It's a bore,' and when explaining to her mother why she didn't want Louis to share her isolation when she had measles, Antoinette uses it too: '*Il aurait été fâcheux qu'il gagnât cette maladie.*' Then again, they shared a sense of humour, whereby Louis was able to check occasional vagaries by Antoinette. One season the Queen took to wearing her hair, man's style, in a massive knot known as a cadogan. Louis said nothing but next time he went hunting put his hair, lady's style, in a chignon. It looks frightful, Antoinette declared, whereupon Louis replied, 'We

---

[1] I have lost: my august daughter
　　Has condemned me to pay;
　　But if she should resemble you,
　　Then the whole world has won.

men have to have a distinctive style; you've stolen in turn our plume, our hat, our long loose tress, our pigtail, and now our cadogan, which doesn't in the least suit ladies.' Next day Antoinette reverted to the chignon.

Antoinette's life underwent a marked change when she was twenty-five and had the Dauphin. She now centred herself on her children. Her daughter, known from her grave expression as *Mousseline la sérieuse*, she educated herself, and for the formation of her second, rather nervous son she was later to write a character-report quite outstanding in its perceptiveness and good sense. She who had been happy in a large family arranged for two little daughters of palace servants, Ernestine and Zoë, to be brought up with her own children and treated exactly like them.

When the Prince de Guéménée went bankrupt and was obliged with his wife to leave Court, Antoinette appointed Gabrielle de Polignac governess to her children. It was a good choice if we are to believe Lady Elizabeth Foster: 'I never saw a mind so firm and yet so gentle;' yet moments of friction arose.

'Lately,' writes Henry Swinburne, an English visitor to Versailles, 'the Duc de Normandie being taken suddenly ill, Madame de Polignac called in the physicians, who ordered leeches. She did not tell the Queen, who was at that time in a critical state of health, two months after her last confinement, but told the King, who approved. The leeches were applied with great medical apparatus, when by chance the Queen came into the room, and saw her child covered with blood, surrounded by physicians, surgeons, and attendants. On learning the cause, she fell into the most violent fury, and vented her anger without reserve on Madame de Polignac. Madame de Polignac stood unmoved, after having in vain attempted to justify herself. At length she left the room, and returned with a cup and saucer, stirring some sugar in it, and offered it to the Queen, saying, "Your majesty had better drink off this orange-flower water." The Queen drank it, and was silent, but twenty-four hours passed in the quarrel, until at last the Queen made it up with her.'

Illness of another kind caused Antoinette great anxiety at this period. Marie Thérèse de Lamballe began having convulsions, sometimes lasting two hours. The Court doctors tried every known anti-spasmodic, from essence of lettuce to Sydenham's laudanum, but without success, whence the Court, always jealous of her, concluded that the Princess had epilepsy and, since epileptics were believed to induce miscarriages, must never again see the Queen.

Antoinette maintained that her friend was merely very nervous, kept her at Court, and was finally proved right when a German nerve-specialist named Seiffert cured her condition completely in eleven months with a light non-fatty diet.

Once peace was signed Antoinette again saw her English friends, including Georgiana and her mother Lady Spencer. One day they were arguing about the most refined English word for *culottes*.

'Small clothes,' said Lady Spencer decisively.

'But the dictionary gives "breeches",' objected Antoinette.

'Not a polite word. But you *can* say "inexpressibles".'

'I like that better.'

In came the Duke of Dorset, Edward Dillon and several other Englishmen; as they were going to the King's hunt, they wore new, rather loud buckskin breeches. Antoinette decided to try the new word, and came out with:

'I do not like dem yellow irresistibles.'

The Princesse de Lamballe, who tells the story, says that Lady Spencer nearly fainted, but that she and the Queen laughed till the tears ran down their cheeks.

As Antoinette's life became increasingly centred on her children and a few close friends, so she renounced her early extravagances. She spent less on clothes now than Aunt Adélaïde and instead of discarding shoes when slightly soiled had them retrimmed. After 1784 she no longer had the books at Trianon bound in blue leather. She continued to gamble, but only for low stakes. Her main pastime was the inexpensive one of embroidering roses on white silk: she worked quickly and produced quantities of chair-covers.

In 1782 Antoinette started developing as a farm land on the other side of the lake from her Trianon garden. She remodelled eight thatched cottages, built a cow barn, stables, a dairy, paddocks, a chicken-run with nesting boxes. She stocked it with sheep, goats, Swiss cows and 68 hens, and she planted fruit trees and bushes, including 200 apricot trees, 100 gooseberry bushes, 100 raspberry bushes and 800 strawberry plants. She went there sometimes to feed the hens, trim the hedges and carry in the milk, but it is wholly mistaken to see the Hameau as a toy. On the contrary, like her aunts' farm, it belongs in the context of the new attempts to improve agriculture, and is a sister-scheme to Louis's raising of merino sheep at Rambouillet. The farm was run on commercial lines and the sale of its produce brought in on average 6000 livres a year.

Trianon meanwhile Antoinette had made a show-place, and it

was there that she entertained for her husband visitors important to France. Of the six costly receptions she gave at Trianon, later so much criticized, one was for the wife of the English ambassador, and four for visiting royalty. The reception that was remembered longest took place in June 1784.

King Gustavus III of Sweden, aged 38, was Europe's leading enlightened despot. A homosexual who loved fine clothes and masquerades, he was also quite a good playwright. He staged his own plays and, to add sparkle to the production, let actors wear the Crown jewels. When Gustavus visited France incognito as the Comte de Haga, Louis asked Antoinette to entertain him lavishly, since Sweden was France's bulwark against Russia.

Antoinette chose a new opera with ballet interludes by Piccini, *Le Dormeur reveillé*, to be given in the Trianon theatre. Based on a story in *A Thousand and One Nights*, it tells how Hassan, an ordinary citizen, becomes a caliph, and then renounces his throne for a beautiful slave girl. It allowed scope for the spectacular costume changes Gustavus liked. Afterwards Antoinette entertained two hundred people to supper. Distinguished guests were offered 48 entremets and 16 roasts, including a special dish of red mullet for Gustavus; but Louis, like Antoinette, had a choice of only four entremets, two of them rabbit, and only one roast: Caux chicken. Antoinette in fact ate nothing but 'did the honours like an ordinary housewife': so Gustavus noted with approval, also that 'she spoke to all the Swedish gentlemen and looked after them with the utmost attention.'

After supper Antoinette had the garden illuminated with log fires and fairy lights, and allowed the public to walk in the garden provided they wore white. Boats were provided to ferry them back and forth across the water to the Temple of Love. Gustavus was dazzled and thought it looked like the Elysian Fields. When the time came for him to leave the reception, he was presented with a copy of the opera bound in green morocco with the arms of Sweden; he spoke about the evening for weeks afterwards and before leaving Paris signed a new treaty on the lines Louis wished.

Among the Swedes Antoinette spoke to that evening was Colonel Axel de Fersen, tall, slim, handsome and energetic, but with the eyes of someone who has been hurt young. He had arrived at Versailles six years before, wearing a uniform designed by Gustavus which Antoinette thought very smart: a blue doublet over which was a white tunic, tight-fitting chamois breeches and a black shako topped by a blue and yellow plume. On his return from America in 1783 Fersen asked for command of the Royal Suédois regiment in the French army and because Fersen's father, a famous Field Marshal, was leader of the pro-French *parti des chapeaux* in the Swedish diet, Louis gave it to him. He thus became part of the Versailles scene.

Fersen was a reserved, introspective person who kept a diary and yet was good at party games. He had an extremely close relationship with his sister Sophie, whom he once said was 'almost a wife' to him. Although attractive to women, he felt he would never marry. He was something of a dreamer, longing to achieve glory, yet felt 'I am not one of those men who will find happiness.'

Fersen liked both Louis and Antoinette, and was liked by them, perhaps because he was more serious than the usual French courtier. Antoinette entrusted the tall Swede with little commissions, including the purchase for her in 1784 of a Swedish dog: 'not a small one', she stipulated. One evening at Madame de Polignac's Antoinette, seated at her pianoforte, sang to a small company an air from Piccini's *Didon*, and as she uttered the words of Dido to Aeneas, '*Ah, que je fus bien inspirée quand je vous reçus dans ma cour!*' it was noticed that she looked across at Fersen. But gossip went no further. No one regarded Fersen as a favourite of the Queen, yet her enemies would have been only too pleased to add this foreigner to the list of Antoinette's supposed lovers. Before the Revolution there is, in fact, not a scrap of evidence to suggest that Fersen was anything more to Antoinette than a well-liked courtier.

In the warm yet brilliant atmosphere of her receptions, and even more in her informal way of life at Trianon, Antoinette created something personal that had not existed before at Versailles. But, as in any creative act, she had to cut back firmly, even harshly, all that jarred with the desired mood. One year, for example, 'The Queen hates orange-colour, and has declared that she will receive no one who approaches her with that colour; for which reason no lady goes to Versailles with orange-coloured ribbon, although they are very common in Paris.'

But it was above all a tone that Antoinette wished to establish, and here her strong-mindedness produced graver consequences than in the matter of orange ribbon, as the following example shows.

The Duc de Fronsac had inherited from his father the post of First Gentleman of the Bedchamber. Fronsac was a tiny degenerate gouty rake. Antoinette could not stand him and when she organized her amateur dramatics at Trianon she decided to put in charge of them not Fronsac but a pleasant, decent, social nobody named Monsieur Campan.

Fronsac sent Antoinette a stream of furious letters declaring that it was his job to look after all royal entertainments, private as well as public. He demanded his rights.

Antoinette's father-in-law had felt obliged to reverse his choice of Mondonville to teach him the violin; Louis had tolerated the hated Vermond, though it is true he did not speak a word to him in ten years; it was part of the order of things at Versailles not to infringe the sacred code of precedence, especially when the person concerned happened to be important. Antoinette violated that code many times, and she violated it again by keeping Campan. So angry did Fronsac become that she had to ask Louis to silence him. Fronsac, however, continued to hang around her boudoir, referring with heavy irony to 'My colleague Campan'. Antoinette would shrug and, when he had left, remark 'It's painful to find so petty a man in the son of Maréchal de Richelieu.'

Fronsac looked for a way to hurt her. He knew that the King responded to the charms of opera singers: for example Antoinette Saint-Huberti, a tall slim blonde whose exceptionally sensitive singing of Piccini's *Didon* Louis rewarded with a pension. One night Fronsac happened to hear Louis praising an opera singer named Mademoiselle Zaccari. Now this girl was Fronsac's mistress. The next night, in his post as Gentleman of the Bedchamber, Fronsac contrived to place her in the King's way.

'There she is, Sire,' he said leeringly, 'the little Zaccari piece.'

Ignoring the girl, Louis turned on the courtier with a look of scorn. 'Get along with you, Fronsac! It's all too plain you're your father's son.'

Fronsac was one of the enemies Antoinette made through deciding to be herself. There were others: Madame de Genlis, whom she excluded from Court balls for indecent behaviour; Madame Du Barry; the Duc d'Aiguillon; several princes of the blood; La Fayette, whose ungainly dancing she had laughed at; even influential patrons of the French musicians to whom she dared prefer Gluck. Antoinette had many friends at Trianon, but in Versailles and Paris she had many enemies. From their underground presses the slanderous songs, leaflets and brochures that had begun soon after she came to the throne grew steadily in number, and when the birth of a Dauphin ended Monsieur's long period as heir to the throne, Monsieur's followers joined in. Louis's self-effacement and that the fact that he did not paw pretty girls provided an all-too easy fulcrum for slandering his wife. In the following song Coigny is the handsome Duc de Coigny. The Queen had shown him no special marks of favour but as First Equerry he saw a lot both of Louis and her:

> *D'un dauphin la naissance*
> *Enchante tout Paris;*
> *Sa subite existence*
> *Trouble le paradis.*
> *'Qui, diable, l'a produit?'*
>
> *Dit le Verbe en colère;*
> *'C'est quelque coup du Saint Esprit;*
> *Car jamais personne n'a dit*
> *Que le roi fut son père.'*
>
> *'Pardonnez-moi, mon maître,'*
> *S'écria le Pigeon,*
> *'Je n'ai pas donné l'être*
> *A ce cher nourrisson.*
> *De ce qu'on voit de beau*
> *La reine est le modèle,*
> *Coigny brûlant d'un feu nouveau*
> *D'amour alluma le flambeau,*
> *Sans m . . . la chandelle.'*[1]

Antoinette suffered from these slanders, whose authors proved impossible to catch. But from the very beginning she, like Louis, had put her trust not in the high and mighty but in the people. If Trianon is one part of Antoinette's life, equally important, though less well known, is her work for those who needed help. Here are a few examples.

Antoinette paid for and superintended the education of five children from destitute families: one was Armand Cagné, the son of a farm labourer, who received musical training and was to become a famous 'cellist. During the severe winter of 1783–4, when Louis set up a 3 million livres' relief fund to be met by a 3% deduction in Court pensions, Antoinette distributed to the hardest hit 250,000 livres of her own money saved from her annual allowances. She and

[1] Paris is enchanted with a Dauphin's birth, but Heaven is puzzled. The Word says angrily, 'Who the devil produced it? It's a trick of the Holy Spirit, for no one pretends the King is his father.' 'Excuse me, Master,' cries the Dove, 'I'm not responsible for this dear baby. He clearly takes after the Queen, while Coigny, burning with love, didn't spare his candle in lighting the flame.'

Louis allowed the poor to come into the palace, to warm themselves in the kitchens, and to take away braised meat and soup. On New Year's Day 1784 she took Mousseline la sérieuse and the Dauphin to the Versailles toy display and explained to them that the money which would have gone on toys for them would be spent that year on blankets and bread for the poor.

The example of Antoinette and her husband made helping the needy almost a fashion. Five hundred well-off Parisians, many from the *grande noblesse*, formed the Maison Philanthropique to help persons over eighty, the blind, and widowers or widows with six or more young children. Branches started in the provinces, and later the King and Queen became patron and patroness of the whole charity.

Antoinette's concern for the unfortunate brought its reward. She might be slandered at Court, but despite her Austrian birth she was now popular with ordinary Frenchmen. When she helped them during the winter of 1783–4 the Parisians built a statue of her in snow and ice, next to one of the King, and put on it this homely rhyme:

> *Reine, dont la beauté surpasse les appâts,*
> *Près d'un roi bienfaisant occupe ici ta place,*
> *Si ce monument frêle est de neige et de glace,*
> *Nos voeux pour toi ne le sont pas!*[1]

As for Louis, his popularity now stood very high. After his Normandy visit Le Havre asked permission to erect a bronze statue to him, but he turned down the idea as a useless expense. Two other towns, however, did put up statues to him: Dole in the Jura, and Perpignan, the latter statue being inscribed: 'Servitude Abolished, America Independent, the Navy Restored, Trade Protected.' These statues were a reassuring symbol to Louis and Antoinette that some at least of the French people had begun to appreciate the efforts of the monarchy to bring them happiness.

---

[1] Take your place near our kindly King, Queen whose beauty surpasses your charms; this frail monument is of snow and ice, but our wishes for you are warmer.

CHAPTER 14

The Temper of the Age:
Science and the Arts

IN order to understand later events of the reign it becomes necessary to pause in the narrative and consider certain topics by subject matter, the first being science, pure and applied.

Louis took a keen interest in science, particularly exploration and shipbuilding. He read the latest books on these subjects and, showing his practical bent, ordered scale models of important inventions. In his apartments he had models of ships, anchors, cranes, the tools used in building a ship; also of a brass mortar for testing gunpowder and a field-forge for repairing guns.

Louis continued his interest in maps. One day, before sending it to the printer, Constant de La Motte submitted a new map of Versailles to the King, and although La Motte was France's best geographer, Louis spotted certain errors. 'This pond is too large,' he wrote in pencil. 'Here a fallow field has been forgotten.'

In May 1777 the Duc de Croy presented Louis with a map he had made of Antarctica, showing the ice line, navigable waters and routes of explorers. The Emperor Joseph was also present. Louis, who had been reading an account of Captain Cook's voyages, examined the map. 'He pointed to all the most notable places and spoke to me about them at length . . .' says Croy. 'It is certain that the King is very learned, and much superior to what people think and to what he appears. The contrast was striking between the Emperor who paraded the little he knew, and the King, who knew a great deal but was too shy and modest to show it.'

From that and similar conversations a dream grew in Louis's mind. Every French King was expected to launch at least one 'great' undertaking, and in 1780 Louis decided that his would be not a war of conquest or a costly palace, but a voyage to the Pacific, the long journey of adventure he would have liked to make had he not been King.

Louis began active preparations after the American War and himself chose the man who was to lead the expedition: Jean François de La Pérouse, an open-faced talkative southerner of forty-four, who was seconded by a laconic Breton, Paul Antoine de Langle. Both officers had proved their worth in 1782 by capturing two English forts in Hudson's Bay. It was Louis who chose the names for their two 500-ton frigates: *Boussole* (Compass) and *Astrolabe*.

Louis drew up the route and their instructions. La Pérouse was to cross the Atlantic and sail to the tip of South America, noting the prospects for commercial whaling in those seas; rounding Cape Horn, he was to make for the west coast of North America, and there obtain samples of furs for possible trade with China or Japan; thence to the Aleutians, to find out what posts the Russians had established there; he was to reconnoitre the coasts of Korea and Chinese Tartary with much circumspection: 'the Chinese Government,' Louis warned, 'is very suspicious;' he was to sail south to Australia, and from there home via the Cape of Good Hope.

The islanders in particular were expected to be friendly, for Bougainville had reported well of Tahiti in 1768 and Diderot, adding to Bougainville's report a dose of Rousseauism, praised the Tahitians as 'more honest and wiser than us'. Louis ended: 'His Majesty will consider the expedition to have been successful in one of its main purposes if it is completed without the loss of a single life.' As a last suggestion he urged that the expedition, which was already carrying as gifts axes, hammers, ribbons, imitation jewels, mantles and magic lanterns, should take on board one copy at least of *Robinson Crusoe*.

The *Boussole* and *Astrolabe* sailed on 1 August 1785. They successfully rounded Cape Horn and made landfall at Easter Island, where, while measuring the statues of giants, La Pérouse noted:

We have made a fuss of the weak and unprotected, especially babies at the breast. We have sowed in their fields all kinds of useful grain. We have landed pigs, goats and sheep, which will in due course breed. We have asked for nothing in exchange. Nevertheless, they have thrown stones at us and stolen everything they possibly could.

La Pérouse concluded that the *philosophes*, safe in their studies, were mistaken in such views as 'Nothing is more gentle than man in his primitive state.'

La Pérouse continued to the Sandwich Islands and from there to Lituya Bay. He coasted western America as far south as Monterey, where he and his crew appreciated fresh beef and partridge. He then sailed to St Peter and St Paul, in what is now the Russian peninsula of Kamchatka. There he set ashore one of his officers to carry his diary and maps overland to Louis: they were to prove valuable in establishing the true position of several Pacific islands.

La Pérouse sailed south to Bougainville's Navigators' Islands – the Samoa group – and there, at Manua, the first disaster struck: Langle and ten men from the *Astrolabe* were killed by hostile natives. La Pérouse sailed on by way of Tonga and Norfolk Island to Fort Jackson. A letter written from Australia on 7 February 1788 was the last heard of him. From later evidence it appears that the *Boussole* and the *Astrolabe* foundered on offshore reefs of Vanikoro in the Santa Cruz group, all members of both crews being killed, perhaps eaten, by cannibals.

La Pérouse's diary entry, already quoted, is the best commentary on his own end. A well-equipped expedition had sailed under the sign of high hope and ended in disaster: for Louis it was a deep personal sorrow, for the historian it is a parable of later events in the reign.

Louis's interest in science was not confined to exploration. An open-air man who liked the country, he knew about horses and dogs, cattle and grain yields. At Cabinet meetings he would surprise Ministers in the midst of political discussion by 'going into details on agriculture and manufacturing'. After the grain riots he was particularly concerned about the need to grow more food.

While a prisoner of war in Germany a pharmacist named Antoine Parmentier had been fed on potatoes, a vegetable introduced in the sixteenth century from Peru, but which did not catch on in ever-conservative France, where the peasants claimed it caused leprosy. Parmentier found his diet of potatoes tasty and far from contracting leprosy put on weight. He came to Versailles, explained that potatoes were cheap to grow, and asked for help.

Louis decided to back Parmentier. He gave the pharmacist 54 acres in the plain of Sablons, and here Parmentier grew a crop of potatoes.

On Louis's feast-day in 1785 festivities were unexpectedly interrupted by the arrival of a tall man with big nose and square jaw, who strode forward to hand the King a bouquet of pale mauve flowers. Louis was surprised and touched.

'Monsieur Parmentier, men like you cannot be rewarded with money. Give me your hand, and come and kiss the Queen.'

Louis then put a spray of the potato flowers in his button-hole, while Antoinette put another on her dress. Next day courtiers were paying up to 10 gold pieces for similar sprays.

'In future famine will be impossible,' Parmentier predicted. The claim was excessive, but potatoes did become a useful subsidiary food. Choiseul invented a curious recipe for cooking the new vegetable: potatoes were peeled, boiled and made into a purée; then divided into croquettes, rolled in beaten egg, fried in boiling oil and served – sprinkled with sugar! The fashion of grilling beef was adopted at this time from England, so that in Louis's reign Frenchmen adopted what was to become their national dish: *bifteck grillé et frites.*

Considering next science applied to manufacturing, we find that France lagged behind England: mainly because the French liked to produce beautiful theorems; the English, machines that worked. In screw-cutting lathes, cast-iron bridges and the coppering of naval vessels, to name only three typical inventions, France trailed fifteen years behind her island neighbour, while the difference in production-power can be gauged from the fact that while England dug 6 million tons of coal annually, France dug only 700,000 tons.

Here again Louis showed that he was aware of the problem and did something – though not enough – to help. In 1783 he founded a School of Mines, initially with eight pupils, to train the engineers who would later develop the coal-fields of Artois and Flanders. In 1775 he sent Brigadier de La Houlière to visit the advanced foundry producing coke-smelted iron at Bersham, Denbighshire. La Houlière reported that during the twenty years since the adoption of the foundry furnace not one English naval cannon had burst, while in the French navy such accidents were so common that the sailors 'fear the guns they are serving more than those of an enemy'.

Louis acted on this report. He persuaded the manager of the Bersham works, William Wilkinson, to take charge of the State ironworks and cannon-foundry on the isle of Indret, near Nantes. In his three years there Wilkinson installed two small cupola furnaces and improved the quality of the cannon. Then Louis moved him to Le Creusot, where he built a coke-furnace for iron-smelting, the first on the Continent.

With Calonne's help, as we have seen, Louis made a determined effort to modernize French manufactories, but even so ordinary French manufactured goods such as scissors and razors could not compete with English and not enough effort was put into tapping new markets. 'At Versailles,' Jefferson noted, 'they think that there is no condition in life where there is less knowledge wanted than in commerce, but they are very much mistaken.' Lack of professionalism meant that manufactories had a low turnover, paid poor wages and were as vulnerable to foreign competition as agriculture was to bad weather and disease. Here were danger signs.

In two fields of science, however, Frenchmen led the world. One was natural history. Georges Leclerc de Buffon began life as a timber expert. He was taken up by Maurepas, when Minister of the Navy, and commissioned to catalogue the King's natural history museum: a task which Buffon's ambition transformed into an account of the whole of nature in 44 quarto volumes. Their style is so pompous people said Buffon wrote wearing lace jabot and lace cuffs, but pomposity did not prove a bar to Suzanne Necker's salon. In his last illness Suzanne lent Buffon her husband's mawkish essay, *On the Consolation of Religion*, and this, the naturalist assured her, though it is hard to believe, turned him from agnosticism to God.

Buffon was the first scientist to treat the facts of natural history as a whole. He broke down the hierarchies established by Aristotle and perpetuated by St Thomas in order to reveal the essential unity of all living things. He even claimed that animals possess souls. Buffon did more than write a scientific masterpiece, he helped change the intellectual climate of his day. He showed in effect that in nature there are no class distinctions.

The other pioneer scientist was Antoine de Lavoisier, a wealthy tax-farmer whose chosen field was gases. 'Your latest experiment, Monsieur,' Louis wrote to him on 15 March 1789, 'again wins my whole-hearted admiration. The Queen and a few persons whom I wish to witness your discovery will gather in my study tomorrow at 7 p.m. You will give me pleasure by bringing your *Treatise on Inflammable Gases*.'

Lavoisier had discovered that certain substances such as phosphorus become not lighter, as previously thought, but heavier on combustion, and they become heavier because they absorb oxygen. Air becomes matter! – it turned most people's ideas of the world upside down and, like Buffon's thesis, created an attitude of eager acceptance for new ideas in other fields, including politics.

Joseph Montgolfier was another who experimented with air and gases. In 1783, helped by his brother Etienne, he devised the first inflated airtight envelope of paper able to float in the air and carry a considerable weight. Louis took an interest in it and asked for a demonstration at Versailles.

On 19 September 1783, after Mass, the King and Queen inspected the balloon and the cage containing the first balloonists: a sheep, a cock and a duck. They then watched a fire being kindled to provide the hot smoke: it was made of damp straw, old slippers and animal carcasses; 'the foul smell,' says a chronicler, 'obliged their Majesties to withdraw.'

At 12.45 Louis gave the signal to start. A first cannon shot announced that inflation was beginning; a second, seven minutes later, that it was complete. At the third shot ropes were released and the balloon rose into the air, watched by crowds on the palace roof.

Louis had arranged for the royal astronomers to make a triangulation, the base of which was the height of the palace, according to which the balloon reached a height of 1500 feet before landing in the wood of Vaucresson, two miles away. The animals were safe, except that the sheep in its fright had kicked the cock, injuring its right wing.

Later, Louis talked to Joseph Montgolfier, ennobled his family and gave him, aptly enough, the Order of the Holy Spirit. But Louis opposed manned flights, considering them dangerous.

Alexandre Charles devised a rival to the montgolfière, inflated with hydrogen and known as the charlotte or caroline. Since Louis was backing the montgolfière, Philippe d'Orléans decided to back the caroline and arranged a manned flight on 1 December. Charles and a colleague ascended from the Tuileries and came down twenty-five miles away, near Nesle. The montgolfière became known as the *globe terrestre*, and the caroline, which went higher and quicker, as the *globe céleste*.

A prettily decorated montgolfière was named after Antoinette, and the following summer she had it demonstrated before Gustavus of Sweden. Manned by Pélâtre de Rosier, it took off from the Cour des Ministres and three-quarters of an hour later landed on an oak-tree in Chantilly. Pélâtre escaped, but the balloon went up in flames.

The most spectacular flight took place on 7 January 1785, when François Blanchard ascended from Dover Castle accompanied by an American physician, Dr Jeffries. They were carried out to sea by a light north-westerly. Twice their montgolfière descended dangerously close to the waves, and to save themselves they had to throw all inessentials out of the car, and finally to strip themselves of their clothing. Two hours after leaving Dover they landed in the forest of Guines, near Boulogne. Antoinette heard about the achievement as she was playing cards. She announced that any win she made on her next card would go to the brave balloonist. She then played and won quite a large sum, which was handed to Blanchard.

The French were proud at having for once forestalled the English, and Monsieur wrote:

> Les Anglais, nation trop fière,
> S'arrogant l'empire des mers,
> Les français, nation légère,
> S'emparent de celui des airs.[1]

Everything from ladies' hats to children's games had to have a balloon motif. Even a new liqueur appeared: *Crême aérostatique.* Somebody wondered why all this fuss about a toy, to which Franklin replied, 'What is the use of a newborn baby?'

It became important to devise a means of steering balloons. One idea was to attach windmill-like sails to the basket, and Artois actually ascended in such a balloon. But the problem of steering was not at this time resolved. Calonne, ever alert to export markets, sent twelve balloons to Peking, but the Chinese grandly waved them aside: their ancestors, they said, had known how to fly *and* steer.

Ballooning gave rise to an unusual lawsuit. A Benedictine abbot, in 1787, prevented one of his monks from accompanying Blanchard in a balloon ascent from the Champ de Mars. The monk took his abbot to court, claiming that a monk should be free to travel by air whenever he wished, adding that he was not cut out for the cloister, and that pressure had been brought on him to take holy orders. The case went to Parlement and, the chronicler adds, 'the Duchesse de Villeroy very generously offered a home to this victim of monkish despotism.'

Man's ability to ascend, so it seemed, to the very heavens and to fly through the air like an angel of God marks an important stage not only in human progress, but also in human self-consciousness. Man sensed in himself a new and exhilarating kind of freedom. Admirable as an achievement, ballooning did however contain seeds of danger. Arguing from the fact that 'the world turned upside down' could produce benefits, many people turned uncritically to irrational theories and behaviour, and the success of air-flight stimulated, in other directions, flight into the unknown.

The most important of these 'flights' was organized by Anton

[1] The over-proud English may rule the sea, but the light-hearted French take possession of the air.

Frederick Mesmer. Born on the shore of Lake Constance in 1734, he studied medicine in Vienna and qualified as a physician, writing his thesis on the planets' influence on the body. He was a man who lived in the clouds, made an unhappy marriage to an older woman and had no friends. His two passions were music – he played the 'cello and commissioned Mozart's first opera – and the books of the Swiss alchemist Paracelsus.

Mesmer wandered for three months in a forest like a Rousseauite savage: 'I felt closer to nature there . . . "O nature," I cried out in those paroxysms, "what do you want of me?" ' Having erased from his mind ideas acquired from society, Mesmer announced that 'to the physical causes of disease must be added moral causes: pride, ambition, all the vile passions of the human mind.' The Church had long recognized illness of this kind and treated it with the sacraments and even exorcism. Mesmer devised more flamboyant methods.

Arriving in Paris in 1784, he set up house in the rue Montmartre, and in the centre of his drawing-room installed an oaken tub about a foot high containing a weak solution of sulphuric acid. From the lid of the tub projected pointed and movable iron branches. Patients sat round the tub, holding in one hand the iron branches, which were said to conduct 'animal fluid' in the form of magnetic currents, and giving the other hand to their neighbour. In subdued light, silent, they sat in concentric rows, linked by cords, while from the next room drifted soft music on a harmonium. Mesmer then appeared: thoughtful brown eyes, squat nose, double chin, wearing a lilac silk coat. Slowly and with dignity he walked round, touching the diseased parts of his patients' bodies with a long beautifully wrought iron wand. Soon some of the patients would go into a trance or convulsions. There would be 'jerking of the limbs, contractions of the throat, twitching, dimness and rolling of the eyes; loud cries, weeping, hiccoughs, and uncontrolled laughter.'

Some emerged from the trance feeling relieved, and a number claimed that Mesmer cured them of illnesses 'of moral origin' ranging from migraine to partial blindness. Among those who backed Mesmer was Antoine Court de Gébelin, director of the Paris museums, a lawyer named Nicolas Bergasse, who in order to spread Mesmer's methods founded a Society of Harmony, and La Fayette, who sailed to the United States to found branches, duly armed with Mesmer's special cure for seasickness – he was to hug the mast, which would act as a mesmeric 'pole'.

When her pet dog fell ill, the witty actress Sophie Arnould took him to Mesmer, who treated animals too. 'If you cure him,' she said, 'I will proclaim your name to the world.' Mesmer put the dog into a trance and presently gave him back, telling Sophie he was all right again. But to Sophie's dismay the dog survived only a couple of days. 'What a consolation I took him to Mesmer! At least the poor animal died cured.'

Despite such setbacks, Mesmerism had a fantastic success and with it the view that man, by merely human means, can overcome moral evil. All the right people began to think in terms of trances and possession. At the King's *lever* one morning a neurotic individual named Millet threw himself at Louis's feet, begging the King to free him from a devil, set on him, he claimed, by Mesmer. Louis turned the man over to a bishop standing beside him. The Princesse de Guéménée, governess of Antoinette's children and a keen dog-lover, would stop in mid-conversation and fall into a trance: a 'mediating spirit' was informing her of the wishes of her dogs. And at one of Antoinette's private concerts four ladies, deeply moved by Steibelt's singing, thought fit to go into convulsions, and had to be removed to the park.

Antoinette was by temperament predisposed to believe in spirits and trances. She considered Mesmer an honest man who could effect otherwise impossible cures. She proposed he should set up a clinic under Government surveillance, and offered him a sum of money, which Mesmer, however, turned down, judging it insufficient.

Louis was more cautious in forming an opinion. On 12 March 1784 he appointed a commission to investigate animal magnetism on behalf of the Académie des Sciences. They studied the patients in a clinic run by Charles d'Eslon, first physician to the Comte d'Artois, and Mesmer's leading French disciple. The commission made two reports, of which only the first was published. It concluded that there was no such thing as animal fluid, and that any benefits patients derived from treatment were merely imagined. Antoine de Jussieu, dissenting from the majority view, held that suggestion, acting on the body through the imagination, could heal certain illnesses. The second report, which remained in manuscript for fifteen years, condemned Mesmerism on moral grounds, because the process of animal magnetism could arouse women sexually.

The Académie des Sciences was not the most far-sighted body in Europe: it had recently rejected vaccination and the lightning-conductor. Louis undoubtedly took their report with a grain of salt, for he allowed Mesmer and d'Eslon to continue practising. Personally he seems to have had doubts about the reality or at least the efficacy of the cures, for he roared with laughter at the Comédie Italienne's skit on magnetism, *Les Docteurs Modernes*, and teased La Fayette: 'What will Washington say now you are Mesmer's journeyman apothecary?'

Louis's brother, Monsieur, considered Mesmer a fraud and had a lot of fun at the expense of those who believed in 'miraculous' cures or doings. For example, there was the man who proposed to walk across the Seine on rubber shoes: he announced his intention in the newspapers, gave a far-fetched, so-called scientific explanation of the rubber shoes, named the day and time of the crossing, and finally cancelled it. The man in rubber shoes was the invention of Monsieur.

In October 1784, at the height of Mesmermania, Monsieur issued a print of a truly terrible-looking animal, described as follows: 'This monster has been found in the kingdom of Santa Fé, part of Peru . . . it appeared by night and devoured the pigs, cows and bulls of the district. It is eleven feet long and has a face like a man's . . . it has two horns twenty-four inches long, like a bull's . . . its hair hangs to the ground . . . two wings like a bat's . . . and two tails. It was captured in large nets . . . and is now on its way to Europe, where, if a female can be caught, it is hoped to perpetuate the species.'

The oddest thing about this odd monster is that many otherwise intelligent Frenchmen believed it really existed. As Monsieur noticed, new scientific discoveries such as Lavoisier's, the success of balloons, and especially Mesmerism had created among the public a climate of gullibility. Later this gullibility was to be exploited against the King.

The conclusion to be drawn from this survey of science is that on the one hand spectacular advances raised high hopes for man's betterment and self-betterment; on the other hand backwardness in applied science meant that the French economy could not, in the near future, satisfy such hopes. Like the *Boussole* and *Astrolabe*, France was blithely sailing into dangerous seas.

In the arts, even more than in science, the King and Queen of France were expected to show a lead. It was their role to set a tone, to encourage artists and writers and to give financial help to those they liked. Louis and Antoinette carried out this part of their royal functions with diligence, and a survey will show their tastes.

Louis XIV in Versailles, Louis XV at the Ecole Militaire and Petit Trianon have left monuments to themselves; Louis XVI, who preferred to spend his people's money more usefully, has left no great building and so contributed, unwittingly, to the image of himself as a nonentity. Yet he did build – the excise wall round Paris, the harbour works at Cherbourg – and even at Versailles made one vital change, though it is not a flashy one.

On his accession Louis found that most of the trees planted by the Sun King a century earlier were past their prime. Some were rotting, others ripped by storms. In 1775 he had several hundred of the trees felled. The felling was a solemn and, though no one knew it, a prophetic event. Hubert Robert painted two pictures of it, one of which shows Louis in red coat and olive breeches, with Antoinette fondling Clotilde and Elisabeth, while Jacques Delille brought the scene into the second canto of *Jardins*:

> O *Versailles! O regrets! O bosquets ravissants,*
> *Chefs d'œuvre d'un grand Roi, de Le Nôtre et des ans,*
> *La hache est à vos pieds et votre heure est venue!*[1]

Louis replanted characteristically with solid, long-lasting oaks many of which survive to this day.

As regards painting, Louis, with his liking for precise detail, preferred the Dutch. He bought for the royal collection some thirty Dutch pictures, including works by Ruisdael and Cuyp. The deeper side of his nature comes out in his purchase of two Rembrandts at a time when that painter was unfashionable: *The Two Philosophers* and *The Carpenter's Home.*

Louis is probably the only king to have taken an interest in frames. At the Salon of 1775 he admired and bought a frame by Boutry depicting the arms of France, trophies, garlands of flowers and foliage. It was the kind of carved woodwork he liked to do in his leisure moments.

Pastels, watercolours and gouaches, formerly considered inferior genres, flourished in this reign, and when he came to order battle scenes of the American War Louis commissioned not oils but gouaches from Louis Nicolas van Blarenberghe. Three of them he hung in his private apartments.

[1] O Versailles, O regrets, O lovely groves, masterpieces of a great King, of Le Nôtre and the years, the axe is at your feet and your hour has struck!

Another of Louis's commissions reflects his interest in classical history. He ordered a series of the Roman antiquities of Provence from Hubert Robert, which were shown in the Salon of 1787. Robert was unusual in being an athletic artist – as a student he climbed for a bet to the top of the Colosseum, and he kept fit with Indian clubs. By temperament gay, he specialized in sad scenes, notably shattered buildings, and was called 'Robert of the ruins'.

Louis's most important artistic commission was not for himself but for his wife. The dairy at Rambouillet is a sober circular building designed by Hubert Robert. In the centre stands a statue of Amalthea, the nymph who fed Zeus with the milk of a goat. Round the walls are white marble medallions showing the milking of a cow, churning of butter, shearing of sheep and distribution of salt. There are also two long white marble bas-reliefs of classical scenes in which children and animals are prominent. The subjects were obviously chosen to please Antoinette, and the sculptor Louis commissioned, Pierre Julien, made of the work a masterpiece of playful innocence.

Louis has the further distinction of being the first King to show part of the royal collection of paintings by putting it on public display in the Gallery of the Louvre, in which he also placed fourteen specially commissioned statues of famous Frenchmen, from Corneille to Montesquieu. Louis must therefore be considered the founder of the Louvre Museum.

Antoinette's preference in painting was for still-lifes. When she had had her private sitting-room done up in 1783, as the main picture, above the door, she chose Oudry's fifty-year-old *Pineapple in a Pot*. She liked Moreau le Jeune, who engraved charming outdoor scenes for Rousseau's *Emile*, and Charles Nicolas Cochin, who engraved the Court festivities. She stood godmother to a son of Joseph Ducreux, a pastellist who painted her as a girl, and encouraged the miniaturist, Jean Baptiste Isabey, when he was still unknown. Vernet, the seascape painter, was another favourite. One year at the Salon, noticing two fine pictures by him, a *Storm* and a *Calm Sea*, she turned to Vernet: '*Je vois que c'est vous qui faites la pluie et le beau temps ici*.'[1]

Antoinette sat several times to Elisabeth Vigée Lebrun, a year older than herself, who produced the gay innocent type of portrait which Antoinette, and the public generally, preferred to the incisive

[1]The play on words is untranslatable. 'I see that it's you who calls the tune here.'

psychological studies of, say, Quentin de la Tour. Madame Lebrun recalls arriving one morning at Versailles, to be told by Monsieur Campan of the Queen's Household, 'Her Majesty was expecting you yesterday. She certainly won't see you now.'

Antoinette, who was finishing her toilet and, a book in her hand, giving her daughter a lesson, overheard.

'Don't leave,' she said. 'I shouldn't like you to have come for nothing.'

She ordered away the painter's calèche and then and there gave her a sitting. Madame Lebrun, in her confusion, knocked over her paintbox. 'Don't worry,' said the Queen, and despite the artist's protests herself picked up the fallen paints.

Elisabeth Lebrun was a sweet person bullied by her husband, and Antoinette, once again showing a taste for unfortunate women, became very fond of her. The painter's husband was a picture-dealer and a wife then had the same status as her husband; this meant that Madame Lebrun was excluded from the Academy, whose members might not deal in pictures, a ban which, said their con-stitution, 'contributes to the glory of the arts'. Learning that her friend longed to join the Academy, Antoinette asked Louis to make an exception for her. Louis did so, and Elisabeth Lebrun became one of the first lady members of the Academy of Painting.

This kindness, as often happened, turned against Antoinette. As an Academician Madame Lebrun might exhibit at the Salon, and in 1783 chose to hang an unusual portrait of the Queen not in royal finery but in a simple Creole-style white gauze dress. Antoinette was bitterly criticized for popularizing such inexpensive clothes and so 'ruining' the Lyon silk manufacturers.

Antoinette's taste rather than Louis's chimed in with French taste generally. The painting of the reign is gay and virtuous. Boucher's nudes, bottoms in the air, have yielded to innocence, or so-called innocence, as in Greuze's *Broken Jug*, painted in 1777, while a crowd of painters sought to discover the charm of ordinary people: customs men in their office, labourers repairing a road. But except in David's *Oath of the Horatii*, a work of genius running counter to the general trend, one looks in vain for depth of feeling and the figures, though bright and gay, cast no shadows.

Louis, as King, was responsible for the great Sèvres porcelain works. He found it losing money, largely because of embezzlements by its managers, Parent and Roger, appointed under Louis XV. Louis imprisoned these two and although obliged in 1778 to withdraw his annual subsidy of 96,000 livres, from 1780 he had the satisfaction of seeing Sèvres make a profit, largely because of good management and personal interest by the King and Queen.

Louis, with his taste for fine craftsmanship, liked Sèvres porcelain and it was one of his little pleasures to unpack personally the crates containing the latest designs when they arrived in time for New Year's Day present-giving. He himself commissioned statuettes in biscuit of famous Frenchmen, four of which – Boileau, La Fontaine, Racine and La Bruyère – he kept on a mahogany table in his study. Louis also commissioned the most sumptuous dinner service ever produced in France. The ground colour is bleu du Roi, and each plate is decorated with a mythological scene. Most of the scenes were painted by Dodin and they include the nymph Amalthea nurturing Zeus, evidently a favourite with the King. To ensure fine workmanship, Louis limited production to about a dozen pieces each year. By 1792 the service comprised 42 plates, 10 crystal *seaux à verre* and fruit-dishes, 14 cups and 10 salt-cellars.

Sèvres issued for Louis's coronation a fine work of the King and Queen joining hands on a globe marked with three fleurs de lis, inscribed 'For the people's happiness', and for the Dauphin's birth a piece by Pajou depicting the Queen with a child in her arms and inscribed 'Venus arising from the waves with a Dauphin for France'. Antoinette was shocked by this representation of herself as the goddess of love and got Sèvres to alter the resemblance.

Antoinette suggested to Hetlinger in 1782 that he should add cornflowers to the stock decorative flowers – roses, tulips, jonquils – and the following year Sèvres produced the first of many sets of porcelain decorated with that flower. For her dairy at Trianon Antoinette bought milk jugs modelled on Etruscan vases newly brought from Italy by Denon, and when Grand Duchess Maria of Russia visited France Antoinette gave her a gilded Sèvres toilet set on which for the first time drops of translucent enamel representing jewels were applied over the gilding. For inventiveness and crafts-manship it is generally agreed that Sèvres reached its apogee in this reign.

Furniture had affinities with porcelain in that floral motives distinguish both, while tables and small cupboards were often inlaid with plaques of Sèvres. Louis's main commission in this field, his library, is one of the handsomest rooms in Versailles. The cupboards for his books, made by the Rousseau brothers, are separated by cascades of roses, dahlias, peonies and marguerites, and surmounted by gilt bas-reliefs: Apollo leaning on his lyre, and France receiving homage from the arts.

Antoinette also liked the warm texture of carved woodwork and wherever possible replaced marble or stucco facings with panelling painted pale blue or pale green, never the grey with which these colours have often been over-painted. The panelling in her living-room at Versailles depicts fleurs de lis and trophies of musical instruments above two squatting sphinxes on either side of a steaming perfume-pan. For curtains and upholstery she chose white satin or white gros de Tours.

The most beautiful artistic products of the reign are the gracefully curved tables, desks and small cupboards inlaid with marquetry flowers produced by Jean Henri Riesener and Georges Jacob. Antoinette bought heavily from both, and Riesener she counted as a friend. It used to be thought that Antoinette had no say in the furniture made for her, but newly discovered evidence shows that she did in fact influence design.

When she wished a new piece of furniture, the Queen asked Gondouin, designer of the Crown furniture, to submit sketches, and on these she gave him her views. Gondouin then made a wax or wooden model three to six inches high; if it was a chair, he made the arms and legs each in a slightly different style. The Queen chose the ones she wanted, and Gondouin made a full-scale model in wax or plaster; some of these models are still in existence. If the Queen approved the model, the chair was then made by one of the royal furniture-makers.

Antoinette had a particular fondness for tables. She had several gaming tables: a triangular one for backgammon, circular for brelan, square for quadrille; she also owned a painting table with containers to hold her watercolours and palettes. For her first confinement she ordered from Riesener and Merklein a mechanical table for taking her meals in bed, its height adjustable at the touch of a button. At the touch of a second button it became a toilet-table, and of a third button a writing-table. She was evidently fond of this beautiful and ingenious piece, for she took it, in her last years, to the Tuileries. It is now in the Metropolitan Museum of Art, New York.

One of the richest works ordered by Antoinette is a secrétaire of oak veneered with thuja wood and purple wood, decorated with gilt-bronze putti and delicate flowers in full relief. It was made by Riesener in 1783 for Trianon and is now in the Wallace Collection, London. Later, when she had to be careful with money, Antoinette arranged for old lacquer from discarded furniture to be used in adorning a secrétaire and commode for her apartment at Saint-Cloud.

After 1780 Riesener's style grows more refined, his marquetry more sober, and the bronzes attain an unequalled precision and sensibility. Pierre Verlet, the expert on royal furniture, attributes the improvement to the influence of the Queen. Whether or not Verlet's view on this point is accepted, the Queen's taste certainly made itself felt in the furniture of the royal châteaux, in Paris, which followed the royal lead, and thence right across Europe. Louis left this field to her, intervening only occasionally to have certain of his chairs decorated with his favourite motif, the sunflower. In furniture at least the Louis Seize style is very much the Queen's.

From her sitting-room in Trianon, with its floral motives, Antoinette could look out on the garden she created. The Trianon garden was her idea, her work of art. Its starting-point was the translation in 1776 of William Chambers's *Dissertation on Oriental Gardening*, which set a fashion for Chinese-style lakes and grottoes. Antoinette, helped by her friend Prince de Caraman, designed a garden centred on a lake, fed from a stream issuing from a precipitous heap of rocks. But there the Chinese-ness stopped. Very European were the two small buildings: an octagonal pavilion decorated by Deschamps with bas-reliefs of the four seasons, and a Temple of Love modelled on the Vesta in Rome, twelve white marble Corinthian columns enclosing Bouchardon's statue, *Love fashioning a bow from the club of Hercules*. Very English were the lawns, which Antoinette wished smooth and close as those described by her English friends, and she brought over in 1784 John Eggleton, recommended by Lord Southampton, to care for them; but, as Blaikie notes with relish, 'he soon was lost and returned in disgrace to England, as he was a Man of no Genius.'

Antoinette made her garden distinctive by filling it with flowers. As Thomson's gazelle marks out its territory with drops of scent, so the Queen delimited her domain with beds of hyacinths and roses, of tulips and irises, grouping them by kind and colour, red, white, yellow and her favourite blue. Orange-trees were another feature of her garden; she planted enough to yield, in a good year, up to 100 pounds' weight of blossom. This was esteemed for making orange-flower water and she made gifts of it to Louis and to her suite.

We are given a glimpse of Antoinette in her garden by Comte

Paroy, a courtier who was also a gifted painter. The Queen watches a gardener who is pushing turf in a wheelbarrow. Remarking that she would like to be able to say that she had worked on her own garden, she takes the wheelbarrow and starts to push it, not realizing that the ground is sloping. The barrow runs away with her, courtiers hurry to help and finally, laughing, she has to let the barrow go. In the house Paroy happened to notice an unfinished watercolour sketch of the garden by Antoinette; he took the liberty of adding to it the scene he had just watched.

Literature during the reign fell to a low ebb. Though everyone was making a parade of sensibility, true sensibility is not to be found, least of all in the work of the more ambitious poets, Delille and Saint-Lambert, whose verse is trivial, bookish and enervatingly tidy. Light verse, rainbow-coloured bubbles such as those of Boufflers, was highly esteemed, and Monsieur wrote reams of it. Sometimes he would indicate certain words by their initial letter, inviting his friends to fill in the blanks.

Louis seems to have taken no interest in either contemporary verse or in the French novel. With rare exceptions such as *Les Liaisons dangereuses* the novel embraced the sentimentalism of English fiction while missing its realism and that richness of life which had found its last abundant national expression in Rabelais. Antoinette read these novels, however. *Ernestine* by Madame Riccoboni was among her favourites – she renamed one of her adopted children after the heroine – and because it typifies novels of the reign its plot is of interest.

The orphan daughter of a German embroidery-maker living in Paris, Ernestine earns a tenuous living painting miniatures. One day she is commissioned to paint the kindly Marquis de Clemenges. He falls in love with her but because he can afford to marry only on the successful termination of a lawsuit he does not tell her. However, he arranges for some money to be made over to Ernestine, without her knowing where it comes from. Ernestine begins to live in style and goes to the opera at Versailles, where she is snubbed by an old friend, who accuses her of being a kept woman. 'What are the world's rash judgments to me,' replies Ernestine, 'so long as I am innocent, and my heart has nothing with which to reproach me?'

Clemenges is so unhappy at being unable to marry he falls ill. Ernestine offers to become his mistress, if that will help. Clemenges – most implausibly – declines. He is then forced by circumstances connected with his lawsuit to become engaged to another woman. Ernestine bears it all with exemplary patience. At the last minute, more illness and the unexpected winning of the lawsuit lead to a happy ending.

It is obvious why Antoinette felt drawn to the sensitive German-born heroine, with whom, in such scenes as the unjust charge of promiscuity, she could identify herself. Less obvious is the reason why hundreds of such highly moral novels were read and re-read in an age of low moral standards. This is a phenomenon we shall meet again in the drama, and it will be analysed there.

The King's most important artistic responsibility was the opera. It was he who subsidized it and was ultimately responsible for both repertoire and quality of performances. Unlike his sister Elisabeth, who composed the well-known touching romance *Pauvre Jacques*, Louis was not musical and could not sing in tune. However, he had inherited a taste for music from his parents, went often to the opera and was a good enough judge of performance to single out Saint-Huberti when she was still little known.

As at Sèvres Louis cut down expenditure, in 1782 reducing his annual grant for music from 499,848 livres to 257,400. He also abolished a fantastic system of hereditary seats, whereby the heir of anyone who had ever sung a role, however minor, in an opera was entitled to a free seat at any performance. To improve quality, Louis founded prizes for libretti and instituted the important Ecole de Chant et de Déclamation, one of the earliest schools of music for the training of opera singers and actors, nursery of the present Conservatoire. These changes helped to raise standards.

In June 1782 the opera house burned down, killing ten people, which did not stop a couturier launching a fashionable new orange colour called *opéra brûlé*: this seems to be why Antoinette did not like orange. Louis immediately ordered the building of a new opera house near the Porte Saint-Martin. Antoinette offered the architect, Lenoir, a bounty of 6000 livres and the order of St Michel if he brought her the key of her box by 31 October. Working round the clock, Lenoir was able to do this with four days to spare. Antoinette, with her vivacious temperament, was a great one for deadlines. In 1786, ordering shutters for one of her salons, she stipulated that they must be 'made, painted, hinged and hung within a week'.

Opera balls were held in Paris; Antoinette often attended them. She was criticized by the Court for mingling with commoners, and by historians ever since her presence at the balls has been seen as yet another instance of a scatterbrained search for pleasure. A closer look suggests a different explanation. In order to break even the Opéra needed up to 150,000 livres annually, and it was to cover this deficit that balls were given. In a year when Antoinette did not attend, the balls produced a total of 34,000 livres, but when Antoinette did attend, a single ball could net 240,000 livres. Antoinette may have enjoyed the balls, but her dominant motive was probably a wish to help her beloved Opéra.

Antoinette had done much to improve the opera by bringing Gluck to Paris, and we have seen that it was to her that he dedicated his masterpiece, *Iphigénie en Tauride*. Piccini too wrote an opera about Iphigenia. Its second performance was marred when Mademoiselle Laquerre, playing the lead, came on tipsy. This prompted the actress Sophie Arnould to murmur, 'Iphigenia in Champagne.'

Antoinette brought the Italian Sacchini, who wrote in the style of Gluck, over to Paris, but her influence on the opera declined about 1785. In that year Sacchini completed his best work, *Œdipe à Colonne*. Antoinette had promised it should be the first opera at the royal theatre during the Court's next residence at Fontainebleau. The time approaching and nothing being said about it, the composer sought an audience.

'My dear Sacchini,' said Antoinette, 'I am accused of showing too much favour to foreigners. I have been so much pressed to command a performance of M. Lemoine's *Phèdre* instead of your *Œdipe* that I cannot refuse. You see the situation; forgive me.' It was a bitter disappointment and three months later, believing the Queen's favour lost, Sacchini died.

Lemoine was a bore; the best of the French opera composers was André Grétry. Antoinette encouraged Grétry: she stood godmother to his third daughter, Antoinette, and whenever she saw her godchild in the audience blew her a kiss. She chose part of Grétry's ballet suite, *Cephalus and Procris*, as one of the tunes played by the prized bronze musical clock in her sitting-room. She and Louis attended Grétry's best opera, *Richard Cœur de Lion*, in 1784: it portrays a King held prisoner in a castle, a curious but by no means unique example of prophecy in the arts.

In light opera Antoinette's taste was much less sure. She insisted on the Comédie Italienne performing *Ernestine*, based on her favourite novel, music by the mulatto Saint-Georges. It proved a flop. The dénouement brought a courtier on stage, where he stood for a full minute cracking his whip, and shouting 'Ohé! Ohé!' It was meant to be dramatic, but the audience roared. Antoinette recognized her mistake and on leaving the theatre parodied the scene by saying to her coachman: 'To Versailles, ohé!'

When he went to the theatre Louis liked to laugh. He was particularly fond of broad parodies, such as Pierre Laujon's *Matroco*, a take-off of chivalry in which ineffective giants boast and splutter, affected heroines go on and on about their virtue, languorous heroes harangue instead of taking action, and the enchanter, Matroco, is a charlatan. Troubled by insomnia, Matroco decides to sacrifice a turkey to the full moon, which he addresses with the splendid invocation: '*Déesse blanche à face ronde . . .*' but at the crucial moment the turkey flies off. In February 1778 Louis pronounced it the funniest play he had ever seen.

Antoinette liked plays about simple country folk such as Favart's *La Chercheuse d'Esprit* and she gave a pension to Sébastien Mercier for his working-class dramas. But both Louis and she liked tragedy. Louis gave a pension to Chamfort for *Mustapha et Zéangir*, about an evil queen who intrigues against her husband in the hope of ruling through her son, and Antoinette called Maisonneuve to her box after applauding his *Roxelane et Mustapha*, which has much the same theme. Incidentally, it is almost inconceivable that Louis and Antoinette would have honoured such plays if Antoinette had really been the political intriguer her enemies were later to say she was.

Beaumarchais wrote *La Folle Journée*, later known as *The Marriage of Figaro*, in 1778. Three years later it was tentatively accepted by the Comédie Française, who passed it to the King for his approval. Louis had it read to him.

The action is set in Spain and turns on the privilege of a Spanish nobleman to take the maidenhood of any bride married on his estate. The *ius primae noctis* had never obtained in France, but it provided a promising intrigue for a play whose object was to show that servants are often cleverer and more worthy than their masters. Beaumarchais succeeded in regenerating this age-old theme because his language is fresh and concrete, the characters closely observed and convincing, and the whole dosed with the author's immense fun and joie de vivre. It was to other social comedies what a cannon is to a bow and arrow.

Louis occasionally interrupted the reading to say, 'That is in bad taste. He keeps using Italian-style verbal conceits.' In the scene when Figaro attacks various aspects of French society, notably

State prisons, Louis rose from his chair. 'That's horrible, it will never be performed . . . This man upsets everything in a Government that ought to be respected.'

'So it won't be performed?' asked Antoinette.

'Certainly not. You can be sure of that.'

Beaumarchais distributed copies to the leading actors of the Comédie Française and enlisted their support for at least one private performance. The hall used for opera rehearsals was secured and tickets went out to everyone of importance for a certain day. On the morning of the performance, when some of the audience were already seated, Louis acted at variance with his usual liberal-mindedness: he signed a *lettre de cachet* forbidding the play to be acted.

'Oppression!' 'Tyranny!' cried the disappointed ticket-holders. Beaumarchais in a fury announced: 'Gentlemen, he doesn't want it performed here, but it will be performed, I swear it, even if it has to be in the choir of Notre Dame.' He then cleverly let word get around that, in a spirit of conciliation and deference to his Majesty's wishes, he had suppressed all the offensive passages. The Comte de Vaudreuil, a friend of Antoinette, then obtained permission from Louis to stage the play privately at his country house. *Figaro* was performed, with of course the offensive passages intact. The audience of courtiers was impressed and talked about it for weeks. When the Czarevitch and his wife visited France, they wanted to attend a reading. Gabrielle de Polignac loved it and praised it to Antoinette. So many people had read it and were talking about it, so many others criticized the King for not respecting an author's freedom, that three years after he had first banned it Louis retracted and allowed the play to be performed publicly. It was a striking example of Louis ceding to his wife and friends, and did him much harm, since it encouraged a belief that on larger issues too he might yield.

The première in April 1784 was the event of that year. Great ladies supped with actresses in the hope of getting seats and at 11 a.m., five hours before the box office opened, the Duchesse de Bourbon sent her footmen to stand in the queue. Doors and even iron gates were broken down by the crowd in its impatience to buy tickets.

The play was given in the Théâtre Française; and because of its originality received only lukewarm applause. Someone remarked that it wasn't suited to a Paris audience, it would fail. 'You're right,' said Sophie Arnould drily. 'It's a play that will flop . . . forty nights in a row.' Even that large figure was surpassed. After the play had been running several weeks Beaumarchais, with his usual flair for publicity, announced that the fiftieth performance would be a benefit in aid of poor mothers with infants at the breast. People murmured approvingly, 'This playwright is *for* society, not against it.'

Everyone said *Figaro* was scandalous and dangerous, but everyone went to see it. It ran and ran, begetting no less than twelve parodies or satires. But contrary to what is usually said, the play probably did little to sap people's faith in established society. The real danger to society from the arts lay deeper.

Summarizing Louis's and Antoinette's patronage of the arts, we may say that except in literature they did a great deal to try to raise standards and, when they found it, they rewarded merit. Their main achievements were in opera, Sèvres porcelain and marquetry furniture: the last two attaining a quality never surpassed.

Nevertheless, taken as a whole, the artistic production of the reign gives cause for grave disquiet. It is, to start with, oversoft, pink and gold and cloying like a too-ripe peach. There are altogether too many flowers: one senses a lack of virility. Portrait after portrait depicts a sweetly smiling lady or kindly peasant, casting no shadows, and we meet these same unbelievable types in the novels. We might be in the garden of Eden for all one hears of evil. And there is an overabundance of happy endings.

Artists, in short, were failing to perform their proper job of sounding the heights and depths of human nature as they found it in their time. Instead they opted for the easy course of flattering their audiences with rosy pictures of oh-so-good people all finding a well-deserved happiness. Their art was soft because they were soft.

To see how deep the rot went it is enough to look at the most influential of the arts in Paris, the theatre. One of the most popular plays in the 1780's was a study of Henri IV called *Henri IV's Hunting Party*. Instead of dramatizing one of the really important acts of that reign, such as Henri's decision to give up his Protestant faith for the sake of national unity, the author chose to show Henri as a hail-fellow-well-met sort of bloke, drinking and singing merrily with peasants, flirting with the girls and occasionally telling Sully to reduce some tax or reprieve some wrongdoer. It was a wishful picture wholly divorced from reality, which Louis could never live up to.

Antoine Blanc's *Marco Capac, First Inca of Peru* was revived in 1782. Here again was a saccharine picture, this time of Peruvians, and according to the Duc de Croy it owed its great success to its claim 'that man in his wild, natural state is superior to man living in society under a government.'

Where in the world was evil? Where was tragedy? It might be thought that it came on stage with the first French adaptations of Shakespeare. Jean Ducis, born in Versailles in 1733 and holder of the pleasant sinecure of Secretary to Monsieur, adapted *Romeo and Juliet* in 1772, *King Lear* in 1783 and, a year later – his most praised effort – *Macbeth*.

The curtain rises on a heath, but no witches appear: Ducis has struck them out of the cast. Duncan and his friend Glamis are plotting to kill Macbeth; learning of the plot, Macbeth, urged and helped by his wife, kills Duncan. Malcolm has no suspicion who the murderers are. He has been brought up by a shepherd whom everyone supposes to be his father, but he shows Macbeth a letter in Duncan's hand which establishes that he, Malcolm, is Duncan's son. Malcolm wishes to return to his former peaceful life in the country, but he and his adoptive shepherd father see Lady Macbeth sleepwalking and trying to wash blood from her hands. They realize that she has been inculpated in Duncan's murder. Lady Macbeth dispatches assassins to kill Malcolm, but Macbeth intervenes to protect the threatened man and is killed by them in error. Lady Macbeth then stabs herself.

Ducis's version of *Macbeth* is a highly moral little play in which Macbeth is a good sort, though weak, who kills Duncan in self-defence. All the supernatural side disappears: witches, Hecate, Banquo's ghost. As Ducis says in his Introduction: 'I worked hard to eliminate horror, which always revolts an audience and would have ensured the play's failure.' He then declares that he has aimed at imparting terror, though 'only to a bearable degree'. In fact the play contains not one ounce of terror. For a few moments at the beginning of Act III Ducis attempts the terrible tone of the original: Macbeth experiences remorse, and precisely at that point, says Grimm, the public began to yawn.

Ducis's *King Lear* was still more of a travesty: he eliminated the Fool and gave the play a happy ending. Even a watered-down storm scene proved too strong for the Parisians, and provoked a parody entitled *Le Roi Lu*, in which Lu and his friend Konkin exchange philosophic platitudes under an umbrella.

Shakespeare never really came to Paris, for the French did not want him. 'Let the English be content with Newton,' wrote Voltaire in his preface to *Irène*, 'without pretending to produce a modern Sophocles.' It was not simply that Shakespeare failed to observe the unities and the classical separation of pathos and humour; Voltaire the Frenchman was guarding naturally good man against one who laid bare the blackness in his soul.

Louis, incidentally, disliked Ducis's sugary versions of Shakespeare, whom he knew in the original, and he commissioned Pierre Letourneur to make faithful prose renderings of all Shakespeare's plays. These, however, were not performed.

On the Paris stage, then, there was no mad fellow to utter, in the language of the common people, deep, dark and necessary truths. Worse still, since Racine and Corneille were out of fashion, there was no tragic hero to sin, suffer and repent. Paris audiences left the theatre as gaily as they entered it, convinced that man is naturally good and that so-called evil is just a misunderstanding.

It is surprising that Parisians chose to ignore the dark side of human experience, for there was plenty under their noses. Mrs Thrale, not a morbid woman, noted: 'There is a place called the Morgue where all dead bodies which have been found in the night, drowned, crushed or assassinated, are carried every morning to be owned and buried by their friends. Here . . . are often to be found six or seven corpses of a morning, but seldom fewer than two.'

These unhappy endings were hushed up, the dirt was swept under the carpet; people did not want to know their own failings. There was in fact a quite staggering moral vanity abroad, and it was nourished by the Parisians' literary diet. Because it was starchy and oversweet, it made for a spiritual imbalance, a lack of tonus. As Ducis says, the stage was kept clear of horror, because horror would have 'revolted' the audience – the verb is his. It might have been better for France if Parisians had not yawned at Macbeth's remorse, if they had been revolted in the theatre rather than elsewhere at a later date, and so been purged vicariously of their more bloodthirsty urges.

CHAPTER 15

The Temper of the Age: Religion and Philosophy

THE moral tone, spiritual values and social conscience of a Christian nation depend largely on the state of its Church. Under Louis XVI, the Church in France gave the appearance of flourishing. The clergy, consisting of some 70,000 secular priests and 60,000 monks, friars and nuns, owned about 10% of the land of France. They enjoyed an annual income of 200 million livres, most of which they spent on schools, hospitals, hostels and food for the poor. Every five years they met in assembly to vote the King a 'free gift', usually 16 millions. When other levies are included, the Church paid to the state about 6% of its income. Apart from a few very rich bishops and abbots, the clergy lived frugally, though not in penury as it was fashionable to pretend, and they performed satisfactorily their job of teaching and looking after the poor.

Closer inspection, however, reveals a deep malaise. To start with, there was a sharp drop in vocations. Between 1770 and 1789 the number of monks and friars fell by 10,000. Many small abbeys hobbled along with only a couple of aged monks. The intake to diocesan seminaries also fell. Young men no longer esteemed the priesthood or else, like Turgot, lost their faith altogether.

The lack of devotion during Sunday Mass in a big Rouen church had already struck Mrs Thrale in 1775: 'Some were counting their money, some arguing with the beggars who interrupt you without ceasing, some receiving messages and dispatching answers, some beating time to the music.' Nine years later: 'I never thought so little religion could be tolerated in a Christian country . . . The crucifixes and Madonnas which used when I was last on the Continent to meet my eyes perpetually . . . are strangely diminished in number, and those there are still standing will not be here long; for nobody repairs them which the weather ruins.'

There was, in short, a lack of faith. How had it come about? Whereas in England the central religious debate had long turned on the authority of Rome, in France it had turned on the power of grace. To what extent does an ordinary Christian require God's grace in order to lead a good life? To a very considerable degree, answered the Jansenists. Man, they held at Port Royal, is a helpless, miserable creature unworthy even to receive Holy Communion, except occasionally after careful preparation. Only the freely given grace of God can raise him from his misery, and for this he must wait in awe and trembling.

Much of this teaching of Port Royal was healthy and needed, but the Jesuits pounced on certain heretical aspects and, because they were a great power in the land, they destroyed French Jansenism. The symbolic moment came in 1712, when, on orders from Louis XIV, the ruined buildings of Port Royal were ploughed into the ground. Certain vital elements then disappeared from French religion: a sense of awe and mystery before the justice of God, the notion of man caught in dramatic tension between his own animal nature and divine grace. Applying Pascal's theory of history, one can say that the fate of France would have been different had not Pascal's name been placed by Rome on the Index, for this meant that his *Pensées*, the book which offers the deepest and most balanced picture of Christianity in French, was published only in one tendentious, abbreviated edition, and completely ignored by both intellectuals and ordinary churchgoing Frenchmen.

The Jesuits meanwhile continued to be an immense power in the Church and remained so during most of the reign of Louis XV. They taught a less austere, more worldly-wise Christianity than the Jansenists, but they taught it effectively. Being supporters of a strong papacy and a strong monarchy, they incurred the hatred of the Parlements, by whom they were destroyed in 1762. Some 4000 Jesuits were obliged to leave France, while Voltaire rubbed his hands: 'In twenty years there will be nothing left of the Church.'

With its left and right flanks routed, the Church's centre was too weak to contain the new rationalism – and irrationalism – stemming from scientific advances. 'Physics, chemistry and technology,' wrote Grimm in 1783, 'have produced more miracles in our day than fanaticism and superstition taught during centuries of ignorance and barbarism.' The authenticity of the Gospels, the miracles and the divinity of Christ – everything came to be doubted. This was happening all over Europe but whereas in a country like England the springs of enthusiasm were still flowing, and in the open-air preaching of John Wesley Christianity found a revived strength, in France for a variety of reasons those same springs failed to well up. There fell on the Church of France a great fear, a wavering, and then a compromise. 'The ordinary priest or curé,' says Chamfort, 'must believe a little, or else he is considered a hypocrite; but he must not be too sure of his facts, otherwise he will be considered intolerant.'

The bishops were another matter. Many of them were quite sure of their facts and did not mind being considered intolerant: a better word would be bigoted. They clamped down, for instance, on any hint of Jansenism. Before he might receive the Last Sacraments a dying man was obliged to obtain a certificate stating that he had confessed his sins to a priest untainted with Jansenist views. These *billets de confession* were denounced by most sensible people and did great harm among ordinary Christians by bringing into disrepute the sacrament of penance.

The bishops' other intolerant action was to call on Louis to burn certain books. In their assembly of 1775 they condemned fourteen works, including Raynal's *Histoire philosophique*, which attacked missionaries, *L'Examiner important*, attributed to Bolingbroke, and Holbach's *Le Système de la Nature*, of which a doctor at the Sorbonne is said to have exclaimed: 'Hateful book! It establishes the truth of atheism.'

They contain [said the bishops] principles objectively false, injurious to God and his august attributes, favouring or teaching atheism, full of the poison of materialism, annihilating the moral code, confounding vice and virtue, capable of disturbing peace in the home, of stifling feelings of family unity, authorizing every kind of passion and disorder, tending to inspire contempt for scripture, to overthrow authority, to strip the Church of the power received from Jesus Christ and to discredit its ministers, calculated to make subjects rebel against their sovereigns, to foment sedition and disturbances, destructive of all revelation, full of calumnies and outrages against our holy law and the adorable person of Jesus Christ our Saviour, scandalous, rash, impious, blasphemous and as offensive to the Divine Majesty as they are harmful to empires and society.

That denunciation is powerful. Had Louis been a weak man he would have yielded to it and to other episcopal recommendations; his would have been a bigoted reign. Let us see what actually happened.

Louis's parents had been good Catholics and from them he had received a sound religious education. He was exact about Mass, the sacraments, fasting and abstinence. His religion meant a great deal to him. But he had no great liking for priests. He said that he did not want any 'sayer of Mass' for the Dauphin's education, and he warned his cousin the Duke of Parma against becoming dependent on priests or, worse still, on monks.

Louis was a believer in personal example. He did not tell people how to lead their lives, as Louis XIV had done, nor did he approve of intolerance by the clergy. In the year of his accession he sent for the Archbishop of Paris who had been demanding *billets de confession*. 'The King my grandfather exiled you several times for the troubles you occasioned in the State; I sent for you to tell you that if you relapse, I shall not exile you, I shall give you over to the rigour of the law.'

Louis turned down the Assembly's request that he burn or outlaw certain books. 'I shall always support religion, but you must not expect the Government to do your work for you. It is your example which is the true support of religion, your behaviour, your virtues are the most effective weapons for resisting those who dare to attack it.'

When the Académie Française offered a prize for the best eulogy of Voltaire, who had recently died, the Archbishop of Paris, in the name of his curés, requested the King to annul the competition. Louis replied: 'It is the job of the clergy to pray for a man's soul, of writers to celebrate his genius.'

Throughout his reign Louis came under pressure from the bishops to expel Protestants. The Breton Bishop of Dol was particularly violent on this subject. One day, according to Chamfort, the Bishop of Saint-Pol asked the Bishop of Dol why he had spoken to the King in the name of his colleagues without consulting them. 'I consulted my crucifix,' the other replied.

'In that case you should have repeated exactly what your crucifix said.'

Louis not only resisted this episcopal pressure, in 1787 he placed before Parlement an edict which would grant civil rights to France's 70,000 Protestants. It was in effect an edict of religious toleration. Parlement opposed it, and Louis had to write to the Chief President: 'My will is that my Parlement shall proceed to the registering of this edict without delay. You will account to me on Wednesday.' Parlement submitted and registered the edict; for the first time in a hundred years Protestants had an official existence in France.

For Louis, being a Christian meant being humane, and this comes out in his treatment of the suppressed Order of Jesuits. For fifteen years individual ex-Jesuits, unable for one reason or another to leave France, had eked out a wretched existence, unable to exercise their pastoral functions. In May 1777 Louis issued an edict allowing ex-Jesuits to possess canonries, simple benefices and parishes; there to minister as their bishops should direct. He forbade them, however, parishes in large towns. 'This last prohibition did not satisfy Parlement, which extended it to include any canonry; and forbade the Jesuits to preach in towns or to leave the diocese of their birth.' As part of his larger political strategy Louis had to grant Parlement this point, but he continued to invite Lenfant, an ex-Jesuit, to preach at court.

Louis's personal life was decent and kindly. It set the tone at Versailles. No minister grew rich in his service, no mistress found places for favourites. In marked contrast to the previous reign, Christian values were a reality in the royal circle.

Many of the nobility regretted this change. The men had less opportunity for intrigue and trading in State secrets, the ladies pouted at finding no easy way to the royal bed. The very decency of the King's life aroused in many a certain hatred. This was particularly true of the King's rich and influential cousin, Philippe d'Orléans.

Since his failure at the battle of Ushant Philippe had been going downhill. Heavy drinking gave him a ruddy complexion, so that on his visits to England, where he gambled at White's and Brooks's, he was known as the Duke of Burgundy. He took a mistress, Madame de Genlis, 'a hen Rousseau', according to Walpole, and very prudish, of whom Talleyrand remarked, 'In order to avoid the scandal of flirting, she consents immediately.' Philippe asked Louis's permission to make this woman English-style governess to his sons: an unprecedented appointment. Louis replied: 'I have the Dauphin; Madame may yet become pregnant, the Comte d'Artois has sons . . . you may do as you like.' But when Philippe wished to send his sons to be educated in England, doubtless at Eton, Louis drew the line: princes of the blood, he said, belonged to France.

In 1783, to stave off bankruptcy, Philippe turned the beautiful Palais Royal gardens into shops, cafés, gambling saloons and brothels. They brought him in half a million livres annually and Louis joked: 'Now my cousin has turned shopkeeper, I suppose we shall see him at Court only on Sundays.'

Philippe had debauched tastes. Having rented 35 Portland Place, he told his agent to leave it unfurnished until his arrival, 'because

I believe that furniture as well as women must be chosen according to the whim of the moment.' In the summer of 1783 he gave a mixed supper party and had the idea of placing under the napkin of each guest a French letter, which in those days were made of pigs' bladders and called 'English overcoats'. Philippe had the French letters inflated very full with hydrogen, so that when his guests removed their napkins they floated up and around the room.

When he succeeded his father in 1785 as Duc d'Orléans, Philippe became first Prince of the Blood, and his debauchery then took on a new and symbolic importance. Because he lived in central Paris, everything he did was talked about. It was Philippe who gave the aristocracy a name for corruption, and the vices the Parisians saw him practise they began to suppose were practised in places like the Trianon which they did not visit. Thus irreligion became a very important political factor.

Moral standards fell even on the fringes of Versailles. 'Pederasty,' writes one observer in December 1784, 'is today the fashionable vice, together with Lesbianism. His Majesty desired to take action against certain noblemen caught red-handed. There is talk of a sort of seraglio of sodomites in Versailles. The King has been warned that the commotion caused by a criminal trial would be very danger-ous, dishonour many great families, and doubtless increase people's desire to experience this sin.' Louis rusticated some of the worst offenders, including Madame's *maître d'hôtel*, who had perverted one of Antoinette's Hungarian subalterns.

A breakdown like this the Church traditionally fights with its shock troops: saints. But Louis's reign produced only one saint, Benoît Labre, and he lived in Italy, a strange silent hairy tramp, forever on the move, sleeping rough, seeking extremes of suffering and derision. In France there were a few outstandingly holy men such as Jacques André Eméry, superior of Saint-Sulpice, but most priests trimmed their sails to the Deist wind. 'In more than one sermon lately,' writes a Parisian, Sébastien Mercier, 'the only things Christian are the sign of the cross and the Gospel citation.' When Father Bonnet, superior of the Lazarists, preached in Nancy, one of his congregation offered to put a gold louis on each place in his sermon when the name of Christ occurred.

Books might have helped, but pitiful were the writings in defence of Christianity. The Assembly of Bishops commissioned second-rate men like Bonhomme and Gourcy to wade through the old apologetic writings and to translate selections therefrom. Snippets of Justin,

Athenagoras and Tertullian against the flashing wit of Voltaire were about as effective as Roman legionaries' shields against 64-pounders.

The salt had lost its savour, but men cannot live without salt and when this happens they seek substitutes. Louis XVI's France produced three synthetic varieties of salt. The first was freemasonry, a speculative system that claims to be based on those fundamentals of faith held in common by all men, and therefore admits adherents of all faiths, provided they believe in the Great Architect of the Universe. Condemned by the Pope and frowned on by the King, it was at this time an underground organization patronized by high society.

Philippe d'Orléans was Grand Master of all the lodges in France. Their declared purpose was 'the improvement of man's lot'. No one could quarrel with this, though it usually meant helping other masons in their careers. Nor was there anything sinister about their meeting-hall, where columns painted on canvas represented the temple of Solomon, and there were pictures of the flaming star, the set-square, the spirit-level. The benign aims and vague ritual obviously lacked a binding force, and this was supplied by an element of secrecy. A mason learned certain truths which he swore never to divulge 'on pain of having my throat cut, my tongue torn out and my heart rent asunder, and buried in the depths of the sea'. Threat of death comes as a surprise in this century of tolerance: it had been hatched in that dark irrational climate which was the freemasons' substitute for traditional religion. In some lodges this threat of death extended to masons' activities in the world and around 1786 one lodge concerned with man's political betterment adopted as its slogan '*Liberté, Egalité – ou la mort.*'

One of the most influential lodges, that of the Nine Sisters, brought together masons distinguished in the arts, sciences and learning. Voltaire was initiated into it during his visit to Paris, supported on one side by Benjamin Franklin – later to become its Grand Master – on the other by that keen Mesmerist, Court de Gébelin. Members included Piccini, Greuze, Bailly, Condorcet, Chamfort, Camille Desmoulins, the abbé Sieyès and Danton.

There were women's lodges also. To join the lodge known as the Mopses a postulant underwent an odd rite: blindfolded, she had to kiss the backside of a little dog. Only at the moment of embrace did she discover that the dog was just a velvet toy. The Mopses divided themselves into four grades: apprentice, companion, mistress and perfect mistress.

The freemasons never conspired to overthrow the Government or society, though they have often been accused of so doing. Freemasonry operated as a disruptive force at quite a different level. It drew men from the mysteries of religion to a purely secular secrecy; it dissipated Christian ideals into deism, pantheism and eventually materialism; it encouraged the belief that man can become perfect by making certain social changes, and that these would best be made outside the Establishment by 'opposition' groups such as the masons.

The second synthetic salt was occultism. The sceptical, pantheist and smiling eighteenth century was also the most credulous of ages. People could not get enough of visionaries and new interpretations of the Bible, all of course extolling the goodness of man, the heights to which he could rise. Two Swedenborgian lodges opened in Paris and two at Toulouse, professing to reveal the esoteric meaning of Scripture. Martinès de Pasqually, the wandering prophet of Mont-pellier, converted hundreds to a cult called Reintegration, while Claude de Saint-Martin taught an illuminism attractive to many. The courtier-poet Boufflers said of Saint-Martin, 'When you listen to him you share his feelings without understanding his ideas.' He meant it as the highest praise.

A lady on the fringes of Antoinette's circle, Eléonore de Sabran, with whom Boufflers was deeply in love, describes a visit in January 1787, to the black, dirty attic of a fortune-teller, 'the favourite of Lucifer and the best informed of his designs'. The fortune-teller's husband happened to be dying in the next room, but the woman was quite unconcerned and this added a shiver of horror to the proceedings. The woman consulted her cards and told her client that the man she loved loved her truly, would make a fortune and marry her. 'Did she speak the truth?' Eléonore asked Boufflers, 'or are you like dreams, that go by contraries?' To make doubly sure, as soon as she left the fortune-teller, she bought a love powder.

Such incidents, taken in isolation, are harmless enough, but multiplied by thousands they reveal a craving for the irrational. How is it that Frenchmen who rejected irrationality in the theatre hungered after it in real life? The answer is that they saw their behaviour not as irrational but, so to speak, as a direct vision of the truth. They felt themselves to be communicating with higher powers, and in the case of illuminists, perfecting themselves. Ultimately occultism was dangerous, for it paved the way for the gullible swallowing of any creed, even a political creed, that offered strong sensations and promised the Ultimate.

The third synthetic salt was futurism: writings in which man, unaided by grace, achieves heaven on earth. Jean Baptiste de Lisle's *The Philosophy of Nature* is a typical example. Voltaire's Deism has been diluted to pantheism; men don't need virtue because they are ignorant of evil; they don't need laws because they all possess 'wise instincts'. It tells us something about this brand of writer that Lisle, in his rooms, displayed his own bust in white marble, inscribed, '*Dieu, l'homme, la nature, il a tout expliqué,*' to which a wit added the line, '*Mais personne avant lui ne l'avait remarqué.*'

The most sustained vision of France in the future is Sébastien Mercier's *The Year 2440*. The King has abdicated freely, after demolishing the Bastille. Versailles is in ruins, 'crushed by its own weight: one man in his impatient pride had tried to bend nature to his will.' France is ruled by a chief magistrate and senate responsible to the States General. Everyone pays 2% income tax, but there is also a chest for free gifts: 'I saw several people with easy, cheerful, contented looks, drop sealed packets into the chest, as in our days they used to drop letters into the post-office.' At the Collège des Quatre Nations 'we teach them little history, because history is the disgrace of humanity, every page being crowded with crimes and follies.' In the Temple of God, which is circular not cruciform, there are no paintings, statues or allegorical figures. An hour's prayer is held there every morning, during which the name of God is repeated a thousand times in different languages: only that, the rest of the time the doors are shut.

Mercier's book is remarkable less for its occasional true prophecies than for its author's conviction that man can and will attain happiness by a definite date. The faith and visionary quality that had once gone into religion are here transferred to social planning. In a similar mood the best of the rising politicians were to bring to their work of reform a blazing and generous idealism.

Mercier, a solid bourgeois, mostly keeps his feet on the ground. Others drifted to cloud-cuckoo-land: for example, the editors of a series of *Voyages Imaginaires, Songes, Visions et Romans Cabalistiques,* 36 volumes published between 1787 and 1789. The first three volumes give an idea of the whole. They are a reprint of *Robinson Crusoe*, but Louis's favourite novel is here accompanied by a tendentious commentary. The philosophy of Crusoe, a matter-of-fact empiricist if ever there was one, consists in 'accepting with docility, though he cannot understand them, the presentiments and stirrings of the heart, for they are promptings given us by pure intelligences which, in a way past comprehension, are in touch with man's spirit!' For good measure the editors add a conclusion to Defoe's novel entitled 'Vision of the angelic world': this declares that man must heed his dreams and act on them, since they are sent by angels.

So many rosy works of this kind appeared that it is often said the shadows in human nature were completely overlooked, or at least not expressed. This is not wholly true. To find the shadows one must turn to the more imaginative authors of philosophical fiction or poetry. For example, in *Le Paysan perverti*, a novel by a writer of peasant origins, Restif de la Bretonne, the stock oh-so-good countryman is set down in Paris, where, however, far from continuing virtuous he becomes totally corrupted by the city's evil influences. In another very popular novel by the same author, *La Découverte australe*, pantheism curdles to blasphemy: 'life is the product of the ineffable copulation of a male God and female Nature;' the devil's existence is firmly denied; true religion is pronounced to be sexual pleasure and celibacy 'a crime on a par with assassination'.

These were warning signs of what might be expected from a major collapse of religious and moral values. But the most revealing of these writings is a long satirical epic by a young Burgundian who later was to become a famous political figure. The author's father died when he was nine; good-looking and gifted, he was made a fuss of by his mother and by the Oratorians who educated him. He repaid their kindnesses by running off with all his mother's silver, an action that cost him six months in prison, from which he emerged convinced that he was a victim of 'tyranny'. A few years later, aged twenty, he published *Organt*, a light, sometimes libertine epic in the style of *Orlando Furioso*, nominally about Charlemagne's war against the Saxons, in fact about France, present and past.

Early in the poem the author imagines himself King of the whole world, and traces his programme. He will raise up the poor, humble the rich, weigh justice in merciful scales. 'I shall have neither guards nor fasces – let Marius announce his presence with terror and the key to tombs! – I shall march without axes, without defence, followed by heartfelt good wishes, not by executioners.' The poet will never make war; he will leave Turk and Huron to worship their own gods, he himself being convinced of the sublime truth that God is nothing more than Wisdom.

There is more in this vein. It is the familiar, goody-goody picture, but soon the mood is shattered, as the author begins to deride aristocrats, priests, nuns and religion generally with a bitterness not only out of key with the poem but astonishing in a youth of twenty. An archbishop makes lewd advances to a Rhine nymph and summons the Devil to help him achieve his goal; a monk lusts after the heroine, is beaten up and stripped of his habit. As the fashionable ladies of the Mopses took pleasure in kissing the backside of a dog, so with sadistic gusto the poet describes the profanation by Saxon troops of a convent of nuns.

But this is as nothing to the attack on Charlemagne and Cuné-gonde, names that hide Louis and Antoinette. The King is a rich, lazy, heavy-drinking fool, his wife sacrifices everything to her lusts, she sucks and then spits out the blood of the people; she is a cruel vulture tearing at the liver of France; their Court is a labyrinth of crimes where the only clues are traces of gold, the nobles' corruption equalled only by the priests'.

One night the King has a terrible dream that his wife is deceiving him. In alarm he decides to wake his confessor and ask him what the dream means. The confessor, who is not alone, hastily reassures the King and gets rid of him, then hurries back to his concubine. The King once more is gulled.

As gaiety and idealism founder in a whirlpool of bitterness, these lines escape the author: 'Man is an animal, like the bear or lion, his characteristics error and foolishness, malice, pride and ambition . . . His heart, compounded of pride and self-interest, fears what it hates and scorns what it loves. It brazenly describes as virtue the muffled crime of pretentious sophism.' In moments of trouble man can count on help from the Devil, and in one startling passage the devils actually get hold of St Peter's key, force their way into heaven and there entrench themselves.

Organt was to be published in 1789. Though it was little read, one day all France would be trembling at the name of its author: the arch-terrorist Antoine de Saint-Just.

Such was the religious or, more correctly, areligious condition of France in the seventeen-eighties. Lack of faith in God had engendered a prodigious faith in man, and in quasi-religious pana-ceas; it had weakened faith not in monarchy but in divine right monarchy. Save among the peasants, there was little churchgoing, yet many a nobleman had his pet theosoph. It was not a healthy state of affairs. A theologian would say that by staying away from Confession and Holy Communion, the French people fell from grace. A psychiatrist would say they failed to exteriorize their failures and failings, which were then allowed to fester; a Jungian that they denied 'the shadow', which would later rear up as an imaginary enemy. A sociologist would say that by failing to gather each Sunday under the same roof with a common aim people lost a sense of community and of loyalty, through their Church, to the Crown. By all accounts some ingredient essential to man's well-being was lacking.

CHAPTER 16

Diamonds

THE years immediately following the end of the American War were particularly happy for the King and Queen. Their third child, a boy, was born in 1785. The harvests of 1784 and 1785 yielded more than enough wheat. Visitors crowded Paris to buy the luxury goods the Court denied itself. New houses were going up and business was good. At last the confidence for which Louis had been striving over the past ten years appeared to have been established, and the stately ceremonial of Versailles to represent a real strength.

In the Marais district of Paris stood a palatial house Louis had never entered. Behind its colonnade were painted rooms crammed with gold plate and Boulle furniture; even its stables were decorated with a masterpiece, Le Lorrain's *Horses of Apollo*. Here lived the Rohans, their motto: 'I cannot be a King, I disdain to be a prince, the name of Rohan shall suffice.' Henri de Rohan had led the Calvinists against Louis XIII, Louis de Rohan had plotted against the Sun King and been beheaded. Now calumny had replaced the sword, but the Rohans were none the less dangerous, and their beautiful house in Paris was an anti-Versailles.

Here, in 1734, was born Louis René Edouard, third child of Hercule de Rohan and his cousin Mademoiselle de Soubise. He grew up to be a pretty fellow with high-bridged nose, rosebud mouth and long-lashed supercilious eyes. His talents were moderate, his ambition high, and to close the gap he relied on his name and wealth.

Rohan entered the Church and at 26 became coadjutor to his uncle, the Archbishop of Strasbourg. In 1771 he was appointed by his rakish friend, the Duc d'Aiguillon, ambassador to Vienna. He entered that city in a specially built coach upholstered in mauve silk, accompanied by twelve footmen, six musicians, five secretaries and his string of fifty thoroughbreds. He gave costly parties, and made friends with everyone, including the Emperor Joseph and the Chancellor, Kaunitz. Everyone, that is, save Maria Theresa.

Maria Theresa disapproved of the new ambassador for the very same reason the Rohans and other great French families disapproved of Antoinette: he flouted convention. Maria Theresa expected a bishop to pray and preach, not to hunt, shoot and cavort with ladies. She particularly disliked the way Rohan seated his 150 dinner guests at intimate tables of six or eight, an innovation she tried – and failed – to stop. One day Rohan's men beat up a Crown official called Gapp, and the Empress put them in prison. 'But their colleagues,' she complained, 'go along to amuse them, and when one of them fell ill Rohan took him home, leaving two others in his place: all this accompanied by intolerable banter, irony and impertinence.'

Rohan conducted his duties in slapdash fashion, failed to foresee the partition of Poland, and then wrote to the Duc d'Aiguillon a letter mentioned earlier: 'I have seen Maria Theresa weeping over the misfortunes of poor oppressed Poland, but she is a past mistress of pretence and can evidently shed tears at will; with one hand she wipes her tears with a handkerchief, with the other she seizes the sword to carve out a third share of the loot.'

Three years passed, and the aged Cardinal de La Roche Aymon died. Louis XV had promised the post of Grand Almoner to Rohan and, on becoming King, Louis XVI had confirmed the appointment. Antoinette, who considered Rohan 'unprincipled and a dangerous intriguer', suggested to Louis that Rohan's younger brother should get the post, and Rohan, who had been relieved of his ambassadorial office, be compensated with a cardinal's hat. But the morning after La Roche Aymon's death, the Comtesse de Marsan had audience of the King. Louis's former governess and a cousin of Rohan was a large, supremely confident lady. Louis told her of his plan to make Rohan a cardinal instead of Grand Almoner.

'No favour,' replied the Comtesse, 'can compensate for the one promised on your Majesty's sacred word of honour. It is the only reward I ask or will accept for the services and care I lavished on your childhood.'

'I cannot fulfil the promise. I have given my word to the Queen.'

'Your Majesty cannot have two words of honour . . . Having made public your word to me, I must also make public that the King has gone back on his word – merely to please the Queen.'

'But would you have me take into my royal household a man distasteful to me and supremely distasteful to the Queen?'

'I pledge myself and all the Rohans to this: if in two years my cousin has not had the good fortune to redeem himself in your eyes and favour, he will resign as Grand Almoner.'

So Louis de Rohan became Grand Almoner, kissed hands with the King, and swore the oath incumbent on officials of the household to inform his Majesty without delay of any suspicious action which might tarnish the good name of the most Christian King or of the Queen. Antoinette shrugged it off, writing to Vienna: 'his new office gives him no dealings with me and he will see the King only at his *lever* and at Mass.'

In 1778 Rohan got his cardinal's hat as well, through the influence of his friend the King of Poland. Now aged 44, with an income of 2½ millions, he divided his time between the Hôtel de Rohan and his episcopal palace near Strasbourg, where he had succeeded his uncle, with occasional visits on feast days to Versailles. As Superior of the Quatre Vingts, a Paris hospital for the blind, he used his own money to help launch an improved building programme. An amateur physicist, he devised a method of extracting saltpetre, an ingredient in gunpowder, from sea-water and tried to interest the Government in the scheme. But his ambition was to become Prime Minister, in the footsteps of Richelieu and Fleury. He saw no hope of winning over the King, but the Queen had a kind heart. Rohan had displeased her by ridiculing the Empress but he felt sure he could win her over.

The Cardinal had a cousin, Princesse de Guéménée, Governess of the Royal Children. He had long been on bad terms with her, but now he made it up and persuaded her to give the Queen a letter. Antoinette read the letter. It was not apologetic – the Rohans never apologized – it was arrogant and asked for an audience. Antoinette acted cautiously: she did not refuse an audience, but each time a date was proposed she had a previous engagement.

In the summer of 1782 Antoinette gave a party in the gardens of Trianon for the Czarevitch Paul. Rohan, who had not been invited, bribed the concierge to let him into the gardens, promising to go there only after the royal family had returned to Versailles. But he broke his promise and entered the gardens at the height of the festivities, partly disguised by a dark frock-coat. The Queen, however, caught sight of a pair of scarlet stockings, became very angry and next day dismissed the concierge. The dismissal had a characteristic sequel. Antoinette's personal maid pointed out that the poor concierge had children, and that he was more sinned against than sinner, and the Queen, touched, reinstated him. None the less, in regard to Rohan she became still more cautious.

For eight years Antoinette addressed not one word to the pushing prelate – a remarkable proof of tenacity. Things might have continued so had not a shady woman entered the Cardinal's life. She had been born Jeanne de Saint-Rémy, the daughter of a poor farmer in the Champagne region who claimed, correctly, to be a direct descendant of King Henri II and therefore the last of the Valois. Jeanne was neglected, went barefoot, minded the cows and often had nothing to eat but the charity soup from the village curé. When her father died leaving her penniless she was taken up by a kindly marquise who had her genealogy authenticated at Versailles. Louis XVI in 1776 awarded an annual pension of 800 livres to this scion of the family which had preceded the Bourbons on the throne of France. He had no obligation so to do: it was an act of kindness.

With her pension as a dowry Jeanne married a soldier of the police militia, Nicolas de La Motte, whom she dubbed Count. She first met the Cardinal when she was twenty-five, a slight woman with white skin, chestnut hair and small breasts, remarkable only for her winning smile and driving will. She told Rohan her hard luck story: wasn't it shameful that a descendant of Henri II should be so neglected by the King? The Cardinal saw this as a useful Court card in that game of poker the Rohans had long been playing with the Bourbons. He said it certainly was shameful, gave her a little money and got La Motte a commission in the Comte d'Artois's bodyguard.

Jeanne and her husband rented two furnished rooms in Paris and two more in Versailles. She wanted to get the Valois estates, but since these had devolved to the Orléans family, was prepared to settle for a sum of money that would allow her to live like a princess of the blood, and to keep a carriage decorated with the royal lilies.

At Versailles distressed gentlefolk were as common as ragwort, and Jeanne met with no success until, one cold December day, in the service quarters of Madame Elisabeth, she fainted. The King's sister heard about the incident, read the petition which Jeanne was clutching when she fainted, and with characteristic kindness had her carried on a stretcher to her lodgings. Left alone, Jeanne summoned her servant. 'If Madame sends for news of me, say I've had a miscarriage and been bled five times.'

Madame Elisabeth twice sent her doctors to see Jeanne, gave her 200 livres and persuaded the King almost to double her pension to

1500 livres. Jeanne then hopefully fainted in the Galerie des Glaces, when the Queen was about to pass. Unfortunately the Queen did not notice, nor did she notice when Jeanne made a show of convulsions under her windows. She then took to sitting down indefinitely in the Finance Minister's office, threatening to stay there until the King gave her money enough to maintain the kind of residence to which, with Valois blood in her veins, she was entitled. Finally she agreed to leave, the richer by 2400 livres. Her debts were mounting and to pay the most pressing she sold her pension for ready cash. To give the impression that honour and riches would soon be hers she hung around the service staircase of the Queen's apartments and told her friends: 'I am the Queen's confidante. She and I are just like this,' and, with a winning smile, she held up two crossed fingers.

Jeanne used to visit Rohan in his beautiful Paris house, known now as the Palais Cardinal. In the intimate chinoiserie salon, where monkeys gambolled on the walls, she listened to Rohan dreaming his dreams aloud. If only he could get into the Queen's graces, he said, his career was made and he would fulfil his ambition of becoming Prime Minister. It occurred to Jeanne that here was an excellent way of getting money. She told Rohan that she had reason to believe the Queen was revising her opinion of the Cardinal. His generous behaviour towards the Prince de Guéménée and other acts of kindness showed, said the Queen, that the Cardinal had a good heart. Jeanne added that she would use her influence to interest the Queen in his career. In May 1784 she persuaded Rohan that the next time he went to Versailles the Queen would show her good will towards him by slightly inclining her head. Rohan, keyed up, thought he saw what he wanted to see. Not once only, but on several occasions it seemed to him that the Queen very, very slightly inclined her head in his direction.

Jeanne meanwhile had taken a lover, a certain Réteaux de Vilette who sang agreeably and wrote a fine hand. On gilt-edged paper embossed with fleurs de lis she caused Vilette to write short notes supposedly from the Queen to her dear cousin, the Comtesse de Valois, in which from time to time Rohan's name was favourably mentioned. These she showed to the delighted Cardinal. Then she told him that the Queen wished him to send her a written justification of his behaviour right back to the fatal letter about the partitioning of Poland. Rohan, completely convinced by Jeanne's winning smile, set to work and after many a rough draft produced a letter that satisfied him. Jeanne promised to deliver it and a few days later handed Rohan a letter on the by now familiar gilt-edged paper embossed with fleurs de lis: 'I am charmed to find that you are not to blame. I cannot yet grant you the audience you desire. When circumstances permit, I shall let you know. Be discreet.'

At Jeanne's suggestion, the Cardinal wrote to express his joy and gratitude, and soon there began a regular exchange of notes.

The Cardinal's gullibility requires an explanation. He had recently fallen under the influence of a Sicilian doctor calling himself Comte de Cagliostro. This man claimed to have been alive under the Pharaohs, and to possess the gift of turning base metals into gold. In a voice 'like a trumpet veiled in crape' he discoursed about the heavens and the stars in their courses, the temples of the Nile, transcendental chemistry, giants and behemoths, and a city in darkest Africa ten times the size of Paris with which he maintained constant touch through numerous correspondents. Cagliostro was virtually Rohan's pet prophet and, when the gilt-edged notes arrived, he announced that they would lead to a change in the Cardinal's fortunes, that soon Rohan would play an important role in the Government and use his influence to ensure the glory of the Supreme Being and the happiness of French masons – for Cagliostro was a mason.

Jeanne was satisfied with the way things were going but she realized that before she could persuade the Cardinal to part with large sums of money he must have some more tangible proof of the Queen's favour. As a theatre-goer Jeanne certainly heard about and probably saw *The Marriage of Figaro*, which had opened in April, a key scene in which shows the Countess Almaviva disguising herself as her maid Suzanne, and representing her at a midnight assignation in the castle gardens with her own husband, the Count. Jeanne decided to adapt this trick to her own needs. She looked around for someone who resembled the Queen and finally found a Palais Royal prostitute with ash-blonde hair, blue eyes and full lips. Jeanne had her to dinner, flashed her winning smile and promised to put the girl in the way of easy money. Obsessed by rank and her own royal blood, Jeanne gave her new prostitute acquaintance the grand name of Baronne d'Oliva, an abbreviated anagram of Valois.

On 10 August Jeanne told the Cardinal that the Queen authorized him to present himself before her the following evening at eleven o'clock in the park of Versailles. It might have been difficult to believe that the Queen of France would give an unattached man an appointment out of doors on a moonless summer night, but so many pamphlets had appeared, some telling how the Queen walked on the terrace and fraternized with strangers, others imputing to her love-affairs with Artois, Coigny and so on, that the Cardinal decided the message was not out of character. He agreed to accompany Jeanne to Versailles, where she would take him to the exact spot for the meeting.

On the evening of the 11th Jeanne and her fellow conspirator drove to Versailles. After a gay dinner at an inn with the apt name of La Belle Image Jeanne instructed the Baronne d'Oliva in her part. She would be approached by a great lord to whom she must give a letter and a rose, saying: 'You know what this means.' Then Jeanne dressed the impostor. A long white dress of frilled lawn like the one Antoinette wore in Madame Vigée Lebrun's much discussed portrait, a wide-brimmed hat with a veil, and the prostitute could fairly pass as the Queen.

At ten o'clock Jeanne and the Baronne met La Motte and Réteaux on the terrace of the palace, to which the public had free access. It was a dark moonless night. After walking on the terrace for a little while Jeanne and her husband led the Baronne d'Oliva down to a grove enclosed by shrubs and trees known as the Bosquet de Vénus. Access was through a leafy labyrinth, and the place was shut away behind a series of overlapping trellises, with, behind, catalpas, tamarisks, tulip trees from Virginia and Judas trees. Then the woman in white was left alone.

A few moments later there came into the grove a tall man in a dark cloak, face hidden by a broad-brimmed hat. This was Rohan. The woman in white became frightened and trembled. Rohan removed his hat, knelt and kissed the hem of her dress. When he got up she handed him the rose, and spoke the words she had been told to speak: 'You know what this means.' As for the letter, she forgot about it and it remained in her pocket.

Before Rohan had time to speak, Jeanne re-entered the grove. She said, 'Come quickly!' while a man who bore a strange resemblance to Réteaux de Vilette hurried up. 'Madame is coming! And the Comtesse d'Artois!' Rohan withdrew, followed by Jeanne.

Later that night, while the Cardinal gazed at the rose secretly given him by the Queen of France, the four conspirators talked over the adventure, which had succeeded as well as could be hoped. They laughed at the idea of the Cardinal kneeling before the Baronne d'Oliva. She had been promised 15,000 livres for her one-night, one-line performance, but Jeanne fobbed her off with 4268 livres.

A few days later Jeanne told the Cardinal that the Queen desired to help a family of distressed gentlefolk with an immediate gift of 50,000 livres. Would he oblige her by giving her that sum by way of her cousin, the Comtesse de La Motte? Rohan treasured his meeting in the Grove of Venus and was having a special box made to hold the rose. Although in debt, he said that of course he would oblige. He turned to a moneylender named Cerf-Berr and eleven days after the meeting in the Grove Jeanne pocketed 50,000 livres. In November she used the same device to pocket a further 100,000, one part of which she used to buy a fine house in her native Champagne, another part to entertain courtiers and to keep up the illusion that she and the Queen were 'just like this'. It was then that another predator struck.

Charles Böhmer of 11 Rue Vendôme, by appointment jeweller to her Majesty, had this in common with Jeanne and the Cardinal: he was a dreamer of grandiose dreams. Böhmer's dream, dating back many years now, was to make and sell the most opulent necklace ever known. He had begun to collect diamonds of the first water, at first a few, then many until at last he had 647 brilliants weighing 2800 carats: twenty times more than the Regent diamond, which the King on state occasions wore in his hat. These he and his associate Bassenge lovingly assembled in a four-tier necklace. First was a choker of seventeen diamonds, five to eight carats each; from this hung a three-wreathed festoon and pendants; then came the necklace proper, a double row of diamonds culminating in an eleven-carat stone; finally, hanging from the necklace four knotted tassels. Böhmer, who came from Saxony, had a heavy taste and the woman he hoped would wear the necklace, Madame Du Barry, liked flashy objects. The necklace, all of fifteen inches deep, was certainly flashy, and also appallingly ugly. Nevertheless, it was a phenomenon, and the price Böhmer asked for it was 1,600,000 livres. But hardly was the necklace ready than Louis XV died and Madame Du Barry left Versailles in disgrace. The future of the necklace depended on the new Queen.

Antoinette liked diamonds but they were not one of her passions. In 1776 she bought a pair of ear-rings for 460,000 livres, paying for them in instalments over six years. Six months later she bought bracelets worth 300,000 livres, but reduced the price by trading in some diamonds in old-fashioned settings. Those were her only two purchases, and she told Böhmer she would make no others.

During the American War Böhmer showed the King his wonderful necklace. Louis took it to his wife and suggested that he give it to her as a present. Antoinette replied that she already possessed some fine diamonds, and that they were worn at Court only four or five times a year. The price asked was too high for a necklace, she said, and, being a good little patriot, she added that the money would be better spent on a ship of the line.

Böhmer tried unsuccessfully to sell his necklace to the King of Spain. Then, a year later, he again offered Louis the necklace, this time on easy terms. The King spoke to Antoinette. She said that he could buy it if he wished as a present for his daughter when the time came for her to marry, but she herself would never wear it, because people would blame her for being extravagant. Louis then told Böhmer that he was firmly decided not to buy the necklace.

Böhmer began to be seriously worried. To make the necklace he had borrowed 800,000 livres from Boudard de Saint-James, official banker to the French Navy, and was finding it difficult to meet interest payments. He obtained an audience of the Queen. A portly man, as soon as he entered the room, he threw himself on his knees at her feet, clasped his hands and began to cry. 'Madame, if you don't buy my necklace I am ruined. I don't want to survive such a terrible misfortune. I'm going at once to throw myself in the river.'

'Stand up, Böhmer,' Antoinette replied in a tone sharp enough to recall him to his senses. 'There is no need for honest men to get down on their knees to plead. If you were to drown yourself I should be sorry but I shouldn't consider myself responsible. I never commissioned you to make the necklace and, what's more, I've repeatedly told you that I would never add a single diamond to those I possess. I refused to buy your necklace for myself; the King offered to buy it for me, and I refused it as a gift. Never mention it again. Break up the necklace and try to sell the diamonds separately – then you will have no occasion to drown yourself.'

Böhmer withdrew disconsolate but he did not follow the Queen's advice. Breaking up the necklace would entail a financial loss but, far worse, it would mean breaking up the dream: the life-work which would perpetuate his name. He let his friends know that he was still determined to sell his masterpiece to the Queen.

On 29 November 1784 Jeanne de La Motte gave a soirée in her apartment in the rue Neuve Saint-Gilles. Here the tone had considerably improved. The furniture was ornate, the service soigné. Her husband played the harp, Réteaux sang, and Jeanne wore some very pretty jewels – all this thanks to the money turned over to her by Cardinal de Rohan. Among the guests that evening was an advocate named Laporte, who knew Böhmer. He said to Jeanne that since she was such a close friend of her Majesty, surely she could help poor Böhmer to sell her his necklace. Jeanne asked if he had seen the necklace. 'Yes,' replied Laporte, 'and it's a marvel.' Jeanne expressed no wish to intervene but her interest had been aroused. She became curious to see the necklace and on 29 December Böhmer's partner Bassenge brought it round to her apartment. As soon as the galaxy of diamonds was spread out before her eyes Jeanne conceived the idea of making them hers.

The Cardinal was away in Alsace. As soon as he returned, Jeanne had an interview with him, during which she convinced him that the Queen desired to buy the necklace without letting the King know and on credit, being for the moment short of money. She would pay for it in three-monthly instalments. She needed an intermediary, well known and highly considered, who could be a firm guarantee to the jewellers in respect of so large a sum, and it was of the Cardinal that she had thought. Jeanne then handed him yet another letter on gilt-edged paper embossed with fleurs de lis, in which the Queen asked the Cardinal to acquire the necklace on her behalf, himself deciding the rates of payment.

Once again this piece of duplicity fell on a mind made receptive by Court gossip and libellous pamphlets. Antoinette had been represented by her enemies as a wild spender, a heavy gambler, despite the fact that for years now she had ceased playing for high stakes; she had been represented as an Austrian agent, acting counter to, and behind the back of the King. In this context Jeanne's story, far from seeming improbable, sounded quite possible, and on 24 January Rohan went to 11 rue Vendôme to inspect the necklace. He found it heavy and ugly, and it surprised him that the Queen with her taste for light, refined objects, should have taken a liking to it.

On 29 January Böhmer and Bassenge came to the Palais Cardinal and agreed on the price: 1,600,000 livres, payable in four six-monthly instalments, the first on 1 August 1785. The necklace would be delivered on 1 February, because, said Jeanne, the Queen wished to wear it on Candlemas Day. The Cardinal himself put this into a written contract, which Böhmer signed and was then handed to Jeanne to take to Versailles. The next day Jeanne came back, saying that the Queen approved the contract but would rather not put her signature to it. The Cardinal, however, insisted, saying that for such an important transaction he must have something in writing. Jeanne again took away the contract. Against each paragraph she got the fair-handed Réteaux de Vilette to write '*approuvé*'. There remained the question of the signature. Jeanne had never seen the Queen's formal signature, which she used only on rare occasions, for example when witnessing a marriage. Jeanne was accustomed to think of herself as Jeanne de France – this was the correct appellation for a daughter of the King, and very grand it sounded – and she now told Vilette to sign the contract 'Marie Antoinette de France'.

On 31 January Jeanne handed the contract to Rohan, saying that the Queen expressly recommended him not to let it out of his hands. Next morning Rohan showed Böhmer the contract, pointing out to him the Queen's signature. As a former ambassador, Rohan should have known that a Queen never signed 'de France' after her official names, but perhaps he was too excited to notice, and it did not strike Böhmer either.

Böhmer handed over the necklace, and that evening the Cardinal drove out to Jeanne's lodgings in Versailles. Then a man arrived, dressed completely in black, who Jeanne said was attached to the Queen's household. He carried a letter in which the Queen instructed the Cardinal to hand over the necklace to the bearer of the letter, who was in fact Réteaux in disguise. The Cardinal did so and returned that night to Paris.

That same night Jeanne took the heavy necklace from its leather case. A royal piece of jewellery had found its rightful place in royal hands: that was how Jeanne saw it, not as the most audacious swindle in French history. Nevertheless, it was incriminating, so she did what the Queen had advised Böhmer to do: broke up the necklace and sold the stones separately. Some of the stones were prised out with a knife by Vilette and sold to a jeweller named Adan at a very low price. The jeweller became suspicious and informed the police. They questioned Vilette but, since to their knowledge no important piece of jewellery had been stolen, he was not arraigned.

Shaken by this, Jeanne sent her husband to London where he sold diamonds 'from a stomacher, a family heirloom' to Robert and William Gray of New Bond Street and Nathaniel Jefferyes of Piccadilly for 240,000 livres. Other diamonds he exchanged for a variety of precious objects, including pearl necklaces, ruby brooches, a silk wallet, snuff-boxes and a pair of tongs for serving asparagus. He returned to Paris in early June, telling his friends that he had had a run of luck at Newmarket races. The Cardinal meanwhile for safety's sake had been hustled off to Alsace with another little gilt-edged note: 'Your absence is necessary in order to afford me the opportunity to make my final preparations for your appointment to that high post to which you rightfully aspire.'

The hour of Jeanne's triumph had nearly arrived. She went to the most expensive shops in Paris and spent lavishly, compensating for her barefoot hungry childhood with draperies and carpets from Tessier, bronze statues from Chevalier, marbles from Adam, crystal glassware from Sikes. These were taken in forty-two waggons to her big new house in Bar-sur-Aube. Jeanne followed in a pearl-grey berlin, its doors painted with the Valois coat of arms and the device: 'From my forebear the King I possess the blood, the name and the lilies.'

Cagliostro, meanwhile, was keeping the Cardinal's hopes aloft. He obtained communications for him from the Invisible by means of an innocent young girl, born under the right star, whom he called 'a dove'. One night he arranged for 'the dove' to come to the Palais Cardinal, where he decked her out in a long white and silver chemise with a big sun in the centre, and round her waist a blue sash. Cagliostro led her into the Cardinal's candlelit bedroom, in which stood a table. On the table was a carafe of water surrounded by cut-out paper stars and figures of Isis and the bull Apis. Cagliostro stood behind a screen. After making passes with his sword, he told the girl to look into the carafe of water. 'Do you see there a woman in white?' The girl answered yes. 'Does she look like the Queen?' Again the girl answered yes. Cagliostro then made her repeat invocations to the Great Cophta and the angel Gabriel. 'Look into the water. Tell me if you do not see the Cardinal on his knees, holding a snuff-box in which there is a coin.' The girl gazed into the carafe and finally said she did see that scene, whereupon the Cardinal in a paroxysm of joy went down on his knees, wept and raised his eyes to heaven.

The first of August drew nearer, fatal date when the jewellers must be paid 400,000 livres, the first instalment on the necklace. Jeanne saw the Cardinal in Paris in early July. He showed surprise and even the beginnings of suspicion because the Queen had not yet been seen wearing the necklace. Jeanne had a ready answer. The Queen, she said, found the price too high and wanted a reduction of 200,000 livres, otherwise she would return the necklace. Rohan understood then that the Queen did not wish to wear the necklace because she did not yet consider it her property. On 10 July he saw Böhmer and Bassenge who, after much resistance, at last consented to the reduction asked for. The Cardinal also suggested that they write to thank the Queen for her kindness in buying the necklace. Bassenge drafted a banal little note which the Cardinal reworded, adding a last elegant phrase of his own invention.

On 12 July Antoinette was returning from the chapel of Versailles, where she had just heard Mass. Böhmer, who had come to the palace that day in order to deliver a baptismal present which the King had ordered for his nephew, approached the Queen and handed her a note. When she got back to her apartment, this is what she read:

Madame,

We are at the pinnacle of happiness in daring to think that the latest arrangements proposed to us, which we accepted with zeal and respect, afford new proof of our submission and devotion to your Majesty's orders, and we take real satisfaction in thinking that the most beautiful set of diamonds in the world will adorn the greatest and best of queens.

Antoinette could not make head or tail of this note. She assumed that Böhmer, who had once threatened suicide, had now gone slightly mad. A lighted candle stood on her desk for melting the red wax with which she sealed letters. 'This isn't worth keeping,' she said and put the note in the flame.

On the eve of the fatal first of August Jeanne sent the Cardinal a note telling him that the Queen could not pay the 400,000 livres until 1st October. He hurried to the jewellers who were already suspicious at having received no acknowledgment of their note from the Queen. They refused to wait any longer. Jeanne realized that the truth was bound to come out. She sent a messenger to tell the jewellers that they had been taken in by a forged signature; then, instead of leaving France, she went quickly to Bar-sur-Aube, leaving the Cardinal to extricate himself from the mess. She believed that rather than appear in the ridiculous role of dupe he would pay the jewellers for the necklace and hush up the affair.

On 5 August Böhmer went direct to Versailles and although he could not see the Queen he spoke to her maid, Madame Campan. A short exchange made clear what had happened. Madame Campan told Antoinette that forged letters bearing her signature had been circulating in Paris, and that somehow the Cardinal had been involved in acquiring a necklace on her behalf.

Antoinette at once realized the seriousness of the affair and sent a special messenger to summon Böhmer to Versailles. Questioning him, she learned how the jeweller had sold the necklace to Rohan acting, he understood, as her agent. Antoinette was astonished and also frightened. She ordered Böhmer to give her a report in writing. As soon as this reached her, on the 12th, she showed it to Louis Auguste de Breteuil, Minister of the Household, equivalent to Home Secretary. A burly ex-ambassador of 55 with a booming voice, Breteuil was strong, honest and efficient. He too took a serious view of the matter, and that same day Antoinette spoke about the fraud to Louis.

Antoinette as yet had none of the details, but she knew enough to be furious with Rohan. She felt sure, as she later wrote to Joseph, that 'the Cardinal has used my name like a vile and clumsy counterfeiter. The probability is that, temporarily pressed for money, he would be able to pay the jewellers the first instalment without anyone's ever discovering the fraud.'

Louis too was very angry. But before taking action he wanted to get further details about the contract. He decided to send for the Cardinal's kinsman, the Prince de Soubise, and to order him to speak to the Cardinal about the contract and learn what he had to say about it. But Soubise happened to be away from Versailles on the 14th, when the King sent for him. Louis and Antoinette then chose what in the circumstances was an extremely mild course: to summon the Cardinal next day, confront him with the evidence and hear what he had to say.

The fifteenth of August was the most important holiday in France, Feast of the Assumption and also the Queen's name day. Earlier than usual, without waiting for her hair to be arranged, Antoinette joined her husband in his private study, where the two Ministers concerned, Breteuil and the Keeper of the Seals, Miromesnil, were waiting. Presently the Cardinal arrived, robed for High Mass, to which he expected to accompany the King, over his scarlet soutane a petit-point alb decorated with medallions bearing the Rohan arms and device, a garment valued at over 10,000 livres.

Louis handed the Cardinal Böhmer's report and told him to read it. Having done so, the Cardinal admitted that the facts in the report were true.

'Haven't you anything to say to justify your conduct?' Seeing the Cardinal look agitated, he added, 'Calm yourself. Go into my room. Write down what you have to tell me.'

The report Rohan handed the King a quarter of an hour later was as confused as could be. One thing was clear. A woman called de Valois had persuaded him that the necklace was to be acquired for the Queen, and that woman had deceived him.

'Where is this woman?'

'Sire, I do not know.'

'Have you the necklace?'

'It is in the hands of that woman.'

Two courses were open to Louis. He could leave the Cardinal at liberty and while probing the affair risk seeing him leave the country, or he could have him taken into custody.

'I beseech your Majesty, out of consideration for my family, to hush up the affair.'

'I cannot,' said Louis, 'either as King or as husband.'

Antoinette then spoke. How, she asked Rohan, could he have believed that she would have chosen him for such a commission, she who had not so much as addressed a word to him since his return from Vienna?

The Cardinal answered with a knowing look. The Queen – didn't she remember? – had made certain signs to him with her head, and he gave a demonstration. Antoinette felt a mixture of fear, surprise and anger; for a moment she thought she was going to faint. Louis, angered by something disrespectful in the Cardinal's glance, and concerned for Antoinette, said to Rohan, 'That is enough. Leave the room.' Then he ordered Breteuil to arrest the Cardinal and seize all his papers.

Breteuil entered the Œil de Bœuf and discreetly told the Cardinal that the King had ordered his arrest. The Cardinal should have halted; instead, he continued walking. 'Not here,' he whispered. 'Can't you keep me in custody as we walk?' Rohan then turned into the Hall of Mirrors, that day crowded with people come to pay their court. Breteuil had good reason to fear that the Cardinal would slip away and be lost in the crowd, so he summoned a young exempt of the Bodyguard. 'By the King's order, arrest Monsieur le Cardinal.' The exempt immediately strode up to Rohan, and escorted him straight to his room.

The first act of the drama was over. Antoinette confided to Joseph: 'I have been really touched by the good sense and firmness the King showed in that arduous meeting.' She added the hope 'that this horror and all its details may be brought to light for everyone to see.'

This hope was to be granted only in part. The Cardinal was a silly man, but he possessed a sense of honour. On being escorted to his room, his first thought had been not of himself but of the gilt-edged letters written to him, as he still supposed, by the Queen. When they were discovered, they would prove his innocence but they would compromise the Queen. So Rohan scribbled a note to his secretary, ordering him to burn all the papers in a certain red portfolio. The consequence of this auto-da-fé was, however, just the opposite of what Rohan hoped. The letters with their obviously forged signatures would have exonerated the Queen at once; while their destruction was to leave the way clear for Jeanne de La Motte to deny having written them, and for a hundred ill-natured theories to be propounded by the Queen's enemies.

'Monsieur de Launay, I am writing to tell you to receive in my castle of the Bastille my cousin Cardinal de Rohan and to keep him there until further order from me.' So wrote Louis. The Bastille was now equivalent to a good Paris hotel, Launay its kindly manager. Rohan was allowed two of his personal valets to serve him, received daily visits from his family and legal staff, and one day served oysters and champagne to twenty guests.

Louis, in theory, could do what he liked with the Cardinal, since all justice flowed from him, as King. He believed the Cardinal to be guilty of fraud – the terms of the sale contract were written entirely in the Cardinal's hand – and knew that a public revelation of that fact would forever sully the name of Rohan. Out of consideration for the Rohans, then, he offered the Cardinal a choice: either to throw himself on the King's mercy, or to have his case judged by Parlement. The Cardinal, who knew himself to be innocent and who had caused to be burned not only all the gilt-edged notes but the contract too, chose to appear before Parlement. On 5 September Louis signed the necessary letters patent: 'Not without righteous indignation have we been able to contemplate such an unheard-of temerity, such an audacious effort to trade on an august name (a name dear to us on so many counts), such a daring violation of the respect due to the royal majesty.'

At first public opinion in Paris blamed the Cardinal. With each new woman in the case, the Parisians said 'Another of the Cardinal's mistresses,' and there were caricatures of Rohan, a money-box in each hand, captioned: 'The almoner begs alms to pay his debts.' But the Rohans set up loud cries of indignation, calling the arrest an act of despotism, while the clergy, then in assembly, protested that a bishop could be tried only by his fellow-bishops. The nobles of course rallied to Rohan, and whispered that a Frenchman of ancient birth had been arrested on the whim of a foreign queen. Soon public opinion veered round, as Fersen reported on 9 September to King Gustavus:

> The most popular theory is that it was all an intrigue between the Queen and the Cardinal; that she pretended to dislike him, the better to conceal their little game; that actually he was very much in her good graces and that she did commission him to arrange the necklace purchase for her; that the Cardinal informed her of what took place at Council meetings, which she passed on to the Emperor . . . ; that the King finally heard about it and made a scene, whereupon she pretended to faint away, claiming the excuse of pregnancy.

Antoinette took this shift of opinion very much to heart. With exceptional force of character she had refrained from addressing a word to the Cardinal for eight years and now people suspected her of having been his mistress. She felt suddenly insecure and, partly in pique, partly to reassure herself, decided to make an expensive purchase. In October she would be leaving for Fontainebleau. The year before, being pregnant, she had gone by river, in a boat lent by the Duc d'Orléans. This year she decided to go by river again, and ordered, at a cost of 100,000 livres, a sumptuous yacht, furnished with mahogany and marbles, and gilded carving. On 10 October, from the top of the tower, the prisoners in the Bastille could see her embark on her expensive new acquisition. Even the abbé de Véri criticized the Queen's untimely piece of extravagance.

Public opinion continued to harden against the Queen. For example, the Pope, much to Louis's annoyance, demanded that Rohan should be tried in Rome by his fellow-Cardinals, and when Louis firmly rejected the demand, temporarily relieved Rohan of his rights as cardinal. According to Véri, the public believed that the Queen had urged this course on the Pope, and 'the Cardinal is taking on the colour of a persecuted innocent.'

The Cagliostros, husband and wife, were charged with conniving in the swindle and sent to prison. Cagliostro protested that he had no misdeed on his conscience unless it were the assassination of Pompey, when however he had acted on orders from the Pharaoh. He further protested at not being allowed to see his wife, a hefty blacksmith's daughter named Lorenza but whom Cagliostro called Serafina. In a letter to Parlement, subsequently printed, he spoke of 'an illness which presently threatens her life. Will she be allowed to perish without even the benefit of her husband's healing arts?' Launay replied: 'The lady in question is not ill at all. She takes her walks daily – is out walking this moment on the platform of the tower. She did suffer a slight sprain to her left wrist some two weeks ago, but even that was so minor an accident as not to have kept her from her embroidery.' Nevertheless public opinion obtained Serafina's release on 18 March, and it became all the rage to flock to the rue Saint-Claude to pay one's respects to Madame Cagliostro. 'It is not unusual on any one night to see the names of 300-odd visitors inscribed on the register at her porter's lodge.'

Criminal procedure, like so much in France, was a mixture of Gothic obscurity and lachrymose humanitarianism. The defendant had to face the examining magistrates alone, without benefit of legal counsel, in utmost secrecy. Only when the examining magistrates had concluded their enquiry did defence counsel gain access to the facts and evidence. But counsel could then publish for his client one or more highly emotional defence pleas, the purpose of which was to stir up public sympathy for the defendant. In theory secret, a criminal trial was as public as the King's Sunday dinner.

Rohan engaged the best lawyer in France, Target, and during the preliminary examination wrote him invisible-ink letters. In one he speaks of Jeanne: 'That wicked woman created quite a scene today with Count Cagliostro, hurling a candelabra at his midriff when he called her a "damned cheat". But retribution was swift, for in doing so she struck herself in the eye with a candle. I am to be confronted with her tomorrow, but I will answer for it that she will dare throw nothing at me.'

Among the witnesses called by the Prosecutor General was Madame Du Barry, from whom Jeanne had solicited money. Her appearance provided a welcome lull in the sordid story. 'Your age?' asked the examining magistrate.

'Now really, messieurs, since when do gallant gentlemen ask a pretty woman her age?'

'If Madame declines to state her age, we have no choice but to record it as fifty.'

'Why not sixty? That would add some fun to the proceedings.'

Midway through the interrogations Antoinette wrote to her brother: 'Writs have been issued for the charlatan Cagliostro and his wife, for the La Motte woman and for a streetwalker named Oliva. What company for a Grand Almoner of France, a cardinal of the house of Rohan!' But the Paris public did not see it like that at all. The most astonishing thing about the astonishing necklace affair is not the dream-worlds of Rohan, Jeanne de La Motte and Cagliostro, nor the swindle itself, but the dream-interpretation put on events by the people of Paris. They literally turned every fact upside down in order to be able to sympathize with the accused. When the defence pleas were published, they became best-sellers: that of Oliva, for instance, sold 20,000 copies, and engravings of the poor innocent girl were in hot demand, particularly after she had given birth, in the Bastille, to an illegitimate son. Jeanne de La Motte was believed when she tenaciously maintained that the Queen ordered the necklace in order to encompass the Cardinal's destruction. As for Rohan, he became a popular hero and gave his name to the fashionable hat in spring 1785, 'Cardinal in the straw': it was shaped like a cardinal's hat, with long red ribbons, but its brim was of straw, symbolic of straw bedding in the Bastille. The straw, of course, was non-existent; in fact Jeanne de La Motte slept on a feather-bed.

On 22 May 1785 sixty-four members of Parlement's Grand' Chambre and Tournelle assembled in the Great Hall of the Palais de Justice, its pepper-pot towers overlooking the Seine, in order to begin examination of the evidence. Sympathies were fairly evenly divided. The President, d'Aligre, was favourable to the King and Queen, the Advocate General, Séguier, neutral. Opposition was led by a small, fat, highly emotional lawyer of thirty-nine named Jean Jacques Duval d'Eprémesnil, who had written a book on Nostradamus, was a confirmed Mesmerist and conducted his private life on the advice of Cagliostro. D'Eprémesnil had already led the public outcry that secured Serafina Cagliostro's release, and was naturally favourable to Cagliostro's friend and patron the Cardinal. He took notes of all that was said and done throughout the proceedings and, though this was illegal, transmitted it to the Cardinal's lawyers, who were able to design a plan of conduct for him to follow in his appearance before the Court.

On 30 May Rohan and the other accused appeared in the Great Hall. Rohan denied the prosecution's charges that he had recognized the Queen's signature on the contract to be forged, and that he had been guilty of negligence in not consulting the King and Queen before purchasing the necklace. He had, he said, just been a dupe of Jeanne de La Motte. As he explained to a friend: 'I employed all the resources of my intelligence to prove that I am an ass.'

Parlement believed him. Rohan had been a dupe. But had he been a culpable dupe? On becoming Grand Almoner, Rohan had sworn to inform the King of any suspicious action which might tarnish the good name of the King or Queen. In the present instance he had failed to honour his oath and so, while Rohan's supporters urged an unreserved acquittal, the Prosecutor General demanded a reprimand for Rohan's 'lack of respect for the Queen's sacred majesty'.

The question turned in effect on Antoinette's character. We know her to have been a woman of principle who would never have stooped to subterfuge. But Rohan had never got to know Antoinette – she herself had seen to that – so all he had to go on was the courtiers' 'image' of the Queen: tittle-tattle about political favourites, lovers and underhand action behind the King's back.

If Parlement had had a true picture of Antoinette's character, they would probably have found Rohan guilty of *lèse majesté* and administered a reprimand. But Parlement, traditionally hostile to the Crown, preferred, like Rohan, to adopt the courtiers' image of the Queen; once they had done that, it followed that Rohan had no grounds for being suspicious of the transaction or for informing the King. On the evening of 31 May, after eighteen hours' deliberation, by twenty-six votes to twenty-three with fifteen abstentions, Parlement unreservedly acquitted Cardinal de Rohan of all charges against him.

While a crowd of 10,000 shouting 'Long live Parlement!' escorted the Cardinal to his house and called him to appear on the balcony, Antoinette broke down and wept. 'The Queen's distress at the outcome of the trial was greater than seemed reasonably justified by the cause,' wrote Mercy to Vienna. But Antoinette saw what Mercy failed to see: by acquitting the Cardinal, Parlement was declaring that the Queen's private life was not above reproach. In the eyes of the French people she was compromised.

Louis was very angry at the Cardinal's acquittal. He felt sure Rohan had known the signature 'Marie Antoinette de France' was a forgery, and had acted throughout in the hope of getting money to pay the family debts. Two courses were open: either he could meekly accept Parlement's verdict and treat Rohan as completely innocent or he could protest against it, and against its implied slur on the Queen, by dismissing the Cardinal. He chose the second course.

Breteuil had come under very heavy attack for arresting the Cardinal in so public a place as the Hall of Mirrors, though in fact he could scarcely have acted otherwise, and as with Turgot and Saint-Germain, the attacks brought on gout. On 1 June he had to be carried in a sedan chair to deliver in person Louis's *lettre de cachet*, ordering Rohan to resign as Grand Almoner and retire to his abbey of La Chaise. 'Indignation,' writes another Minister, 'at the monarchy's punitive measures against the Cardinal was widespread and outspoken. Cries of "Tyranny!" went up from every rank of society, directed primarily against the Queen.'

Louis was not deterred by this outcry from taking action against Cagliostro also. He had emerged from the trial as quite clearly a charlatan, and dangerous too, his Masonic apron being embroidered L.P.D., standing for '*Lilia pedibus deride* – Trample the lilies under-foot.' Louis wrote to Breteuil: 'You will order Cagliostro to be out of my city of Paris in eight days' time, and out of my kingdom of France within three weeks. You may show him this letter bearing my seal.'

The Sicilian's very considerable vanity was deeply hurt and from London he wrote a 'Letter to the French people' which proved damaging to the monarchy: 'I have been hunted like a criminal from France. A *lettre de cachet* of the King has banished me, although the King has never heard my case; an unworthy Minister wielded that dread instrument of royal power.

'The question has been asked of me whether I would return to France if the King's exile order were to be rescinded. "Assuredly yes," I replied, "on one condition – that the Bastille, where I languished for six interminable months, be razed to the ground and a public promenade erected on its ruins." '

Jeanne de La Motte was condemned to be branded with a 'V' for *voleuse* and imprisoned in the Salpetrière for life. The Duchesse d'Orléans initiated a public collection on her behalf, while day after day carriages were waiting outside the prison with so many highly placed well-wishers it is not surprising that she escaped two years later to England. There she took revenge on the Queen by publishing her *Memoirs*, 3000 copies in English, 5000 in French.

'With my dying breath,' wrote Jeanne de La Motte, 'I will main-tain that illicit relations existed between the Cardinal and the Queen

. . . His Eminence found it strenuous to live up to the amatory standards of his royal paramour and made arch admission that he resorted to a variety of stimulants, first fortifying himself with a dose of Cagliostro's famous aphrodisiac, then stimulating himself further by a visit to the love-nest he maintained in Passy.'

Even more damaging to the King and Queen were the witty songs which originated in Paris during and after the trial. Hundreds of them circulated and the police were powerless to catch their authors, fly-by-night journalists. In one song the Queen reprimanded the prostitute Oliva:

> *Vile donzelle; il te sied bien*
> *De jouer mon rôle de reine!*
> *– Point de courroux, ma souveraine,*
> *Vous faites si souvent le mien.*[1]

In another, '*Fureurs utérines de Marie Antoinette*', the Cardinal is the real father of the Queen's latest child:

> *Toinette des Bourbons augmente la famille;*
> *Ce commerce à Louis est à peu près égal:*
> *Mais nous qui nourissons et père, et mère, et fille*
> *Pouvons nous écrier avec le cardinal*
> *Que les reines catins ont toujours fait du mal.*[2]

The most audacious libel was perpetrated by friends of Rohan. They contrived to smuggle a new die into the royal mint of Strasbourg, and in 1785 the mint began to issue gold louis d'or with the King's head on the obverse, similar to other louis d'or save in one respect: from the head of Louis XVI sprang a cuckold's horns.

The necklace affair as well as saddening Louis and Antoinette personally did great harm to the monarchy. In ordering the arrest and imprisonment of a man subsequently declared innocent, and later in rusticating him, Louis – or rather his Ministers, for Louis himself remained a popular figure – were held to have acted despotically; *lettres de cachet* and the Bastille became hated signs of that despotism. The grande noblesse became more hostile than ever,

---

[1]'Harlot, you dare to take my role
And flaunt yourself as a queen,'
'Do not be angry, Majesty;
For you mine was not too mean.'

[2]Toinette adds children to the Bourbon family; Louis hardly cares a fig; but we who feed father, mother and daughter declare with the Cardinal that sluttish queens have always been up to dirty tricks.

while the belief that the Queen had connived with the Cardinal, then stamped on him, weakened the average Frenchman's respect for the crown.

For Louis and Antoinette the end of the trial marked the close of the two and a half years of happiness which followed the American War. Louis must have realized the harsh truth lying at the heart of the necklace affair: that uneducated people deduce from any given event what they wish to deduce; the facts count for less than the climate of opinion. It became imperative therefore to win over that opinion by continuing speedily to work for the happiness of his people. As for Antoinette, when Böhmer's note had arrived, she had been learning her part for Beaumarchais's *Barber of Seville*, but she was no longer in the mood for comedy, and she stopped the private theatricals at Trianon. As Madame Campan says, 'It was farewell forever to those brilliant fêtes and galas which served as showcase for all the glittering splendour, the sparkling wit, the exquisite good taste of French court life.'

CHAPTER 17

An Ace is Trumped

EVERY New Year's Day Louis was accustomed to balance his books and personally take stock. On that day in 1786 he was aged thirty-one and had ruled France for eleven years. He had three children: Madame Royale (Mousseline la sérieuse), aged seven; the Dauphin, four, and the Duc de Normandie, nine months; and Antoinette was expecting a fourth child. He continued to divide his time mainly between State affairs, Court functions, his family, hunting and reading. He was giving more time to charity, attending for example a gym display by blind children, and the evenings to his friends. After each party of faro or intimate supper, he would take a playing card and on it record the date and the names of his twenty or so guests.

In autumn he moved to Fontainebleau for the hunting he so much enjoyed. In the interests of economy only a few courtiers now received lodging, and the rest stayed away, so it was usually a small gathering. Madame de Staël, Necker's daughter, was one of those involved and gives a revealing glimpse of Court values: 'It is amusing to hear courtiers say, when the King does not hunt or go to the theatre: "His Majesty is doing nothing today," by which they mean that he is working all evening with his Ministers.'

When he came to assess the state of France, Louis could feel he had accomplished much. He had ended the *corvée* in most provinces, improved communications, hospitals and prisons and effected more humanitarian legislation than any of his predecessors. He was fast building up manufacturing. In September 1786 Calonne signed a commercial treaty with England, which lowered tariffs on French wines and luxury products in England, and on English goods, mainly textiles, in France. Though for the moment it caused problems, competition would in the long run make overprotected French workshops more efficient.

Louis, however, was not content to rest there. In his persevering way he wished to extend to all France the provincial assemblies he had already established in three provinces, to end the *corvée* altogether, and to reduce internal customs barriers. Above all, he wished to make taxation more equal. Income tax at around 10%, known as the *vingtième*, was unevenly levied, so that some nobles and all the clergy were exempt, while others paid less than they should. Louis intended to rename the tax *subvention territoriale* and, he wrote, 'to levy it with the utmost equality on all householders without exception'. This was such a sweeping reform that Malesherbes, who came back into the Government in 1787, called it 'the King's revolution'.

Equal taxation was conceived as an act of justice, but Louis saw that it could also set the finances in order. Inflation was now gathering pace. It forced up basic Government expenditure and made it necessary to tax more at a time when people were finding it difficult to make ends meet. It was Louis's tragedy that he had to face the very grave problem of inflation which others, including Necker, had avoided.

Louis's own spending accounted for only 6% of State expenditure, interest on the national debt, much of it incurred in the American War, for 49%. Louis believed the limits of borrowing had been reached – Calonne, raising 80 millions in 1786, had to pay the very high rate of 9% – and he wanted to have done with anticipating. The new tax structure plus a growth in industry would permit that.

Knowing that Parlement would balk at these measures, Louis astutely decided to win public opinion by calling, as Henri IV had done, an assembly of notable Frenchmen to discuss and comment on his plans. He chose 144 altogether, ranging from princes and dukes to bishops and mayors. The day he announced the assembly Louis told Calonne, 'I could not sleep last night I was so pleased.'

Louis opened the assembly at Versailles on 22 February 1787. 'Gentlemen,' he said, 'I have chosen and assembled you, following the example of the head of my branch of the family, whose memory you love. My plans are far-reaching and important. I intend to relieve the people, increase tax revenue and diminish obstacles to trade. I have decided on these measures because I see that they are necessary; but I shall listen to, and ponder, your comments on them.'

Calonne then explained the new land tax which, payable in kind, would amount to between $2\frac{1}{2}\%$ and 5% of income, depending on the richness of the soil, and stated the budget deficit, 112 millions. Calonne had a good presence, a musical voice and, unlike Turgot and Necker, spoke the tactful language of polite society. He had most of the Court behind him and Louis felt confident of success.

The notables divided into seven sections, each presided over by a prince of the blood. On provincial assemblies, they disapproved of Louis's plan to make commoners, nobles and clergy sit together and vote by heads; they wished nobles and clergy to sit apart, and a vote by orders, which would always assure them a majority over the commons.

On taxation, the notables were more accommodating. Eighteen out of 22 in Artois's section, for example, approved equality of taxation. But they and their like were hard hit by a rise in their cost of living between 1736/41 and 1785/9 of 62%: Rohan's penury and the Prince de Guéménée's bankruptcy were not isolated events, even Choiseul was 14 million livres in debt and had to sell his town house. So the notables, while agreeing in principle to equality, criticized this particular way of going about it. 'Sire,' they said in effect, 'make us poor but not yet.'

Opposition came mainly from the fourteen bishops, led by Loménie de Brienne, Archbishop of Toulouse, who wanted to replace Calonne. 'Equality is all very well,' said Brienne, 'in Republics or in Philadelphia . . . but in France all assemblies must be presided over by the clergy.' Archbishop Dillon of Narbonne attacked any idea of taxing the clergy: 'M. de Calonne again wishes to bleed France, and is merely asking us whether to make the incision on the feet, the arms or the jugular vein.'

The clergy's opposition set the tone, and soon the notables were enjoying themselves charging Calonne with mismanagement and overspending. The Press took up their cry and headlined not the basic fact that most people would pay less but that the total would be more. A fashionable embroidered waistcoat showed Louis enthroned amid the notables; his left hand holds a sign announcing 'The golden age', while his right hand is dipping into the waistcoat pocket.

After four weeks the notables were still maliciously criticizing the proposed reforms and challenging Calonne's administration on points of detail. Calonne was half-killed, even working in his carriage and at home, sitting up late by candlelight checking figures, his feet in hot water. At last, in exasperation, Calonne decided to appeal to the people. After all, La Fayette had written to George Washington on 13 January: 'The King and his Minister deserve our thanks, and I hope that gratitude and good will reward this measure in favour of the people.'

Calonne therefore published a pamphlet explaining clearly the good points of his land tax: 'More money will be paid to the Government, it is true, but who will pay it? Only those who haven't been paying enough.'

One would expect the pamphlet to have been greeted with enthusiastic cheers. Not at all. The silence was deafening. No one raised a voice in favour of the King's great reforming measure.

Why? The answer is to be found in France's moral and spiritual mood, which has already been examined, and in a tendency to think only of rights, not duties, noticed a few years earlier by Véri. Having made the point that Frenchmen were far better off than in his boyhood, Véri remarks that no one would think so. 'Everyone's mouth is full of complaints . . . From the throne down to the shepherd's crook there are whines. Man is not what the philosophers say he is, a reasonable animal, but a complaining animal.'

So the people and press failed to rise to Calonne's pamphlet. No one wished to believe that the Government intended to help the have-nots. That would have run counter to the growing view that all monarchy tends to despotism. Much worse, the notables, led by the clergy, took the pamphlet as a personal insult. Archbishop Dillon found a curious term of abuse, calling it 'a seditious appeal to the people', while the moderate Duc de Nivernais, whom Louis esteemed and was soon to take into the Government, said 'Monsieur de Calonne must have gone off his head.' They began to step up their attacks. On 31 March Brienne's friend the Bishop of Langres 'declaimed a long diatribe on stock-jobbing: right off the subject in hand, and plainly an indirect attack on the Controller General's administration.'

It was a central article of Louis's political creed that the three orders must work in harmony. So he would have disapproved anyway of Calonne's pamphlet, and when the pamphlet alienated nearly every one of the notables, he saw that Calonne had ruined his chances. If the reforms were to be saved, Calonne must go.

During the Holy Week recess Louis received a memorandum from Brienne approving the land tax in principle, but suggesting certain modifications: for example, it should be collected in cash, not in kind, which would have entailed expensive building of storage barns. Brienne made clear that the clergy would co-operate in the King's reforms if he were to replace Calonne.

Brienne was a smooth, respected bishop-administrator, sixty years old, liberal to the point of agnosticism, who had opened his fine library to the people of Toulouse and built a canal linking the canal du Midi to the Garonne that still bears his name. Turgot had said, 'I'll be consoled for my disgrace if the Archbishop of Toulouse some day fills my post.' Louis, who disliked worldly prelates, had prevented Brienne getting the see of Paris: 'The Archbishop of Paris must at least believe in God;' moreover, Brienne was delicate and suffered from eczema. However, in the circumstances he was the obvious man for the job. Louis dismissed Calonne and on 30 April appointed Brienne to head the Council of Finances.

Calonne was burned in effigy outside Parlement and hounded from France. It was an undeserved fate but what mattered to Louis was the disrepute into which his imprudence had brought the Government. When Madame de Chabannes, one of Calonne's lady friends, sought permission to join Calonne in England, Louis said crossly to Breteuil, 'Tell her to get stuffed!' whereupon Breteuil murmured, 'Very good, sire. I shall tell her that your Majesty approves her request.'

With Brienne's appointment opposition in the notables lessened, though La Fayette, belying his letter, did all he could to embarrass the Government by calling for a committee of ordinary Frenchmen to control State spending. Again, lip-service was paid to equality of taxation, but only one of the seven sections, that presided over by Monsieur, actually approved the new land tax. Louis dissolved the notables on 25 May, and that summer presented his package to Parlement. This would be the real test.

Parlement, reflecting public opinion, was now in a highly critical mood. Several of its leading members were ardent Mesmerists, and around the magnetic tubs where Dr Mesmer achieved with his wand cures denied to the medical authorities they dreamed up equivalent political remedies. Duval d'Eprémesnil made it his aim in life to 'debourbonize' France: an advocate of tolerance, he was none too tolerant where his own beliefs were concerned and he tried unsuccessfully to move heaven and earth, including Louis, to ban *Les Docteurs modernes*, a skit on Mesmerism.

Another Mesmerist Parlementaire was Adrien Duport, twenty-eight years old, a cold man who made short, cutting speeches and wished to give power to the bourgeoisie, guided by the liberal nobility. Duport held meetings in his Paris house of a group of thirty influential friends, through whom he kept in touch and in some respects directed anti-Government circles throughout France. A third influential Mesmerist was a lawyer named Bergasse; financed by the rich banker Kornmann, he presided over a secret society which, under guise of magnetic experiments, subsidized Brissot, Carra and other journalists to write pamphlets against the Government.

Louis's package consisted of the provincial assemblies – modified in deference to the notables' criticism so that the presidency was shared between the nobility and clergy, but with the commons providing half the total members – the ending of the *corvée*, the lifting of remaining barriers to a completely free corn trade and the land tax, which Brienne had reduced to 80 millions, making up the amount of the reduction by quadrupling the stamp tax on contracts and patents.

Parlement approved the first three measures but in a stormy seven-hour session, led by d'Eprémesnil and Duport, rejected the stamp tax. Only Monsieur and Artois, whom Louis had won over to his reforms, voted in favour of the stamp tax, with one other member. On 30 July Parlement also rejected the land tax. When d'Aligre and the two High Court presidents brought him Parlement's objections, 'the King, standing in front of his chimney-piece, said angrily: "I shall let you know my decisions;" then, turning his back on them, went into the next room, slamming the door.' Four days later Louis summoned Parlement to a *lit de justice* and obliged them to register this land tax.

Again, it might be thought that this extraordinarily liberal measure would have delighted the ordinary citizen. But no. 'Carica-tures, placards, bons mots,' wrote Jefferson to Adams, 'have been indulged in by all ranks of people. For some time mobs of 10; 20; 30,000 people collected daily, surrounded the parliament house, huzzaed the members, even entered the doors and examined into their conduct, took the horses out of the carriages of those who did well, and drew them home.' Playing up to this mood, on 10 August Dupont carried a motion instituting criminal proceedings against Calonne for corruption – almost tantamount to indicting Louis – and three days later by 80 votes to 40 Parlement denounced the *lit de justice* as 'contrary to the nation's rights' and announced that Louis would obtain no further taxes. Furthermore they published these conclusions, which was contrary to the law.

Louis viewed all this with angry dismay and deep frustration. He had had enough of the red-robed lawyers who put their own bank accounts and popularity with Parisians before the welfare of France, forced him to take stern measures, and then called them 'despotic'. He decided to rusticate Parlement, and in view of the stormy scenes in Paris, it was a decision of courage. Between midnight and 2 a.m. on 15 August officers of the Gardes Françaises woke each of the magistrates and handed him a *lettre de cachet* ordering him to Troyes, a hundred miles away.

Louis then went ahead fast with his 'revolution'. He employed the abbé de Véri to set up provincial assemblies, 24 in all, to levy the new land tax, with no one exempt: in so doing, says the liberal abbé Morellet approvingly, the King 'is giving up the prerogative which he and his predecessors have enjoyed for nearly two centuries, of administering the kingdom alone and through his intendants.' In Troyes Parlement seethed and denounced but to no avail.

Louis then had a stroke of bad luck. Profiting from France's domestic crisis, England and Prussia joined to stir up trouble against the republican or Patriot party in Holland, which Louis had long subsidized and through which he played a predominant role in Dutch affairs. Frederick William of Prussia took as a pretext a quarrel between the Patriot party and the English-backed Stadt-holder to mobilize 20,000 troops. If France continued dangerously divided, England and Prussia would almost certainly attack Holland. Louis realized this, and it was solely in order to reduce the chances of war that in early September he proposed to withdraw the land tax provided Parlement extended income tax for five years and allowed no exemptions therefrom. Thus he preserved his principle of equal taxation. Parlement agreed and returned to Paris.

On 19 November Brienne had to ask Parlement for authority to raise the agreed money: 420 millions over the next five years. Louis went in person to the Palais de Justice to see that the edict was registered. Instead of a *lit de justice*, he decided to hold a 'royal sitting': an unusual but not unprecedented procedure whereby he would sit on an armchair, not on a throne under a dais, members might speak, but no vote would be taken. All the royal pomp and pageantry was duly observed; then at the end of the debate the Keeper of the Seals was about to pronounce the registration of the edict when one of the princes suddenly rose. It was Philippe d'Orléans.

Philippe was now actively supporting Parlement's opposition through the masonic lodges and by employing malcontents such as Laclos, author of *Les Liaisons dangereuses*, to write against the Government. Philippe seems to have wished to show that Louis, enslaved to an Austrian whore, was unfit to reign; he may even have hoped to play in France the role the Prince Regent played in England.

Philippe stood up in the great hall and declared that Parlement ought to have voted on the edict. 'Sire,' he said, 'I consider this registration illegal.'

Louis replied, 'It *is* legal, because I wish it.'

'The King and his brothers left [wrote Antoinette to Joseph]. The Duc d'Orléans remained in Parlement and – it is this that shows his evil intentions – pulled from his pocket a protest written beforehand. He did not succeed in getting it adopted in entirety, but he had the registration declared technically illegal. The King has exiled him to Villers-Cotterets, and forbidden him to see anyone but his family and servants. Two councillors of Parlement, M. Fréteau and the abbé Sabbatier, who had spoken insolently in the King's presence, have been imprisoned. I am sorry that these blows for authority have had to be struck; unfortunately they have become necessary, and I hope they will inspire respect.'

Antoinette's hope proved vain. 'From the moment of his exile people forgot the debauches, the avarice, the swindling of the Duc d'Orléans. The people saw only an illustrious victim of arbitrary power.' Orléans played up to this, but he was to be more a catalyst than a danger himself, for, as someone who knew him well remarked, he liked 24-hour conspiracies; longer than that he got cold feet.

Louis was deeply upset by Orléans's opposition, as was Brienne. Both fell ill: Brienne lost his voice and Louis contracted erysipelas, a feverish condition that turns the skin red, and was out of action for a week. When he got better he took to sweating out his indignation hunting the stag for hours on end and returned almost dropping with fatigue. This produced the slander from Orléans's hacks that the King of France was fuddled with drink.

On 29 April 1788 Parlement went back on its word, and refused to collect income tax from those formerly exempt. The tug-of-war between King and Parlement had now reached breaking-point. At the beginning of his reign Louis had reassembled Parlement, long suspended, on the understanding that it would co-operate with him in the task of reform. Parlement, it seemed to Louis, had broken its contract. On 8 May Louis summoned the magistrates to a *lit de justice* and through his Keeper of the Seals informed them that he suspended not only the Parlement of Paris but the twelve provincial Parlements also. He then set up plenary courts to carry out the Parlements' judicial functions.

The outcry was immediate, far-flung and furious. All the provincial Parlements declared their suspension illegal. The nobility denounced the ending of tax exemptions. Pamphleteers claimed that Louis was trying to circumvent the will of the people, although it was precisely the Parlements that had opposed taxes to favour the people. Louis was so upset that, according to his sister, in early June he thought of retracting: 'he is always afraid of being mistaken; his first impulse passed, he is tormented by fear of doing injustice.' However, in the event he stood firm. Whatever the privileged classes and writers might say, he believed he was acting in the interests of France.

That summer opposition switched from Paris to the provinces, notably Dauphiné, Brittany, Burgundy and Provence. Here the Parlements had refused to levy income tax, and when Louis went over their heads to the new provincial assemblies, consistently blocked its collection. The nobility, particularly the *noblesse du robe*, were already faced with a declining standard of living because of rising costs, and resolved to cling to their privileges, even small ones, such as the right of a Dauphinois nobleman to be judged by his peers, which Louis's new plenary courts would abolish. Partly from regional pride, partly because of 'liberal' feeling against central authority, the middle class in Dauphiné supported the nobility. In June outcry became revolt in the so-called 'Day of Tiles'.

The military commander in Dauphiné, Charles, Duc de Clermont Tonnerre, sixty-eight years old, had a good record in two wars and long experience at his job, which was hereditary. He had married a lady-in-waiting to the late Queen, who was also a cousin of Louis's firm Minister, Breteuil. On the other hand, he had showered attentions on Rousseau when that writer visited Dauphiné and he was Grand Master of a Freemasons' Lodge.

Clermont Tonnerre received orders from Versailles to exile members of the Grenoble Parlement for having denounced the King's edicts. He chose to implement his orders on a market day, 7 June, and this, according to Véri, was an error of judgment. Many townsmen foresaw ruin for Grenoble, whose law courts were being replaced by Louis's central plenary courts; others clung to the traditional view that Parlement was their best defence against royal authority. Anger finally flared up in the Place aux Herbes among the women selling fish and vegetables. Five-year-old Henri Beyle, the future Stendhal, heard one of the women shout '*Je me révorte, je me révorte*'. A crowd of 200 entered the house of the Parlement's president, whose bags were packed to leave, and cried they would not let him go.

Clermont Tonnerre ordered two companies of infantry to clear the house. He gave them no ammunition and told them not to use bayonets. At two in the afternoon they were attacked by twenty townsmen with stones and ordered by their officer to charge. Young Stendhal, watching from his grandfather's window, saw a hatter wounded in the small of the back by a bayonet thrust staggering along supported by two friends, his white trousers stained with blood. He climbed to his sixth-floor room; there he collapsed and died.

Anger swept Grenoble. People climbed on the roofs near Clermont Tonnerre's house and pelted the troops with heavy stones and tiles. Clermont Tonnerre came out and told his soldiers to disperse the crowds but on no account to shoot. Despite this, one detachment did open fire. The rooftop guerrillas continued to hurl down tiles, the tocsin was rung, and several hundred peasants arrived armed with hoes, axes and pistols.

Clermont Tonnerre had four battalions. Twenty of his men were wounded, two of the rioters killed. By ordering his troops to fire he could have quelled the riot but humanitarianism, perhaps the strongest force of the age among educated men, acted as a safety-catch which nothing, not even loyalty to the King, could push back. At four o'clock Clermont Tonnerre called off his men and sent a message to the President saying he might remain in Grenoble. The crowd then broke into Clermont Tonnerre's cellar, drank his best wine and insulted Louis's representative, the Intendant. They then escorted the members of Parlement in triumph to the Palais de Justice. So ended the Day of Tiles.

Louis had some experience of hostile crowds. A couple of years earlier 2000 angry Savoyards had marched on Versailles to protest against a Government order and to present Louis with a memorandum, whereupon the commanding officer turned out the guard. Louis returned from the day's hunt: 'passing through the avenues [he] could not conceive what such preparations meant, and on his arrival at Versailles was informed of the cause of them, upon which he immediately ordered the guards from their posts, and laughed exceedingly at the great precautions taken, adding at the same time to his Capitaine de la Garde, "*qu'il n'y avait pas de quoi fouetter un chat*" [that it was just a storm in a tea-cup].'

Louis therefore was not unduly alarmed by the Day of Tiles.

Through his War Minister he blamed Clermont Tonnerre for having punished the officer whose detachment opened fire and told him to take firm action against any more demonstrations. But as Clermont Tonnerre wrote, 'the whole province is united in a common cause' and he failed to prevent a hundred local dignitaries meeting in Grenoble's Hôtel de Ville, where they composed a letter urging Louis to recall the Parlements.

Louis replaced Clermont Tonnerre by the tough Maréchal de Vaux, with orders to stop a protest meeting of all three orders called for 21 July. Vaux tried to talk the nobility into staying away, doubtless explaining that Louis's provincial assembly would allow them as much say as they had had in Parlement. But he made the fatal mistake of admitting a repugnance to use force: he actually said he would 'shut his eyes'. On the appointed day in the château de Vizille 165 nobles, 50 clergy and 276 commoners reaffirmed their opposition to the provincial assembly and again demanded the recall of Parlement. That the meeting took place at all was a blow to Louis's authority.

The revolt of the nobility, and bloodshed, were not confined to Dauphiné. All around France nobles and magistrates joined forces, nominally to defend their Parlements, in reality to stop equality of taxation, which would emerge from Louis's provincial assemblies. Riots broke out in Brittany, Béarn, Burgundy and Provence; in Rennes and Pau the provincial Parlements met in defiance of the King's orders. This revolt of the Parlements and nobles against the King's economic policy and social reforms constitutes the first phase of the French Revolution.

Louis reacted as he had done in Dauphiné, ordering his provincial commanders to stand firm and uphold the law. He set an example by sending to the Bastille twelve leading Bretons who brought him a written protest from nobility of that rebellious province. But the army commanders proved as soft as Clermont Tonnerre, while the nobles by boycotting the provincial assemblies were able to bring local administration to a standstill and to reduce taxes to a trickle.

A call had gone up from the Parlements and from leading commoners that the King should summon the States General, elected representatives of all three estates, in order to vote a new tax structure. Louis knew that the last States General in 1614 had solved nothing. Nobles and Third Estate each accused the other of grabbing too much of the national wealth, while Gallican clergy feuded with ultramontanes. For long Louis XIII could not get them to disband, and when he did they had effected no reforms of value.

Louis resisted the call for a States General as long as he could, knowing that it would make inroads on his authority, but by mid-summer this seemed the only concession that would calm the disturbances, and on 8 August Louis announced he would hold such an assembly next year. The news was greeted with approval, but the provincial nobles still shook their fists, taxes dried up altogether and the funds slumped.

Louis had appointed Brienne in order to win over the clergy, but Brienne, with his eczema and faint voice, was rapidly losing his grip. When he summoned the clergy to a special assembly and asked them for the 8 million livres he needed in order to hold on, they refused to give more than one million, reasserted the Church's immunity from taxation and, breaking a long tradition of fidelity to the Crown, urged Louis to recall the Parlements.

Louis now found himself in check to knight and bishop. Trade had virtually ceased, public confidence fell to a new low. In the second half of August with a mere 400,000 livres in the Treasury Brienne announced that he would have to print paper money to pay civil servants. This amounted to national bankruptcy and an admission of personal failure.

Louis dismissed Brienne on 25 August. Three turbanned ambassadors, recently arrived from Mysore, learned of 'the grand vizier's' disgrace and, licking their lips, asked to see his head, to which a wag replied, 'Brienne didn't have a head.'

If this was a time of ordeal for Louis, it was equally so for Antoinette. The Dauphin was showing symptoms of curvature of the spine, and in the summer of 1787 the last-born of her children, a daughter named Sophie, died suddenly aged eleven months. Charged with grieving too long for so young a child, Antoinette explained through her tears, 'She might have grown up to be a friend.' Sophie's death was followed in December by that of the King's Aunt Louise, seventeen years a Carmelite, whom Antoinette greatly admired. In her pain at these losses the Queen turned to what Versailles called 'the path of devotion': she went more often to Holy Communion and still further simplified her way of life. Véri, grown cynical in later years, put a false interpretation on Antoinette's piety: 'The Queen does not like the Parlements any more than the King does; she knows that the clergy are not fond of her; this way believers will give her their support, and by running the Court with agreeable decorum she will conciliate the great military families.'

After the diamond necklace affair, slanders that had formerly been confined to the drawing-rooms of courtiers began to circulate, and to be believed, among ordinary Frenchmen. In June 1787 Mallet du Pan noted in his diary, 'The Queen went to the opera a week ago and some insolent people shouted, "There is the deficit." ' When Calonne was burned in effigy, he held a scroll accusing Antoinette of having sent Joseph 100 millions in three years, an absurd slander, since Joseph was actually reproaching his sister with having become too French, and for having nothing German about her but her face.

Just as in the opening scenes of the Reformation reformers launched their attack on the Church obliquely by claiming that Mary was usurping the role of God, so now they accused Antoinette of usurping the role of the King. Because the abbé de Vermond was a friend of Brienne, they accused Antoinette of fiddling his appointment, though she had done no such thing. She played so minor a political role that when she wished to have galleries erected so that she and her ladies could watch the assembly of notables, as Marie de Médicis had done in 1614, Louis refused point blank, saying, 'You are not regent.'

With the fall of Brienne, however, Antoinette almost for the first time did intervene in politics. People were now clamouring for Necker. Forgetting his dishonest account in 1781, they saw only a soft-hearted wizard who could run France on loans. Antoinette had always thought well of Necker and she now saw a chance of regaining her good name. She went to Louis and urged him to take back the Swiss banker.

Louis was none too pleased with Necker, and had recently rusticated him for helping to topple Calonne. He seems also to have felt that the Swiss was at heart not a monarchist. However, he came over to Antoinette's view that a concession over Necker would create a serener atmosphere for the States General.

'I have just written three lines to M. Necker,' Antoinette informed Mercy, 'asking him to come here tomorrow at 10 o'clock . . . I tremble – forgive me for this weakness – at the thought that it is I who am recalling him. My fate is to bring bad luck and, if infernal machinations make him fall again or if he weakens the King's authority, I shall be still more detested.'

Louis reappointed Necker on 25 August and, the people's

happiness being so much in the air, let fall the remark, 'For years I've had no lasting happiness,' upon which Necker airily promised the King should have some soon. He lent the Government 2 millions of his own and got an advance of 75 millions from businessmen and bankers. But his system could function only if taxes were paid, and clearly they would not be paid until the Parlements were recalled. Reluctantly, and only to stave off another bankruptcy, in September Louis recalled the Parlements.

'Today,' wrote the Marquis de Bombelles on 26 September 1788, 'the King received a packet of letters while hunting. He went into a copse to read them, and was soon seen seated on the ground, arms resting on his knees and face hidden in his hands. His squire and other persons heard sobs and went to fetch M. de Lambesq [the First Squire], but when he approached, the King told him brusquely to go. He insisted on staying: then the King, dropping his hands and showing a face bathed in tears, said in a kindly tone, "Let me be." '

What were in those letters? Almost certainly news that Parlement, on its return, had been accorded a tumultuous triumph. That the people of Paris should prefer the lawyers who opposed justice to the King who proposed it – for Louis it was a last twist on the rack of humiliation. This immensely strong man was so upset that he could not sit his horse and had to be carried back to Versailles on a chair.

The victory of Parlement and the nobles had wider implications. It encouraged the middle class to take a stronger line in *their* claims for a bigger share in the Government and when Louis invited political theorists to express in writing their hopes for the States General, a spate of pamphlets appeared demanding with force and sometimes in extreme language a voice in taxation and even an end to feudal privileges.

One day the bluff old botanist-lawyer, Lamoignon de Malesherbes urged Louis to reflect on Charles I. 'Your position, like his, lies in the conflict between the earlier customs of authority, and the present demands of the citizens. Fortunately, religious disagreement is not involved.'

'Oh yes, there we are indeed fortunate,' said Louis, taking Malesherbes's arm. 'So the ferocity will not be the same.'

'Besides, the gentler ways of our time guarantee you against the excesses of those days . . . I will answer for it that things will not reach the stage they did with Charles I; but I won't answer for the absence of any other forms of excess. You must turn your mind to warding them off.'

Louis evidently took to heart the lawyer's well-meant warning. While making a mental note of the principles on which he would stand firm, he determined to make the States General a success, and for this it must be a truly representative assembly of the whole nation. Though Parlement (to the shocked amazement of Parisians), the nobility and all the princes save Monsieur wished the States to be constituted as at its last meeting in 1614, each order having the same numerical strength and each possessing a single vote, from which it followed that clergy and nobility would always be able to outvote the Third two to one, Louis decided in a Cabinet meeting on 27 December 1788, attended by Antoinette, that the Third Estate should have as many deputies as clergy and nobility combined. This implied that voting, at least on matters of general concern, would be by heads, though Louis for a reason unknown did not explicitly state this. He also decided, in a no less liberal gesture, that the franchise should be extended to almost all male tax-payers over twenty-five.

These concessions increased Louis's popularity with ordinary Frenchmen to a point where Malesherbes's warning of excesses seemed pure fantasy. Camille Desmoulins, a high-minded young Picardy barrister prevented from practising by a stammer, voiced the general mood: 'I regarded Louis XVI with admiration because he had virtues, because he did not follow the same path as his fathers, was not a despot and convoked the States General. In the depths of my province I had read in the papers his beautiful words: "What matter if my authority suffer, provided my people are happy." '

CHAPTER 18

The States General

LOUIS decided that a building used for storing theatrical scenery and props known as the Hall of Lesser Pleasures would be a good place for the States General to meet, and as inexpensively as possible gave it a look of splendour with imitation columns, gold and white paint and tasselled hangings. True to his sense of history, he laid down that as in 1614 each order should wear distinctive dress. For the 1200 deputies he had rooms reserved in Versailles town, restaurants stocked up, new latrines dug and vinegar laid in to disinfect them.

Louis's homework for the States consisted in reading a representative selection of the 55,000 *Cahiers de doléances* – Lists of grievances, drawn up by each group of voters. These were the authentic voice of his people. Country districts complained about seignorial rights and the tithe they had to pay their parish priest, towns demanded guarantees of individual liberty and freedom of the press. Nobles and clergy wished to keep social distinctions between the orders, the Third wished to end them. But on two fundamental points nearly all the Cahiers agreed. They wanted what Louis had been striving for for years: a fairer incidence of taxation. They also wanted to retain in essentials the Catholic monarchy that gave Louis the initiative in the making and sanctioning of laws, and on all matters the final decision; these powers furthermore they would like embodied in a written irrevocable constitution.

Louis strongly sympathized with the first demand and was not unsympathetic to the second. His chief hope from the States was that deputies of all orders would call for fairer taxation. Then, since they were just a deliberative body, it would be for him as King to issue the necessary laws.

On Saturday 2 May Louis welcomed the deputies. He received the clergy first, and the double doors leading to the Hall of Mirrors were open wide, the King being traditionally always available to the clergy; the nobility second, one door being closed; and the Third Estate last, both doors being initially shut in their faces.

Among the clergy Louis recognized Archbishop Loménie de Brienne, Bishop de Talleyrand with his twisted leg, the abbé Maury, a cobbler's son with a guardsman's physique who sometimes preached at Versailles and was a staunch monarchist, and the courtier-priest who had so much harmed the monarchy, Cardinal de Rohan.

Then came three hundred noblemen in black satin suits with white plumed hats, sword at hip. Here Louis recognized loyal supporters such as the Duc de Montmorency Luxembourg and the Marquis de Ferrières, liberals such as La Fayette, Lauzun, now Duc de Biron, and Lally-Tollendal, enemies such as Philippe d'Orléans, the yellow-faced Duc d'Aiguillon, and his two bitterest opponents in Parlement, Adrien Duport and Duval d'Eprémesnil.

Finally Louis received the Third Estate, some six hundred citizens in black cloth suits and tricornes. Among those known to Louis were Turgot's able secretary, Du Pont de Nemours, Antoine Barnave, 'the Tiger', who had stirred up open resistance in Dauphiné, and Isaac Le Chapelier, who had done the same in Brittany.

The Paris deputies, who because of election delays were to arrive late, included Jean Sylvain Bailly, a Pierrot-faced astronomer, kindly Dr Guillotin, who was to propose the adoption of a humane machine for taking life, and the abbé Emmanuel Sieyès, a Provençal who had lost his faith and turned from an austere idealism to politics. Rejected by his own order, Sieyès just scraped last place among the deputies of the Paris Third.

The most striking man among the Third was also an outcast from his order. Honoré de Mirabeau had a big pock-marked head, thick shaggy hair, protuberant eyes and the look of a mastiff. Imprisoned early in life for heavy debts, he had eloped with the prison governor's wife, fought a running battle with his difficult father, committed incest with his sister, piled up more debts, spent three years in Vincennes; altogether Louis had had to issue 17 *lettres de cachet* against him. But Mirabeau proclaimed himself verbally and in lucrative pamphlets a victim of despotism, and had been elected by the Third Estate although a Comte. 'I am a mad dog,' he said, 'from whose bites despotism and privilege will die.'

These were the men Louis faced when on Monday 4 May he entered the Hall of Lesser Pleasures to shouts of '*Vive le Roi!*' He wore a suit of cloth of gold and in his hat the Regent diamond; Antoinette, who followed him, wore a white dress with silver spangles, a heron plume in her hair. After taking his seat on a velvet-covered throne Louis rose to read a carefully prepared speech.

'Gentlemen, the day I have been awaiting eagerly has at last arrived, and I see myself surrounded by the representatives of the Nation it is my glory to command.' Louis had first put 'happiness'; 'glory' was suggested by Antoinette. Louis then spoke of the inequality of taxation, paying a tribute to the clergy and nobility for their offer, made on 20 December 1788, to renounce their financial privileges, and expressing the hope that all three orders would co-operate with him for the good of the State. According to a peg-legged American, Gouverneur Morris, who heard Louis, 'The tone and manner have all the *fierté* which can be desired or expected from the blood of the Bourbons.'

Louis's programme was sketched by his Keeper of the Seals, Barentin: the King desired to see the burden of taxation shared by the clergy and nobility, to introduce greater freedom of the press, and to bring about reforms in the punishment of crime, a clear reference to *lettres de cachet*. Necker then gave a detailed account of the finances. After this the Estates divided. As in 1614 each order was to verify the credentials of its deputies separately, after which the States would again meet in common.

The clergy and the nobility set about this task immediately. The Third did not. They took the view that verification could be valid only if done by all the members in common assembly. They flatly refused to verify their credentials separately. On 11 May, when the nobles had finished, the Third had not even begun. What made these ardent reformers drag their feet?

France's urgent need, we know, was to produce more and distribute it fairly. But the Third did not see it like that. Out of 621 members only forty were working-class and a handful manufacturers, while no less than 360 were lawyers: men who did not themselves produce and cared less about economics than about politics. What these young lawyers wanted was social equality. They believed that all men were 'naturally' equal and that only class distinctions prevented them from being truly brothers. Free men from class distinctions, they said, and the rest would follow.

This was an immensely powerful idea, with much truth in it, and tallying with changed attitudes in many areas of intellectual life from science to the arts. It was propounded not by the selfish reactionaries of Parlement but by men of great honesty and determination. Whatever he may have thought of social equality, Louis could have no doubt that a majority of the Third shared his intense concern for the welfare of the people as a whole. In a real sense they were his natural allies, and he had given them a gage of alliance by doubling their numbers.

When he saw that the Third were from the start making a show of strength, Louis should have taken this as a warning bell and acted to head off a clash. He should have invited their leaders into his apartment and talked to them. Behind the scenes he could have reassured them about several matters: that he took his own decisions and was not a tool of the nobles, that *lettres de cachet* were not used despotically, but to plug loopholes in a Gothic legal system. He could have made himself known as a person, not just as a bust on the gold louis.

There was one big obstacle: etiquette. The laws of Versailles, all the more rigorous for being unwritten, decreed that while a nobleman might speak to the King standing up, a commoner must go down on bended knee. Louis knew that men like Barnave or Le Chapelier would consider this humiliating. He could have waived it, as for the procession to the Church of St Louis on the day before the opening of the States he had waived the canopy traditionally held over the King's head. But he did not waive it, and it is sometimes said that he feared to infringe one of the nobility's little marks of rank. The true reason lies deeper: Louis distrusted himself with strangers. After fifteen years as King he still had not learned the art of small talk and striking up an easy relationship. With his mind he trusted the people, but now, at a crucial moment, he would not trust himself to them as a person, and so etiquette, like the useless statistics in his diary, became a refuge from threatening reality.

Louis's failure to get to know, and perhaps win over, leaders of the Third had two important consequences. In the first place it meant that he had no opportunity of rebutting slanders now filtering down from Court enemies. Antoinette, for example, had arranged for deputies to attend performances of operas and plays, and to visit Trianon. There they demanded to be shown the room encrusted everywhere with diamonds and adorned by pillars covered with rubies and sapphires. Louis was told of this by Antoinette, and suggested to her that the origin of the myth might be found in the paste stones with which Louis XV had decorated the theatre at Fontainebleau. But he did not speak up and personally demolish the myth, with the result that deputies left Trianon convinced that this example of royal extravagance had been hidden from them.

The second result of Louis's failure to communicate with the Third was that it caused a vacuum of personality, into which the more militant deputies, such as Mirabeau, now inevitably moved. Not only did they still decline to verify their credentials, fearing that if they started by meeting separately they would be condoning the class system, but they denounced the other two orders for refusing to join them for verification in common and began to call themselves the Commons, a medieval term for all citizens possessing rights of self-government.

On 28 May Louis mediated. He set up a joint commission, which announced a compromise procedure for verifying deputies' credentials. But now it was the nobility's turn to drag their feet. Galled by the Third calling themselves the Commons, they rejected the compromise procedure. The Third, who had arrived hoping to make a heaven on earth, were deeply frustrated that after almost a month the States still had not got down to business – though the fault, initially, had been their own.

Louis now faced a serious situation. The Third were certainly being provocative, but since they represented the people at large had a special call on his sympathy. Throughout his reign Louis had put his trust in the people. He had recalled Parlement in 1774, with all the strains that had imposed, in order to win over the people. Whenever the people had been in distress, he had thrown thrift to the winds and spent lavishly – he was doing so at that moment, to provide low-cost bread after a harvest shattered by hail. But there was a second principle to Louis's kingship. He wished to be just. At his first Cabinet meeting he had said: 'Everything unjust is impossible.' Now the Cahiers disagreed about class structure. The clergy and nobles wanted it, the Third did not. That meant the deputies were about equally divided, and it would be for them, when the States got under way, to deliberate and vote on such an important point. If he took sides now, he would be prejudging the issue.

Louis decided finally in favour of strict justice. It was in his nature so to do. Order, legality, precision of speech, the exact balancing of accounts: these were his characteristics. Even at the time this decision was seen by many to be an error: Louis's second failure in a month. What he should have done is to have expressed the wish that clergy and nobles sit with the Third to verify their credentials as the sole means of launching the States, and, if necessary, imposed that wish by appearing personally in full session. He was, after all, King, and his word in such matters had the force of law.

An unexpected event, almost a fatality, had several times queered Louis's life: the partition of Poland had acerbated his early marriage, the Dutch crisis had obliged him to parley with Parlement in 1787. Now another such fatality occurred. The Dauphin, an exceptionally sweet and intelligent boy, was heir not only to the throne but to the family disease: King's evil. 'One hip is higher than the other,' wrote Antoinette; 'the vertebrae of his back are out of place and protruding.' For weeks he had been bedridden and in pain. On 4 June, to the intense sorrow of both his parents, he died. He was laid out in a white coffin, with his crown and gold spurs, while two rows of monks chanted the Office of the Dead, then buried inexpensively at Saint-Denis.

This loss coincided with an important political development. On 3 June the tough Paris delegation arrived. Its tone was set by the abbé Sieyès who in a famous pamphlet had asked 'What is the Third Estate?' and answered, 'Nothing.' 'What should it be?' 'Everything.' The first answer was untrue, for Louis by creating the Provincial Assemblies had associated the Third in the government of France, but no one bothered about that, and the double question and answer was already a political battle-cry. The arrival of Sieyès among the Third, frustrated almost to desperation point, spelled political danger, and indeed within a week Sieyès was to issue an ultimatum: clergy and nobles must at once join the Third if they wished to be considered 'representatives of the Nation'.

Here was another dilemma for Louis. As a family man he wanted to mourn his son; as King he needed to keep a close eye on the Third. In the event he chose to follow his heart. He locked himself up with his grief: first at Versailles, then, on 14 June, withdrew for a week to Marly. This constituted a third and fatal failure, for it meant that the drama of the States was to unroll without the King.

The nobles had a special room in which to meet; so had the clergy; but there was none big enough to seat the 621 members of the Third, and for economy's sake Louis had not built a new one. Instead he had them hold their private meetings in the Hall of Lesser Pleasures. It was more than a detail of décor: it gave visible shape to an idea, which Sieyès, Mirabeau and the militants were proclaiming, that the Third, by themselves, represented the whole nation; and this notion was strengthened by the absence of the King.

On 17 June, in the Hall of Lesser Pleasures, the Third held an important meeting. They had been joined now by nineteen curés, and because spectators in the public galleries had interrupted earlier meetings, guards stood on duty. Sieyès rose to speak. Believing that the Commons were the nation, he demanded that they and their adherents should now take the name of 'National Assembly'. Mirabeau spoke against the motion, pointing out that the name National Assembly had previously been applied to the States General as a whole. After a long debate the Third voted in favour of Sieyès's motion by 491 to 89. The self-styled National Assembly then announced their intention of framing a constitution, implying that they would begin this task without the King's consent.

This announcement was given visible dramatic shape three days later in the palace indoor tennis-court, where all the Commons save one pronounced a solemn and curious oath. Louis David's recent painting showed the Horatii, right arm in the air at forty-five degrees, swearing to defend Rome, and this served as a model now. In front of Bailly, their 'dean', who stood on a table, each stepped forward, stretched out his right arm and swore, not on the Gospels but so to speak by that Roman episode, never to disband until France had a constitution.

By assuming the name 'National Assembly' without asking the King's permission and by implying that the framing of a constitution might be begun without the King's consent, the Third Estate had taken a decisive step. They were saying that there existed another source of sovereign authority – the people – and that they embodied it. Their action in this respect constitutes the second phase of the French Revolution.

Louis heard the news at Marly. He saw that the Third were about to contest his supreme power and that to do nothing, as the British ambassador noted, would be 'to lay the crown at their feet'. Two main ways opened before him, and it was within Louis's character to follow either.

The first way was to use force: dissolve the States, occupy the Lesser Pleasures with troops, arrest leading deputies such as Sieyès; garrison the Bastille with a battalion of picked troops under a war veteran, occupy the Hôtel de Ville and that centre of anti-Government propaganda the Palais Royal, imprison the militant leaders of Paris's electoral assembly, place regiments and cannon at the bridges and gates, and finally himself carry through the reforms generally called for by the Cahiers. What would be the long-term results of such action? Louis could tell because two of his friends had tried it.

On his mother's death in 1780 Joseph II became sole ruler of Austria. Completely self-confident, he rode down opposing views and ruled as an enlightened despot. He freed the serfs from all duties save the *corvée* and tithes, made taxation more equitable and modernized the legal code. He granted freedom of religion to his Orthodox and Protestant subjects; built hospitals and orphanages; dedicated every minute to making Austria a model state. What was his surprise to find that his reforms aroused bitter opposition! All his non-German subjects disliked the centralization of government in Vienna, though it made for efficiency; his educational reforms, especially the closing of episcopal seminaries, brought the Netherlands into open revolt. 'Why am I not loved by my people?' sighed Joseph, as he lay ill of fever contracted while winning glory for Austria against the Turk. The answer is that this was the late eighteenth century and people resented reforms granted from above, not wrested from below. From 1789 Joseph was actually obliged to cancel many of his best measures, and a year later the Emperor who had done so much to make his people happy died unmourned.

Gustavus III also chose the way of enlightened despotism. In the summer of 1772 he overthrew Sweden's creaking constitution by a hereditary coup lasting twenty minutes and assumed almost absolute power. Less hard-headed than Joseph – he consulted fortune-tellers and dabbled in the cabbala – Gustavus nevertheless ended a long period of anarchy and pushed through reforms that delighted his friends Rousseau and Voltaire. About Gustavus's benefits to the Swedish people there can be no question. But the nobles hated him because he curbed their power. They declined to wear the costume Gustavus himself designed as a mark of national unity, and they undermined his schemes. In March 1792 a discontented noble, Anckarström, arrived at a masquerade ball, pulled out a pistol and shot Gustavus in the back, fatally.

Louis was more reflective than Joseph or Gustavus, but he could act when required. What made him reject the use of force now? Probably he saw the lesson implicit in Austria and Sweden, and spelled out at various times in the France of his own day: no king could successfully thrust happiness down his subjects' throats.

Louis chose therefore to take the second way, that of conciliation. Within the now narrow limits set by his three failures in six weeks, he decided to bid for alliance with the Third by making almost every sacrifice he could make, short of alienating the rights of the Crown.

On 23 June the States gathered for what was called a royal sitting.

Their mood had changed since the King had first spoken to them seven weeks before. The faces of deputies showed worry and frustration. No one now expected instant happiness: the place where they sat was a Hall of Lesser Evils.

Louis entered with the usual pomp and read a short speech in which he deplored the States' delay in getting to work and the divisions by which they were rent. Those divisions he intended to end.

Barentin then rose and read a declaration by the King annulling the actions of the Third on 17 June as 'illegal and unconstitutional'. The three orders were to be maintained and all three, not one alone, were 'representatives of the Nation'; with the King's approval they might deliberate in common, though not about the prerogatives of the first two orders, or the constitutional form of future States.

Louis then spoke a second time. He was going to institute certain reforms, which would be announced. 'I do not intend to circumscribe your zeal, for I shall be pleased to adopt any other project for the public good that the States may propose.' Barentin then read thirty-five reforms. The first declared: 'No new tax will be levied, no old one renewed, without the consent of the Nation's representatives.' Another declared that Louis would publish an annual budget. Louis promised also to sanction the ending of fiscal privilege as soon as the clergy and nobility had so voted. Provincial States would be set up, half their members to come from the Third, to administer hospitals, prisons and social welfare. *Lettres de cachet* would be abolished. The Press would be free.

The contents of this programme were certainly generous. As Louis himself said: 'Never has a king done so much for any nation.' Talleyrand, speaking as a nobleman and bishop, with his usual perceptiveness went to the heart of Louis's principles: 'Your Majesty could not have gone further without ceasing to be just.' To an impartial observer, the English agriculturist Arthur Young, 'the plan was a good one, much was granted to the people in great and essential points.'

What of Louis's manner in presenting it? This was the one occasion, late though it might be, when a Henri IV by his sheer likeable presence, or some other king with poetry and personal aura, could have lifted up the nation to their way of thinking. But aware now of the Third's hostility and grief-stricken for his son, Louis had lost the assurance of the opening session, and he made his speeches in an 'unsteady' voice. He failed to carry the deputies with him. He ended by saying that if they abandoned him in so fine an undertaking, he would act for the good of his people alone; but his hesitant manner negatived the bold words.

Louis gave orders for the States to disperse and followed this up with a tactical mistake. Knowing the Third's mood and that the tennis-court meeting had been held against his wishes, he should have remained at his throne and seen the deputies off the premises. Instead he walked out of the hall.

The Third were not satisfied by Louis's concessions. As Arthur Young put it, many 'will accept of nothing as the concession of power: they will assume and secure all to themselves, as matters of right.' But in a group of six hundred some were defiant, others conciliatory, some brave, others timid. One, however, had spent a lifetime in open disobedience to all authority. He had known two kinds of hell: enslavement to passion and imprisonment, and so, in adopting the generous ideas of the reformers, he gave them a dark aggressive tinge they were never to lose. It was Mirabeau who spoke for the Third in a magnificent booming voice.

'Gentlemen, I admit that what you have just heard could well be the salvation of the *patrie*, if the gifts of despotism were not always dangerous. We are being dictated to in an insulting manner. The guards constitute a violation of the nation's temple, and you are being ordered to be happy. Who orders you? Your mandatory! Who gives you imperious laws? Your mandatory! It is he who ought to receive laws from us, gentlemen, clad as we are in an inviolable political priesthood . . . I demand that you put on your legislative powers and withdraw into the religion of your oath: it allows us to disband only after having made the constitution.'

The Master of Ceremonies stepped forward: Henri Evrard de Dreux Brézé, only twenty-three but assured and urbane: being the King's representative he kept his hat on as he repeated the King's order to disperse.

'Yes, sir,' replied Mirabeau, 'we have heard the intentions that have been suggested to the King . . . If you have been told to clear us from this hall, you must ask orders to use force, for we shall leave our seats only at bayonet point.'

The speech was clever. Although he knew that bayonets were there only to protect unpopular deputies from the restive public, Mirabeau made them seem a threat, first having assured his colleagues that they had a quasi-religious 'inviolability'. Not only did he dispute the King's title, recognized by all the Cahiers, to be the one true representative of the nation, but he insinuated that the King was merely echoing grey eminences behind the throne. So both the timid and the honest members of the Third believed that by remaining in their places they were not disobeying the King with the unsteady voice. They were disobeying only the Queen and reactionary Ministers. So they did as Mirabeau urged: by 493 votes to 34 declared themselves inviolable, that is, above the law; and again urged all the nobles and clergy to join them.

Meanwhile, young Monsieur de Dreux Brézé hurried to tell Louis that the Third Estate declined to leave the Hall. 'The King went pale with anger and swore roundly. "Then clear them out by force," he said. *"Qu'on les chasse."* Monsieur de Dreux Brézé returned to execute this order, but found that the deputies had by then dispersed.'

Louis now found himself isolated. What support could he expect from the nobles who had revolted in 1788, from curés who by birth and milieu were closer to the Third than to the Crown? He could do nothing but wait and it came as no surprise to him when on 24 June a majority of the clergy took their seats with the Third, a momentous event which Bailly compared to 'two great rivers mingling their waters in order together to irrigate the countryside'. Next day 47 noblemen, including Philippe d'Orléans, also went over to the Third.

It was Louis's turn now to feel frustration. He saw no possible course but to accept a *fait accompli*. On 27 June 'for the safety of the State' Louis ordered all the clergy and nobility to sit with the Third. It was an admission that he had now completely lost control of the States General.

The action now radiates like shock waves from the Hall of Lesser Pleasures to Versailles town and Paris. Many ordinary citizens took the Third's victory as a sign that they could now do as they pleased. One group stoned the carriage of the Archbishop of Paris because he had opposed joining the Third, while in Paris, according to a Breton visitor, 'people are attacked in full daylight. "Are you for the Third?" they are asked. If you don't raise your hand to signify "yes", you are beaten black and blue. In the streets there are no longer patrols or guards. It is pure anarchy . . . On Saturday a woman leaving the Variétés on her husband's arm was blinded in one eye by a firework. This is what they term rejoicing; I call it a calamity.' There was imminent danger of order breaking down completely.

Louis may have lost control of the States General but he had no intention of losing control of Versailles and Paris. The question of increasing France's police force by 300 men had arisen in 1779, and on the grounds of economy been decided in the negative, much to Véri's anger. So Paris had a mere 1500 police, and a garrison of 5000 troops known to be disaffected: not enough to protect key buildings and ensure the regular distribution of bread. Having no more police at his disposal, on 26 June Louis summoned six regiments from the eastern frontier, mainly Swiss and German mercenaries. He also summoned from Alsace his best general, Victor François de Broglie, hero of the Seven Years' War, and entrusted him with both the troops and his own personal guard. After serious riots on 30 June, during which Parisians broke into a military prison and the dragoons sent to disperse them 'thought it better to drink with the rioters and return back to their quarters', Louis summoned a further ten regiments.

The first troops reached the heights round Paris on 6 July. From Versailles Broglie wrote to his second-in-command, the courtier-general Besenval, stationed in central Paris: 'The King wishes you to collect all the troops on whom you can count in order to defend and keep control of the Royal Treasury and the Discount Bank.' Broglie stationed strong detachments at the bridges of Sèvres and Saint-Cloud, linking Versailles with Paris. From these and other orders by Broglie it would seem that the role of the new regiments was to have been entirely defensive: there is no hint of action against the Assembly.

On 8 July Mirabeau made a speech that was to win him the nickname 'Thunder'. 'A large number of troops already surround us,' he boomed. 'More are arriving each day. Artillery are moving up . . . these preparations for war are obvious to everyone and fill every heart with indignation . . . Why this array? To keep order? . . . Never have the people had better reason for keeping calm and patient than now, when they have representatives to assert their rights and complaints, and about to better their lot.' The King, said Mirabeau, was not responsible, it was his Ministers. 'Do they realize with what horror this good King will eye those who light the torches of sedition, and cause him to shed his people's blood?'

This was the moment for Louis to stride into the Assembly, square his shoulders, thrust out his chest, and declare that he personally had summoned the troops and why. But it was not in his character. He made do with receiving a deputation a couple of days later and explaining to them that the troops were there in a purely precautionary role: 'If the States are alarmed', he added, 'let them sit at Noyon or Soissons.' That was a good point, but what was needed was thunder.

So again Louis failed. Nevertheless he did act resolutely in spheres where his character allowed. He ensured adequate food supplies for Paris by spending 25 millions on grain, as Necker reported to the Assembly, and after 4 July, to economize on wheat, he and his household ate only rye bread. He carried on with his daily routine, showing no signs of the tension he felt, and receiving with outward assurance distinguished visitors, such as the Devonshires and Lady Elizabeth Foster, who describes their first dinner as 'silent and thoughtful such as I have never seen at Versailles'.

Antoinette also put on a brave face. She arranged to see the Devonshires one afternoon at two, but they were not dressed in time, so she obligingly put it off till six. Then 'hearing we wanted to be in Paris to see *Nina* at the Comédie Italienne, she put herself out of her way to see us at five . . . She receiv'd us very graciously indeed, tho' very much out of spirit at the times . . . She is sadly altered, her belly quite big, and no hair at all, but she has still great éclat.' Only once did she let her anguish show. When the Duke of Dorset remarked to Lady Elizabeth that 'the Queen ought to have another son,' and the remark was translated, Antoinette retorted, 'Why should I? So that Monsieur d'Orléans can have him killed?'

Antoinette had another cause for anguish. When urging Louis to recall Necker, she had trembled lest he might 'weaken the King's authority'. By pointedly absenting himself from the royal sitting Necker had done just that. Ordinary people assumed that this sentimental man without a title opposed class distinctions, and they treated him as a hero.

Louis meanwhile stuck to his decision to act firmly. He saw the issue as one between order and anarchy. Necker did not. He wanted Louis to yield whenever and wherever the good people asked him to yield: to buy popularity however high the price. Differences grew: four times Necker expressed the wish to resign; four times Louis kept him on. But finally the King decided Necker was too flabby for the job in hand and must go.

The Swiss banker had boasted to friends that Louis would never dare dismiss him but early in the afternoon of 11 July he received Louis's letter dispensing with his services and asking him to leave Paris quietly. Necker believed that the dismissal of a Minister as popular as himself would cause resentment, that after failing as a personality before the States, it was too late for the King to show firmness, and that disturbances would grow. After his first surprise at the King's letter Necker bundled himself and Suzanne into their carriage, without trunk or even overnight bag, and instead of taking the long route across France to Switzerland, headed at full speed for nearby Belgium.

CHAPTER 19

Captured

PARIS in 1789 was still a largely medieval city of narrow winding muddy streets, small wooden houses and a few splendid modern buildings such as the Ecole Militaire. Its population, like the population of France, had risen by over fifty per cent since 1730, and now stood at 650,000. This made it very overcrowded. Paris crowds have already appeared in Louis's life: they got out of control at his wedding celebrations and more than a hundred were crushed to death. When he attended a ball in Paris in 1782, huge crowds pressed in on him, shouting, 'Long live the King!' 'If you want him to live,' Louis remarked, 'don't suffocate him.'

The crowds were denser now because of unemployment. The commercial treaty of 1786 had flooded France with superior and cheaper English goods: everything from woollen cloth to scissors and tumbler locks. In Carcassone one thousand workmen in the light cloth industry had to be laid off, and elsewhere workers smashed jennies and other English machinery in the belief that such inventions were putting them out of a job.

Paris was suffering not only from English competition, but also from a drying-up of Court spending. By supporting the Parlement in its insistent demands for cuts in royal spending, the tradespeople of Paris were really cutting their own economic throats, and one example is that the Queen's dressmaker, Rose Bertin, had recently gone bankrupt. Furthermore, the many riots staged by Parisians in the past two years had frightened away the rich foreigners who were usually good regular customers. By July 1789 about half of Paris's workers were unemployed.

To this was added a second problem. On 13 July 1788 a hailstorm swept the Paris region. It was of quite exceptional severity, with hailstones sixteen inches in circumference. Windows were smashed, big trees uprooted, 1200 villages damaged, and much of the harvest ruined. A year later wheat had become scarce and the usual fears came into play when it was moved from country to town. The Government were doing everything possible to ensure that people had enough to eat, spending on grain imports between August 1788 and November 1790 the huge sum of 74 millions. Nevertheless France was not organized for effective distribution of essential supplies. The price of a 4 lb. loaf of bread rose in July 1789 to 14½ sous; outside the bakers stood housewives in a long line, called by the new word 'queue'.

Necker had been popular with Parisians because of his policy of borrowing instead of taxing, and the confidence with which he inspired the stock-market. Brienne, in 1788, had had to declare a national bankruptcy, and when the news of Necker's dismissal reached Paris on 12 July, the rentiers believed another bankruptcy was imminent, which would hit them hard, while the artisans and workers who had considered Necker 'the father of the poor' feared that work and bread would become even scarcer.

Political malcontents congregated in the cafés, clubs and shops of the Palais Royal; since these were the private property of Philippe d'Orléans, the police were not allowed in. Here underground presses turned out one new pamphlet every hour, denouncing unemployment and the food shortage, while crowds of up to 10,000 gathered to hear speakers attack the Government. One of the crowd, Camille Desmoulins, supported the attacks but disapproved of certain propaganda methods; he wrote home that 'an intelligent, well-brought-up child of four went round the garden in full daylight, at least twenty times, on the shoulders of a porter, shouting "Decree of the French people: 'The Polignac woman exiled to ten leagues from Paris. Condé ditto. Conti ditto. D'Artois ditto. The Queen . . .'" I dare not tell you the rest.'

The mood in the Palais Royal during early July is described by two foreign observers: 'The novelty of the situation has turned the brains of the people; each thinks himself a Brutus, and sees a Cæsar in each noble.' 'Three months ago the sight of a soldier excited awe – now they speak of attacking whole regiments.'

When news of the Government changes reached Paris at noon on 12 July Desmoulins climbed on to a café table. 'Citizens,' he shouted, 'you know that the nation asked for Necker to stay, for a monument to be erected to him, and now he's been driven out! Can they defy you more insolently? After this, they will stop at nothing. Tonight they are plotting, perhaps preparing, a St Bartholomew's massacre of patriots.'

By placing 25,000 troops in and around Paris Louis had taken his first firm action after a long period of granting whatever the people wished. It came as an unpleasant shock to many. Everything Louis had done in fifteen years suggested that the troops had been placed merely to keep order and defend Versailles. But Desmoulins and many others preferred to hold the more exciting view, invented by their own propaganda, that all kings at heart were tyrants, that they were living, and might soon die, under a tyrannical government. In self-defence, therefore, they began to search for arms. First armourers' and gunsmiths' shops were raided, then, on the morning of 14 July, 7000 Parisians attacked the Invalides.

General Besenval, now in full command, had enough troops to guard this key building – three regiments of Swiss, 100 cavalry and a battalion of gunners – but sensibility would not let him use them. He saw the crowd attack but did not shoot – it may be said that his powder was wet with humanitarian tears. The crowd seized 28,000 muskets and some cannon. By stealing arms they had put themselves in the wrong and they now began to fear they would be punished. The sensible course would have been to send a deputation to the Assembly and negotiate from strength. But the situation did not present itself to them like that. Picturing a wholly mythical tyranny, they believed they must crush it or themselves be crushed. The symbol of that tyranny in Paris was a fourteenth-century fortress, and so the cry went up: 'To the Bastille!'

The governor of the Bastille was Bernard de Launay, aged forty-nine. He had held the post since 1776, like his father before him, and was paid 60,000 livres annually. He had looked after Cardinal de Rohan and his only battle to date had been a verbal one with Cagliostro, who claimed, falsely, that Launay had withheld some of his wife's jewels after her detention. Launay was a civilian not a soldier, and dressed in a grey frock-coat. He had a garrison of 32 Swiss and 82 pensioners, 17 cannon and an ample supply of muskets to defend the powerful rectangular fortress of eight round towers joined by courtines 100 feet high.

At noon Launay received a deputation from a municipal body, the Electors of Paris, who asked him to remove the cannon from the towers, because the people considered them a threat, and not to resist in case of attack. Launay replied that he would resist any attack to the death. However, he did remove the cannon and closed the embrasures with planks.

Some eight hundred men had gathered round the Bastille. Mostly they were small workshop masters, craftsmen and journeymen. They included 49 joiners, 48 cabinet-makers, 41 locksmiths, 28 cobblers, 11 wine-merchants, 10 hairdressers and wig-makers. They began the attack shortly after midday, using muskets and cannon, including some that were a gift from the King of Siam, captured in the Invalides. They demolished the first of two drawbridges and brought their guns into position against the second. Making a smoke screen by burning two carts of dung, they pounded the gate, and although the garrison had killed almost a hundred of the assailants, their position began to look serious. The commander of the Swiss contingent, Louis de Flue, wished to surrender but Launay said he would rather blow up the Bastille. He actually took the mesh from a cannon in order to set alight 20,000 pounds of gunpowder, but two NCOs snatched it from him. Then Flue scribbled a note, offering to lay down arms if the garrison was spared. He passed it through a loophole; a plank was swung across the moat and a young ex-soldier named Stanislas Maillard advanced along the plank, grabbed the paper and delivered it to one of the crowd's leaders, an officer of fortune named Elie. Elie read the message aloud, and shouted, 'On my word as an officer, we accept. Lower the drawbridge.'

Without orders from Launay, four pensioners lowered the draw-bridge, and the crowds rushed in, killing those few of the garrison who had not already downed arms, smashing the windows and furniture of the officers' quarters, and releasing the Bastille's seven prisoners, including a mad Irishman with a three-foot beard who believed he was God – a delusion that others, in the next few months, were to share.

Launay was arrested by a wine-merchant named Cholat and marched off towards the Hôtel de Ville. This royal official who, according to the British ambassador, 'always treated the prisoners committed to his charge with every degree of lenity and humanity', was molested by the crowd. Some tore out his hair, others jabbed him with swords. Finally a cook named Dénot cut off Launay's head with a butcher's knife, later boasting of his prowess and saying he deserved a medal for it. The dripping head was skewered on a pike, and this officer who had merely done his duty was described on a placard as 'Governor of the Bastille, disloyal and treacherous enemy of the people'.

At Versailles meanwhile the early part of the day had passed off calmly. At his *lever* Louis received the officers of the Nassau and Bouillon regiments, recently arrived, and spoke for some time to those in command. He also saw the officers of the artillery regiment that had been stationed in the Queen's stables. In the early afternoon he was conferring with his Ministers when news arrived of the attack on the Invalides. A deputation from the Assembly came to ask him to withdraw troops stationed in Paris; Louis had already ordered Besenval's troops to withdraw from the Champ de Mars, and he explained this to the deputies. Then the Vicomte de Noailles galloped up with news of the fall of the Bastille, followed at 10.30 p.m. by a new deputation. 'Gentlemen,' said Louis, 'you rend my heart yet more with your account of the misfortunes in Paris. It is inconceivable that orders given to the troops are the cause.'

Louis was genuinely puzzled. He could not see why an act of defence had been interpreted as an act of aggression. Himself highly rational, he could not understand that the Parisians, under the pressure of various fears, were behaving irrationally. He continued to believe that they were being misled.

Louis had a strong intuition that he ought to leave at once for a garrison town, perhaps Metz. He consulted Maréchal de Broglie, who said, 'Yes, we can go to Metz, but what shall we do when we get there?' With officers who dared not shoot, the best troops became chocolate soldiers. Monsieur was even more strongly opposed to flight. He begged his brother not to leave, and Louis, who still esteemed Monsieur's intelligence more than his own, let himself be dissuaded. 'I missed the right moment,' he was to tell Fersen later.

Next day, the fifteenth, Louis went to the Assembly and in a short, moving speech asked its members to intervene to prevent further bloodshed. At the request of the Assembly, he then dismissed his Government and recalled Necker.

Louis had had to capitulate. He knew it, and the Parisians knew it. At the Palais Royal the crowds, having got away with murder, now placed a price on the heads of Artois and all those they most hated. So Louis, more prompt about others' safety than his own, ordered Artois to leave France with his wife and sons, and the Polignacs too.

A painful farewell scene took place at Versailles on the evening of 16 July: Louis deeply upset to part from a brother who, whatever his faults, had always been very close to him, Antoinette in tears at saying goodbye to her loyalest friend. Not for the Trianon theatre this time, Gabrielle disguised herself as a chambermaid. As she entered her carriage a purse from the Queen containing five hundred louis d'or was handed to her and this note: 'Goodbye, tenderest of friends. What a frightful word. But it is necessary. Goodbye. I have strength only to embrace you.'

The atmosphere in Versailles was now one of alarm, with the

Princesse de Lamballe fainting right and left. On 17 July Louis had to go to Paris, unescorted, for a civic reception, and he made his will first. Almost alone in the deserted palace of padlocked doors, Antoinette felt sure he would not return. Yet she needed him now in a way she had never done before. She ordered horses ready to take her to him and even wrote and memorized a short speech imploring the Assembly to let her and her children remain with the King.

The reception went far better than either of them expected. Louis was bewildered by the warmth of his welcome from well-ordered crowds, who were confident they had reconquered their King by freeing him from the influence of evil counsellors. Louis accepted the tricoloured cockade, in which the white of the Bourbons was wedded to the red and blue of Paris. It suggested that the situation was not beyond redemption. When in the evening he returned unharmed, he and his wife embraced with the new tenderness born of danger. 'Happily there was no bloodshed,' Louis told her, 'and I swear French blood will never be shed by my order.' He repeated this several times.

After the Assembly had abolished feudal rights and privileges, Louis went there on 12 August to receive the title of 'Restorer of French liberty'. But the occasion can have given him little pleasure. Target, a famous jurist, began to read the address: 'Sire, the National Assembly has the honour . . .' only to be shouted down: 'No honour! We don't want that word.' Target resumed: 'has the honour to lay at his Majesty's feet . . .' Furious shouts greeted this, making the windows shake, and Mirabeau cut in with a mocking sally that was greeted with prolonged applause: 'Majesty has no feet.'

As the smoke cleared from the Bastille, Louis could see more clearly the various groups with whom he had to contend. First came those deputies with generous ideals: there were many of them, none more winning than Jean Joseph Mounier, thirty-one years old, from Grenoble. Slim, handsome, with a sensitive face but a weak voice which had obliged him to give up practising as a barrister, he was a man with many friends and known as 'virtuous Mounier' because of his devotion to equality of rights, and his belief in an English-style constitutional monarchy.

A second group comprised those who wished for the destruction of the old order from less generous motives. Most of these men were personally unhappy: Talleyrand, for example, the lame bishop who did not believe in God, Philippe Duc d'Orléans, the failed sailor who felt slighted by Louis and hated Antoinette.

A third group comprised the writers, those who influenced the crowd. Young Camille Desmoulins, now editor of *Révolutions de France*, was among the most idealistic. Equality of rights was not enough for him, he wanted also an end to all authority. He hailed the ending of feudal privileges in a passage modelled on the Holy Saturday liturgy: 'This is the night that has ended masterships and exclusive privileges. Anyone who wishes may now go to India, or open a shop. The master tailor, the master cobbler, the master wig-maker will weep; but their employees will rejoice and in their small attic windows there will be illumination.' Ended too was the hated List of Barristers; 'Now every man conscious of his strength and trusted by his clients will be able to plead.'

Another influential writer was Jean Louis Carra. While still at school he served two years in prison for theft. On his release he furnished Voltaire with articles for the *Encyclopédie*, stolen from an earlier reference work. He wrote a book attacking monarchy, but through his friend Cardinal de Rohan obtained a job in the King's library. He edited the *Annales politiques*, which preached political extremism. This and similar clandestine newspapers went beyond Rousseau to blasphemy, atheism and, via Mesmerism, to the theory that nothing is impossible to man.

For some in these groups Louis was still God's representative, a kindly father, inviolable. Not so the Queen. She came under increasing attack from the newspapers, and from anonymous pamphleteers, who drew on and amplified old Court gossip. A new feature of the pamphlets was their obscenity. The *Essais historiques* accused Antoinette of having numerous lovers, including Dillon, and the Duc de Coigny, father of her first child. *Les Amours de Charlot et Toinette*, in verse, begins:

> *Une Reine jeune et fringante*
> *Dont l'époux très-auguste était mauvais fouteur . . .*

She takes her pleasure alone until one day Artois makes love to her on her sofa, not noticing however that a bell-pull has got caught under the cushions, so that each bounce produces a ring of the bell. Another, 'The Austrian Woman on the Spree', cast in the form of a play, begins with Artois pinching the Queen's bottom in the presence of Madame de Polignac, as a prelude to orgies by all three.

Sexual envy is often linked with cruelty and bloodshed, as the Marquis de Sade was at that very moment demonstrating. The call for bloodshed, which started as a murmur, grew within days to a

full-throated shout. In a description of how he had stormed the
Bastille, Humbert started with this epigraph: 'It is glorious to purge
the earth of the monsters which lay it waste, and to redden it with
their blood.' Robespierre, describing the same event in a letter,
already uses his key words: 'punish', 'terror', 'victim'. Blood, the
pride and proof of aristocracy, had to be shed; it was like a secret
that had to be made public, violated, poured out. One of many such
sheddings was noted by Gouverneur Morris in his diary:

22 July. After Dinner walk a little under the Arcade of the Palais
Royal waiting for my Carriage. In this Period the Head and Body
are introduced in Triumph. The Head on a Pike, the Body dragged
naked on the Earth. Afterwards this horrible Exhibition is carried
through the different Streets. His crime is to have accepted a
Place in the Ministry. This mutilated Form of an old Man of
seventy-five is shewn to Bertier, his Son in Law, the Intendant
of Paris, and afterwards he also is put to Death and cut to Pieces,
the Populace carrying about the mangled Fragments with a
Savage Joy. Gracious God, what a People!

This from the most civilized and perhaps most humane society
on the continent of Europe! How it came to happen has already been
suggested. Young people had been brought up to pamper their
feelings and, sometimes without knowing it, their aggressive feelings
too. But they no longer had lurid public executions to attend, for
these had been suppressed on humanitarian grounds; at the theatres
there were no vicarious tragedies to purge their violent emotions,
and they no longer went to church where, for centuries, a cruel
death had been sublimated in the sacrifice of the Mass. Only those
whose hands were daily red with animal blood were immune from
the growing blood-lust: butchers, for instance. They were one of
the most numerous trades in Paris, yet only five butchers attacked
the Bastille, and no butchers took part in the subsequent killings.
In the same way Louis the killer of stags was the most averse of
men to shedding human blood. The cry for human heads came
most violently from men seated at desks, who had never in their
lives looked on mangled flesh.

In the two and a half months after the storming of the Bastille
Louis did what he could to counter these new enemies, to try to
get through to the people and to show that he had their interests at
heart. He allowed the President of the Assembly access to his
bedroom, which was considered a great honour, and – so far was the

King from thinking the Revolution would end otherwise than happily – he bought for the Crown *Brutus*, painted by an admirer of republican Rome, Louis David. He saw to it that the royalist newspapers stated his policy and answered slanders against him and the Queen. On 24 September, to relieve the shortage of bread, he and Antoinette sent their table silver to the mint.

Louis, equally, was concerned to maintain some balance of forces in France, and to protect the ancient rights of the Church and the nobility; hoping that time would show deputies the need for amendments to them, he delayed accepting the 'abolition of feudalism' and the Assembly's first fundamental statements of constitutional principle.

This kind of behaviour would have suited a normal situation, but it proved inadequate at a time when passions were aroused. Louis again came under suspicion and his enemies, not least the gutter journalists, watched for any action by the King that could be used to whip up more hatred and bloodshed. They found what they wanted at last in an incident on 1 October, when Louis and Antoinette gave a banquet for the Flanders Regiment in the opera house at Versailles. Such banquets were traditional when a new regiment came into garrison. The officers toasted the royal couple, the band played a sentimental royalist song: '*O Richard! O mon Roi! l'univers t'abandonne*', and later the soldiers sang and danced under the King's windows. Desmoulins and others played this up in their newspapers, adding untrue details, such as the troops trampling the tricolor cockades underfoot. They described the banquet as a sacrilegious orgy – for the Nation, spelled with a capital, was deemed sacrosanct – and Desmoulins called on Parisians to bring the King to Paris.

The price of the 4 lb. loaf had dropped to 12 sous, but owing to a drought the new harvest was slow in coming through the watermills, and bread in Paris was still scarce and of poor quality. Suspicion of the King's intentions had become acute, since he had again called troops to the Paris area. On the morning of 5 October fishwives and women stall-holders of the market converged on the Hôtel de Ville, demanding bread; after seizing the guards' arms they decided to march to Versailles, a distance of twelve miles, and found a leader in the tall black-haired consumptive who had stormed the Bastille, Stanislas Maillard.

Antoinette spent that afternoon walking for the last time in her Trianon garden. She was preoccupied by the drop in the little stream feeding the pond of the Hameau. Louis went shooting and bagged twenty and a half brace. At three a messenger galloped up with a note from Saint-Priest, Minister of the Household. Louis considered it. 'They're asking for bread. Alas, if I had any, I shouldn't wait for them to come and ask me for it.' He was just going to mount his horse when a new messenger rode up, this time straight from Paris, and threw himself at the King's feet. 'Sire, they're only women. I beg your Majesty not to be afraid.'

'Afraid!' Louis retorted. 'I've never in my life been afraid.'

Louis called a Cabinet. Necker characteristically proposed to grant whatever the crowd should demand; Saint-Priest suggested the King place himself at the head of his troops and defend the Sèvres bridge. Others suggested he retire to a loyal province. Louis chose neither the bold nor the feeble course; he waited quietly for the crowd, instructing the Bodyguard on no account to fire.

The women arrived at five o'clock, joined now by men, including *agents provocateurs* paid by the Duc d'Orléans: 7000 altogether, the women in red cottons and white caps armed with scythes, pitchforks, pikes, muskets and daggers; shouting that they would tear the Queen to pieces to make cockades. They swept into the Assembly, where Mounier chose twelve of them to go to the Palace.

Louis received the women in his Salle de Conseil and asked them to tell him their wishes.

A pretty flower-seller of seventeen from the Palais Royal, Louison Chabry, replied, 'Sire, we want bread.'

'You know my heart,' answered Louis. 'I will order all the bread in Versailles to be collected and given to you.'

This was too much for Louison, who fell to the floor in a faint. Smelling-salts were brought; Louison revived and begged to be allowed to kiss the King's hand.

'She deserves better than that!' said Louis, whereupon he embraced the flower-girl. Once outside, Louison was in danger of her life for her conversion to the Court, the crowd threatening to strangle her with her own garters.

The *agents provocateurs* immediately got to work. As Mounier was to testify, they gave the impression that Louis was powerless; the aristocrats – a term of hatred just coming into use – and the Queen would withhold the bread. 'Thus,' says Mounier, 'they associated with the feeling of want the feeling of vengeance.'

In every town of France a citizen militia had been formed, answerable to the Assembly and known as the national guard. The Versailles national guard, who were hostile to and jealous of the

King's troops, welcomed the horde of Parisians and at nine that evening provoked a clash with the King's Bodyguard, posted around the palace. Soon shots were being fired. 'In the Œil de Bœuf,' says the Swedish ambassador, 'there was a typically French agitation – brave men begging to risk their all for the King and promising to make him master of events' – but in the whole palace there was only one company of troops who could be relied on. While the women bivouacked outside the gates, La Fayette arrived at the head of 20,000 Paris national guards. Louis questioned him and asked for an assurance that the royal family were now safe. This La Fayette gave. At two in the morning Louis and Antoinette, in their separate apartments, went to bed.

At 5.30 a.m., entering by a gate usually kept locked, whose key could only have been got through treachery, armed women broke into the palace, killed and cut off the heads of two guards, and made for the Queen's apartment, shouting 'Death to the whore!' Mio-mandre, an officer of the Bodyguard, was on duty. Before being cut down he just had time to fling open the antechamber door and shout: 'Save the Queen.' Her ladies-in-waiting heard, locked an inner door, and rushed to the Queen's bedroom. In her shift and petticoat, with her stockings in her hand, Antoinette hurried to the King's apartment. Minutes later the crowd broke in and with sabres slashed the sheets on her bed to shreds. Meanwhile Louis had gone by a private staircase to look for his wife. When he returned he found Antoinette waiting for him, and a few minutes later they were joined by their children.

Throughout the attack and killing La Fayette lay sleeping on a sofa: as Rivarol was to put it, 'he slept against his King.' But once wakened he quickly cleared the palace of assailants. Then a crowd gathered in the marble courtyard, clamouring for the King. Louis showed himself. Then came the cry, 'The Queen! The Queen!' With a yellow-striped dressing-gown on and her hair in disarray, Antoinette stepped on to the balcony with her son and daughter. 'No children! No children!' She made her children go back into the room and stood alone for two minutes. Muskets were levelled at her, but she did not flinch, whereupon the crowd's mood swung round and they shouted enthusiastically, 'Long live the Queen!'

A voice cried, 'The King to Paris!' and was taken up by the crowd, who thought that the King's presence among them would ensure sufficient bread. Louis consulted with his Ministers, who had arrived on the scene after the palace had been cleared of assailants.

The previous evening Antoinette and Saint-Priest had urged him to flee, but Louis had refused with the scornful phrase, 'A fugitive King!' Now flight had become out of the question: Necker, Montmorin and a majority of his Ministers advised him to fall in with the crowd's wishes as the only way of avoiding further bloodshed. Louis agreed. It was compromise – 'for the happiness of the people'. But he insisted on taking his family with him. Going on to the balcony, he called out in a loud voice: 'My friends, I will go to Paris with my wife and children. I confide all that I hold most dear to the love of my good subjects.'

At 1.25, avoiding the main bloodstained staircase, Louis went down to his waiting carriage. Leaves on the oak trees he had planted were turning yellow; his library and maps, his model ships and locksmith's forge – when would he see them again? Before getting in, he turned to the Comte de Gouvernet, an officer he trusted: 'You are in charge here. Try to save my poor Versailles for me.'

Louis saw that a huge disorderly procession had formed round his carriage. It was headed by the national guard. Then came the fishwives, some carrying branches trimmed with ribbons, others flags; some wore grenadier bearskins and shouldered muskets. Those too drunk to stand sat astride the guns. Loaves of bread were stuck on bayonets, carts of flour drawn by the King's finest thoroughbreds. At the rear came carriages carrying the few remaining courtiers, retainers and belongings. 'The only sound to be heard in the Château was the fastening of doors and shutters which had not been closed since the time of Louis XIV.' The palace of Versailles was never to be inhabited again.

The procession started off. In the royal carriage sat Louis, with Antoinette, their daughter aged eleven, their son aged four, Monsieur, Louis's sister Elisabeth, and the children's governess, Madame de Tourzel. Round the carriage eddied the fishwives and soldiers, firing off muskets and chanting songs, 'like a Saturnalia' thought the Saxon ambassador. The fishwives danced on the muddy road and some shouted threats at the Queen. 'Let's soak her arms and hands in the smoking entrails of her Bodyguard!' The Dauphin clasped his hands at the carriage window, crying *'Grâce pour Maman! Grâce pour Maman!'*

Louis showed no alarm. His behaviour now was probably similar to that noticed by an English observer on 17 July: 'he was accustomed to throw his head very much back on his shoulders, which, by obliging him to look upwards, gave a kind of stupid character to his countenance, by increasing the apparent breadth of his face, and by preventing that variety of expression which is produced by looking about.'

'I returned to Paris in one of the carriages that followed the King,' Fersen wrote home a few days later. 'We were six and a half hours on the road. May God preserve me from ever again seeing so heart-breaking a spectacle as that of the last few days.' Louis and Antoinette were obliged to go to the Hôtel de Ville, where in a ceremony in which no one seemed to notice the irony, the new Mayor, Bailly, handed Louis the city keys. Among those watching was Artois's Scots gardener, Blaikie:

> The people was all roaring out '*Voilà le Boulanger et la Boulangère et le Petit Mitron*' saying that now they should have bread as they now had got the baker and his wife and boy. The Queen sat at the bottom of the Coach with the Dauphin on her knees in this condition while some of the blackguards in the rable was firing there guns over her head. As I stood by the coach one man fired and loaded his gun four times and fired over the Queen's head. I told him to desist but he said he would continue but when I told him I should try by force to stop him and not have people hurt by his imprudence some cryed that it was right and so he sluged of very quietelly and after the corte went on and they lodged the King and his family in the Thuilleries.

This dark sixteenth-century palace had been uninhabited since 1665, though Antoinette had occasionally slept there after a late party in Paris. Its furniture was stiff and old-fashioned, its windows small, and until 1782 its largest room had served as a theatre for tragedies.

'It's very ugly,' complained the Dauphin.

'Louis XIV lived here,' Antoinette told him, 'and was comfortable. We must not be more demanding than he.'

They ate supper and went to bed exhausted – Madame Royale had to sleep on a sofa.

Antoinette found that the hair at her temples had begun to turn grey from shock. Yet both she and Louis retained their faith in the ordinary Frenchman. 'There are evil men,' Louis said next day to the Dauphin, 'who have stirred up the people, and the excesses committed are their work; we must not bear a grudge against the people.' And Antoinette wrote to Mercy: 'Despite the unkind things done to me, I hope to win over the healthy, honest section of the bourgeoisie and people.'

CHAPTER 20

Diminishing Freedom

THE move from Versailles to the Tuileries brought important changes to Louis's life. At the personal level he was none too pleased at being forced into an old-fashioned uncomfortable house, stifling in summer, icy in winter, far from his favourite park and woods, and at being obliged to stop hunting. The Assembly, it is true, offered to let him continue his favourite sport, but Louis said that in such difficult times he did not wish to. Though he rode occasionally in the Bois de Boulogne, his constitution required long exhausting hunts, and it suffered from the new regime. He began to get a pot belly and a pronounced double chin.

Louis chose a suite of rooms overlooking the Seine on the first floor of the steep-roofed three-storey grey stone château. Here the rituals of the *lever* and the *coucher* continued as though the Court was still at Versailles, but with one obvious difference: Louis was followed everywhere, even into the garden for his daily walk, by six armed national guards answerable to the Assembly.

Louis was no longer an absolute monarch. According to decrees he had signed in early October, he was 'King of the French' in accordance with a constitution still being drafted, and 'the source of all sovereignty resides essentially in the nation.' Louis still held the supreme executive power, but his law-making powers had been assumed by the Assembly, though he could still veto for several years a law of which he disapproved.

Louis had been deeply shocked by the violence of October 5th and 6th. He told Bailly that he hoped his stay in Paris would 'bring peace, concord and submission to law', and he wrote privately to his cousin the King of Spain lodging a protest against 'all the acts contrary to royal authority wrung from me by force since 15 July'. It was in this mood that during the autumn and winter he went to ground in the Tuileries. He seems to have been deeply depressed and the depression emphasized the weaknesses in his character: a reluctance to force things to conclusions or to become too involved. Perhaps also his extra weight diminished his energy. He resumed his lock-making, saw a lot of his children, and in the evenings played whist with Monsieur. He seems to have been wearied with the whole political business and for almost four months kept away from the Assembly.

From his windows Louis could see the new red, white and blue flag embroidered with rods and axes and the words, 'Freedom. Nation. Law. King.' Freedom came first, King last, and, as reports reached to him of each new debate in the Assembly Louis began to realize that unless he asserted himself the whole notion of King would be squeezed out. That he did not want. He became alive again to his responsibilities and began to bestir himself. He must act with the Assembly in order to retain his powers, then use them in order to preserve a just balance of interests within the State.

On 4 February 1790 Louis walked across to the Riding School where the Assembly now met. It had changed character since Versailles, for a hundred moderates – the men with whom Louis could most easily have worked – had been hounded out by violent Parisians, among them Lally-Tollendal and Jean Joseph Mounier, who escaped assassination nineteen times. The remainder sat, according to their views, on one side or the other of the president: this being the origin of Left and Right.

'It is time, gentlemen,' Louis said, 'that I should associate myself more closely and in a still more direct and open fashion with the successful carrying out of all that you have planned for the benefit of France.' He spoke of the need to establish the new order calmly and to work for the good of all. He pledged himself to defend freedom: 'I will do more: in agreement with the Queen who shares all my sentiments, I will educate my son in the new principles of constitutional monarchy and freedom with justice.'

Louis's speech was cheered and he was escorted back in triumph. But as the weeks passed it became clear that between Louis and the Assembly there lay a fundamental tension. Louis's title was 'by the grace of God and the constitutional law of the State King of the French' and while he emphasized the first phrase, the Assembly emphasized the second. Louis wished to act freely in the name of the nation, of whom he was the supreme representative; the Assembly wished him to be their rubber stamp. This tension came to a head in May when Alexandre de Lameth introduced a motion proposing to transfer the power to declare peace and war from the King to the Assembly.

Now Louis had always taken a close interest in foreign affairs and made important decisions personally. He was one of France's most peaceful kings and had three times averted an imminent threat of European war. He considered the prerogative under debate an essential part of a monarch's powers. But how was he to make his case heard? The Assembly had passed a law forbidding him to take Ministers from among their number – a striking example of their deep suspicion of the monarchy as such – and so the Government could take no part in the debate. Louis was obliged therefore to subsidize several deputies to speak on his behalf, the most influential being Mirabeau, who now believed that without a strong monarchy France would become enslaved to extremists. Heavily in debt, Mirabeau was glad to take the 6000 livres a month Louis agreed to pay him.

So the crucial debate opened. Alexandre de Lameth's brother Charles denounced the wars waged by Louis's ancestors, while Barnave argued that Pericles had destroyed Athens by launching the Peloponnesian War. Meanwhile, as usual, a mob terrorized the Assembly. 'People with haggard eyes, faces drawn and blue with anger,' writes one ambassador, 'circle the Assembly hall, shouting, "You're a bunch of milksops! If the Assembly favours the King, we'll at once take up arms . . . Let the Assembly watch out, we'll put Paris to fire and sword rather than let the nation be deprived of its rights." '

Mirabeau ran this gauntlet of threats in order to speak against the motion. 'You have referred to Pericles making war in order to cover up his heavy spending. To hear you speak, one would think Pericles was a king. Just the contrary, he was a man who knew how to flatter the people's passion and to buy applause. Whom in fact did he persuade to launch the Peloponnesian War? . . . The National Assembly of Athens.' 'By giving all power to the Assembly,' Mirabeau concluded, 'you are falsifying the spirit of the Constitution . . . Better no king at all than an impotent, useless king.'

It was admitted to be one of Mirabeau's most powerful speeches, but the deputies were unconvinced, and they deprived Louis of his power to make peace or war. The most they would grant was that the King should *propose* peace or war, leaving them to issue the actual decree.

Louis was extremely disappointed. He resented the fact that the Assembly, while reverently uttering the word 'freedom' a hundred times a day, should diminish the freedom of action of one whom the Cahiers all agreed was the nation's supreme representative. However, he continued to try to work with the Assembly, hoping that things would improve.

Antoinette, meanwhile, was also trying to adapt to diminishing freedom. She, like her husband, was tailed by six national guards, while deputations were constantly popping into her rooms: fish-wives to protest their loyalty and to say that *they* had had no part in the October Days, patriotic citizens who wished to see the Dauphin – 'a very pretty, good-natured-looking boy' according to Arthur Young – and so ensure he had not been smuggled out of Paris. On these occasions Antoinette had Marie Thérèse de Lamballe by her, but the departure of Gabrielle de Polignac was a loss she felt so deeply she could hardly pronounce the name. When Georgiana asked if she had any message for Gabrielle, 'she said in a low, trembling voice, "Tell her that you have seen a person who will love her till her life's end."'

Antoinette, like her husband, tried to work for conciliation. To a commission questioning her about the October Days, she said: 'I saw everything, I heard everything, I have forgotten everything.' The phrasing sounds as though suggested by Louis, but that it reflects Antoinette's feelings is shown by a letter of the same period: 'We must inspire confidence in this unhappy people. It is only immense patience and the purity of our intentions that can bring it back to us.' And so she launched into a life centred more than before on public welfare. To her, days among the hyacinths of Trianon succeeded visits to manufactories, hospitals, asylums, orphanages.

Louis wished to strengthen Mirabeau's attachment and, knowing his susceptibility to women, asked Antoinette to meet him. Although she considered 'his whole existence is nothing but deceit, cunning and lies,' Antoinette consented. In great secrecy, half-fearing assassination by the Court, Mirabeau made his way to Saint-Cloud where Louis and Antoinette were spending the summer, and on 3 July was driven by his nephew to the garden gate, whence he was led to the Queen's apartments. Here Antoinette received him in her husband's presence.

The Queen was losing her looks but suffering had increased her charm, and to this Mirabeau willingly succumbed. After a conversation that has not been preserved, the ageing roué, partly from gallantry, partly from a southerner's sense of theatre, asked permission to kiss her hand. Antoinette extended it, Mirabeau fell on his knees. 'Madame, the monarchy is saved.'

Outside, on his way to his carriage, he confided to his nephew in a voice trembling with emotion: 'She is very great, she is very noble and very unfortunate, but I shall save her.' Mirabeau did indeed try to save her, and to strengthen Louis's powers, but the Assembly noticed Mirabeau's improved living standards, drew the obvious conclusion and declined to be moved by his rhetoric. So in the long run Louis gained little from his deal with the chivalrous but dissolute Comte.

Louis and Antoinette were now plainly where the French people wanted them to be. Louis's freedom of action was curtailed, Antoinette separated from supposed reactionaries like Artois and the Polignacs. Both were guarded by the people's militia, and spied on through keyholes. They were co-operating in the new order; everything they said showed a desire to see it work. It might be thought, therefore, that having achieved the political changes they desired, the people too might have settled down to make the new order work, and so they might have done had their revolution been only political. In fact it was far more. Politics constituted only one aspect of a more fundamental disturbance arising from the principles, feelings and conception of man considered earlier. In changing the political structure political leaders thought they had cured the disease; in fact they had only removed the chief symptom.

Symptom-removal is one of the most dangerous forms of medical intervention, for the disease spreads almost invisibly. Text-book signs are no longer there to warn of deterioration; there do arise, however, troubling forms of irrational behaviour.

The first was already in evidence and relates to the Queen. On any rational interpretation the sewage of libels against her would now have ceased or at least dropped to a trickle: in fact it swelled both in quantity and virulence. One duct still carried the sexual excesses of *l'Autrichienne* – the name had scurrilous as well as xenophobic overtones, since *chienne* means 'bitch'. An illustrated pamphlet shows the Queen holding in her arms a grenadier of the National Guard: '*Bravo, Bravo! La Reine se pénètre de la Patrie.*' Another names more than thirty of her lovers, including at the age of twelve and a half an affair with the future Cardinal de Rohan, and includes an admission by Louis that he is not the father of Madame Royale and the Dauphin. A new, heightened version of Madame de La Motte's *Memoirs* accuses Antoinette of Lesbianism. The Queen turned her eyes, Jeanne is represented as saying, 'on what she smilingly called my "outstanding attractions", then her lips, her kisses following her greedy glances over my quivering body . . .

What a welcome substitute I made, she laughed, for the lumpish, repulsive body of the "Prime Minister" – her mocking name for the King.'

Still more damaging were the strictly political slanders. One common charge was that the Queen passed money to Austria: how much truth there was in it may be gauged from a letter of Joseph to his brother Leopold: 'They cannot get away from the idea that my sister has secretly sent me millions, whilst I do not know why or how I should have asked for them or how she could have got them to me; I have never seen a sou from France!'

Another kind of mud stuck – and has stuck to this day. With the 1789 harvest, bread became plentiful but, writes an English observer, 'such is the enmity of the people against the Queen that they circulate letters written in her name, said to have been intercepted, in which she is made to say to the Comte d'Artois, "Everything goes well, we shall end by starving them" – many people believe in the authenticity of these letters.'

A third political theme runs through the pamphlets: the Queen hates the Revolution and is plotting to overthrow it. Now in August 1790 Mirabeau secretly advised Louis to withdraw to Normandy, rally the army and fight it out with the minority of the extreme Left. This ruthless plan was welcomed by only one member of the royal family, Elisabeth, who wrote to the Marquise de Bombelles: 'I regard [civil war] as necessary . . . Anarchy can never end without it, and the longer it is put off, the more blood will be shed.' Antoinette's opinion of the plan appears in a letter to Mercy: 'How could Mirabeau or any other thinking being believe that the moment would ever come, especially at the present time, for us to provoke a civil war?'

So widespread as to be believed even in villages of remote Auvergne, these slanders constituted an important political fact. For Louis, his Queen was no longer the brightest jewel in his crown but a serious liability. He had told the Assembly that 'the Queen shares all my sentiments' and Parisians interpreted everything he did in terms of Antoinette's sinister influence. Antoinette, involuntarily, contributed to diminish her husband's freedom.

Two groups actually tried to separate Louis and Antoinette. One group saw this as a means of weakening the Crown. The pamphlet containing Louis's admission that he is not the father of her children, went on to say that 'leading prelates, generals and great lords' advised Louis to repudiate his wife and pack her off, with the children, to Vienna. 'They are planning to legalize divorce,' writes the Spanish ambassador, 'then separate the King and Queen . . . and shut her up in a convent for the rest of her days.'

The other group hoped the removal of the Queen would make Louis a more effective King. Its leader, La Fayette, came to see Antoinette about it at Saint-Cloud. He 'used the most odious means to agitate her soul; he even went so far as to tell her that, in order to obtain a divorce, they would try to take her in adultery.'

Louis unhesitatingly rejected all such attempts to take away Antoinette. He went further. It was probably at this time that he gave his wife an assurance never to separate himself from her and their children. Shared suffering had strengthened their affection, if we are to judge by a note of deeper tenderness on both sides. Antoinette wrote to Leopold: 'In order to re-establish peace and happiness, [the King] has sacrificed his opinions, his safety and even his freedom. I cannot believe that so many misfortunes and so many virtues will not one day be rewarded;' while in a postscript to one of Antoinette's letters to Gabrielle de Polignac, Louis wrote: 'Your friend is very unhappy and very misjudged; but I feel that one day justice will be done her.'

The Assembly could not long remain immune from this suspicion of the Queen. They were infected with it indirectly through whispering campaigns and directly through demonstrations: when Mirabeau spoke for the monarchy he had to push his way through a hostile crowd shouting 'Traitor! *A la lanterne!*' An image grew of a sexually voracious Austrian draining his strength from the people's King in order to impose on him her plot for counter-revolution.

How could sensible men believe this? The answer lies in the atmosphere of gullibility created by the equation 'deep feeling = truth'. Here is one typical example from hundreds. Brissot, a former Mesmerist, denounced the following dire and dangerous 'plot': two men received a reactionary programme from Madame Thomassin, 'a somnambulist with aristocratic connections', who had received it from the Virgin Mary, and they came to Saint-Cloud to 'imprint' it in a state of trance, by means of a mesmeric fluid, on Louis's brain. The two men were arrested – much to their surprise, as they had believed themselves invisible – and Brissot solemnly warned against a 'counter-revolution by sleepwalkers'.

Believing that Louis was under constant pressure to foil the Revolution, the Assembly took extraordinary precautions to parry his blows, and this meant in effect still further diminishing his freedom. Now according to one of their own laws, the King's Ministers should have had full responsibility for action within their departments, but during 1790 and early 1791 the Assembly nullified the law by appointing no less than 31 standing committees to supervise Ministers and by issuing their own instructions for the application of general decrees. Louis in his study overlooking the Seine gave, through his Ministers, one set of orders, while a stone's throw away in the Riding School the distrustful Assembly issued a contrary set. Sooner or later a conflict was bound to arise.

Discipline in the armed forces had been lax when Louis acceded: it had now grown vastly laxer. Even Louis's guard at the Tuileries 'were so insolent that a soldier at the King's door gave a box on the ear to his Sergeant, and a kick in the stomach to the Corporal, notwithstanding which he was not punished, nor any notice taken of it.' Agents of the left-wing Jacobin Club encouraged such behaviour, with the result that in August the army mutinied at Nancy and in September the navy mutinied at Brest. Louis through his Ministers acted firmly but with his usual concern to minimize bloodshed, and both mutinies were with difficulty brought under control.

The Left in the Assembly roared disapproval. They resented the fact that Louis, through his Ministers, had acted independently of them, though it was they who had passed the law saying 'the supreme executive power resides in the King.' They launched an attack on his Ministers – whose appointment the previous year they had warmly approved – and declared them 'aristocrats', 'slaves of the Court'. Smears, threats, even a projected indictment so heightened fury against them that on 21 October 1790 the whole Ministry tendered Louis their resignation.

Louis would not accept it. In a letter made public he denied the charges against them: 'I have always seen you act as friends of the people, of order, justice and the laws.' Louis persuaded the Ministry to stay, but within a month the Ministers of War and of the Navy and the Keeper of the Seals found their places too hot and quit. Louis with difficulty found successors, but the pattern of distrust, slander and forced resignation was to be repeated with sickening frequency, hence Louis's later declaration: 'The complete absence of freedom has stultified every step I have taken since the month of October 1789.'

Had the curtailment of Louis's freedom been confined to politics, he and the Assembly might eventually have found a *modus vivendi*. But it now moved to a wholly different sphere.

The Assembly had found a quick way of remedying France's shortage of money. 'All the temporal lands, which men devout have given to the Church, would they strip from us:' the French clergy could echo Shakespeare's Canterbury as all Church land, in November 1789, was nationalized. It was valued at 3000 million livres, and in the next year and a half assignats for 2500 million livres were issued. Financially, the French were now in clover.

Having seized its property, the Assembly, it might be thought, would leave the Church alone. Not at all. Some of its lawyer members held a strongly Gallican, anti-papal tradition, others mocked in the vein of Voltaire. Many – probably a majority – denied the basic Christian conflict between man's conscience and his natural desires, between grace and gravity. They believed man's problems could be resolved by the State; that natural man had no need of the supernatural, and therefore that there was no room for a spiritual authority at the elbow of the secular ruler. Some, such as Mirabeau and Robespierre, even made of the State a new religion, and when Mirabeau came to die the Assembly buried him, with Voltaire and Rousseau, in a gaunt building known as the Pantheon. Once a pantheon had been in honour of all the gods: the gods now were patriots, and this was the first temple of *la Patrie*.

The Assembly's religious views would have been of scant political importance had they not been backed up and reinforced by widespread anti-clericalism. The people in their new mood had come to hate the clergy as representatives not only of the old order but of order in general: of restraint, rationality, gentleness; and here again the Revolution is seen to have impulses far deeper than the merely political. A glance at the Paris theatres reveals the mood: *Les Rigueurs du Cloître* showed girls forced to take vows and the terror of convent life; *L'Autodafé* painted a lurid picture of the Goa Inquisition; while at the Théâtre Français Chenier's *Charles IX* showed the Cardinal de Lorraine, in full pontificals, blessing the daggers with which Catholics are to assassinate Protestants. Was it, asked Burke, 'intended to make the Parisians abhor persecution and loathe the effusion of blood? No, it was to teach them to persecute their own pastors.'

The Assembly began by appointing a committee on Church affairs, led by Treilhard, a Voltairean, and Camus, a crypto-Jansenist who spent hours praying before a lifesize crucifix in his bedroom and from the tribune attacked the nobles – he raised one of the rare laughs in the Assembly when he called the nobility's country houses '*ci-devant châteaux*.' The committee first proposed the suppression of virtually all monasteries and convents, and when this had become law, a complete restructuring of the Church. Bishoprics were cut from 130 to 83; bishops and parish priests were to be elected – even atheists might vote; bishops were to be 'guided' by twelve or sixteen episcopal vicars, and no longer to be invested by the Pope. These changes were called the Civil Constitution of the Clergy, but that is a misnomer, for several changes such as the curtailing of a bishop's powers affected the nature of spiritual authority.

On 12 July 1790 the Assembly passed this bill and struck out its committee's recommendation that Louis should negotiate all details with the Pope. Then they sent the law to Louis. He could either sanction and publish it or, if he disapproved of it, impose his veto, which would have the effect of suspending the law for the lifetime of two legislatures.

Louis was a believing and practising Catholic but as King he had taken little interest in Church affairs. Like all monarchs of his day, he considered the Pope a political nonentity and when Pius VI had written to him demanding that Cardinal de Rohan be tried in Rome, Louis had replied sharply that a Pope should not meddle in French affairs.

When the Civil Constitution of the Clergy arrived on his desk, Louis consulted his Cabinet. His Keeper of the Seals, Archbishop de Cicé, advised him not to sign immediately but to work out some arrangement with Rome but a majority of the Cabinet, led by the Foreign Minister, Montmorin, advised Louis to sanction the law at once. On 22 July Louis did so.

Two days later Louis received a letter from Pius, written of course without knowing that Louis had already signed the law. 'We expressly declare,' said the Pope, 'that if you approve the decrees relating to the clergy you are leading your nation into schism.'

Pius's strong line came as a surprise, but Louis stuck to his decision. He was ready, he told Pius, to receive the Pope's comments on the law with due respect, but asked him to take into account the present condition of the Church in France; 'the chief object of religion now is the avoidance of schism.' In effect he was asking Pius to acquiesce in a *fait accompli*.

The Assembly, meanwhile, far from being content with Louis's approval of the Civil Constitution, stepped up its fire. First it rejected a compromise proposed by a highly respected archbishop, Boisgelin of Aix, accepting the principles of the new law but referring details to a joint commission of clerics and laymen; then on 27 November it voted a decree forcing every priest in the land to swear on oath to observe the Civil Constitution.

This law was much clearer-cut than the first. It expressed the Assembly's determination that even in spiritual matters there must be no authority higher than itself. Louis did not like the look of the law. Discussing it with Fersen, who had recently urged him to flee to some provincial town, Louis remarked, 'As things stand now, I would rather be King of Metz than King of France.'

Louis knew what the priests of France did not yet know: that Rome disapproved of the Civil Constitution. So as soon as the new law arrived on his desk he wrote to Pius asking for speedy guidance. Three weeks passed and no answer arrived. On 23 December Louis received a sharp demand from the Assembly for immediate sanction of the law. Louis asked a little more time, as the Pope's reply had not yet arrived, whereupon Camus the Jansenist rose. The Pope, he thundered, has no right to interfere with the French Church, and he proposed that a second and final peremptory demand for his signature be sent to Louis. This was agreed.

The crowds that had urged a strong line on the Assembly from the public gallery now headed across the courtyard to the Tuileries. There they furiously shouted at the King to hurry up and sign and hurled threats at the Queen.

Louis turned for advice to the best of the clerics in the Assembly, Archbishop Boisgelin. He recalled the Assembly's demands and, it appears, expressed concern for the Queen. Boisgelin replied that a majority of the clergy would weakly take the oath, and therefore that Louis should compromise before the Assembly's demands, which, he wrote, amounted to constraint. He advised Louis to sign, and again to urge Pius to accept another *fait accompli*.

On Christmas Day Louis seated himself at his desk in front of the new law and Boisgelin's letter of advice. He faced perhaps the most painful possible dilemma: the one between truth and charity. Louis believed that the new law infringed traditional Catholic truth by giving the State undue power in spiritual matters, and yet it was the will of the people, *his* people who put their trust in him. His veto would alienate the Assembly, divide France and, as an English agent predicted, it was probable that the Seine would ebb 'a crimson current to the sea'. On the other hand, in sanctioning the law he would be going against his conscience – yet about this he could not be absolutely certain, since the Pope had not replied. Which stood higher: the King concerned with peace, or the man concerned with conscience? On 26 December, with a heavy heart, Louis made his choice and at the bottom of the law signed 'Louis': the letters are tight and flattened, like an animal at bay.

The New Year, 1791, arrived and astonished everyone, not least Louis and Boisgelin. Outside the Riding School a crowd howled '*A la lanterne*, all who refuse the oath,' but of the forty-four bishops in the Assembly all save two refused to take the oath, and barely a third of the clerical deputies took it. Though in Paris a majority did take the oath, in the rest of France most of the clergy refused. In Strasbourg three priests only took the oath, in Rennes two, in Nîmes one, in Montpellier none. In the absence of papal guidance, it was a remarkable demonstration of loyalty to the Holy See.

Parisians showed their anger by breaking into St Sulpice, whose curate refused to take the oath, and forcing the organist to play their new song, '*Ça ira, ça ira, les aristocrates à la lanterne!*', while they sang and danced to it in the nave. Though article 10 of the Declaration of the Rights of Man, proclaimed in 1789, laid down that 'no one must be disturbed on account of his religious opinions,' they threatened the lives of non-juring priests, denounced by the Assembly as 'refractory' and 'fanatical'.

Louis's Aunt Adélaïde, living near Paris, heartily detested the Civil Constitution of the Clergy and, as reprisals worsened, she and her one surviving sister, bagpipe-playing Victoire, decided France was no place for them and asked Louis for passports to Rome. Louis issued them and on 19 February 1791 the two elderly spinsters set off secretly, without even a change of linen. Ordered by the Assembly to be arrested, they were held for eleven days in Burgundy, Adélaïde writing gaily to a friend that she and Victoire played piquet all day, then washed their chemises and went to bed early, to give them time to dry.

It was Louis who bore the brunt of public anger. More crowds swirled around the Tuileries, pressing him to recall Mesdames; deputations came in to see that the royal aunts had not kidnapped the Dauphin. Once again the mob had the upper hand, and only a forceful speech by Mirabeau prevented the aunts being brought back to Paris under guard.

When his aunts had safely crossed the frontier and the crowds dispersed, Louis took to his bed. His nerves were frayed, his conscience too was deeply troubled. He sensed that he had taken the wrong decision on Christmas Day. He who was rarely ill now lay feverish for three weeks, coughing and spitting blood. In his anguish he found again his boyhood devotion to the Sacred Heart of Jesus, a symbol of Christ's overflowing love for man – denied by the Jansenists – and of loyalty to the Holy See. 'O God,' he wrote, 'You see all the wounds that tear my heart, and the depths of the abyss into which I have fallen,' and Louis vowed, as soon as he was in a position to do so, to build a church in honour of the Sacred Heart.

Hardly was he up and about when Louis at last received a reply from Pius. The Pope pronounced the Civil Constitution schismatic, and suspended every priest who took the oath to it unless he retracted within forty days. He declared the election of State bishops null and void, and their consecration a sacrilege.

The Pope had spoken; it was for each French Catholic, having searched his conscience, to obey or disobey. Louis personally had no doubts left. He dismissed his confessor of the past fifteen years, who had taken the oath in February, and replaced him by a holy Norman, Fr Hébert, who shared Louis's devotion to the Sacred Heart. He then asked a learned theologian, Bishop Bonal of Clermont, whether he could receive Easter Communion from a Constitutional priest – for the curé of his parish church, St Germain l'Auxerrois, had taken the oath – and whether he must publicly retract his sanction of the law signed on 26 December. Bonal replied that Louis was under an obligation not to receive Communion from a Constitutional priest but not to retract his sanction of the law.

When the Pope's decision had been made public in a Brief, Paris reacted by burning Pius in effigy and, when the Nuncio protested, by throwing into his carriage the head of a decapitated policeman. Fishwives broke into a convent in the Faubourg Saint-Antoine and beat up the Grey Nuns: an action which Louis publicly condemned. The Directory of Paris, a municipal body, called on Louis to dismiss Fr Hébert, while on 17 April the Club of Cordeliers circulated a pamphlet, '*Great Treason of the King of the French*', denouncing Louis – untruly – for having received Communion from a non-juring priest and thereby showing himself 'refractory to the laws of the kingdom'.

Louis saw that this campaign must come to a head on Easter

Sunday. The crowd would then try to force him to receive Communion from a Constitutional priest, and this in conscience he could not do. He decided therefore to go to Saint-Cloud – his doctors had ordered a rest – and there quietly receive his Easter Communion from the hand of a priest loyal to the Holy See.

On Monday of Holy Week punctually at half past eleven Louis and Antoinette, with their children and the children's governess, arrived at the door of the Tuileries, expecting to find their carriages. Several minutes passed. Soon it became apparent that the carriages had been stopped by a large crowd gathered outside the gates. Antoinette then proposed that they should get into a berlin standing in the main courtyard. This they did, and the coachman drove to the gates.

Here the national guard, commanded by La Fayette, stood on duty, but, won over by the crowd, they refused to open the gates. La Fayette swore at them, and Bailly added his own meek voice, but the guard refused to budge. Finally Louis put his head out of the carriage window and said:

'It would be surprising if I, who have given freedom to the nation, should not be free myself.'

To this the crowd responded with a hail of invectives: 'You f——aristocrat!' 'You great hog; we pay you twenty-five millions a year; do what we tell you.'

Antoinette appealed to the crowd, but she too was insulted. Louis's attendants surrounding his coach were dragged away with violence; Amédée de Duras, First Gentleman of the Bedchamber, was so roughly handled that the Dauphin burst into tears and cried: 'Save him, save him!'

La Fayette asked Bailly to proclaim martial law by hoisting the red flag; Bailly refused. Still the gates remained shut. The upshot was that for an hour and three-quarters Louis sat in the berlin, vainly waiting to drive to his country house. At 1.15 Louis ordered the coachman to turn back. At the door of the Tuileries he and his family got out and returned to their apartments.

During that hour and three-quarters in his stationary coach, threatened and insulted, Louis saw that he was now no longer a free agent. Sooner or later these people who had adopted the new religion of *la Patrie* would try to force him to receive Communion from a schismatic priest. Louis would go a long way, a demeaning way if necessary, towards political conciliation, but he would not let them do this. During the long months of diminishing freedom he had been urged by friends to break out of Paris; again and again he had resisted their advice, hoping to establish trust between himself and his people. Now he decided enough was enough. He would make a dash for one of his provinces and there, he hoped, he would find the freedom he needed not only in order to do his job properly as King but to follow his conscience as a Christian.

CHAPTER 21

Flight

ALL palaces are to some extent prisons; the Tuileries was now an actual prison, guarded by 600 national guards with muskets and bayonets, some pacing the corridors outside the Queen's bedroom on the ground floor and the King's on the first. Anyone wishing to enter the royal apartments had to show a blue pass. Many of the staff were paid spies. In order to conduct a private conversation Louis first had to open the doors to make sure no one was listening at keyholes, and speak low. Private letters he had to write in cipher and smuggle out. Always, day and night, he and Antoinette were watched, not perfunctorily but by people on whose nerves the newspapers constantly played.

'In the Tuileries,' warned Marat in *L'Ami du peuple*, 'a perverted Queen incites an imbecile King . . . Traitors, traitors, traitors everywhere. And the arch-traitor, crowned and inviolable, is the King! A subterfuge! He attends the Assembly. A subterfuge! He only seeks in this manner to cover his flight. Watch out! A great betrayal is maturing!'

Louis and Antoinette realized that if they were to escape they needed a friend working outside the palace. The Polignacs, Vaudreuil, Guines, Breteuil had had to emigrate. Only one of Antoinette's intimate circle remained, immune from popular hatred because a foreigner: Axel de Fersen.

He was now the same age as the Queen: thirty-five, tall, dark-eyed, still handsome, cool in manner and energetic. When the Bastille fell, he had been at Valenciennes with his regiment, but in the autumn he came to Versailles and on 6 October went to Paris in one of the carriages following the King. There he decided to remain, explaining to his father the Field Marshal: 'I am attached to the King and Queen and I owe it to them for the kindness they showed me when they were able, and I should be vile and ungrateful if I deserted them now that they can do nothing for me and I have the hope of being useful to them.'

Fersen gave up his military duties and was appointed by King

Gustavus to act as intermediary between him and Louis. He conveyed the Kings' letters to each other and enabled them to exchange their views. In his official capacity he naturally also met and talked to the Queen.

Fersen deeply sympathized with the plight of Louis and Antoinette, whom he described to his sister Sophie as 'an angel in her courage and sensitivity'. He kept emphasizing this spiritual quality: 'She is an angel and I try to console her as best I can. I owe it to her. She is so perfect for me.'

That was Fersen's chivalrous side. But the Swede had a strongly sensuous side too, and this provided a second motive for remaining in Paris. In the rue de Clichy lived a full-fleshed Italian brunette of thirty-nine named Eléonore. Beginning life as a circus acrobat, Eléonore had bounced her way into numerous gilded beds, including those of the Duke of Württemberg, of a rich Anglo-American named Sullivan, who married her, and eventually that of Quintin Craufurd, a Scots millionaire who now kept her in diamonds. Fersen was sexually attracted to Eléonore, and whenever he got the chance, slept with her. If this affair darkens the picture of a Swedish Galahad, it made Fersen a first-rate escape accomplice, expert in smuggled notes, disguises and secret assignations.

The nature of the relations between Fersen and the Queen is a question around which controversy has long raged. Between 1778 and 1789 it is now generally agreed that the two were never more than friends, but from the October days until the flight to Varennes the question becomes more difficult.

One source only – the Memoirs of Saint-Priest – suggests that Fersen was then more than a friend. Saint-Priest says that Fersen came nearly every day to the Tuileries, passing by an entrance which La Fayette purposely left unguarded, with – Saint-Priest suggests – the malicious intention of putting the Queen in the wrong. Saint-Priest further states that whilst the royal family were at Saint-Cloud in summer 1790, Fersen used to come and go at all hours of the day and night and on one occasion was nearly arrested by a palace guard at three in the morning. Even if this was true it proves nothing against the Queen; it was naturally safer to discuss secret plans at night. Saint-Priest himself relates that the Queen so little imagined any evil construction could be placed on Fersen's visits that when he, Saint-Priest, told her they might prove dangerous, she answered carelessly: 'Tell him so if you think it advisable. As for me, I think nothing of it.'

It is Saint-Priest's belief, however, that the Queen and Fersen were lovers for some or all of the time between October 1789 and June 1791. What trust is to be placed in his evidence? Saint-Priest was a rancorous ex-Minister belonging to the Court faction hostile to Antoinette, and his wife had for a time been Fersen's mistress, so he had a motive for disparaging both the Queen and the Swede. His Memoirs, written many years after the events they purport to describe, repeatedly conflict with known facts and are among the less reliable sources of the period. In this particular section it is doubtful whether Saint-Priest is correct in saying that Fersen frequently visited Saint-Cloud in summer 1790, for on 28 June that year Fersen wrote to his sister Sophie, from whom he hid nothing: 'The King and the royal family are at Saint-Cloud . . . No one goes there but those in attendance and I have not been there.' Never once in his letters to Sophie that summer does Fersen speak of going to Saint-Cloud.

Against Saint-Priest has to be set the fact that no contemporary voice ever suggested that the Queen was having an affair with Fersen and neither then, nor later at her trial, did any person – equerry, page, maid or spy – step forward to accuse her on the score of Fersen. Yet all the while she was continually watched by national guards, one of whom slept in her ante-chamber. There is not a scrap of evidence in any known paper surviving today that could be used to prove that Fersen, during the period before the flight to Varennes, was anything other than an ardent friend of the Queen.

When he was approached about a proposed escape, Fersen gladly agreed to help Louis and Antoinette. But escape, he pointed out, would be costly. Since Louis had no private resources and Antoinette only her jewels, which could not readily be sold, Fersen generously offered to lend the King and Queen all he had – 600,000 livres – and to borrow a further 240,000.

Louis and Antoinette were determined to stick together, with their children and with Elisabeth also, so their escape coach would have to be a large four-wheeled berlin drawn by six horses. Fersen ordered such a vehicle from a fashionable coach-builder named Jean Louis. The bodywork was painted dark green, the wheels lemon. Inside it was upholstered in leather, with taffeta cushions, the windows were provided with green taffeta blinds, and it was furnished with walnut coffers. Fersen tried it out by driving fast along the Vincennes road. The Duc d'Orléans, out for a drive with his newest mistress, happened to meet Fersen. 'What the devil are you doing, my dear count? Trying to break your neck?' 'Just running in my new carriage.' 'But why such a large one? Are you taking all the chorus girls from the Opéra?' 'No, my lord, I leave them to you.'

Louis needed also a devoted general who still retained firm control of his soldiers. He found the man he wanted in the Marquis Louis de Bouillé, commanding the army in the east. Louis decided he would go by coach to Montmédy, 194 miles from Paris. There, joined by Bailly and his army, he would rally his loyal subjects round him, recall those who had been forced to emigrate, and address a manifesto to France declaring that he planned to rule in accordance with the principles of the royal sitting on 23 June 1789. Should he fail to win sufficient support, Montmédy lay close to Switzerland and to the Netherlands.

Louis made elaborate arrangements with Bouillé for military protection on the second half of his journey. Forty hussars were to be posted at Pont de Sommevelle, 110 miles from Paris; forty dragoons at the next staging-post, and so on: altogether 723 soldiers. Louis got Fersen to communicate these and other arrangements in cipher. Fersen proved extremely efficient, but on one occasion, having based his cipher on a certain page of Montesquieu's *Greatness and Decadence of the Romans*, he failed to specify which page, so that it took seven hours to decipher his message.

To command the forty hussars at Pont de Sommevelle Bouillé chose a young officer, the Duc de Choiseul, nephew and heir of the Minister who had caused Louis such trouble during the early years of his reign. The methodical Fersen objected to Choiseul on the grounds that he was muddle-headed, but Bouillé insisted that Choiseul was the right man for the job.

Louis wished to take three of his old bodyguard with him. One was to ride in front of the berlin, one on the box, one behind. Fersen bought them yellow liveries once worn by the Prince de Condé's servants and going cheap since the Prince had emigrated. Fersen also brought to the Tuileries a grey wig, a brown suit and a green overcoat for the King.

Louis faced the problem not only of what to take with him but of what to leave behind. In May he ordered a locksmith with whom he had often worked, François Gamain, to construct an iron cupboard in the wall of a passage between two doors of his apartments. In this skilfully concealed hiding-place, to which only he had the key, Louis locked all his papers.

On 27 May Louis wrote to Bouillé saying he had decided to start between midnight and 1 a.m. on 19 June. But the King's will was no longer omnipotent. One of the royal household staff, a woman who looked after the bathrooms, happened to be the mistress of a leading revolutionary and was known to spy for him. This woman had been due to go on holiday on the 12th but after Louis had made his plans she decided to take her holiday later, on the 20th. Louis hurriedly wrote to Bouillé that the escape must be postponed until the night of the 20th.

On the morning of that day, a Monday, Louis worked in his study and received various deputies. Antoinette installed her son in a railed-off part of the garden where, with toy tools, he played at digging and raking. She attended Mass and afterwards sent for her hairdresser, Léonard, who lived in. Léonard was a small, neat, serious young man, who alone knew how to arrange prettily her dry, thin, greying hair. Antoinette asked whether she could depend on him and when Léonard swore she could, she handed him a letter to deliver to the Duc de Choiseul at his house in the rue d'Artois: Choiseul would entrust him with her jewels, which he was to carry to Montmédy.

After their one o'clock dinner Louis revealed to his sister that they were all to escape that night. After her first surprise Elisabeth, a brave young lady, showed herself delighted. Later Fersen came in to make last-minute arrangements. As he left Antoinette burst into tears and Louis said: 'Whatever happens, I shall never forget all you are doing for me.'

After supper Monsieur and his wife called. They were to escape that night too, in separate cabriolets, making first for Brussels, whence they would rejoin the King once he had established himself at Montmédy. Antoinette was by now in a bad state of nerves, and gently asked her brother-in-law to abridge his long rhetorical farewell. As he left, the pious Elisabeth slipped Monsieur a holy picture.

At ten o'clock Antoinette left the drawing-room and woke her children. To the Dauphin she whispered: 'We are going away, to a military town. We'll see a lot of soldiers.' The Dauphin was pleased, then puzzled as he was made to put on a frock and a girl's bonnet. Antoinette and the children's governess, Madame de Tourzel, led the Dauphin and Mousseline la sérieuse along a passage and downstairs to the apartment of Monsieur de Villequier, the King's First Gentleman, who had recently emigrated. It opened on to the main courtyard, and this door, being that of a vacant lodging, was not guarded. When Antoinette opened the door, there was Fersen, disguised as a cabbie. He led the governess and royal children to a waiting hired carriage, while Antoinette retraced her steps.

At eleven Louis and Antoinette went to their bedrooms. In the presence of high dignitaries, including La Fayette, Louis undressed, but he made clear that he did not wish to linger in conversation, and at quarter past eleven the dignitaries departed. Most went home, but La Fayette had been warned by Bailly that Paris was flooded with rumours of an impending escape, so he went to double-check security.

Louis got into bed, the heavy blue curtains were drawn closed by his valet. The moment his valet had left the room Louis got out of bed and went down a private staircase to Antoinette's bedroom, where his travelling clothes were laid out. He put on the brown suit, green overcoat, grey wig and a round hat. The Queen was already dressed in a brown dress, black coat and black hat with a veil.

Louis left first. Carrying a cane and escorted by one of his bodyguard, he walked down the grand staircase and out of the main door. For a fortnight the Chevalier de Coigny, who was in the secret and bore a likeness to the King, had left the Tuileries every night dressed in just such clothes as the King now wore, so the guards paid no special attention to him. In fact when one of his shoe-buckles worked loose Louis even knelt to tighten it two paces from a passing sentry. Then he walked out to the courtyard, where Fersen led him to the carriage, one among many waiting to take palace officials home.

Antoinette left soon after the King, by the unguarded door of Villequier's apartment. Hardly was she outside than she met the carriage carrying La Fayette on his security check. She drew into the nearest wall, but the carriage passed so close she could have touched its wheel. Upset by this narrow shave, she took a wrong turning and lost her way in a maze of courtyards and narrow streets. When she finally reached Fersen's carriage a precious half-hour had been lost.

It was a considerable achievement for four adults and two children to have left unseen so closely guarded a palace, and Louis doubtless felt a stir of elation as Fersen whipped up the horses and they were at last on their way. Instead of leaving Paris directly Fersen drove north to Craufurd's house in the rue de Clichy. Here he got out to make sure that Moustier, one of the King's three bodyguards, had in fact collected the berlin from Craufurd's courtyard and left for the rendezvous. This detour set the travellers back another half-hour.

It was two o'clock in the morning when the royal party finally left Paris by the Porte Saint-Martin. A little beyond the customs post Fersen began to look for the berlin. It was a moonless night and at first he could not find it. Louis got out to help him. Presently they saw it. Fersen drove his hired carriage alongside so that his passengers could transfer to it without stepping down. Then, having ditched the carriage, he jumped on to the box of the berlin and ordered his coachman, Balthazar, to whip up the horses. The berlin rattled over the cobblestones, gathered speed and in less than half an hour arrived at Bondy. Here Balthazar unharnessed Fersen's horses, while postilions from the post-house led out six fresh horses, ordered in advance by the third of the bodyguards. When the traces were buckled, Fersen begged to be allowed to continue. Louis had already rejected this idea, for should he be caught it would not look well for a foreigner to be with him, and he repeated his refusal now. Fersen then bade an affectionate goodbye and rode fast for Belgium.

The berlin headed east, with Louis now in sole charge. At the next posting station, Claye, he found, as arranged, a cabriolet waiting, in it two of Antoinette's lady's maids. The little convoy was now complete, and Louis disposed it for the long journey ahead. First rode one of the bodyguard in his impressive yellow livery, to warn the next relay post that horses were needed. Next came the cabriolet with the lady's maids. Then came the berlin, with one of the bodyguard on the box, one or more postilions on the post-horses, which, at the next relay, would be unharnessed and led home. The third bodyguard rode an escort beside the berlin. Every dozen or so miles the horses in the berlin would be changed.

Louis began to relax. 'Once I have my buttocks in the saddle again,' he announced, 'I'll be a new man.' As the dawn light played on their unfamiliar dress, they chose names. Madame de Tourzel was a Russian lady, Madame de Korff, as her passport stated, travelling with her two children Amélie and Aglaë. Antoinette was their governess, Madame Rochet. Louis's sister was a friend, Rosalie. Louis was the steward, Durand.

After passing Meaux at six o'clock, the travellers began to feel hungry and opened their provisions. There was cold veal and *bœuf à la mode*, bread, a bottle of white wine and five bottles of water. They ate some of the meat on hunks of bread, washing it down with water.

Louis then read aloud a copy of the declaration he had left in the Tuileries. He began in general terms: deploring the destruction of the monarchy and the lawlessness prevailing in France. All that he had done and proposed to do for the people's welfare had been consistently distorted. He then criticized the Constitution in detail, pointing out, for example, that although he was supposed to have complete charge of Foreign Affairs, in fact he could not even choose his ambassadors. As for finances, the deficit was running at a level ten times higher than when he had controlled them. Turning next to religion, Louis declared that he had been forced to dismiss the priests who served his private chapel and to attend the Mass of a State priest in St Germain l'Auxerrois. He ended by calling on Frenchmen to rally to him and to a Constitution that he could freely accept, one guaranteeing 'respect for our holy religion'.

For Louis any journey, even one like this, had its pleasures. He had brought with him a map and a gazetteer, and with these followed the route attentively, noting the time they were making. At eight o'clock he remarked, 'La Fayette must now be feeling very embarrassed.' After passing La Ferté they all got out to stretch their legs and relieve themselves, and at Fromentières Louis, again getting out, went so far as to speak to peasants on their way to bring in the hay. 'When we've passed Châlons,' said Louis, referring to the one considerable town on their route, 'there will be nothing to fear. At the stop after that we shall find the first detachment of troops.'

At an average speed of eleven miles an hour, Louis and his family reached Chaintrix, the stop before Châlons, at two-thirty in the afternoon. The postmaster's son-in-law, Gabriel Vallet, had been to Paris the previous summer and at a public ceremony seen the King, whom he much admired. He recognized him again now, and at once the whole family showered attentions on the travellers, inviting them in to rest, while the postmaster's daughters served them hot clear soup. When it was time to go, Antoinette gave the daughters two silver porringers, one engraved with interlaced L's.

Vallet insisted on accompanying them to the next post-house. But on the way out of Chaintrix, crossing a narrow bridge, one of the berlin wheels struck a stone corner-post, the traces broke, and the horses fell. Half an hour was lost repairing the damage. Finally they reached Châlons, where Antoinette had briefly stopped twenty-one years before, on her way from Vienna to Paris: perhaps she remembered that a group of girls had sung her a welcoming song. Now she went unrecognized, and after a quick change of horses the berlin clattered on to the village of Pont de Sommevelle.

For eighteen hours Louis had been travelling unescorted and

vulnerable. Here at last, in Pont de Sommevelle, he would find the protection of soldiers. It was with considerable excitement, there-fore, that he looked out of the berlin window for the sky-blue, fur-trimmed jackets of forty hussars. As he entered the village he could not see them; doubtless they were further on, at the post-house. But when he arrived there, and changed horses, he could still see no sign of Choiseul's hussars. Soon it became clear that there wasn't a single hussar anywhere in the village. It was a shattering discovery. 'I felt,' Louis later recalled, 'as though the whole earth had fallen from under me.'

Louis knew that something had gone seriously wrong. He was to discover exactly what only later, but for the purposes of the story it is necessary to explain here. The Duc de Choiseul had arrived in Pont de Sommevelle shortly before eleven that morning by cabriolet from Paris. In a room of the post-house he changed into his uniform. At noon his forty hussars galloped in. After a meal, Choiseul had them saddle and stand by in readiness. He knew that Fersen had written to Bouillé: The royal party 'will be at Pont de Sommevelle on Tuesday at 2.30 at the latest. You can count on this absolutely.'

Two-thirty came and went. Choiseul nervously consulted his watch and sent one of his hussars down the road. Three-thirty and still no sign of the berlin. The delay in normal circumstances would not have mattered, but some of the local farmers were behind with their rent, and, disbelieving Choiseul's explanation that his men were there 'to escort a treasure to pay the army of the East,' they felt sure the hussars intended to collect the Duchesse d'Elbeuf's overdue rents. As the afternoon wore on, hundreds of angry peasants gathered, brandishing pitchforks and muskets. With every quarter of an hour tension increased. By four-thirty Choiseul became alarmed. The King was now two hours overdue. It looked as though the escape had miscarried. Even if it had not, an armed clash between the peasants and his hussars seemed imminent. If that happened, the King's coach would certainly be stopped and searched.

The sensible thing would have been to disperse his hussars in the countryside, while remaining himself on the road with his sergeant. If and when the King arrived, he could send his sergeant to gather the hussars on the road beyond the village, where they would provide the promised escort. Choiseul, however, inex-perienced despite his thirty years, acted in a muddled way. Summon-ing Léonard, whom he had brought with him from Paris, he handed the hairdresser a hurriedly scribbled note, telling him to show it to the leaders of the other detachments stationed between Pont de Sommevelle and Varennes. Choiseul's note read: 'There is no sign that the treasure will pass today. I am leaving to join M. de Bouillé. You will receive new orders tomorrow.'

While Léonard set off by calèche with this message of alarm, Choiseul waited until five-thirty, then, giving up all hope of seeing the King, he led his hussars out of the village into the Argonne forest, where, as night fell, they were to become hopelessly lost.

Half an hour after Choiseul's departure Louis arrived. He wanted of course to know whether troops had been there and left, but out of prudence he could not ask. He decided to continue without the hussars. Horses were changed, the berlin continued along the white chalky road, and at eight o'clock rolled into Sainte-Ménehould. Again Louis looked expectantly out of the window, this time for 33 dragoons. But he could see no sign of them.

Captain d'Andoins, commanding the dragoons, had spent a difficult day. The town had its own national guard and resented the presence of unfamiliar troops. All day d'Andoins had had to appease suspicious crowds and when he received Choiseul's message it was with some relief that he stood down his dragoons, who dispersed in search of a drink. When the berlin eventually arrived and Louis put his head out the window, d'Andoins sidled up, saluted and whispered to the King: 'Plans have misfired. I am going to stay far away from you so as not to arouse suspicion.'

Louis had to content himself with that cryptic message. The horses were changed and the berlin was about to leave when the postmaster came in from the fields. A sharp-eyed young man, Jean Baptiste Drouet had seen the Queen several times during his army service. He thought he recognized her now in the berlin, but before he could be sure it had driven away. Drouet confided his suspicions to his wife, but she advised him to say nothing.

When the berlin had left, Captain d'Andoins ordered his bugler to sound the command to mount. But by now the townspeople were suspicious. First, talk of a treasure, then, instead of treasure travellers who were evidently important, for d'Andoins had saluted before whispering to them. As soon as the bugle sounded for the dragoons to turn out, from the direction of the town hall came the rolling of drums and a call to the people to assemble. National guardsmen only too pleased to assert themselves quickly overpowered the dragoons, most of whom had been drinking freely, and prevented them leaving.

Louis, meanwhile, was travelling towards the next village, Cler-mont, puzzled that d'Andoins had not joined him with his dragoons. The twenty-first of June is the longest day of the year, and so it must have seemed to the royal party, travelling now for more than twenty hours and aware that something serious had gone wrong. Louis was dismally aware that without an escort the royal party would be an easy prey for anyone who cared to stop them. Pursuers must long ago have left Paris. Montmédy lay forty miles ahead. Could they get there before being overtaken?

At seven o'clock that morning, in the palace of the Tuileries, the King's valet had entered the royal bedroom, announced the time, drawn the blue curtains and found the royal bed empty. A pro-longed search having failed to reveal the King, at eight La Fayette was told. He hurried to the Tuileries, while Bailly summoned the Assembly. Several hours must pass before the deputies could gather; meanwhile, what was to be done? La Fayette dictated an order declaring that 'the enemies of the Revolution have seized the person of the King' and in the name of the Nation called upon all good citizens to rescue him and 'return him to the bosom of the Assembly'. Copies were made and handed to a score of messengers, of whom one, Captain Bayon, chose the road east.

Bayon rode flat out for six and a half hours. At Chaintrix he felt too exhausted to continue, so he scribbled a message ordering the King to be stopped. When the message reached Sainte-Ménehould, Drouet saw that his suspicions had been correct. He and another good horseman named Guillaume the Shaggy were ordered by the municipality to pursue and stop the berlin. They set off shortly after nine: ahead of them lumbered the berlin with a lead of about ten miles.

So far Louis had been following the main road, which led to Metz. But after Clermont he turned off on a minor road, which led through Varennes to Montmédy. The sun had set, the berlin's lamps were lit. Having changed horses at Clermont the bodyguard seated up on the box shouted to the new postilions 'Take the Varennes road!' As chance would have it Drouet's postilions overheard, and on their way back, when they met their boss and Guillaume the Shaggy, were able to impart this precious information. Without it, Drouet would certainly have continued on the main road towards Metz.

About eleven o'clock Louis sighted the lights of Varennes: only thirty miles now from his final destination. Varennes was divided by the river Aire into two parts: the upper town, where the berlin now arrived, and down a steep slope, then across a stone bridge, the lower town. Since Varennes was not a posting station, two officers, Raigecourt and Bouillé's son, the chevalier de Bouillé, were supposed to be waiting in the upper town with eleven fresh horses.

Louis's outrider could not find the horses. Louis, Antoinette and Elisabeth then got out and began searching. Louis rapped on the door of a shuttered house, but the inmates without opening shouted that they knew nothing of any horses. Louis then tried to persuade the postilions to continue to the next staging-post, Stenay. They replied that their horses were needed next morning to bring in hay from the fields. Finally Louis offered them money, and here he made a mistake. Instead of offering them say ten livres, he offered them a hundred louis, a sum which alarmed the postilions. They refused absolutely to continue. In the midst of this argument, two horsemen galloped past – Drouet and Guillaume.

At last Louis persuaded the postilions to continue at least as far as the lower town, guessing that the eleven fresh horses would be somewhere there. This guess was correct, for owing to a blunder by the officers the horses were waiting across the river, at an inn called *Le Grand Monarque*.

The berlin slowly descended the steeply sloping village street. Ahead stood a church, from the wall of which a massive stone arch projected across the street. Hardly had the berlin reached the archway when figures sprang out from its base, and the travellers heard the cry they had dreaded all that day to hear: 'Halt!'

Louis told the postilions to continue, but men barred their way, crossing their bayoneted muskets in front of the horses: 'One step more and we fire!' A tall, imposing, middle-aged man came forward, holding a lantern. This was Jean Baptiste Sauce, whom Drouet had wakened, procurator in the commune of Varennes, population 1500. Sauce asked to see their passport. Madame de Tourzel handed it through the window. Entering an inn, the *Bras d'Or*, which stood close by, Sauce examined the passport, which covered Madame de Korff and her party, and saw that it was in order. Having some knowledge of the law, he was inclined to let the berlin proceed. But Drouet drew him aside. 'I tell you, the King and Queen are in that carriage. If you let them pass, you will be guilty of high treason.' As he was hesitating, dozens of villagers ran up, alerted by the cry of 'Fire!' which Sauce had caused to be raised.

Sauce returned to the berlin and informed the passengers that in view of what he termed 'all the emotion in the place' it would be better if they waited until morning. Muskets were rattled. 'This is armed arrest!' exclaimed Madame de Tourzel, and Louis protested to Sauce. Where, he was wondering, were the sixty hussars stationed in Varennes precisely in order to rescue him from just such a situation as this? In fact the hussars were asleep in a building on the edge of the village, their commander having been told by Léonard the hairdresser that the King would not be arriving that day.

As more and more armed villagers came to bar the way, Louis realized that it was impossible to go further. The best he could do was to play for time. He and the others got out of the berlin and were invited by Sauce to rest in his house, which stood nearby. On the ground floor of the wooden building was a shop where Sauce made a living selling groceries and candles; up a narrow winding stairway with a dirty rope handrail were two small bedrooms. Into one of them Sauce led the mysterious travellers. Here the children were put to bed, Antoinette seated herself on a straw-bottomed chair, while Louis paced the room, watched suspiciously by Sauce and an improvised guard. Someone had gone to fetch a villager who had lived several years at Versailles. Presently this man arrived. He took one look at Louis and bent his knee to the floor, exclaiming 'Oh, Sire!' Louis made the best of it. 'Very well then, I am indeed your King.'

Louis saw that the villagers were overcome with awe: he was after all still the father of all Frenchmen. He embraced Sauce and, one by one, the improvised guard. Then he explained why he had left Paris. Sauce appeared moved and promised the King he should have an escort to continue to Montmédy at first light.

At this moment Choiseul rode in with a company of hussars. Hurrying up to the little bedroom, he drew Louis aside and proposed, there and then, a daring escape: Louis, with the Dauphin in his arms, on one horse, Antoinette on another, the rest of the party on other horses belonging to his troops. Louis considered the plan for a moment. 'You have forty men,' he said, 'but there are seven or eight hundred in the street, many armed. How can I be sure that the Queen, my children, or my sister might not be killed by a bullet in such an unequal battle?' 'If I were alone,' he added, 'I would willingly take your advice and win through.'

Louis still hoped that General de Bouillé, informed of his arrest, would hurry from Montmédy with sufficient troops to effect a rescue. He waited anxiously in the small crowded room, while his children slept, and the villagers watched him with awe and suspicion. Presently troops did arrive, but they were not Bouillé's. Sauce had sent messengers to neighbouring towns for help, and all through the night detachments of national guards began to march in, some dragging cannon.

At five in the morning two couriers from Paris entered the bedroom: Bayon, who had been joined now by Romeuf, official messenger of the Assembly.

'Sire,' cried Bayon, 'you must return to Paris! Throats are being cut there. The lives of our women and children are threatened. In the interests of your people you must return to the capital at once.'

Paris in fact had remained calm, and perhaps Louis suspected this. He drew himself up and in a cold voice asked Bayon if he had orders to support his contention that the royal family should return to Paris.

'My companion has them,' replied Bayon and pointed to Romeuf.

Romeuf handed Louis a decree in which the Assembly ordered the royal family to be prevented from continuing their journey. According to the Constitution, the person of the King was inviolable, and Louis recognized the decree's implications.

'There is no longer a King in France!' he said.

Then Antoinette read the decree. 'Insolence!' she exclaimed and when Louis laid the paper on the bed, she swept it to the floor: 'I will not have my children defiled!'

Louis ordered the room to be cleared of all but Bayon and Romeuf. He then appealed to the two officers, asking them to let him stay until Bouillé and his regiment of troops arrived to escort him to Montmédy. Romeuf, who was devoted to the Queen, agreed. Bayon did not commit himself but as soon as he was down in the street he incited the crowd by announcing that the King refused to leave, and that Bouillé and a cavalry regiment would soon be opening fire.

Louis and his family ate a simple breakfast provided by Madame Sauce, and accompanied by advice from the same woman. Louis, she said, should return willingly to Paris: 'After all, the Nation pays you twenty-five millions. Anyone who wanted to give that up would have to be pretty queer in the head.'

Louis learned that some six thousand armed men had collected in Varennes, and he could hear them clamouring for him to return to Paris. Against such numbers Bouillé would be powerless to effect a rescue. So after breakfast Louis reluctantly agreed to leave, and shortly before six he and the royal party re-entered the berlin.

Surrounded by the crowd, they set off, up the steep street and into open country. Half an hour later Bouillé arrived on the outskirts of Varennes and saw in the distance the royal carriage and procession. But the bridge had been barricaded, the river was too deep to ford. When it was pointed out to him that six thousand armed men surrounded the King's carriage, he sounded the order for retreat and rode for Luxembourg.

During the return journey Louis had plenty of time to reflect on why the escape had failed. Choiseul had made a fatal blunder by sending that message of despondency down the line of troops; for the second time in his reign Louis had suffered from a Choiseul. But, at bottom, Choiseul's blunder was a flaw in the structure of the old regime. He owed his command to wealth and birth, not to experience or merit, and under strain had cracked like ill-tempered steel. The other fact leading to failure had been the slow berlin. But such a vehicle was implicit in Louis's decision to keep Antoinette and the children by him. Ever since 1789 he had been obliged to travel heavy and therefore slow. He was not only King, but family man, and therefore vulnerable in a way that Fersen, say, or his brother Monsieur, who escaped successfully, were not.

Suppose Louis had reached Montmédy, what then? The poor discipline of those troops deputed as an escort, and the hostility to them of the national guard suggest that a stand by the King would have met with little success. The balanced constitution proposed by Louis held little popular appeal in face of the emotional slogans being tossed around by the political clubs in Paris. Within weeks Louis would have been obliged to leave France, forfeiting his crown.

As it was, would he still retain his crown – or rather, the travesty of it still left? He would know in Paris. For the moment he faced humiliation, within and without the coach. Now more than ever he must appear a failure to Antoinette, to Elisabeth, to his children. He could do nothing to reassure his wife, who was terribly afraid that their bodyguards and the officers who had tried to help them would be put to death. At Sainte-Ménehould the mayor thought fit to make a speech, or rather a reprimand, to which Louis replied that he had had no intention of leaving France. Open-air altars decked with flowers were being erected for the procession of Corpus Christi, reminding Louis of his religious dilemma, still unresolved.

At three o'clock an elderly man on horseback, armed with two pistols and a gun, rode up to salute the King. The white and gold

cross of St Louis gleamed on his breast. As Louis acknowledged his
salute, the crowd grew angry and closed threateningly round the
horseman. He in turn made his horse rear and tried to approach the
berlin. It was the Comte de Dampierre, a local nobleman, who
wished to speak a loyal phrase to the King. The crowd closed round
him; one of the boldest tried to pull him off his horse. The word
'aristocrat' rang out. With a final salute to the travellers, Dampierre
turned and spurred his horse across the fields. Part of the crowd
pursued him and above the heavy tread of footsteps several shots
were heard.

'What's happening?' Louis asked.

'Nothing. They have killed a lunatic.' Dampierre had fallen from
his horse, a bullet in his back. His assailants tried to carry him to the
berlin in order to kill him under the King's eyes, but were hindered
by a deep ditch. There they finished off their victim, tearing him to
pieces.

Louis was appalled by this brutal killing; Antoinette found it
abominable, the more so since Dampierre was known to have been
a man who did much good on his estate. Louis and Antoinette
continued to speak of the incident with grief, even on the following
day, when they were joined by three members of the Assembly,
two of whom got into their carriage.

One was 'Tiger' Barnave, a sincere and honest young man with a
plain, prognathous face and turned up nose. In Mirabeau's day he
had seemed to the King and Queen one of their bitterest opponents
but now, with even more violent attacks coming from the extreme
Left, he ranked as a moderate.

The other deputy, Jérôme Pétion, did belong to the extreme Left
and was a friend of Robespierre. Born in Chartres, thirty-eight years
of age, Pétion was a fat, lazy fellow with a round face and receding
brow who fancied himself as a lady-killer, and also as an orator.
While Barnave sat between the King and Queen on the rear seat,
Pétion installed himself between Madame Elisabeth and Madame
de Tourzel. He was later to write an account of the journey.

The Dauphin, seated on Antoinette's knee, spotted the inscription
on the brass buttons of Barnave's coat, *Vivre libre ou mourir*. Eager
to show that he could read, he spelled out the words and pronounced
them. Barnave smiled and complimented the boy's parents.

Pétion had been prepared by Leftist propaganda to find Louis an
idiot. He was therefore much surprised to notice that every remark
the King made was to the point and sensible. While following their

route on the map and from time to time announcing their exact position, Louis began speaking about English manufactures and English business skill. No subject was more important for French prosperity since even the buttons on national guard uniforms had to be imported from England, but Pétion knew nothing about the subject and as a good patriot did not want to know. When Louis dropped the conversation Pétion put it down to shyness.

The weather was blazing hot and dust from the road filled the overcrowded carriage. When the time came to take a meal, Antoinette lowered the blind. At once the crowd protested. Elisabeth was about to raise the blind, but Antoinette prevented her. 'We must show character,' she said. She calmly ate her leg of pigeon and only when the crowd had stopped murmuring did she raise the blind, to show that she did so freely. Throwing away the pigeon leg, she said as though giving herself advice, 'We must show character right to the end.'

Pétion noted all this and also the fact, which impressed him, that the Queen and Madame Elisabeth were twelve hours without relieving themselves. At Meaux the royal family slept in the bishop's palace, into which the newly elected constitutional bishop had moved. It had been necessary to obtain beds from the Ursuline convent who were storing the episcopal furniture, and linen, plate and china from a hostelry. When the bishop apologized for his unfurnished palace, Louis could not resist saying, 'You are wrong to apologize. When a man is not *chez soi*, he does well not to over-spend.'

Pétion kept up a conversation with Madame Elisabeth and although in fact he was boring her, he felt sure that he was fascinating her. Each time her arm touched his, he fancied she was making overtures to him. 'I sensed a certain abandon in her attitude, her eyes were moist, melancholy mixed with a kind of physical pleasure . . . I think that had we been alone she would have fallen into my arms and yielded to the dictates of nature.' 'Was Madame Elisabeth,' Pétion asked himself, 'perhaps determined to sacrifice her honour in order to lead me into forfeiting my own?' 'Yes,' he decided. 'At Court people will stop at nothing; the Queen could have concocted the whole scheme.'

Pétion's conceit is interesting because, although a mediocre man, he so successfully played to the gallery that in 1792 he was elected Mayor of Paris and became a hero of the Left. His picture was to be seen everywhere, side by side with Robespierre's, and his Life was to be written by a certain Regnault, who compared Pétion to Jesus Christ: Christ, according to Regnault, would have made a good mayor of Jerusalem. There was only one difference between these two friends of humanity: Christ had succumbed to the high priests, whereas Pétion would triumph over them: 'under his ministry evil citizens will hide, because crime sleeps when virtue is alert.'

Barnave spoke much to the Queen and according to Pétion met with indifference. In fact, however, Antoinette warmed to the sincere young lawyer from Grenoble, while he, like Mirabeau before him, began to feel respect, even sympathy, for this lady who had been depicted to him as a harpy and who turned out to be so dignified and brave. At Meaux they strolled together in the garden of the bishop's palace. By the end of the journey the Queen had made an unexpected conquest, one that was to have some influence on future events.

On the third day after leaving Varennes, amid threats and insults Louis and an exhausted Antoinette re-entered the Tuileries. Their bid for freedom was over. La Fayette, having placed his guards, was making to withdraw, and asked his Majesty's orders. Louis replied bitterly, 'I seem to be more at your orders than you are at mine.' Then he went to write up his diary. For 23 June he put: 'At 11.30 Mass was interrupted in order to hasten our departure. Luncheon at Châlons. Dinner at Epernay. We met the agents of the Assembly near Pont à Binson. Arrived at eleven o'clock at Dormans. Dinner. Slept three hours in an armchair.'

While Antoinette wrote to Fersen, giving him news and telling him not to worry, Louis sent a letter to Bouillé, characteristically taking the blame. His words form perhaps the best commentary on the flight to Varennes: 'I am aware that to succeed was in my hands; but it is needful to have a ruthless spirit if one is to shed the blood of subjects, make armed resistance and thrust France into civil war. The very thought of such contingencies tore my heart and robbed me of all determination.'

CHAPTER 22

The Choice

ON 26 June 1791 the Assembly provisionally suspended Louis from his royal functions. The Left-wing Jacobin Club demanded the abolition of the monarchy, but a majority in the Assembly were against this. They would have their long-awaited Constitution ready in seven weeks, and it called for a King, indeed it would be unworkable without one. The Assembly were most anxious that Louis should accept the Constitution and in so doing resume his royal functions.

Louis saw three courses open. First, he could decide that France had become ungovernable, and he could abdicate, much as his fellow King, George III, had planned to do in 1783, forced, he wrote, 'by the obstinacy of a powerful party that has long publicly manifested a resolution not to aid in the service of the empire unless the whole executive management of affairs is thrown entirely into its hands'. Abdication would be the easiest course and the cleanest break. But then his six-year-old son would become King – Louis could not legally renounce the throne on the boy's behalf – probably under the Regency of the Duc d'Orléans, or Egalité as he now styled himself. So by abdicating he would just shift his responsibilities on to the shoulders of a man he knew to be weak and unprincipled.

The second course would be to sign the Constitution, but instead of resuming his royal functions in full accept what crumbs of authority happened to fall from the Assembly's table. He would then become what the Assembly at heart wished him to be: a civil servant without will or conscience who merely nodded assent to the Assembly's decrees, however unjust; in effect, a rubber-stamp of his own signature.

The third course would be to accept the Constitution and to exercise his royal functions conscientiously. This would call for courage, yet without the satisfying flourish of courage, for his main role would be the negative one of veto. If and when he saw injustice, he could shake his head and go on shaking it – that was kingship in 1791. This he must do while a prisoner, his family prisoners, and outside the gates of the palace-prison crowds chanted the *Ça ira* and shouted 'Austrian whore to the lanterne!'

Louis seems to have considered these three courses with his customary precision. Back in early June he had believed France did not want the newly-completed Constitution, but since then, on the journey to Varennes, he had seen for himself the support it enjoyed from ordinary Frenchmen. As he told the Assembly's commissioners when they questioned him, 'My journey to Varennes has convinced me that public opinion firmly favours the Constitution.' Louis himself thought the Constitution far from perfect, but the people clearly wanted it, and he had always been ready in political matters to implement public opinion. So he chose the third, and most difficult, course. Prisoner though he was, he would exercise his powers as King fully and conscientiously.

Louis signed the Constitution and on 14 September 1791 drove to the Assembly to deliver it to the President. He made a speech, promising to remain in Paris, and announcing that he would work for conciliation: 'Frenchmen living under the same laws must recognize as enemies only those who infringe them.' Characteristically, he then proposed a political amnesty. This the Assembly granted; after which, having completed its task of giving France a Constitution, it dissolved itself.

At the beginning of October a newly elected Assembly met for the first time. It was called the Legislative Assembly, since its task was to enact laws that would give flesh to the bare bones of the Constitution. Since previous deputies had declared themselves ineligible for re-election, all its members were new to their job.

At one o'clock on 7 October Louis drove to the Riding School to inaugurate the Legislative Assembly. Some 200 deputies sat on the right, 350 in the centre, and on the left only 136, but these belonged to the Jacobin and Cordelier clubs, and were the best organized single group. In his speech Louis declared that France was now returning to order in a period no longer revolutionary but constitutional. He foresaw peace abroad and prosperity at home. He even suggested that people instead of frequenting the clubs might do some work for a change, and also pay their taxes. Barnave had drafted the speech, but Louis made important corrections in his own hand. Instead of asking the deputies merely to 'respect' property and religious beliefs, Louis used the verb 'protect'.

Louis's speech was warmly cheered, and it did look as though the new Constitution was going to work. The King drafted plans for improving education, the legal system and social welfare. 'The great majority of people,' Antoinette wrote to Fersen, 'are tired of disturbances; they aren't sure whether they want this regime or another; what they do want is peace and quiet.'

Antoinette had forgotten too soon the insults, obscene abuse and sheer hatred directed against herself; these were not a by-product but an essential part of revolutionary feeling. Militant patriotism could be kept at fever pitch only by hatred, and for hatred there had to be public enemies. The Queen was one but others were needed.

All over France parish churches stood deserted, while Catholics flocked to hear masses said by priests loyal to the Holy See, either in the open or in convent chapels. On the very day of Louis's speech of conciliation an Auvergnat deputy named Couthon, a cripple obliged to speak seated in his wheelchair, denounced these priests as counter-revolutionaries and public enemies. It was an easy charge to make, but was it true?

In the typical diocese of Angers the bishop, de Lorry, and all the best educated clergy refused to take the oath. The brilliant young Père Etienne Bernier, parish priest of Saint-Laud, went quietly on with his duties, undeterred by patriots' threats to blow out his brains in the pulpit if he made impudent remarks about the Constitution. When anti-clerical watch-dogs packed the pews on Sundays, 'At least I've drawn to my sermon,' Bernier observed, 'people who don't come very often.'

When the new laws obliged him to vacate his parish, Bernier prepared his State successor a whimsical welcome. He locked away plate and sacred vessels, doctored candles so they would not light, sewed up the hems of priestly vestments and hitched bell-ropes aloft out of reach. That was hardly counter-revolution and, while the municipality prepared new street names for Angers – rue de la Croix, here as in many towns, was to become rue de la Constitution – Bernier took to the woods, serving loyal Catholics who would otherwise have been deprived of the sacraments. The heart of the matter was stated by former Bishop de Lorry to a curé who had taken the oath: 'We differ, but thought is free! and I would no more ask you to sacrifice your opinions than I would sacrifice to you my own.'

At Couthon's suggestion the Assembly sent a commission to the most Catholic part of France, the Vendée. It reported that nothing could 'either destroy or modify' the religious convictions of the peasants there, adding that it would be both clumsy and dangerous to make martyrs of the non-juring clergy.

The Jacobins had already taken the lead in making patriotism not only a new, but the only religion – the *patrie* was depicted on coins as an altar, the Constitution kept in a cedar-wood ark of the covenant – and it was they who demanded that very action against the priests which the Assembly's commission considered 'clumsy and dangerous'.

The moderate mayor of Paris, Bailly, who, as an astronomer, saw political events with a certain calm detachment, has a comment which is relevant here. 'When everyone,' he says, 'is taking the lead simultaneously, this is what happens: each wants to win the prize for patriotism and zeal, the man who proposes the most extreme measures wins the most support, and you get government by auction.'

This is what happened in the Assembly. First came a decree permitting priests to marry – the claims of nature must take precedence over religious vows – a gratuitous and insulting break with fifteen centuries of Christian life in France. Then, on 29 November, came a punitive decree. All refractory priests were to be deprived of their pensions and expelled from communes where disturbances had occurred; Catholics, moreover, were deprived of their right to hire or buy churches unless they too took the oath endorsing the State Church which Pius VI had declared schismatic. There was no conscience clause, no loophole for those who wished to be faithful both to Church and country. This decree the Assembly sent to the Tuileries for Louis's sanction.

Louis's heart must have sunk when he received the decree, for he had come to realize that the religious problem was the crux of this stage of the Revolution. The Assembly claimed that the oath was an innocuous formality, but when Louis turned back to Pius's Brief, this is what he read: 'Just as Henry VIII pretended that the form of oath that he proposed for the Bishops amounted to nothing but civil and secular loyalty, whereas it really contained the destruction of Papal authority, similarly the assembly that dominates France has actually denied the supreme head of the Church all power . . .'

Louis, who often sought parallels in English history, would have perceived that the present parallel was not, as courtiers glibly claimed, with Charles I, but with the reign of Henry VIII. During the summer of 1536 the Tudor King had held prisoner his own daughter, the Lady Mary, and by a mixture of bullying and blackmail forced her to admit that he was indeed Head of the English Church. Louis, also a prisoner, was being asked to make a similar admission regarding the Assembly.

It was argued by some of his Ministers that, being a State official, Louis must leave out of consideration his personal beliefs. Even if that were true, and Louis did not admit it, could he sanction a decree which penalized more than 20,000 French clergy for their religious views, and which would make it well-nigh impossible for a majority of Frenchmen, say fourteen million, to practise their religion? The Constitution specifically guaranteed 'Freedom to every man . . . to practise the religion of his choice.' Even on non-religious grounds he could uphold the Constitution only by vetoing this decree.

As Christmas approached, the Press howled and threatening crowds gathered outside the palace, just as had happened the previous Christmas. Louis knew that if he sanctioned the decree, he would continue to be popular; if he vetoed it, he would not only lose his popularity but have to fight, single-handed, a majority of the Assembly and all the influential Left-wing clubs. Louis nevertheless took the unpopular decision, and this time he had the support of all his Ministers.

On 19 December Louis informed his Cabinet that he intended to veto the decree. One of his Ministers, alarmed for his safety, advised Louis to take State priests for his private chapel and the Queen's. 'Don't speak to me of compromise,' Louis replied. 'Since there is freedom of religion in France, I must benefit by it as much as anyone.'

When the President read out to the Assembly Louis's decision that, as regards the decree on priests, he 'would examine it' – the eulogism for the suspensive veto – there was a moment of shocked silence, then the Jacobins urged that the will of the Assembly be proclaimed law, regardless of the King. Under the Constitution this of course was impossible, so the Jacobins turned to their powerful newspapers. They began to launch against the King and Queen a campaign of slander and hatred so violent it has never been equalled before or since. As such it constitutes a new stage in the Revolution.

Two editors were particularly irresponsible. One was the Swiss-born son of a Sardinian Calvinist and a Genevan mother, by name Mara, though he called himself Marat. A very small man, barely five feet tall, he had a suspicious nature and believed anyone who opposed him to be dishonest. Before the Revolution he had been physician to the Comte d'Artois's Guard and written books about electricity, which he claimed offered an explanation of the universe superior to Newton's. When the Academy of Sciences pooh-poohed his claims and declined to elect him a member, Marat denounced the Academy as 'dishonest'. He started *L'Ami du Peuple* in September 1789, purporting to support the people, but in fact Marat considered the people 'vile slaves' worthy only to be ruled by a supreme dictator, someone who should be a true 'friend of the people', in other words himself.

Marat wore an open-necked shirt, a bandage round his head and pistols in his belt. He suffered from prurigo, and that itch extended to politics. He scratched and clawed at every constructive measure, and denounced everyone who disagreed with him as 'dishonest'. He who had once excused himself on the grounds of sensitiveness from attending a post-mortem, proved to be the most bloodthirsty of journalists. This man who was not even French wrote that he wanted France 'flooded in blood', and on 27 May 1791 demanded precisely 50,000 dishonest French heads, adding that 'perhaps 500,000 will fall before the end of the year.'

The other militant journalist was Jacques René Hébert: by an odd coincidence he had the same surname as Louis's confessor. A failed dramatist who had become box-office assistant at the Variétés theatre, Hébert, like Marat, was a very small man, but well-mannered and cleanly dressed, smelling of musk and married to an ex-nun. Hébert possessed a cruel streak, remarked on by all his colleagues, and in order to express it adopted an *alter ego*: a large, square, pipe-smoking stove-maker named Père Duchesne, and through this devil-may-care figure Hébert urged the Parisians to crime with bawdy jokes, as Marat did with threats. Hébert specialized in blasphemy and peppered every paragraph with four-letter words. It was he who found savage names for the royal family: Madame Elisabeth was Big-bum Babet; Antoinette the Austrian bitch, Madame Veto, the she-wolf, the new Médicis; Louis was royal cuckold and drunkard, fat Colas, Gilles Capet, and now particularly Monsieur Veto. Three times a week, month after month, Hébert ranted against a King who had accepted the Constitution only to overthrow it. 'Could you ever believe the King would keep his word . . . and that his wife would pardon you all your snubs? Vengeance never dies in the heart of Kings . . . So that a nation determined to be free – f—— it all – must cut into the living flesh

. . . We must do what the English did: till then we'll never have happiness.'

In any highly charged situation extremes of hatred usually carry the day, and gradually the mass of Parisians came to believe the lies dreamed up by Marat, Hébert, Desmoulins and a dozen others, rather than the facts in the Royalist papers established by Louis. Louis, who had always followed the Press closely, was under no illusions. He knew that if he continued to act as a conscientious King, his enemies were quite ready to kill not only him, but his wife, his sister, his children.

This was a new situation and called for a new decision. Realizing that escape had now become impossible, Louis saw only one way of protecting the lives of his family. He must get in touch with his fellow Kings and persuade them to take a concerted stand in his favour: not provocative, for that would alarm the French people, but firm enough to dissuade his enemies from violence. Here is Louis's plan, as outlined to Fersen by Antoinette: 'The King believes that open force would be of incalculable danger not only for himself and his family but for all the French in the kingdom who are not supporters of the Revolution . . . The King wishes that the good will of his family, friends, allies and fellow sovereigns should be demonstrated by a congress and by negotiation. Of course there should be an impressive force to support them, but always far enough behind the frontier so that it could not provoke crime or massacre.'

Was Louis, in acting thus, 'betraying the Revolution'? Surely not. He remained loyal to the new order: indeed it was partly to preserve the Crown, coping-stone of the new order, that he acted as he did. Left-wing suspicions about darker intentions fall to the ground in view, for example, of a letter from his Foreign Minister to Louis: 'This winter [1791-2] submissively and with courage I obeyed the order to do everything possible to keep foreign armies and émigré forces out of my country: such was your will, and therefore my duty.'

Gustavus of Sweden was eager to help, but Leopold, who had succeeded Joseph as Emperor of Austria, dragged his feet, behaving, complained Antoinette, less like an Emperor than a petty Duke of Tuscany. As for Monsieur, instead of accepting Louis's invitation to return to France and strive, like him, to make the Constitution work, he issued an open letter, declaring that Louis, a prisoner, had been forced to accept a Constitution in which he secretly disbelieved. This letter inflamed hostility against the émigrés, and added to Louis's troubles by casting doubts on his sincerity generally and, in particular, on his motives in vetoing the decree against the priests.

Louis took Antoinette completely into his confidence and allowed her at last to play a political role. It was she who kept on friendly terms with the moderates, through her admirer Barnave, she who wrote the ciphered letters in invisible ink, smuggling them out sometimes in chocolate boxes. 'I'm exhausted from writing,' she told Fersen. 'I've never done such work before and I'm always afraid of forgetting something or making some stupid mistake' – which, as she well knew, could cost her her life. 'Sometimes I barely recognize myself and I have to pause to realize that this person is really me.' Secretary was one new role; another, still less congenial, was having to behave respectfully to politicians she despised – and there was no Trianon now to retreat to. 'My God,' she wrote to Mercy, 'is it possible that I – born with character and so aware of the blood flowing in my veins – should be fated to spend my days in such an age and with such men! But don't think I'm losing my courage . . .'

Antoinette found also that she and Elisabeth often disagreed. Elisabeth, like Monsieur and Artois, wanted Austria to invade France and rescue the royal family whereas Antoinette, like Louis, strongly opposed any idea of invasion. The two women could not talk without quarrelling and Antoinette confided to Fersen: 'Our home life is a hell.'

Louis too gave her cause for worry. When a man finds that every gesture, every word he speaks is misinterpreted he begins to doubt his sanity. A time may come when in order to keep his senses he sometimes has to relapse into silence. This is what Louis did that winter. Day after day he spoke no word save the few syllables needed for his evening game of backgammon with Elisabeth. For ten days he continued in this fashion. Antoinette could do nothing to cheer him and began to wonder whether he was heading for a complete breakdown. Then, as suddenly as he had become silent, Louis began to talk normally again. He had managed to surmount his fears.

Antoinette had always put friendship top of life's pleasures, and she was particularly hurt by the perfidy of friends. It pained her that the Versailles set, now in Koblenz, should sneer at Louis and call him King Log, after the inert monarch in La Fontaine's fable; even Mercy, she realized, did not at heart care about her plight. And so she treasured pathetically any sign, however slight, of friendship. Blaikie, Artois's outspoken Scots gardener and a man of no political importance, happened to speak solicitously to Elisabeth, telling her 'that they had to do with a bad set of people who wished to sacrifice them'. Learning of this, Antoinette drove specially to the Bagatelle. 'I know your thinking,' she told Blaikie, 'and I shall never forget you. I have known you long. I will go and see your house which I hear is neat and clean.' So she did and after-wards, says Blaikie, 'when she went off, she repeated she would not forget me.'

One man remained wholly devoted to her: Axel de Fersen. For thirteen years now he had been part of her life. At Versailles he had partnered her in minuets and country dances, and played party games with her; they had attended the same operas, listened to the same concerts. And then, almost alone of the Versailles crowd, he had stayed on after the joys to share her sorrow. As he organized the flight to Varennes, she had seen him show a generosity and self-assurance she had always admired in men, and the courage that was so much part of her own character. At the same time she would have become aware of his feeling for her. By April 1790 Fersen had fallen in love with Antoinette, or was very close to love. He wrote to his sister: 'She is the most perfect creature I know and her behaviour has won everyone to her side. I hear nothing but praise of her everywhere. You may imagine how happy this makes me . . .'

Then came Varennes, Fersen had to leave her, and Antoinette began to realize the extent of her feelings for the tall, dark-eyed Swede. In August, via Esterhazy, she sent him one of the royalist gold rings which for a moment were popular in Paris, inscribed '*Lâche qui les abandonne*', telling him that she had worn the ring herself for two days.

In September they began their secret correspondence and this provided a new link, all the stronger because they were risking their lives, and Antoinette found new cause to admire Fersen as, energetic-ally and almost single-handed, he tried to persuade Gustavus, Frederick of Prussia and Leopold of Austria to act together on her and Louis's behalf. Antoinette now began to confide in Fersen her alarms, including her deepest fear of all, a sort of recurrent nightmare that she who felt she was 'on a battlefield' would be considered spineless by the émigrés because she had chosen to work with, rather than against, the Revolution. And here too Fersen was wonderfully sympathetic. 'I pity you for being forced to sanction [the Constitution],' he wrote to her in October, 'but I feel your position, it is dreadful, and there was no other line to take.' While émigrés circulated a rumour that she was sleeping with Barnave, Fersen maintained his confidence in her unshaken, continually sending her messages not only of reassurance but, a rarer thing, of sympathy at the deepest level for her plight and of admiration for her courage.

That winter Fersen began to become for Antoinette more than a fellow-agent, more even than a symbol of the freedom that filled all her dreams; by his loving devotion, sympathy and activity on her behalf he won Antoinette's heart. From a friend and a deliverer from danger Fersen became the man who, had she been free in such a matter, Antoinette might have chosen to marry. In part of a letter written in cipher, undated but certainly belonging to winter 1791–2, Antoinette gave Fersen a glimpse of her feelings: 'I can say that I love you, and have time only for that. I am well . . . Goodbye, most loved and loving of men.'

As fury mounted over the veto Fersen suggested coming to Paris, perhaps intending to arrange a new escape. Antoinette answered that it was absolutely impossible – she knew he faced certain death should he be caught – though she had 'an extreme desire' to see him. Then, early in February, her feelings got the better of her and she sent Fersen a note saying that conditions were favourable.

On 11 February 1792 Fersen, wearing a wig and disguised as a courier, carrying letters he had written himself purporting to be messages from the King of Sweden to the Court of Portugal, set forth with his orderly and his little dog, Odin, on his dangerous journey. He reached Paris at half-past five in the afternoon of 13 February. He went to the house of Goguelat, the Queen's secretary, and by Goguelat was taken, at seven in the evening, to the bayonet-bristling Tuileries. Fersen wrote in his diary: 'I went to her rooms by my usual route. Afraid of the national guard. Her apartment very fine. Did not see the King . . .'

What happened between Antoinette and Fersen that evening can only be conjectured. First, they probably exchanged their news, then discussed security in the palace. Fersen realized that Antoinette was so closely guarded as to make escape impossible. This immediately put their meeting in a new light. Antoinette was in grave danger; within hours he would have to leave her; in all probability they would never see each other on earth again.

Fersen stayed all night hidden in Antoinette's apartment. His cool exterior hid a passionate nature. He loved Antoinette and probably made advances to her. She, for her part, found herself alone with a man she loved, and who had proved his love for her in a hundred ways. Louis, who at best had never shown much sexual drive, in the present difficult circumstances doubtless came to her bedroom very seldom, so that Antoinette, lonely, tense, highly strung, felt a strong pent-up desire. This, and the fact that Louis need never know, probably combined to break down her moral inhibitions.

There are three telling pieces of evidence. The first is a word in one of Antoinette's letters to Fersen. He had evidently asked her not to speak of her feelings for him, and in June 1791 she replied: 'I have made this painful effort in order to obey you.' 'Obey' is a strong word, rarely used by Antoinette: it suggests that she recognized Fersen as her master and was prepared to yield to him.

Secondly, after writing in his diary, 'Did not see the King', Fersen wrote another phrase, which was later inked out by his heirs. It is clearly composed of two words, of which the second seems to be less than three letters. The phrase may well have been 'Resté là', an expression Fersen habitually used in his diary to indicate that he had spent the night sleeping with a woman. Thirdly, when he later recalled his last meeting with Antoinette, Fersen described not what the Queen told him or what he told her but spoke of his own 'sensations' – a word never applied to his other meetings with the Queen, and which suggests physical pleasure.

Probably, therefore, Antoinette and Fersen slept together that night in the prison-palace. If they did, Antoinette would have found in Fersen a passionate, expert lover, remembered by his mistresses with esteem, and Fersen too, unlike Louis, was a free agent, therefore full of hope and dash: in his arms Antoinette was perhaps able to find the strength she so much needed.

Morning came, and with it the need for furtiveness. Fersen hid in the apartment all day and at six in the evening saw Louis. The King refused to envisage escape, having promised the Assembly not to leave Paris and, says Fersen, 'he is a man of his word.' Louis was depressed and felt the need to defend himself to Fersen. 'I know that I am charged with weakness and irresolution,' he said, 'but no one has ever been in a position like mine;' he added that he had missed the moment on 14 July 1789 and had never found it since.

Fersen told Louis and Antoinette that he would continue to Tours and Orléans, as though making for Portugal, then double back to the safety of Belgium. At 9.30 he said goodbye.

The immediate sequel to that night in the Tuileries Antoinette never knew, and perhaps it is just as well. Instead of taking the Tours road, Fersen hurried to 18 rue de Clichy and his mistress, Eléonore. When Craufurd returned in the evening, Fersen would retire to a maid's attic room and read novels – he read five altogether. After seven days of furtive pleasure with Eléonore Fersen wrote a letter that he had his orderly deliver to Craufurd, announcing his imminent return from Tours and Orléans. He then left the house by the back door, and presently re-entered by the front. Craufurd was completely taken in. 'We played our parts well,' Fersen wrote in his diary, 'and he believed us.'

Ever since the storming of the Bastille Frenchmen had been expecting other nations to applaud and imitate. Daily they awaited news that in London, Vienna, Berlin and Rome the good people had broken their chains. No such news arrived. The silence was deafening, to be followed, in time, by powerfully argued criticism, such as Burke's *Reflections*, or by amused incredulity that the so-called sophisticated French could swallow the view that man is virtuous in inverse proportion to the size of his house and that truth is the prerogative of those who make most noise.

France's neighbours had no intention of going beyond criticism. They were quite content to watch France lapse through internal strife to the level of a second-rate power. True, Austria protected the French émigrés, who from Koblenz shouted aggressive slogans, but less than 200 were under arms – a derisory number that only very gullible people, worked on by propaganda, could consider a threat. In response to Louis's appeal, his fellow Kings massed no army, concerted no action; the best they were able to do was to issue, on 27 August 1791, the feeble Declaration of Pillnitz: the Emperor Leopold and the King of Prussia declared themselves ready to restore Louis to a situation in which he would be free to strengthen the foundations of monarchical government – but only if other sovereigns joined them; such a condition, as they and France well knew, would never be fulfilled, and Antoinette was correct in her comment: 'The Emperor has betrayed us.'

Since no one was threatening France, it might be thought that Frenchmen would have concentrated on their countless domestic problems and turned a deaf ear to criticism from abroad. It was not so. They reacted to it in a way not strictly rational, and to understand why we must go behind the gay political banners with their rational slogans, 'Liberty and Equality', to two of the deeper motive forces.

The first is a condition some would call swelled-headedness, others demonic pride. It expressed itself in the belief that Frenchmen had discovered Truth with a capital T. The way for this kind of thinking had been prepared by Cagliostro, Mesmer and a hundred recent prophets. Frenchmen now believed they had entered into those promised higher spheres, that they, and they alone, held a monopoly of political wisdom.

This pride, which had been so characteristic of both Cagliostro and Mesmer as persons, took the form of a touchy intransigence. An 'either-or' attitude was adopted towards lesser mortals and other nations, expressed, to take one small example, in the motto on the deputies' buttons: '*Vivre libre ou mourir*.'

The French people may have felt that some form of attack was the best means of defending the Revolution. But one cannot rule out another interpretation. Since 1789 whatever they had asked for they had got, even though eight centuries of tradition had been broken in the getting. They had been allowed in particular to get away with murder. An unease set in, then the kind of hysteria children feel when they have done something wrong and go un-detected. Subconsciously they may have longed for a show-down, perhaps even for punishment.

This may partly explain the call for bloodshed which rose like a madman's shriek from every class. A young student in early 1792: 'Our freedom can rest assured only on a mattress of corpses . . . I consent to become one of them,' and Madame Roland, the other-wise intelligent wife of a future Minister: 'Peace is a retrograde step . . . we can be reborn only through blood.'

The man who most passionately preached the virtues of bloodshed was Pierre Brissot. Son of a Chartres pastry-cook, he had left school at fifteen, drifted into journalism, been a paid agent of the Duc d'Orléans, and finally become a convinced Mesmerist. It was in Dr Mesmer's salon that Brissot first felt the excitement of soaring beyond the merely human condition, and of curing man's ills in strange new ways that the uninitiated might call mad. Brissot carried over this thinking to politics, expressing it first in his extremist newspaper, *Patriote français*, then in speeches where logic was replaced by rapturous emotion. On 20 October 1791 Brissot made an important speech to the Assembly, in which he drew a dark picture of France's evil neighbours, particularly her hereditary enemy Austria, now protecting the émigrés. Then Brissot blew his hunting horn: 'You must yourselves attack the powers which dare to threaten you. The picture of liberty, like the head of Medusa will strike terror into the enemy armies.'

Louis was one of the very few not to be carried away by the shouts for blood. He had always personally been a man of peace. As in 1777, he did everything in his power to stem the movement towards war, though, as he wrote to his agent in Vienna, the ex-Minister Breteuil, war against Austria would at least be less of a catastrophe than the civil war threatening France. In March 1792 Louis dismissed the most war-minded of his Ministers, Narbonne. This was met by a cry of treason from the Brissotins, who obliged the rest to resign and Louis to take what they called a 'patriot' ministry, in other words one committed to war. Every département in the country urged 'a holy crusade' or 'the march of a free people against the unjust attack of a King', though such an attack was non-existent. All his Ministers voted for war, and the movement became irresistible.

On 20 April 1792 Louis went to the Assembly and proposed what Frenchmen demanded, but he declined to rhapsodize about France's motives. 'The National Assembly,' said Louis with just a hint of irony, 'and many citizens all over the kingdom, rather than watch any longer the dignity of the French people being outraged . . . prefer war.'

It is to the credit of one deputy, Louis Becquey, that he braved the warmongers: 'We shall earn the reputation of being an aggressive and restless people, who disturb the peace of Europe, and disregard treaties and international law.' Becquey was shouted down. With only seven dissenting votes, the Assembly declared war against Austria: not for twenty-three years would there be peace in Europe.

Louis had not wanted war, but once it was a fact, he showed great energy in recruiting, equipping and feeding an army eventually numbering 400,000. He increased pay and in the one month of May raised 47 battalions composed of volunteers from the national guard. He did this in face of obstacles. For instance, just as he had pains-takingly completed the clothing of the regular army, all of a sudden the Assembly decided that the white uniforms must be discarded and that all the soldiers must be given blue ones.

The war came as a disaster to Louis and Antoinette personally. Many Frenchmen were convinced that in fleeing to Varennes Louis and Antoinette had been trying to reach Austria, and they put the worst construction on everything the royal couple did. In future any unpopular action Louis might take would be denounced as 'pandering to Austria', while Antoinette became in effect an enemy alien, whom it became an act of patriotism to hate. As soldiers ran away, massacring their officers, Carra, in the *Annales patriotiques*, accused an 'Austrian committee' composed of Antoinette, Louis, certain priests and the émigrés. Patriotism more and more became the one true State religion; it was logical, therefore, that on Good Friday a State bishop should successfully move a decree prohibiting the wearing of clerical dress or Christian emblems. Forty-two départements ignored Louis's veto and enforced the decree of 29 November, arresting and imprisoning hundreds of priests. Louis's Keeper of the Seals protested that 'these administrative detentions bring *lettres de cachet* and the Bastille into the bosom of fredom,' but he was powerless to reverse an irrational movement against 'secret enemy agents'.

In the last week of May the Assembly passed a new and far more terrible version of their 29 November decree. Any priest denounced by twenty citizens – which, given the war hysteria, meant any one of 20,000 priests still loyal to the Holy See – was to be deported to Guiana, a colony riddled with malaria and leprosy, from which few could hope to return. This decree was sent to the Tuileries for Louis's sanction.

Louis's leading minister was now a brave stocky soldier, Charles Dumouriez. He took office on 1 March. The King had been depicted to him, he says, 'as a violent, angry man, who cursed and treated his Ministers roughly. But during the three months I worked with him in very tricky circumstances, I always found him polite, moderate, affable and even very patient.' He was particularly struck by Louis's 'great firmness'.

Louis was strongly advised by Dumouriez to sanction the decree deporting priests. If you don't sanction it, he argued, 'you'll be putting a dagger to the throats of these wretched priests,' who would be killed by their fellow Frenchmen. His arguments were endorsed by Jean Marie Roland, Minister of the Interior, who made Louis very angry by reading aloud in Council a letter drafted by his meddlesome wife, who considered priests to be charlatans and Christianity 'absurd'. This letter, which came very close to blackmail, suggested that the King should take a State priest as his confessor, and declared that in case of a veto he, Roland, would unleash against Louis 'the implacable defiance of a saddened people who would consider the King the friend and accomplice of conspirators'.

Finding no support in his Cabinet, Louis consulted Antoinette. She who had advised such conciliatory measures as the reappointment of Necker in 1788 again showed herself less resolute than he. Antoinette urged Louis to sanction the decree, since a veto would arouse the fury of Paris against them both, and they had recently been stripped of their strong personal guard.

Louis disregarded both Antoinette and his Cabinet. He saw that the decree was iniquitous: a thousand times more intolerant, and more ominous of future tyranny, than any decree in his own reign or that of his grandfather. True, he had too little power to prevent the decree being implemented in defiance of his veto, just as the milder decree of 29 November was being implemented. It was a matter now only of principle, of conscience. He knew that he was risking his throne, what little freedom he still had, perhaps his life. He took the risk. On 19 June he vetoed the decree of deportation, and another decree establishing an armed camp of 20,000 men in Paris. Then he wrote to his confessor, Père Hébert: 'Come to see me. Never have I needed the consolation of religion so much. I have finished with men; my trust now is in heaven. Disasters are foretold for tomorrow; I shall be brave.'

The same day leaders of the militant Parisians gathered. Prominent were Antoine Santerre, a brewer who had become rich selling English-style ales and porters, and Legendre, a big butcher with powerful lungs and a loud voice who boasted of his lack of schooling; 'my education is not man-made,' he said, 'it is natural: expect from me only the explosion of feeling.' They decided to lead the Paris crowd into the Tuileries and force the King to withdraw his veto.

On the afternoon of 20 June a large angry crowd arrived at the Tuileries and swept into the palace, the five battalions of national guards offering no resistance. Louis waited upstairs in an ante-room, guarded by a dozen grenadiers. Antoinette set off to join him, but was held back by one of the younger courtiers, the Chevalier de Rougeville, who warned her she'd be killed. She and her children were led by Rougeville to the Council Room, where he barricaded them in with furniture and set a guard.

The crowd surged upstairs and broke down the ante-room door with pikes. They saw Elisabeth clinging to Louis's coat and threatened her with their pikes until they realized she was not the Queen. Louis was helped by the grenadiers on to a window seat. 'Don't be afraid, Sire,' one of them said, and for answer Louis took the soldier's hand and placed it on his heart: 'Feel here if there are any signs of fear.'

Legendre, addressing the King, gave vent to one of his 'explosions of feeling.'

'Monsieur, you're a traitor, you've always deceived us, and you're doing so now.'

He then read a petition, while the crowd chanted, 'Sanction the decrees! Down with the veto! Down with the priests!'

Louis was strong enough to pick up the biggest man in the crowd and throw him out of the window. On the other hand, he was embarrassed before this horde of strangers, bad at impromptu speeches, and in the jammed room suffering from the heat.

The crowd too were both strong and weak. They had the advantage of numbers, and some were militants who carried miniature working models of the guillotine, but they were all somewhat uneasy to be in the palace.

Louis listened to their demands. The refrain was familiar: a patriot King must do as the Nation wished. All his reign Louis had been keeping his ears strained for voices from the heaths of Brittany, the gorges of the Pyrenees, the snow-bound Alps. Frenchmen there, no less than the crowd before him, comprised the Nation. And so, each time they demanded he withdraw the veto, Louis refused. He would not deport 20,000 innocent men for following their consciences on a religious issue.

'I have acted according to the Constitution,' Louis said.

'Long live the Nation!' they shouted accusingly.

'The Nation has no better friend than me.'

'Prove it then. Put on this.' Someone thrust forward on the end of his pike a red cap, symbol of militant patriotism.

'Very well.'

Louis tried to put on the red cap, found it too small, but after a grenadier had stretched it on his knee was able to pull it on to the back of his head. Then a man handed him a bottle of wine, inviting him to drink. 'It is poisoned,' someone whispered, but Louis raised the bottle and called out:

'People of Paris, I drink to your health and to that of the French nation.' Then amid applause he put the bottle to his lips.

By wearing the red cap and drinking their red wine Louis won over many of the crowd, yet he stood firmly by his principles. The more militant continued shouting slogans, but clearly an impasse had been reached.

It was the job of the mayor of Paris to keep unauthorized Parisians from entering the palace and, should they force a way in, to eject them. But the mayor now was Jérôme Pétion, who had accompanied Louis back from Varennes and cared only about being popular. Just before six he entered the room and blithely announced to the King, 'Sire, I have this minute learned of your plight.'

Louis flung him a look. 'That is surprising, since it's lasted all of two hours.'

Pétion faced the crowd, aware what he ought to do, but fearing to be unpopular. Only when twice urged by a municipal officer did Pétion pluck up courage enough to tell the crowd to leave, otherwise, he added appeasingly, 'enemies of the public good might question your respectable intentions.'

The crowd saw that they had failed. The King quite plainly was not going to yield. Grudgingly they left the palace. When all was quiet, Louis threw himself into an armchair, the red cap, which he had forgotten, still on the back of his head, and thanked those who had stood by him.

Antoinette, in tears, threw herself at his feet with the children, and later wrote to Fersen: 'I'm still alive, by a miracle. The twentieth was a frightful day. It's not me they're after now, it's my husband's life, and they don't hide it. He showed a firmness and strength which carried the day, but the danger can begin again at any moment.'

The full extent of Louis's victory emerged in the days following, when addresses began to arrive from all parts of the kingdom and all the armies in the field, bearing tens of thousands of signatures; they congratulated and thanked Louis for having defended the Constitution, asked that those who had abused him should be punished, and demanded the closure of the clubs that had fomented the trouble. This was an unprecedented swing in favour of the monarchy; all Louis needed to consolidate his position was a military victory, and there were signs that this might be on the way, for French troops, in mid-June, captured the important town of Tournai in Belgium.

The provinces' support for the King and the *status quo* is a vital fact in the extremely complex situation that now began to develop in Paris, and which here can be stated only in simplified terms. The chief protagonists in the coming drama were the Jacobin Club, led by Robespierre, the club known as the Cordeliers, because it met in a disused Cordeliers convent on the Left Bank, led by Georges Jacques Danton, barrister and powerful demagogue, Desmoulins, Marat, Hébert and another anti-Christian hate-merchant, 'Anaxagoras' Chaumette, and some of the politically conscious lower-class Parisians who resented restriction of the franchise and their exclusion from full civic rights. It was the aim of these groups to overthrow the monarchy and the Legislative Assembly, which they identified with an essentially undemocratic system of government. Since they could not achieve this by legal means, they decided to foment an insurrection. Their chief device was to play, as never before, on the widespread, basically irrational fear of counter-revolution. Since he refused to deport priests loyal to Rome, that is to a hostile power, Louis was a counter-revolutionary. The Tuileries was a forward outpost of the invading armies, the Queen a she-wolf about to slink out of her lair and, helped by her lovers, priests and enemy agents, massacre every patriotic Parisian in his bed. These crowned counter-revolutionaries would not, must not, last beyond the fall of the leaves.

The organizers of the insurrection demanded arms of their mayor; this was like holding lighted tinder to a barrel of gunpowder, but 'Jesus Christ' Pétion said Yes, certainly, and sanctioned distribution from the arsenal of up to 50,000 arms. A highly organized attack on the Tuileries was then planned by the armed forces of the Paris wards and substantial contingents of 'federal' troops, notably from Marseilles and Brittany, who, against the King's will, had been called to Paris, ostensibly to defend it in case of invasion, in fact to strengthen the lower-class Parisians.

Soon after midnight on 10 August the tocsin sounded. At five in the morning commissioners elected by the Paris wards went to the Hôtel de Ville and installed an insurrectionary Commune – in effect a provisional Government. Danton himself arrested the Commander of the national guard and replaced him by his friend, the brewer Santerre. According to one eye-witness, the Place Vendôme was filled with a crowd carrying human heads on pikes. 'I noticed with horror,' says one observer, 'young people, in fact children, throwing the heads in the air and catching them on sticks.'

Louis, who had been up all night, himself organized the defence of the Tuileries, posting 900 gendarmes, 2000 national guards and 900 red-uniformed Swiss guards. Of these only the Swiss were absolutely reliable, but, owing to a shortage caused by the war, each had only fifteen to twenty cartridges. Louis refused to wear a bullet-proof waistcoat specially made for him and armed himself with a pistol. At eight o'clock he was told that some 20,000 Parisians filled the Carrousel and nearby streets, ready to attack. He sent a message to the Assembly, informing them of the danger and urging them to send a deputation to the palace.

The Assembly left this message unanswered and sent no deputation. Braver than the deputies, members of the département of Paris, a moderate body that disapproved of the Commune's violence, entered the Tuileries. Their leader, a cool-headed young lawyer named Roederer, noticed that the national guards had begun to fraternize with the crowd. He urged the gunners to do their duty bravely, but for answer they ostentatiously unloaded their cannon.

Roederer went straight to the King's study, where Louis, Antoinette and the Ministers were gathered. He told them what he had seen, and declared the troops unreliable. If they stayed where they were, the King, his family and the Court would inevitably be killed. Their only hope, said Roederer, was to hurry to the National Assembly. Antoinette replied that the palace could and would hold out. She did not want to leave. Everyone turned to Louis. The decision was his.

There were two precedents. On 6 October 1789 at Versailles people in a violent mood had stormed the palace by force and been ejected by the national guard, still loyal. Seven weeks ago, on 20 June, the crowd, in a quieter mood, had entered the palace with the national guard's tacit approval. The situation now combined the worst features of both. Louis already had his doubts about the national guard, and what Roederer had seen confirmed them. As for the Assembly, it plainly feared to intervene. If he had been alone, Louis might have decided to hold the Tuileries, but once again he had to consider his wife and children. They were like hostages, placing him at a continual disadvantage. He decided to leave. '*Marchons!*' he said, raising his right hand. 'There's nothing more to be done here.'

Louis, Antoinette, holding her two children by the hand, members of the Court, and the departmental authorities set out from the palace, protected by a guard of Swiss Grenadiers. 'We walked over the leaves which had fallen in the night,' says Roederer, 'and which the gardeners had piled up in heaps across the path followed by the King. We sank up to our knees in them. "What a lot of leaves!" said the King. "They've begun to fall very early this year." ' The Dauphin amused himself by kicking the leaves into the legs of those walking in front of him.

They arrived in the Riding School. 'I have come here,' Louis said to the Assembly's president, 'to avert a great crime, and I think that there is no safer place than among you, Gentlemen.' The Assembly was gratified that the King should entrust his safety to them, but since the law forbade them to meet in his presence, the King and the royal family were huddled into the stenographers' box, ten feet square, six feet high, from which, through iron bars, they could see and be seen.

Louis doubtless believed that by leaving the Tuileries in full view he had rendered an attack on the palace pointless. But the 900 gendarmes and some of the national guard left their posts, fraternized with the crowd and invited them in. Then twelve cannon brought up by the crowd began firing, and a group of armed Parisians charged the palace, shooting at the red-uniformed Swiss. The Swiss fired back and repelled them. John Moore, an English physician then in Paris, and a most reliable source, says: 'After the King and Royal family had forsaken the castle I can see no motive which the Swiss could have for firing, but self-defence.'

Louis heard the firing. Several cannon bullets struck the roof of the Riding School and some musket-shot entered the windows. Then came a lull, followed by the arrival of men warning of another attack. Hoping to avoid a massacre of his Swiss Guard, Louis wrote an order – his last as King: 'The King orders the Swiss to lay down their arms immediately and to withdraw to their barracks – Louis.'

This was carried to the Tuileries, where the second attack had begun. It seems to have had little or no effect, for the Swiss were already doomed by their shortage of ammunition. Within minutes they were overwhelmed by vastly superior numbers and most of them died at their posts. Some sixty of them, taken as prisoners to the Hôtel de Ville by the Marseillais, were massacred by the mob there in cold blood.

Then the assailants entered the palace, killing everyone they found. Some were thrown from top-floor windows, some impaled on pikes, some mutilated obscenely. The wine cellar was looted, chandeliers and looking-glasses smashed, plate and carpets carried away. Wooden buildings adjoining the palace having caught fire, the fire brigade was called and, when it arrived, shot at. Altogether, nearly 900 of the defenders died, while the assailants suffered losses of 376, mostly wounded.

Others of the crowd arrived in the passageway outside the stenographers' box, threatening to break in the door. Helped by a loyal national guard, Louis wrenched out the iron bars of his 'cage', so that should the crowd enter he could get his family out.

Men and women poured into the Assembly hall, laying the objects of their pillage, as offerings to the Nation, on a table in front of the president. Among the treasures they brought were Antoinette's jewels and – final sacrilege – the gold ciborium from the royal chapel tabernacle, containing consecrated hosts.

Only a third of the deputies were present. The rest, who might have been more loyal to the King, had been kept away by threats. Louis watched and listened as this minority discussed the sudden turn of events. The insurrectionary Commune expressed the wish that the King should at once be suspended, and the Assembly, terrified by the Commune's proof of power, fell in with its wishes. Without hearing the King's side of the story, they solemnly decreed the suspension of Louis, King of the French.

For two days Louis, Antoinette and their children remained in the stenographers' box; the nights they spent in the cells of a nearby convent. On the 10th Louis ate nothing save a biscuit and a glass of lemonade, Antoinette a bowl of soup. On the subsequent days their dinner was brought by a caterer. Their sole occupation was hearing the debates. Among those watching the Queen from the public gallery was Dr John Moore. 'A person near me,' he writes, 'remarked that her face indicated rage and the most provoking arrogance. I perceived nothing of that nature [but rather] dignified composure.'

The Assembly decided that Louis and the royal family should be detained in Monsieur's former house, the Luxembourg, but the Commune insisted that the place of detention should be the fortress known as the Temple, and again the Assembly acquiesced. Preparations were made for the move.

While the Commune struck a medal inscribed – incredibly – 'In memory of the glorious combat of the French people against tyranny at the Tuileries,' Hébert, alias Père Duchesne, rapturized about Louis's fall and asked, 'What are we going to do with the fat measled pig which has cost so much to fatten?' Put him in a convent, perhaps? It hardly mattered now that he had been rendered powerless. 'Let him drink, let him get drunk . . . Since Nature has given him a porker's character, let him live on as a porker.'

CHAPTER 23

The Assembly's Sentence

THE Bastille had been razed as a hateful place of arbitrary detention; three years later the prisons of Paris were crowded with men and women arbitrarily detained. Now to their number were added Louis, Antoinette, Elisabeth and the two royal children. They were taken to the Bastille-like Temple, a twelfth-century fortress that had once belonged to the Knights Templar. Their imprisonment was a violation of the Constitution, which declared that no one might be detained more than twenty-four hours without being charged.

Louis's manservant, Jean Baptiste Cléry, has left an account of the royal family's life in prison. Louis got up at six. He washed but at first could not shave, being forbidden a razor. He usually dressed in black silk breeches and a frock-coat of the golden colour still known as 'the Queen's hair', though shock had now turned that hair grey and in places white. Then for three hours he read: books of travel, Montesquieu, Buffon, Hume; Tasso in Italian; Tacitus, the breviary and the *Imitation of Christ* in Latin. Louis read on average twelve books a week. At nine he breakfasted with his family, then went down to Antoinette's room, where he spent the day. In the morning father and mother gave lessons to their children: Louis making the Dauphin recite Corneille and Racine and teaching him geography according to a method he himself had devised. The countries of the world were cut out of maps and the Dauphin had to fit them into the right position.

At one o'clock they all went for a walk in the adjoining avenue of horse-chestnut trees; the Dauphin ran about and played football or quoits. At two they ate a plentiful dinner, Louis drinking wine, Antoinette water and Elisabeth almond milk, which is an aperient. After dinner they played at piquet and backgammon. At four Louis took a nap, and when he woke watched Cléry give the Dauphin writing lessons. Louis Charles was a good-looking boy, with blue eyes and long chestnut hair, gay but nervous, and very fond of his sister: 'every time something pleases him,' Antoinette had noted, 'like going somewhere, or if someone gives him something, his first impulse is to ask for the same thing for his sister.'

Seven was a high point of the day, for then a friendly news-vendor shouted the latest news from across the street loud enough for them to hear. As evening fell and candles were lit, Antoinette and Elisabeth would read to Louis from a book of history. Then came the children's supper, during which Louis amused them with conundrums from back numbers of the *Mercure de France*. At nine o'clock Louis supped alone, and afterwards read till midnight. The relief Louis found in books Antoinette found in embroidering white chair-covers with scattered roses and in playing with her black Scottie, a gift from the Princesse de Lamballe. Antoinette called the Scottie Odin, evidently because Fersen had a dog of that name, and allowed him to sleep in her bedroom.

The locks which had been such a feature of Louis's life had now closed in on him with a vengeance. He and his family lived behind no less than eight locked iron doors. Yet one morning a mason arrived to make holes in the wall of Louis's ante-chamber so that, as a further precaution, huge bolts could be added to the door. During the mason's lunch-break Louis showed the Dauphin in a thoroughly professional manner how to use hammer and chisel. The mason remarked to the King in a kindly tone, 'When you get out of here you can say that you worked at your own prison.' 'Ah,' replied Louis, 'when and how shall I get out?' On another occasion he astonished Cléry and the guards by his dexterity in making houses out of dominoes.

Antoinette felt more afraid than Louis at being in prison and made a greater effort to conciliate the authorities. One day she asked to be given the music of the *Marseillaise*, and when a commissioner next visited the Temple, she who had so often trilled gay little arias in her boudoir at Versailles sang to him the stern, stirring words of Rouget de Lisle's battle hymn.

Louis and Antoinette had to put up with a few discomforts, such as icy stone walls, smoking chimneys, confined space and absence of privacy, but what hurt them most were the petty humiliations. Louis was allowed so few clothes he had become 'a king of shreds and patches', and Elisabeth had to wait till he went to bed in order to darn them. When new linen was allowed in, it was found to be worked with crowned letters, whereupon the guards ordered Antoinette and Elisabeth to pick out the crowns. One day Antoinette told Cléry to make a multiplication table, but a guard took it away, saying that she was showing her son how to talk in cipher.

By a curious irony, the press on which Louis as a boy had set up and printed his little book on *Télémaque* had been found in the Louvre and given to Marat, who was now using it to print his *L'Ami du Peuple*. Perhaps when he saw the paroxysms of hate in that newspaper Louis recalled one of his schoolboy notes on *Télémaque*: 'We ought to respect kings and, even when we disapprove of them, treat them kindly.'

The tone in Paris was being set by such newspapers, by cartoons depicting Louis as a tool of the priests and Antoinette as a harpy tearing up the Declaration of Rights with her claws, and by plays such as *Les Victimes Cloîtrées*, 'a piece,' says John Moore who saw it, 'written to inspire horror and indignation against the priesthood, and to place monks in particular in the most atrocious point of view.'

The guards, mostly simple men, took their cue from this kind of propaganda. One had the habit of puffing smoke from his pipe into Louis's face, knowing he disliked it. Others, behind his back, made fun of the King because, owing to lack of exercise, he had grown fat and snored loudly. When Louis and Antoinette returned from their walk, they would find graffiti: 'Strangle the cubs', or a drawing of a guillotine captioned, 'Louis spitting into the basket'. One evening Louis was given a newspaper by the guard on duty; he thought this was an act of kindness until he read in the newspaper that a gunner had publicly demanded permission to load his cannon with Louis's head and fire it at the enemy.

On 2 September, in the third week of their imprisonment, this hatred spilled over. News arrived that the Prussian army was advancing on Verdun, whereupon the Commune called the people to arms, sounded the tocsin and flew the red flag of emergency. Some Parisians thought they would be very patriotic, very brave. They broke into nine prisons and for five days killed in cold blood the helpless creatures they found there. Altogether they butchered some 1400 people, of whom 225 were priests, and 37 women. Louis's former Foreign Minister, Montmorin, was impaled and carried, still wriggling, to the Assembly; his chaplain, Père Hébert, was murdered in cold blood. The authorities condoned the massacres and when someone protested to Danton, Minister of Justice, he retorted, 'To hell with the prisoners! They must look after themselves.'

This cowardly act of mass cruelty was followed by something

even worse. According to a reliable eye-witness, the lawyer Maton de la Varenne: 'It was about two o'clock when the butchers, tired out and no longer able to lift their arms, though they were continually drinking brandy into which Manuel [the procureur of the Municipality] had put gunpowder to stimulate their fury, were sitting in a ring round the corpses lying opposite the prison to take breath. A woman with a basket full of rolls of bread came past. They took them from her and soaked each piece in the blood of their palpitating victims.'

Louis and Antoinette were aware that Paris was in turmoil; they had heard the tocsin and the crowd moving like a storm-swept sea. A commissioner arrived and told Louis: 'The enemy is at our gates, they want blood, they're asking for heads . . . well, yours will be the first!' Louis for the first time lost his nerve: his eyes filled with tears, he went pale and began to tremble.

Next day at dinner they heard shouting out in the street, and calls for Antoinette to appear. She did not go to the window, but Cléry, on a lower floor, looked out and saw a pike on which was impaled a woman's head: 'though bloody, it was not disfigured; her blond hair, still curling, floated around the pike.' Then a national guardsman strode into the royal family's room and told Antoinette to look out of the window; the people had brought her something nice, to show how they avenged themselves on tyrants. When Antoinette did not move from the dining-table, he uttered these terrible words: 'The head of the Lamballe woman.' Antoinette fell to the floor unconscious.

The princess, a captive since August in the La Force prison, had been dragged from her cell by the crowd and killed. They stripped her of her belongings, including a little red morocco *Imitation of Christ*, a picture of the Sacred Heart and a ring containing a lock of the Queen's hair inscribed 'Misfortune has turned it white.' They then tore off her clothes and raped her. They cut off her head and her genitalia, which they stuck separately on pikes. They had come to the Temple, dragging the body through the cobbled streets and holding the pikes aloft; their intention had been to make the Queen kiss her friend's severed head.

The days following were overshadowed by thoughts of the terrible massacres; then Louis and Antoinette turned their attention to an event long expected and long dreaded. A new elected Assembly, calling itself the Convention, abolished the monarchy and began to consider what should be done with the deposed King.

The Assembly opened a tense debate by asking two questions: can Louis Capet be tried, and if so, by whom should he be tried? Morisson of the Vendée said: 'No one can be condemned save in virtue of a pre-existing law. So long as you cannot show me the text of a law applicable to the deeds for which Louis is blamed, I say that you cannot try him.' Rouzet of Toulouse said: 'Citizens, let us be under no illusion, we are judges and also parties to the action. Would you wish a great nation to degrade itself by practising the maxims of despots? . . . Louis XVI is already judged and punished more severely than the Constitution required.' Many speakers pointed to the definite statement in the Constitution that 'the person of the King is inviolable and sacred.' Faure of the Seine Inférieure wished Louis to be brought to the Assembly and told: 'We were your children and you wished to cut our throats; you deserved death; nevertheless we grant you your life.' Necker, never slow to express an opinion, issued from Geneva a pamphlet against putting the King on trial. During the seven years he had worked with Louis, said Necker, every one of the King's sentiments had shown compassion for the people, and a gentle, merciful, moderate character. True, he had sometimes followed bad advice, but a King, Necker argued pertinently, 'can devote to our service only the means and gifts with which Nature has endowed him; so we agree tacitly to accept his mistakes and sympathize with his weaknesses.'

On the other side Legendre proposed that the Convention should pronounce sentence without hearing the King, while the Calvinist pastor, Saint-André, declared that the King had been judged and condemned by the people on the tenth of August, and that the Convention had nothing to do but order his execution.

At one o'clock on 11 December Chaumette came to the Temple and read a decree summoning Louis Capet to appear before the Convention.

'Capet is not my name,' said the King. 'It was the surname of one of my ancestors.'

He walked to the waiting carriage and was driven to the Convention. There he came forward and stood at the bar. There were shadows under his eyes and his face looked almost bruised, like a boxer's during the final rounds of a long and punishing fight.

'Louis, you may sit down,' said Barrère, the President that day, then continued: 'Louis, the French Nation accuses you of having committed various crimes to re-establish tyranny on the ruins of liberty; the National Convention has decreed that you shall be tried – and the members who compose it are to be your judges.'

To a person less intimately acquainted than you are with the history of human affairs [Gouverneur Morris wrote to Jefferson], it would seem strange that the mildest monarch who ever filled the French throne, one who is precipitated from it precisely because he would not adopt the harsh measures of his predecessors, a man whom none can charge with a criminal or cruel act, should be prosecuted as one of the most nefarious tyrants that ever disgraced the annals of human nature . . . Yet such is the fact.

Louis then heard the general act of accusation read out, a mixture of specific charges and vague denunciations, ranging from cornering the Hamburg sugar and coffee market in order to raise prices to three times firing on the people. Louis's secret iron cupboard in the Tuileries had been discovered and certain papers therein were cited as evidence. The most damaging recorded payments to his disbanded bodyguard. Louis had made these in order to alleviate hardship, but the Convention felt certain that he had been paying an underground army.

Louis believed that Charles I had made a fatal blunder in refusing to accept the competence of Parliament, so he had already decided to accept the Convention as a tribunal. To each charge he made a brief, pertinent reply. Only once did he lose his composure. When the President said, 'You distributed money among the populace for the treacherous purpose of acquiring popularity and enslaving the Nation,' Louis was so astonished by the maliciousness of the reasoning that it took him several moments to find his words. 'I always took pleasure in relieving the needy, but never had any treacherous purpose.'

Louis was granted counsel. 'Ladies ambitious of defending their Sovereign's cause have even offered their services;' but Louis chose Malesherbes, the bluff-friendly lawyer-botanist who had been such an able Minister of the Household. Now aged seventy-one, Malesherbes was helped by Tronchet and a younger lawyer, Romain de Sèze. Counsel had only ten days to put together a defence.

Louis went a second time to the Convention. He had been allowed to shave, and he sat while Sèze went to the bar. Silence fell, but even this was not quite impartial, since it served to emphasize a piece of statuary dominating the hall: a bust of Brutus. Sèze began by re-asserting the King's inviolability. Article 8 of the Constitution declared 'that after his abdication whether actual or legal the King will take his place among the class of citizens, and can be accused and judged like them for acts posterior to his abdication.' In other words, while King, Louis had not belonged to the ordinary class of citizens. However, since some speakers had said that the King was inviolable only in respect of those acts which he had decided with his Ministers, Sèze went on to answer specific charges, the gravest being that on 10 August Louis had carried out a carefully prepared act of aggression on the people of Paris. Sèze showed that the very reverse was true and gave details of how the coup had been prepared. 'In this very hall where I speak members have disputed the honour of having planned the insurrection of the tenth of August.'

Sèze had prepared a peroration which moved Malesherbes to tears, but which Louis told him to omit: 'I don't want to play on their feelings.' So Sèze concluded with these simple words: 'Louis came to the throne at the age of twenty . . . he was thrifty, just, severe; he proved himself the constant friend of the people. When the people desired the destruction of a crippling tax [the *corvée*] he destroyed it. When the people demanded the abolition of servile labour, he began by abolishing it himself on his own estates. When the people asked for reforms in criminal law, to ease the lot of accused persons, he made these reforms. When the people wished thousands of Frenchmen to enjoy the civil rights of which they had long been deprived, he made the appropriate laws. When the people wished for liberty, he gave it them. He took the lead in making sacrifices, and yet in the name of this same people you are today demanding . . . Citizens, I leave the phrase unfinished; I stop before History; remember that it will pass judgment on your verdict and that its judgment will endure.'

Louis added a few words, refuting the charge of having wished to shed the people's blood, particularly on 10 August. 'I confess that the repeated signs I have given that I love the people, and my behaviour throughout my reign seem to me abundant proof that I was not afraid to spare any trouble in order to prevent bloodshed, and forever to banish such an imputation.'

While Louis was driven back to the Temple prison, the members of the Convention, which they liked to call the Temple of Law, broke into violent vituperation, charges and counter-charges. The uproar became such that on one day the President broke three bells, ringing for silence. It might have been thought that Louis's inviolability had been clearly established, as well as the failure to point to any specific law which he had broken. But there were those deputies, on the highest seats to the Left known as the Mountain, who would not be deterred by facts.

Their leader was Maximilien Robespierre. He came from a middle-class family of Arras, had been a choirboy in Arras cathedral and owed his education to the generosity of the bishop. Continuing his schooling in Paris, he had recited verses in praise of Louis XVI on the occasion of the King's solemn entrance to that city. A small, slim bachelor of thirty-four, Robespierre had neat features which reminded some of a cat, hair that was always well-combed and powdered, spotless linen. He was short-sighted and wore spectacles to read. He lodged with a carpenter's family, to whom in the evening he read his beloved Rousseau. In other leisure moments he would play with his dog, Brount. He possessed a strong will, worked hard and was an excellent, lucid speaker, both in the Jacobin Club, of which he was the leading member, and in the Convention. He was greatly admired in the provincial Jacobin clubs and considered by many a perfect specimen of the austere, dedicated patriot.

Yet as a person Robespierre was not liked and he had no friends. To discover why one must go behind these impeccable appearances. When he was nine his mother died and his father walked out on the children. So Maximilien was deprived of love in his formative years and grew up incapable of affection, while the lack of a father resulted in a refusal to brook authority and vanity of exceptional dimensions. In an early letter to a friend Robespierre said: 'I have always had infinite *amour propre.*' 'Infinite' is a characteristic word: Robespierre was forever vowing infinite and eternal allegiance to vague abstractions such as: Humanity, Virtue, the *Patrie*, and, according to one German observer, 'sees himself as the chosen one of heaven; on other men he throws a look of contempt.' Robespierre believed in a Supreme Being, but for mere servants of that God, ordinary priests and nuns, he felt only hate. He seems to have suffered from sexual repression, for though himself unmarried he felt a curious urge to make other men marry. He had recently tried – though without success – to carry a motion obliging all priests to marry.

Robespierre strikingly embodies a characteristic common to most of the Revolutionary leaders from Mirabeau to his own associates, Saint-Just and Marat. Each suffered from some inhibition or passion that crippled his personal fulfilment. Robespierre was blocked by his loveless childhood, his vanity and his belief-to-the-death in Rousseau's rosy world, from having normal relations with other men, and, as Mirabeau's associate Dumont noted, Robespierre never looked you in the eye. 'Freedom!' these men cried, and finding themselves still not free, they shouted with growing hysteria, 'Freedom, freedom!' As they struggled in vain to slip out of their own spiritual strait-jackets, they lashed out at those around them. If they still had not attained freedom, it was because they were being plotted against or enslaved. That is why, throughout the Revolution, happiness and freedom are never there – yet always just around the next corner.

When the question first arose whether or not Louis should be tried, Robespierre took the lead in declaring that a trial was unnecessary. From the very beginning the barrister from Arras treated Louis not as a living, breathing human being, partly good, partly bad, but, philosophically, as the Arch-enemy of Freedom and, at a subconscious level, as the father-figure who had betrayed his children and whose authority he, Maximilien Robespierre, had never accepted. 'Louis cannot be put on trial,' Robespierre cried, 'he is already condemned; either he is condemned or the Republic is not absolved.' Religious imagery is fundamental to Robespierre's thinking; but God has been replaced by the *Patrie*, so that another sentence from the same speech is not ridiculous but fatally logical: 'The people do not pass sentence, they hurl lightning.'

By putting Louis to death, the French people would not be extirpating the monarchy, since the Dauphin would still be alive, not to mention Louis's brothers. What then were Robespierre's motives? The '*Marseillaise*' had already called on children of the *Patrie* to irrigate their fields with 'impure blood'. The political thinking here is as irrational as it is ruthless, but Robespierre took up the same notion now: 'Louis must die in order that the *Patrie* may live.'

Robespierre was now what Louis had once been: the most powerful man in France. 'The bloodthirsty party of Robespierre,' wrote the British ambassador, 'exert every nerve to excite the Convention and the people to terminate the days of their unfortunate monarch.' They whipped up hatred in Paris and the section of the Théâtre Française declared itself in a state of insurrection until Louis should be put to death, its members taking the following oath: 'We swear by the rights of the people, by the memory of the victims of the tenth of August, by the need to be free; Louis must die, or no Republican will survive.'

Much was made of those victims. Orphans, widows, wounded men hobbling on crutches were one day paraded through the Convention in a scene cunningly devised to move members' feelings; no one thought to mention that the 'heroes of the tenth' had broken into property that was not theirs, and that armed rioters must expect to get hurt. But who now cared for the facts? Speech after speech was made without a single reference to proved fact, and when the Convention put up for competition the painting of the tenth of August, Gérard won the prize with a picture showing the Assembly deliberating the King's fate, while Louis guzzled a chicken held uncouthly in both hands.

Necker had pointed out that when the act of accusation against Charles I was read and the clerk pronounced the words 'Accusation in the name of the English people', the voice of Lady Fairfax was heard to cry out, 'Not a tenth part of them.' Moved by that or similar considerations, on the day after Louis had made his speech to the Convention two members, Buzot and Salle, called for a referendum on the King's fate. This would have been the fairest course of all, but Robespierre denounced it on two main counts: first, to doubt even for a moment that Louis was guilty was to doubt the legality and necessity of the insurrection of the tenth of August; a referendum would be tantamount to accusing the Nation. But Robespierre also foresaw, though he was careful not to admit it, that the provinces would show more mercy than Paris; not only that, they might even transfer the Convention somewhere outside Paris, and this would 'doom the Republic'. Robespierre feared a referendum because he no longer believed in majority rule; that is why he said in this speech, 'On this earth virtue has always been in a minority,' and he ended by saying: 'I demand that the National Convention declare Louis Capet guilty and deserving of death.'

On 15 January the Convention began voting to decide the fate of the King. Each member was to come to the rostrum and give his opinion, which would be printed and distributed throughout France, on three questions:

1. Is Louis guilty of plotting against the Nation's freedom and of a criminal attempt on the general security of the State?
2. Shall the sentence, whatever it is, be sent to the people for ratification?
3. What is the penalty to be?

It is hardly necessary to insist on the vagueness of question one, and on the omission from question three of the proviso 'in case he should be found guilty'. It was already clear that this was less a Temple of Law that a court of political action.

The first deputation to vote was that of the Haute Garonne. Its leader, Jean Mailhe, stepped up to the rostrum and declared that in his opinion Louis was guilty and, without consulting the people, should be put to death. Mailhe added: 'If a majority vote for death, I think the Convention should consider a stay of execution.'

One by one members voted. Many recommended detention or banishment. Lehardy said that history teaches 'the death of kings has never been useful to liberty.' Roland Saint-Etienne thought that 'Louis dead will be more dangerous to the people's freedom than Louis living in prison.' Izarn-Valady declared that they must stand by the Constitution of 1791, a contract into which they had freely entered. Bresson, from the Vosges, said 'We are not judges; judges wear an ice-cold headband on their brow, whereas we are devoured with a burning hate of Louis.'

At four o'clock in the morning, after eight hours' voting, came the turn of the Paris deputation. Robespierre, their leader, made no mention of the charge or of specific evidence; he had already formulated the case in his own terms: 'You are not passing sentence for or against a man, you are carrying out an act of national providence.' In a short speech, he declared that he had been deputed by the people to cement public freedom by condemning the tyrant: 'I vote for death.'

Danton, Marat, Desmoulins and sixteen others voted likewise: twenty out of twenty-three. Last came the turn of the Duc d'Orléans, who now called himself Philippe Egalité. He rose, walked to the rostrum and read from a slip of paper: 'Concerned only to do my duty and convinced that all those who have made or will make an attempt on the sovereignty of the people deserve to be put to death, I vote for death.' A horrified hush fell on the house, and when Louis read in the newspaper of his cousin's vote he said to Cléry: 'I didn't believe there were such men.'

Saint-Just, the young author of the poem *Organt* and now deputy for the Aisne, demanded that Louis should die, but with a different argument: not because of anything Louis had done, but simply because he had been King. 'It is impossible,' said Saint-Just, 'to rule innocently.'

After a continuous sitting of thirty-seven hours, voting was complete. Of 749 members, 28 had been absent; and on the first question thirteen abstained. All the others unanimously found Louis guilty. On the second question a majority of 141 decided against ratification by the people. On the third question 387 voted for death unconditionally, 334 for detention or for a suspended death sentence; a majority of 53 for death.

The news was brought to the Temple by Malesherbes at nine in the morning of 18 January. Louis, who with his sister had for long believed that the Convention considered him 'a victim necessary to their own safety', took the news calmly, but Malesherbes broke into sobs at Louis's feet. Louis helped the old man up: 'My dear Malesherbes, don't begrudge me my one remaining refuge.'

One hope, however, remained to Louis. On 19 January the Convention debated whether there should be a stay of execution. Brissot was now beginning to regret his ill-considered war, and he now pointed out that killing the King would alienate world opinion. 'No republican will ever be brought to believe that, in order to set 25 million men free, one man must die . . . that, in order to end the office of King, the man who fills it must be killed; for it would then follow that we must kill also all those who can fill it. So obvious is that, that if the question was raised in America I dare say that out of four million inhabitants not one would vote for death . . . Then again, if Louis is executed, tomorrow we shall have to vote war against England, Holland, Spain, against all the tyrants of Europe, because they will be preparing war on us . . . Are you ready for this general war?'

It is to the eternal credit of the English-speaking people that the one English-speaking member of the Convention, Thomas Paine, born in Thetford, long resident in Pennsylvania, and now a deputy for the Pas de Calais, should have voted against the death penalty, and come out now in favour of a stay of execution. Paine stood silent on the rostrum, while a secretary read a French translation of his speech. After the first few sentences Marat broke in: 'Thomas Paine mayn't vote on this. He's a Quaker; his religious principles are opposed to the death sentence.' To follow one's religious principles had become, in Marat's eyes, treason. But this time the little yellow croaker went unheeded, and Paine continued through his interpreter: 'The man you have condemned to death is regarded by the people of the United States as their best friend, the founder of their freedom. That people is today your only ally; well then, it comes in my person to ask you to suspend the sentence you have decreed. Do not give the despot of England the pleasure of seeing on the scaffold the man who delivered our brothers in America from tyranny.'

Such speeches had little effect for, as Lord Gower noted, 'there were some thousands of armed men parading in different parts of the city ready to commit any sort of riot, and threatening destruction should the King not be put to death.' Throughout the trial the September Massacres were at the back of every deputy's mind, and from the public gallery every appeal for mercy was hooted. When the deputies came to vote, there was a majority of 70 against a stay of execution.

Louis was wakened in the early hours of 20 January to be told that he was to be put to death on the following day. He again took the news calmly. He asked the Convention to look after his family; and for himself, a non-juring priest. A further request, for three days' grace to prepare his soul, was refused.

Louis had already, on Christmas Day, made his will, writing in his own hand, with characteristic prudence, two copies. It is a dignified, elegant and uncomplaining document, the key word of which is not, as might be expected, 'injustice' but '*malheur* – misfortune'. Louis asked Elisabeth to be a mother to his children, should they have the misfortune to lose their own mother. He recommends his son, should he have the misfortune to become King, to remember that he must dedicate himself entirely to the happiness of his fellow-citizens. He must feel no hate or resentment about the misfortunes his father is suffering, and is to care for those persons undergoing misfortunes on his father's account.

For Antoinette Louis wrote: 'I beg my wife to forgive me for all the ills she is suffering for me, and the griefs I may have caused her during our marriage, just as she may be sure that I keep nothing against her should she think she has anything for which to blame herself.' The last phrase was a stock formula in wills, not a reference to Fersen. Louis almost certainly knew nothing of Antoinette's liaison.

Louis gave his son this political advice: 'A King can make the laws respected and carry out the good which is in his heart only in so far as he possesses the necessary authority; if he is hampered in his activities and inspires no respect, he serves a harmful, not a useful purpose.' Louis was here not criticizing the Constitution of 1791; he was saying that he had been prevented from exercising the powers granted him under that Constitution, and that France was better off with no King rather than a mock-King.

As a general statement on government Louis makes the point that a King's job is to make his people happy, but in so doing he himself will be unhappy. Louis's own life had shown why: in an age volatile but suspicious of authority, his motives are misinterpreted, he is thought to act too slowly, too firmly, too prudently, and finally he comes to be considered an enemy of the people.

When drawing up what in effect was a balance-sheet Louis doubtless reflected long on the country to which for eighteen years he had tried to bring happiness. Was his death at least going to benefit France? Dr John Moore wrote in December: 'Four years after the first insurrection, instead of the blessings of freedom, the unhappy people of France are, under the name of a Republic, suffering more intolerable oppression than they ever did under the most despotic of their monarchs.' You could now be thrown into prison for absent-mindedly calling a national guardsman 'Monsieur' instead of 'Citizen'. Louis's death would plainly contribute nothing to ending the present oppression; any good it might do would lie in the future.

The priest arrived that afternoon, a tall, strikingly good-looking man in lay dress, for the soutane was now forbidden, and after being searched right down to the snuff in his snuff-box, was admitted. His name was Henry Essex Edgeworth. Born in county Longford, educated in Toulouse, he was now aged forty-seven, had devoted his life to the very poor and was respected by all who knew him for his holiness. He had long been confessor to Madame Elisabeth and by her had been recommended to Louis. He had hidden during the September Massacres in his mother's rooms and still led an underground life, for on Louis's deposition a new law had been passed obliging all non-juring priests to leave France within a fortnight or face deportation to Guiana. Yet as soon as he received Louis's note asking him to come 'as a favour', Edgeworth had accepted.

Louis was so touched that one man at least, and a foreigner, should have braved Parisian opinion to help him that his composure gave way, and tears came to his eyes. Then he recovered and said, 'Forgive me, sir, a moment's weakness.'

Louis questioned Edgeworth about the state of the French Church and learned that a mass exodus had begun; soon 10,000 priests would be refugees in England, a Catholic counterpart to the Huguenot diaspora of 1685. Louis, says Edgeworth, 'deplored the fate of his clergy, and he expressed the greatest admiration for the people of England, who had mitigated their sufferings.' He enquired after the non-juring Archbishop of Paris, de Juigné, a holy man he had appointed personally: 'Tell him that I die in his communion, and that I have never acknowledged any bishop but him.' When Edgeworth spoke of saying Mass next morning in the Temple Louis's reaction was characteristic: 'though he desired it most ardently,' says Edgeworth, 'he seemed afraid of compromising my safety.' Finally they agreed that the abbé should try to obtain the necessary permission.

Louis had been separated from his family for six weeks but on that last evening of his life he was allowed to see them. It is bad enough to go to the scaffold unjustly, incomparably worse when you leave your children, wife and sister in prison defenceless and probably also doomed. Louis had always been sensitive to the sufferings of those dear to him, and it is not difficult to imagine his feelings as he saw his family for the last time. Antoinette threw herself into his arms, she and the others were in tears and for a quarter of an hour they freely expressed their mixture of love and pain in embraces and sobs.

Louis spoke to each in turn. From his son, who tomorrow in the eyes of many would be Louis XVII, he exacted a solemn promise not to avenge his death. He urged him and fourteen-year-old Marie Thérèse always to be close friends, and obedient to their mother. To Elisabeth, Louis said that he was counting on her to be a second mother to his children. She was the one who needed least comforting, for a life of self-sacrifice had prepared her for tribulation, and her firm faith made her certain that Louis was leaving her only for a short time, and that their happy relationship would continue in another life.

Of the five prisoners Antoinette was the one who had suffered most. She had aged alarmingly and lost so much weight that all her clothes had had to be specially taken in. She felt keenly her degradation and the injustice done to her, and had never been able to feel the resignation that brought Louis and Elisabeth a measure of serenity.

Louis knew that Antoinette would probably follow him to the scaffold, and that by dying first in a sense he was abandoning her. He felt deeply sorry for her, and also guilty. To his counsel he said that he regretted the French people had never come to know her good qualities. 'Poor woman! She was promised a throne and it has ended like this.'

Politics had made them husband and wife, politics was about to set them asunder. At the beginning they had not been in love, yet slowly they had come to feel a solid mutual affection. It had grown out of the esteem they felt for each other as parents, from facing danger together and at last from shared life in the Temple, for ironically they had seen more of each other in an average day in prison than in an average day at Versailles.

Antoinette asked Louis to spend the night with her and the children. Perhaps he wanted to spare them the pain of so prolonged a farewell, perhaps he felt the need to strengthen himself for the morning's ordeal by a period of recollection and a good night's sleep; anyway, he said No. He stayed with them for an hour and three-quarters; then he gave his children his blessing, kissed them all for the last time, and walked with them to the narrow spiral staircase that led to their rooms on the floor below.

Louis went late to bed, slept soundly and was wakened at five. Though Edgeworth does not mention it, he almost certainly went to confession. These are the words Hébert put into the King's mouth in *Le Père Duchesne*: 'I confess to having always deceived my fellow men, of having put on the mask of a decent bugger, when in fact I was a rotten f——. I confess to having let my bourgeois subjects put on my head horns bigger than those of the biggest stag in Fontainebleau; I confess to having emptied the nation's money-boxes . . . and of having caused my brothers, cousins and fellow Kings to plunge France into fire and blood . . .'

Louis heard Mass, kneeling on the floor without a cushion or *prie-Dieu*, and received Communion. He had been planning to say a last goodbye to his family, but gave up the idea when Edgeworth said he doubted whether the Queen could support the shock of another parting. Instead he took off his gold wedding ring and asked Cléry to give it to the Queen.

As morning began to dawn, in all the sections of Paris the rattle of drums was heard. Edgeworth felt as though his blood was freezing but Louis, he noticed, commented quite calmly on each happening. 'It's probably the national guard beginning to assemble.' Presently detachments of cavalry entered the court of the Temple; voices of officers and the trampling of horses were heard. Louis said, 'They seem to be approaching.'

At eight o'clock Santerre and his national guardsmen arrived, together with commissioners of the Commune. They informed the prisoner that it was time to leave. Louis had made a few belongings into a packet and, turning to one of the men, asked him if he would give it to the Queen; then, quickly correcting himself, said 'to my wife.'

The man happened to be Jacques Roux, an ex-priest who led the *enragés*, wildly vindictive politicians. 'I am not here to do your errands,' he said, 'but to take you to the scaffold.'

'That is true,' said Louis, and turning to another man who seemed more compassionate, he gave the packet to him.

Louis was led out to a closed carriage. Edgeworth went too, an act of kindness on which Louis had not been counting. It was a grey, wet morning. The streets were lined with citizens carrying pikes or muskets, and the carriage was escorted by 1200 guards, so that it moved at walking pace. Louis asked Edgeworth to lend him his breviary and to show him the psalms for the dying. These the two men recited during the two-hour drive to the great square which had been laid out by, and named after, Louis's grandfather.

On a platform in the centre of the square stood the city of Paris's executioner, Charles Sanson. The office of executioner was, like monarchy, a hereditary prerogative, descending from father to son, and Sanson, like the King, was a man apart. In the past he had been a hangman, but now beside him stood the new instrument of execution, two grooved wooden posts fifteen feet high joined at the top by a third from which hung a heavy steel blade twelve inches wide.

The guillotine had been introduced as a humane means of execution but just as the humanitarianism of the 1780s had degenerated into anarchy, so the guillotine was already less a humane machine than a speedy one, making it possible to kill ten times more quickly than by hanging. But the guillotine's significance went beyond this: it was a machine for cutting off heads. The head being the reasonable part of man, its severance by the guillotine subconsciously symbolized the Revolution's faith in the human heart and the heart's naturally good feelings. Since the victim now was to be the former head of State, the father of all Frenchmen, whose person according to the Constitution was sacred, the execution would have a still deeper significance. The thousands of armed men in the square were to witness a supreme drama: the ritual killing of the father-figure.

When the carriage stopped and the door was opened, Louis put his hand on Edgeworth's knee. 'Gentlemen,' he said to the guards, 'I recommend to you this good man, take care that after my death he suffers no insult – I charge you to prevent it.'

Louis got out of the carriage. 'Three guards surrounded him and would have taken off his clothes, but he repulsed them with haughtiness.' Louis removed his own hat, coat and jacket, then untied his neckcloth and opened his shirt. The guards seized him, and Louis shook them off. Then, at Edgeworth's recommendation, he submitted. They tied his arms and cut his hair, leaving the neck exposed.

Leaning on Edgeworth's arm, Louis walked to the scaffold. On the top step he let the abbé's arm go and walked alone firmly across the platform. Silencing by his look alone the fifteen drummers placed opposite him, he addressed the crowd in a very loud voice:

'I die innocent of all the crimes laid to my charge; I pardon those who have occasioned my death; and I pray to God that the blood you are now going to shed may never be visited on France; and you, unfortunate people . . .'

The rest of Louis's words went unheard, as an officer on horseback ordered the drums to beat. The time was twenty minutes past ten. Sanson and his aides seized Louis and tied him to the upright plank. The plank was tipped over and he felt the heavy wooden collar fixed round his neck. Sanson pulled the cord and the blade fell. Because Louis's neck was so fat, instead of slicing through, the knife penetrated comparatively slowly, and a scream was heard.

'The youngest of the guards, who seemed about eighteen,' says Edgeworth, 'seized the head and showed it to the people as he walked round the scaffold; he accompanied this monstrous ceremony with the most atrocious and indecent gestures. At first an awful silence prevailed; at length some cries of "*Vive la République!*" were heard. By degrees the voices multiplied, and in less than ten minutes this cry, a thousand times repeated, became the universal shout of the multitude, and every hat was in the air.'

The King's body was taken to the cemetery of the Madeleine and placed in a pauper's coffin, head between the legs. While two State priests chanted the Office of the Dead, the coffin was lowered into a deep grave and covered with lime.

The sense of outrage not to be expected in France revealed itself in England. As soon as the news was announced the audience at one of the London playhouses stopped the play and ordered the curtain to be dropped, while in Parliament Pitt spoke of 'the foulest and most atrocious deed which the history of the world has yet had occasion to attest'.

CHAPTER 24

The People's Sentence

THE King was dead; his death had been voted by France's rulers and had taken place in full view of the people. It might be thought that the itch for royal blood was now satisfied. But it is one of the character-istics of the Revolution that the blood which was going to solve all problems never did quite solve them. In theory Louis's death had absolved the Revolution and firmly established the ruling power, but in fact it by no means satisfied the Government, which from April 1793 was the pitiless Committee of Public Safety, meeting secretly in the Green Room of the Tuileries.

Louis had gone to the scaffold with dignity, protesting his innocence. He had continued to rebut charges against him of con-spiracy and tyranny. To those who could look beneath the surface, the King had died defending freedom of conscience against a State which increasingly claimed to control men's lives and beliefs. Not only to the free peoples of the world but to many also in France the King's death seemed a kind of victory.

The Government therefore and the Commune of Paris, represent-ing the sans-culottes and spoken for by Hébert, determined to deal more effectively with the widow Capet. They determined to break her will and make her confess to heinous crimes, so that in her personal collapse monarchy as such would be seen to tumble. They began to look about for the best means to this end.

There is no doubt that her husband's calm had been a great source of strength to Antoinette. Together they had faced the storming of royal palaces, the flight to Varennes, the war of nerves over the veto. Whatever the circumstances, he had been there to lean on. Now she had no husband to stand between her and her abased condition. Long ago Antoinette had set herself 'to show character': but what was her character now, without throne, without husband? Selecting a role had once been part of the fun of Trianon theatricals; now it was an urgent need, something on which would depend her sanity.

Antoinette chose, quite simply, to be a mother, in particular to her seven-year-old son. She would bring up carefully this intelligent and attractive boy: that would be her new life. So the lessons Louis had given Louis Charles became Antoinette's task; it was she who taught him the new geography, with France divided into départements, and the old mathematics, she who heard him read and taught him to write a clear hand. Since he was now King, she made him sit at the head of the rough table, and be served first. But equally she taught him to be considerate, and one day when he passed a kindly gaoler without a word, she called him back, scolded him and made him say a polite 'Good morning'.

As well as this close relationship with her son, Antoinette felt the need of being in touch with her gaolers, and of trying to make them like her. In this she was much more feminine than Elisabeth, who rose above such matters to the higher realms of piety.

Antoinette made friends with two guards: a young former kitchen assistant at Versailles named Turgy and a pedantic Latin don named Lepitre. But a third guard, named Dorat Cubières, a literary man who had once been a pensioner of the King and now wrote odes to Robespierre and Marat, resisted all her efforts to win him over.

Antoinette said one day to Turgy, 'I've broken my comb, please will you buy me another.'

'Buy her one in horn,' Dorat chipped in. 'Boxwood is too good for her.' Antoinette pretended not to hear.

Turgy bought a tortoiseshell comb, similar to the broken one. Antoinette said, 'You've ignored Dorat's orders. He claims boxwood is too good for us, yet he, but for the King's goodness . . .' She left her sentence unfinished.

'Madame, many people pretended to pay court to the royal family, but only for money.'

'You're right, Turgy.'

Another of the guards, a southerner named Toulan, was a ferocious fellow who had led a battalion against the Tuileries and came to the Temple full of animosity against the Queen. Within a couple of weeks he was won over by her patience and dignity. Soon he began doing her a few small services and ended by carrying her messages to her former private secretary, the Chevalier de Jarjayes.

Jarjayes worked out a plan for all the royal prisoners to escape in disguise. Antoinette corresponded with Jarjayes over a long period, and when the fourfold escape had to be abandoned because of passport difficulties, she finally refused to leave alone, without her son. She wrote Jarjayes a letter of thanks, in which the new dominant themes in her life found expression: 'You will always find that I have character and courage but the interests of my son are the only ones that guide me.'

Another whom Antoinette sought to win over was the only woman gaoler, Madame Tison. Antoinette sensed that this woman was at heart kindly but forced by a brutal husband to act as a spy. Madame Tison continually warned the authorities that Antoinette and Elisabeth, whose relations in adversity had become close, were carrying on a secret correspondence with persons outside the Temple. One day she removed from Elisabeth's room a candlestick, pointing out to the authorities an incriminating spot of red sealing-wax on the candlestick: it had fallen in fact when Elisabeth was sealing a letter to her confessor. Madame Tison also denounced Toulan and other officers who had 'truckled' to the widow Capet.

Madame Tison presently became a prey to remorse. Certain that everyone she had denounced would perish, she alternated between long periods of shrieking and scenes at Antoinette's feet. 'Madame, I ask your Majesty's pardon. I am very unhappy. I am the cause of your death, and Madame Elisabeth's.' Antoinette tried to calm her, assured her that she had her forgiveness, and sent the unfortunate woman a bowl of broth that had been prepared for her. Nothing helped. Filled with a sense of guilt that no words could ease, Madame Tison went mad and was carried away, struggling, by eight men to the Hôtel Dieu hospital.

Antoinette took Madame Tison's breakdown to heart and kept asking for news of her. Partly she sympathized, partly she was very much afraid. She had seen how quickly in this atmosphere of terror, suspicion and lies a woman could lose her sanity. And then suddenly, with no warning, her own sanity was put to the test.

At ten o'clock on the night of 3 July the lock of Antoinette's door was turned and into the dark room, carrying candles, strode a party of municipal officers. One of them – and his voice trembled – read a decree of the Commune ordering the son of Capet to be separated from his mother. It was a gratuitous act of cruelty whereby the Commune hoped to break not only the she-wolf but the cub too.

As two of the officers started towards the boy's bed, Antoinette flung herself in front of them. 'You cannot do it!' she cried. 'I won't let you.' She clutched her son to her side; he woke up and began to cry.

The officers threatened to call up the guard and use force. An hour then passed in discussion, in menaces, in tears and pleading.

Antoinette was all the more distressed because in May her son had been ill with a strange pain like a stitch in his side. Finally, says Madame Royale, who was there, 'my mother consented to give up her son and, bathing him with her tears as though she realized she would never see him again, she handed him over to the officers. The poor boy kissed us all tenderly and left in sobs with the guards.'

Young Louis was taken to the room below, where Antoine Simon, an illiterate cobbler aged fifty-seven, had instructions to bring him up as a good sans-culotte. For two days Antoinette heard her son sobbing. Not only had she lost the person she most loved, but no one could tell her why he was sobbing, and the way was clear to fearful imaginings. She felt she no longer had any purpose, and fell into that profound despair which, because it is so perilously near to madness, has been called the sin against the Holy Ghost. 'God Himself has forsaken me,' she confided to Elisabeth. 'I no longer dare to pray.'

Antoinette just had time to begin to adjust to this loss, and to find some comfort in Elisabeth's strength, when the Committee of Public Safety, which Robespierre had entered four days earlier, dealt her a new blow. The whole of the Vendée and most of Normandy had risen against the repressive and anti-religious measures of the Government, and the Committee considered it necessary to whip up more anti-royalist hatred. In a decree of 1 August it ordered 'the tombs and mausoleums of the *ci-devant* Kings in the church of Saint-Denis and elsewhere, throughout the length and breadth of the Republic, to be destroyed.' The bodies of Louis's ancestors, including the Sun King and Louis XV, were dragged from their coffins and tipped into a lime-filled common grave. Even the body of an English King, James II, suffered this ultimate act of *lèse-majesté*.

As part of the same psychopathic decree the widow Capet was ordered to be taken to the prison on the Ile Saint-Louis known as the Conciergerie. The Committee's intention was twofold: to level down the former queen to the common ruck of political prisoners, and, by parting her from Elisabeth and her daughter, to tighten the strain on her already overwrought nerves.

This parting also took place in darkness. In the early hours of 2 August Antoinette was wakened by four officers and ordered to dress. She was allowed to take with her a parcel of clothes, a few belongings, and, because she now suffered from spells of faintness during her period pains, a bottle of smelling-salts. Tangible mementoes had always meant much to her, and she managed to smuggle also a watch given her by her mother and a yellow glove belonging to her son. She kissed Marie Thérèse goodbye and confided both her and her son to Elisabeth. Then she went down the stone spiral staircase. At the bottom she struck her head on a low beam. One of the guards was concerned. 'Did you hurt yourself?'

'No,' she answered, 'nothing can hurt me now.'

Antoinette's cell, much smaller than her room in the Temple, was eleven and a half feet square. According to Fersen, who sought out details from a man who had seen it, 'the cell was small, damp and fetid, without stove or fireplace; there were three beds, one for the Queen, another beside it for her woman attendant, the third for the two gendarmes who never left the cell, even when the Queen had to satisfy the needs of nature.' There were no dividing curtains to give her privacy, just a battered screen.

Antoinette was never alone now, yet continually alone, for with the gendarmes and her attendant she might not converse. She was in a prison known as the death-block, yet she did not know whether she was going to be put on trial. Rumour had it that she might be exchanged with the Austrian Government for important French prisoners. 'If I could save her by my blood,' Fersen wrote in his diary, 'it would be my soul's greatest happiness,' and he was straining every nerve to persuade the Austrian Government to snatch her from danger. But Antoinette did not know this. She was confused and frightened, suspended between life and death, no longer a wife, no longer a mother; without any visible continuity in her thirty-seven years. She was too tired now to try to be brave; it was a question of fighting day and night just to retain a shred of identity.

Tiny things became of the utmost importance. It mattered enormously to her that she found for her few possessions – a bottle of dentifrice, a swansdown puff and a wooden box of powder – a cardboard box. It was given her by a prison servant, and because it unified what would otherwise have been dispersed, she took it, says the servant, 'with as much satisfaction as if it were the most beautiful treasure in the world'.

Antoinette tried to keep up her self-respect by being neat in her appearance, though her once glorious hair had now become a worry. She parted it in front, after putting on a little scented powder. Her attendant caught the ends with a piece of white ribbon, four feet long, knotted it firmly and then handed the ends to her; these

Antoinette tied herself and pinned on top of her head so as to form a loose chignon. Her dress was plain, either black or white, but she allowed herself one concession to fashion, a pair of plum-coloured, high-heeled shoes known as Saint-Huberti shoes, after the opera singer.

In the Temple she had kept her head by hour after hour making embroidered seat-backs. Here, as part of the campaign to break her spirit, she was allowed no needles. At first she spent hours walking up and down her cell, or sitting staring into space, twiddling the two rings on her fingers. She felt an overwhelming need to prove herself by making something, however insignificant. Noticing that the stone walls were hung with cloth nailed to wooden frames, Antoinette pulled out threads from the cloth, polished them by rubbing them between the palms of her hands and, using pins, crocheted them into a kind of lace.

From time to time she needed also mental escape. At the Trianon she had occasionally read history or novels, but now she felt the need for something much stronger – terrifying adventures. She read several books of this sort, including the *Travels* of Captain Cook, and *A History of Famous Shipwrecks*.

One day at the end of August Antoinette's cell was opened and in strode Michonis, the prison administrator. A former lemonade-seller, then an ardent revolutionary, he had come to respect the Queen and even shown signs that he would like to help her. With him was a short, round-faced man in his thirties wearing a dark suit and holding a carnation. Antoinette recognized him as the Chevalier de Rougeville, the brave courtier who had led her to safety when the crowd invaded the Tuileries. She gave a start, flushed and began to tremble.

Rougeville, for his part, barely recognized this thin, hollow-cheeked woman as the Queen. Michonis exchanged a few insignificant words with his prisoner, then while he was looking the other way, Rougeville tossed his carnation behind the stove, telling Antoinette in a low voice that it contained a note. Then he and Michonis left.

Presently her woman attendant began playing cards with the gendarmes. Antoinette then picked up the carnation and read the note concealed in its petals. It said in effect: 'We have men and money at your service. I will come on Friday.'

Antoinette's excitement may be imagined. In weeks of near-despair this was the first flicker of hope. Tearing up the note, she pondered how to reply. She had to let Rougeville know that she was willing to try to escape, but she possessed neither pen nor pencil. In the morning at Versailles she had been accustomed to place pin marks beside samples of the dresses she intended to wear that day; perhaps recalling that ritual, she now took a pin and pricked a scrap of paper with seventeen words: '*Je suis gardée à vue, je ne parle à personne. Je me fie à vous. Je viendrai.*'[1]

Antoinette then took one of the gendarmes, Gilbert, into her confidence and entrusted him with the note, which he passed on to Michonis. Either he or Rougeville bribed Gilbert and the other gendarme, Dufresne, to lend themselves to the plot and by 2 September – the Friday mentioned in Rougeville's note – everything was ready.

Shortly before eleven o'clock on Friday night Antoinette's cell was unlocked and Michonis came in. He told the gendarmes that he had an order from the municipality to conduct the widow Capet back to the Temple. Antoinette doubtless guessed that this was a pretended order and that the hour of escape had come.

Flanked by the two gendarmes, and preceded by Michonis, Antoinette stepped out of her cell and began to walk down a long corridor, pausing every so often while a series of wicket gates were opened. She and her escort had reached a point where they had only to pass through one more gate before reaching the main exit, and there Rougeville was waiting with a carriage to whisk her out of France.

They passed through the last gate. Ahead lay safety. Then, without warning, the gendarme Gilbert stopped, turned and threateningly barred Antoinette's way. Later depositions are confused but it seems that Gilbert took fright at the possible consequences and changed his mind. Michonis, aware that sentries on the main exit were looking suspicious, decided the game was up. Antoinette was led back from the frontiers of freedom to her cell. Once again she found herself in darkness, all the more total now for her few days of hope.

Rougeville escaped from France, but Michonis was arrested and Antoinette too suffered from their well-meant plot. In mid-September she was moved into solitary confinement. Her new cell, the former dispensary, smelled of medicines. It was tiny and dark. At night it was unlit, save by a glimmer from the lamp in a courtyard outside the single window. Here she could neither work nor read; she had no news of her children. In every respect it was her dark

[1] I am watched, I speak to no one. I trust you. I shall come.

night of the soul. Yet here, against all the odds, she was accorded what she described as an act of God's mercy.

Among the Conciergerie prisoners was a remarkable non-juring priest, the abbé Eméry, whose holiness was of the undeniable kind that moves the hearts even of enemies. The gaolers allowed Eméry to minister to the condemned and to receive visits from another non-juring priest, the abbé Magnin, who brought Eméry consecrated hosts in a pyx. One night the gendarmes on guard agreed to let the abbé Magnin into Antoinette's cell. There he heard her confession and, assembling a very small chalice made up of several pieces, he celebrated Mass on a portable altar-stone only two or three inches square, and gave Antoinette Holy Communion. She found consolation in this and a strength she was soon desperately to need.

At a secret session of the Committee of Public Safety the Queen's most violent enemy, Hébert, speaking as deputy procureur of the Commune of Paris, demanded that the prisoner in the Conciergerie be brought to trial. 'I have promised my readers Antoinette's head. If there is any further delay in giving it to me, I shall go and cut it off myself.' The sans-culottes, Hébert continued, 'will kill all our enemies, but their zeal must be kept on the boil, and you can do that only by putting Antoinette to death.' After an all-night debate the Committee agreed that Antoinette should appear before the Revolutionary Tribunal. The public prosecutor, Fouquier-Tinville, was called in and, having warned the Committee that five jurymen would be favourable to the Queen, was told to replace them. He also complained of a shortage of evidence.

The anti-Christian side of the Revolution had now come uppermost. On 5 October the Christian calendar was abolished; Antoinette found herself living no longer in the year of Our Lord 1793 but in year II of the Republic. Sunday disappeared, and very soon most churches were closed down or turned into Temples of Reason, where actresses paraded as Liberty or performed blasphemous parodies of the Mass. Such was the background against which two violently anti-Christian politicians, Hébert and Chaumette, set out to provide Fouquier with the evidence he lacked.

On the second floor of the Temple young Louis was being turned into a patriotic citizen by Simon the cobbler. Lessons stopped; the boy was encouraged to sing indecent songs and to use foul language. He was given wine to drink and sometimes brandy. If he showed signs of resistance, Simon threatened him with the guillotine. Sensitive by nature, Louis seems to have suffered intensely; he continually asked for his mother and was terrified into doing what was demanded of him to avoid further ill-treatment.

Simon had instructions to bring up Louis as a good sans-culotte. Probably on Hébert's orders, it seems likely that Simon took the phrase literally, in the sense that he removed the boy's trousers; he then taught him how to practise self-abuse. In the course of these revolting lessons it seems that one of the boy's testicles was hurt, and had to be bandaged.

Simon now had the boy completely in his power, and began to turn him against his mother. Antoinette had herself noticed that young Louis 'is very indiscreet and easily repeats what he has heard and often, without meaning to lie, he adds things suggested by his own imagination.' She had tried with some success to correct this fault, but now, under pressure from Simon, it came to the fore. The boy began to ape Simon and to speak against his mother.

At this point Hébert and Chaumette arrived in the Temple and began interrogating Louis. Hébert knew that in moments of danger Antoinette, as a safety measure, had taken her son into her own bed. Hébert spoke of this now and doubtless asked Louis whether he had enjoyed the experience. Louis answered that he had. Slowly Hébert, who was a professional persuader, insinuated ideas into the mind of this defenceless, imaginative boy, cowed by months of ill-treatment. What Hébert did has since become known as brain-washing, and this is the first recorded experiment upon a child.

Hébert drafted a confession. In the first part Louis was made to say that his mother had taken part in counter-revolutionary activities both in the Tuileries and in the Temple. Then followed a second section:

'He declares that Simon and Simon's wife, who were ordered by the Commune to watch over him, several times found him practising self-abuse in bed, and he told them that he had been taught these pernicious habits by his mother and aunt, and that several times they took pleasure in seeing him perform them in their sight, and that very often this took place when the women made him sleep between them.'

Probably under threats the boy was obliged to sign this appalling confession with a cramped and broken 'Louis' quite unlike the neat writing in his exercise books. But Hébert had not finished. In the margin he added an even more revolting charge, with which he was to confront Antoinette during her trial. Finally, he gave orders to Simon that from time to time a prostitute was to be brought to

Louis's room. The boy was too young to have intercourse, but the prostitute would sap his strength and eventually perhaps infect him with syphilis.

Six days passed. Late in the afternoon of Saturday 12 October Antoinette began to suffer such severe menstrual pains that she went to bed. Since coming to the Conciergerie these monthly pains had been so pronounced that on one occasion she fainted twice in a single day, and had had to drink a soothing potion made up by the prison apothecary, containing lime-flower water and Hofman's drops. Her hæmorrhages were known to the authorities, and it was probably in order to place her at a physical disadvantage that the public prosecutor, although still complaining of lack of documents, decided to hold her trial at this time.

At six o'clock in the evening of 12 October Antoinette was wakened, told to dress, and led across the courtyard and up a stone staircase to the former Grand' Chambre of Parlement, a late Gothic hall paved with squares of black and white marble. Here her husband had held several *lits de justice* – it was the great battlefield of magisterial opposition to the Crown – and here Cardinal de Rohan had been tried and acquitted. A painting of the Crucifixion had been removed and replaced by busts of Brutus and Marat. It was now the seat of the Revolutionary Tribunal and known without irony as the Hall of Freedom.

The only light in this huge room was cast by two candles, so that to Antoinette's other terrors was added the terror of darkness. At a table sat the examining magistrate, Nicolas Hermann, aged 34, not a bad man, but one of the new anti-Christian patriots – he named his baby son after the Greek general Aristides – who had been promoted to his present job by Robespierre. Beside him sat the public prosecutor, Antoine Fouquier-Tinville, aged 47, a pale man with thick black eyebrows, low forehead and jutting chin. He and Hermann wore black, and a medal round their necks inscribed *La Loi*. Their round hats turned up at the front were topped by tall black plumes, like a macabre jest on the prisoner's past.

Antoinette was seated at a bench opposite the table. She could see Hermann, Fouquier-Tinville, and a stenographer. But in the darkness she could hear but not see spectators, and the stenographer wrote that 'this alarmed Antoinette.'

Antoinette knew that the Revolutionary Tribunal was a court without appeal, and that in this preliminary examination questions would be fired at her on any and every subject, with the aim of forcing an admission, trapping her in a contradiction or in an unpatriotic statement. She intended to be loyal to her husband, yet somehow to save her life. Unlike Louis, she would not resign herself to the possibility of death.

Hermann began the accusation. Antoinette, he said, had sent millions to the Emperor 'to be used against the people who fed you'.

'Never,' she replied. 'I loved my husband too much to squander my country's money. Besides, my brother had no need of money from France.'

'In November 1791, when Louis Capet was considering the decrees against his brothers, the émigrés and fanatical, refractory priests, was it not you, despite the protests of Duranton, Minister of Justice, who persuaded Louis Capet to affix his veto?'

'Duranton wasn't a Minister in November. Besides, my husband didn't need anyone to urge him to do his duty. These matters were decided in Council, of which I wasn't a member.'

It began to look as though Hermann was deliberately mixing truth and falsehood in his questions. So it was when he referred to Varennes. 'You were the chief instigator of Louis Capet's treason; it was you who advised and perhaps persecuted him into trying to leave France.'

'My husband never intended to leave France.'

'You admit that it was you who opened the doors and saw that everyone left; so there's no doubt that it was you who ruled the actions of Louis Capet and persuaded him to flight.'

She replied, 'I do not think that an open door proves that one is constantly ruling a person's acts.'

Perhaps her tone was slightly ironical, for Hermann exclaimed violently: 'Never for one moment have you ceased wanting to destroy liberty. You wanted to reign at any price and to reascend the throne over the dead bodies of patriots.'

'We had no need to reascend the throne: we were there! But we never wished for anything but France's happiness.' When Hermann turned to her and said that if this had been true she would have kept her brother from making war on France, Antoinette reminded him that it was France, not Austria, who had declared war. Time and again it was she who had to put the record straight.

After a specific question about the banquet of October 1789, when, it was alleged, they had 'trampled underfoot the tricolour cockade', Hermann again returned to generalities.

'Do you think that kings are necessary for the people's happiness?'

'An individual cannot decide such matters.'

'No doubt you regret that your son has lost a throne which he might have ascended if the people, finally conscious of their rights, had not destroyed that throne?'

'I shall never regret anything for my son when his country is happy.'

After several trap questions about her time in prison, Hermann ended the examination. There had been thirty-five questions, some containing errors of fact, and to each Antoinette had given a sensible, yet guarded answer. The examination proved, if nothing else, that the old slander of light-headedness had no truth in it. In fact, that night, when he drew up the indictment Fouquier was able to use only one of her replies, and even this he had to falsify: 'The widow Capet admits in her interrogation that it was she who arranged and prepared everything for their escape' to Varennes.

Antoinette's counsel, Chauveau-Lagarde, aged 28, arrived at the Conciergerie the following afternoon, Sunday. The trial was scheduled for Monday. He saw that it was impossible to prepare a defence to the eight-page indictment in that short time, so he wrote a letter, which Antoinette signed, to the President of the Assembly, asking for a delay of three days. He took the letter to Fouquier. A delay would have given Fouquier time to collect much-needed documentary evidence. He promised to send the letter to the President, but in fact he did not do so. Why? Evidently because he was determined that the prisoner should stand trial during her menstrual period. He passed the letter to Robespierre, who did nothing about it, for after Robespierre's death it was found with other papers under his mattress.

At eight o'clock on Monday morning Antoinette was again taken to the Grand' Chambre. This time it was crowded and there rose a murmur of surprise at the Queen's thin and haggard appearance; if suffering can purify, it also ages. There were five judges, presided over by Hermann, and seated on the right a jury of twelve, all zealous patriots, which meant that they had swallowed whole the pamphlet and newspaper slanders that had been circulating since the Diamond Necklace case eight years before. One of the jurors, a joiner named Trinchard, in a note to his brother, the spelling of which is like that of an eight-year-old, described the prisoner as 'la bête féroche, who has devoured a great part of the Republic'.

Antoinette listened as the indictment was read; it was noticed that she moved her fingers on the arm of her chair 'as though over the keyboard of her clavichord'. She was accused of conspiring with her brother against France and of sending him money; of organizing a counter-revolution; of forcing Louis Capet to veto the deportation of priests; of appointing 'perverse' Ministers; of hatching the plot of 10 August 'by keeping the Swiss guards continually drunk' and 'by herself biting shut their cartridges'; and generally, of starting civil war. Two of the charges were specially odd. Antoinette was accused of printing pamphlets slandering herself 'so as to arouse pity abroad'; and of engineering the famine of October 1789, 'the proof being that immediately she came to live in Paris the famine ceased'.

Beneath these disjointed charges ran an underlying theme. Antoinette had not been a true and loyal wife to her husband: she had dominated him. It was therefore the nature of her married life that was being called in question.

To support their charges the prosecution submitted no documentary evidence of any consequence, but instead called forty-one witnesses. The first was Laurent Lecointre, who had been second-in-command of the national guard at Versailles, and who for two hours described 'feasts and orgies' at the palace. The second witness, Roussillon, declared that on 10 August he had seen, under the accused's bed, some full and empty wine bottles, 'which led him to suppose that she had been making the Swiss guards drunk'.

The fourth witness was Jacques René Hébert. He described a visit to the Temple during which he had found among the accused's effects a missal in which was a card depicting a flaming heart transfixed by an arrow: it was, he said, 'a counter-revolutionary emblem'. He declared the accused had passed messages in her linen and shoes. He then, without warning, announced that 'Simon had surprised the young Capet in self-pollutions that were bad for his health. When Simon asked him who had taught him to do such things he replied that it was to his mother and aunt that he owed his knowledge of this baneful habit. From the declaration that young Capet made in the presence of the Mayor of Paris and the Prosecutor of the Commune it was revealed that these two women often made him lie down between them; that there then took place acts of the most uncontrolled debauchery. From what young Capet confessed there had been, between mother and son, an act of incest.'

What Antoinette felt at this charge can only be conjectured. Probably she found her mind reeling. Since the birth of her son she had dedicated her life to bringing him up as a Christian; indeed, if there was one achievement of which she could justly boast it was that she had always been an excellent mother. What hope did she have in a world where white was called black? But Hébert had not finished. Attributing to the accused his own motives, he declared:

'There is reason to believe that this criminal intercourse was dictated not by pleasure but by the calculated hope of enervating the child, whom they still liked to think of as destined to occupy a throne and whom they wished to be sure of dominating morally. As a result of the efforts he was forced to make he suffered a hernia, for which a bandage was needed.' Hébert's last sentence was the most brazen of all in its distortion of the facts: 'Since the child has been away from his mother his constitution has become robust and strong.'

Antoinette made no answer. She doubtless recalled Louis's advice during the Necklace affair: by answering an insult you make things worse. The charge was in fact related to the main theme of the prosecution: Antoinette, the unnatural wife, was also an un-natural mother.

Hermann said, 'What reply do you make to the witness's deposition?'

'I have no knowledge of the incidents Hébert speaks of.'

Hermann questioned her about messages from prison, when one of the jurors rose.

'Citizen President, would you observe to the accused that she has not answered the charge brought by Citizen Hébert regarding what happened between her and her son.'

Antoinette usually answered sitting, but now she rose from her chair, and according to the stenographer she was very much moved.

'If I have not answered, it was because Nature refuses to answer such a charge against a mother.' Then she turned to the spectators. 'I appeal to all mothers in this room.'

Antoinette was, in effect, answering the charge of unnatural vice by an appeal to the revolutionaries' own two criteria: Nature and the people.

A murmur of sympathy ran through the crowd. There were even some shouts of approval and the court-room had to be called to order. Antoinette turned to her counsel. 'Was there too much dignity in my answer?'

'Madam, be yourself and you will always do right, but why do you ask?'

'Because I heard a woman of the people say to her neighbour, "See how proud she is!" ' It is clear that Antoinette was trying not only to answer the charges but, with her acting experience, to create a favourable impression on the Court; and the self-control implied in this dual role astonished her counsel.

One of the remarkable features of the trial was that almost every charge originated, years before, in the slander and calumny of Versailles. D'Aiguillon first mouthed the story that Antoinette was her brother's agent at the French Court and sent French gold to Austria. It was repeated now by a former maid at Versailles with the grand name of Reine Millot.

One day, said Reine Millot, she had had a conversation with the former Comte de Coigny. 'Will the Emperor go on making war against the Turks?' she had asked him. 'Heavens, it will ruin France, on account of the great sums the Queen sends her brother – 200 millions at least.'

'You are not mistaken,' Coigny replied. 'It has already cost more than 200 millions and we have not finished yet.'

No other evidence was offered on this charge, but the President, in summing up, was to compliment the witness on the exactitude of her memory.

Monday's sitting lasted until eleven at night. Tuesday was to prove even more exhausting: Antoinette was in court, with only one break, for eighteen hours. The prosecution contented itself with dropping highly-charged names: Polignac, Lamballe, Trianon.

'Where did you get the money to have the little Trianon built and furnished, where you gave parties at which you were always the goddess?'

'There were funds especially for that purpose.'

'The funds were evidently large, for the little Trianon must have cost immense sums?'

'It is possible that the little Trianon cost immense sums, perhaps more than I could have wished. We were gradually involved in more and more expense. Besides, I am more anxious than anyone that what happened there should be known.'

'Wasn't it at the little Trianon that you knew the woman La Motte?'

'I have never seen her.'

'Wasn't she your victim in the famous affair of the necklace?'

'She cannot have been, since I did not know her.'

'You persist in denying that you knew her?'

'I have no system of denial. It is the truth that I have told and will persist in telling.'

A former member of the Convention named Valazé said he had seen a letter from Dumouriez, Minister of War, to Louis, asking the King to communicate to the accused the plan of campaign against Austria. The letter had since been mislaid and was not produced in court. This was the nearest Fouquier came to the accused's one vulnerable point. Antoinette had in fact obtained and made use of the campaign plan. On 30 March 1792, three weeks before France declared a wholly unjustified war on Austria, and aware that her life and her husband's depended on Austria's ability to resist invasion, she had written in cipher to Fersen: 'They plan to attack through Savoy and the Liège country and hope to gain something this way, because the two flanks cannot be protected. It is essential to take precautions on the Liège flank.'

Some will judge this letter treasonable, others an act of self-defence justified by the circumstances. But it has to be remembered that the letter was unknown to Fouquier and was to be published only many years later. The court had only Valazé's undocumented statement to go on. Fouquier used it in order once again to ram home the main theme of accusation.

'It seems to be proved, despite your denials, that through your influence you made the former King, your husband, do whatever you wished.'

'There is a great difference between advising that something should be done and having it carried out.'

'You made use of his weak character to make him carry out many evil deeds.'

'I never knew him to have such a character as you describe.'

Of the forty-one witnesses nineteen had nothing to say since they were ignorant of the business in question. No material proofs were brought, but instead a mass of hearsay evidence mixed with false-hoods. During the long hearing, despite her sufferings, Antoinette had not once faltered. It was after midnight when Fouquier finally turned to her and asked if she had anything to add to her defence before the hearing was closed.

Antoinette rose. 'Yesterday I did not know the witnesses and I did not know what they would testify. Well, no one has uttered anything positive against me. I conclude by observing that I was only the wife of Louis XVI and I was bound to conform to his will.' It was a justification of her marriage. She had been, according to the rules of the society in which she lived, a submissive wife. The charge of 'ruling' her husband, with its corollary, that Louis had been weak, was rejected: she had not behaved unnaturally in this respect any more than she had indulged in unnatural passion for Madame de Polignac or her son.

Antoinette's counsel then spoke in her defence. Their speeches have not been recorded – no one wanted to know – but they were probably appeals for mercy: according to Hébert in his *Père Duchesne*, 'they said to the judges that it was enough to have punished the fat pig and that at least his trollop of a wife should be pardoned.'

Finally, Hermann gave his summing-up. It has to be borne in mind that the law required him to do so impartially, and to point out any facts that told in Antoinette's favour. The prisoner, said Hermann, is accused by the French people of having instigated most of the crimes for which the last tyrant of France has already been found guilty. The jury has to judge the whole political life of the accused since she came to be seated beside the last tyrant of France. If the French army has suffered temporary reverses, these are the end-result of trickery in the Tuileries instigated by Antoinette of Austria. She had the King's confidence. She was consulted on political issues. She played a leading role in incidents against the people from the orgy of 1 October 1789 to the night when she bit cartridges shut with her teeth in preparation for the massacres of 10 August. In the Temple the accused had shown a tone of revolt against the people's sovereignty. She had been found with a picture of a heart, a well-known counter-revolutionary sign, since it had been found on nearly all those struck down by the Nation's vengeance. After the tyrant's death, she had treated her son as though he were King. It was for the jury now to decide whether the accused had helped France's enemies with money and information, and secondly, whether she had taken part in a plot to start civil war.

While the jury retired, Antoinette was led to a nearby room. Her throat dry from anxiety, she asked for a glass of water, and then she waited. Antoinette knew she was innocent; but would the jury find her so? Not a scrap of documentary evidence had been produced to prove her guilty; only the tittle-tattle of kitchens, backstairs and gaolers' common-room. From her first years in France even the dresses she had worn had been interpreted as hostile gestures; so now, her life had been reviewed in terms of the old xenophobic slanders first circulated by idle courtiers. But of positive proof the court had been given not one shred.

After deliberating for an hour the jury unanimously found the accused guilty on both counts. After reading the verdict Hermann asked the prisoner whether she had anything to say. She replied by shaking her head. Hermann then announced that the tribunal condemned her to death.

Antoinette gave no sign of emotion. She felt calm, knowing herself to be innocent. She had remained firm, confessed nothing. All she wanted now was to display in her last moments the same firmness as Louis. She was led back to her cell, and although the hearing had lasted twenty hours, she asked for paper, pen and ink. She would not make a will, for she had no possessions, but she felt the need to survive a little in a brief written message. She addressed it to Elisabeth, and the key words in it are 'affection' and 'friend'. She spoke first of her children, urging them to be united, since 'happiness is doubled when one can share it with a friend.' She had three friends left: Fersen, Gabrielle de Polignac and Elisabeth. Without naming them, she wrote: 'The idea of being separated for ever from them and their troubles forms one of my greatest regrets in dying.'

When she had finished, she lay down on her bed for an hour and cried. The first light of her last day came through the barred window. She changed her blood-stained linen and put on a white piqué dress, a muslin shawl, a white bonnet and her plum-coloured high-heeled shoes. She drank a cup of chocolate sent from a nearby café, known as a mignonnette. Shortly after eleven in the morning a tall man entered her cell: Henri Sanson, deputizing for his father, who had executed Louis. He tied Antoinette's hands behind her back and with a large pair of scissors cut her hair, pocketing the tresses in order later to burn them.

She was led out of her cell. In the courtyard she caught sight of the waiting tumbril. Perhaps she had been expecting to be taken to the scaffold, like Louis, in a closed carriage; at any rate at sight of the tumbril fear suddenly seized her and all her carefully patched-up dignity collapsed. She asked Sanson to undo her hands, then squatted down in a corner of the wall and relieved herself. Her arms tied again, she was made to sit in the tumbril, facing backwards.

The journey by cart lasted almost an hour. Antoinette sat erect and unflinching. Shortly after noon she reached the big square where, a young bride, she had been cheered by the crowd, men had thrown their hats in the air, and a friend had whispered, 'Two hundred thousand people have fallen in love with you.'

She had to be helped out of the cart, and in her pretty plum shoes slowly climbed the ladder to the scaffold. Saints had been abolished and the word was reserved now for the thing that towered over the thin figure in white: Saint Guillotine and the widow Capet. Exposed there on the platform, she was overcome by exhaustion and began to tremble in all her limbs. The executioner seized her and tied her to the plank. Four minutes later she was dead. A triumphant whoop came from Hébert: 'The greatest joy of all the joys experienced by Père Duchesne came after seeing with his own eyes the head of the female VETO separated from her f—— crane's neck.'

The body of Antoinette, former Queen of France, was carted away and buried in the same cemetery as Louis, but not beside him, in a grave unnamed and without a cross. Few in France cared, and even many of the émigrés in Brussels wore only half-mourning.

But two weeks after the execution Duchess Georgiana wrote to her mother: 'The impression of the Queen's death is constantly before my eyes . . . Besides the admiration that is universally felt for her and horror at the barbarians, her answers, her cleverness, composure, greatness of mind blaze forth in double splendour, and the horror of making the child depose against her is what one should have hop'd that the mind of man was incapable of.'

Fersen was another who mourned. The Queen's face, he wrote in his diary, 'follows me wherever I go. Her suffering and death and all my feelings never leave me for a moment. I can think of nothing else . . . It fills me with horror that she was alone in her last moments with no one to comfort her or to talk to her, with no one to whom she could give her last wishes.'

CHAPTER 25

Afterwards

ANTOINETTE's last thoughts were of her children, her sister-in-law and her friends. Let us see briefly what became of them.

Madame Elisabeth remained in the Temple and there, in the mood of Marie Leczinska, coolly embroidered a picture of a skull inscribed, 'This is my only thought.' Six weeks after the Queen's death Robespierre wanted the Committee of Public Safety to force every girl over fifteen either to marry or to be 'delivered to the public', that is, prostituted. This, says an English spy, was aimed at Madame Elisabeth and Madame Royale, who traditionally could marry only princes. As regards Elisabeth, the Committee preferred more direct methods. In May 1794 the King's sister was indicted before the Revolutionary Tribunal, which by now needed no documents, no examination, no witnesses, and was found guilty of plotting 'to murder the people, annihilate freedom and restore despotism'. Her decapitated body was flung into a grave at Monceaux with twenty-four others, naked, because her clothes were a perquisite of the State. Found among her effects was 'a silver medal representing the Immaculate Conception of the *ci-devant* Virgin'.

Louis XVII, aged eight when his mother died, was locked up in solitary confinement. For six months his food was pushed through a small barred guichet in the lower half of the door, his window was never opened, his shirt, stockings and bed-linen never changed, so that they crawled with lice, his excrement never removed. During those six months no one spoke to him.

When she was visited by Robespierre in May 1794, Marie Thérèse, already showing strength of character, wrote on a piece of paper a demand that a doctor should be sent to her brother, who a year earlier had begun to complain of a stitch in his side. The demand was ignored.

Even with fresh air and good food the unusually sensitive Louis might not have recovered: in the fetid cell he developed a painful skin disease, and his wrists, elbows and knees began to swell. Then his legs and arms grew disproportionately long, his shoulders rounded. He too had the family disease: tuberculosis of the bones.

Royalist groups had tried unsuccessfully to rescue Louis XVI, and later Antoinette. They may now have tried to rescue the boy King and leave in his place a deaf-and-dumb substitute. Certainly many royalists at the time believed that Louis XVII had been smuggled out of the Temple, and eventually thirty-two different 'pretenders', including one black, were to appear in various parts of Europe. Even to this day in western France one hears stories about the boy King that have been handed down from father to son in royalist families: one I have been told claims that Edgeworth and a boy with fair curls arrived by night at a certain Norman port and at dawn sailed in a fishing-boat for England.

Whereas none of these stories is very convincing, Louis XVII's death in the Temple on 8 June 1795 is well attested, notably by the death certificate, and there is no good reason to doubt it. After an autopsy the little twisted body was buried, without prayers, in a common grave in the cemetery of Sainte-Marguerite.

Marie Thérèse remained in prison throughout the Terror. A stalwart girl with a sense of her own dignity, she stood up well to suffering. When at last Parisians had had their fill of blood, and the mood swung round to tearful sentimentality, in a display of emotion hardly less sickening than their previous cruelty they slobbered over 'the orphan of the Temple'. No longer 'the she-wolf's cub', she became a poor innocent lass alone in the world, and crowds would gather under her barred window to sing tearful songs. To the Government she became an embarrassment. In December 1795 this French Iphigenia was driven to the frontier and exchanged for a prisoner of the Austrians: Jean Baptiste Drouet, the postmaster who helped capture Louis and had since become a deputy for the Marne. Marie Thérèse was to marry the Comte d'Artois's elder son and return one day to the Tuileries.

Of Antoinette's closest friends, Gabrielle de Polignac contracted a sudden illness in December 1793 and within twelve hours was dead. Axel de Fersen lived on to become an important political figure in Sweden: first, Minister to the Congress of Rastadt, where Bonaparte refused to treat with him on the grounds that he had 'slept with the late Queen', then Grand Marshal of the Court and on four occasions Lieutenant Governor of the kingdom. But he did not find happiness. He never married and lived quietly with his sister, remembering the past. He wished that he had accompanied the King and Queen on their flight and had been killed making possible their escape. The anniversaries of their deaths he remembered devotedly. On 21 January 1799 he wrote in his diary: 'I have been sad all day. I cannot forget that today is the anniversary of the death of Louis XVI and all my life I shall be devoted to the memory of that prince.' Of Antoinette he wrote, 'Eléonore will never replace her in my heart: what sweetness, tenderness and kindness; what a loving, sensitive, delicate heart.'

In 1810 the heir to the Swedish throne suffered an apoplectic stroke, fell from his horse and died. Political enemies accused Fersen of having poisoned him and stirred up the people of Stockholm against the powerful Grand Marshal. During the prince's funeral, on the nineteenth anniversary of the flight to Varennes, Fersen was pulled from his carriage by the crowd, insulted, stoned and eventually kicked to death.

Louis had expressed the hope that his execution would heal divisions between Frenchmen. How far this was from happening appears under the Terror. '*Liberté, Egalité, Fraternité . . . ou la Mort*' became the only admissible truth; Chamfort said it meant 'Be my brother, or I'll kill you.' A decree went out, for example, ordering all portraits of Louis XVI to be destroyed, whereupon one working-class man who had a portrait of the King on his snuff-box stuck a piece of paper over it. As he was taking his midday meal in a wine-shop, police searched him, pulled off the paper and found the King's portrait. He was immediately arrested, tried and condemned to death.

Few of those who had been involved with Louis and Antoinette, even distantly, could slip through so fine a net. Madame Du Barry went to the guillotine, as did 'Madame Etiquette', the botanist-lawyer Malesherbes, Antoinette's early admirer Armand de Lauzun, and moderates like Barnave and Bailly. The bloodthirsty too paid with their lives, not from any royalist reaction but because they were seen as impediments to that complete freedom that was always just around the corner. Louis's Minister of the Interior Roland and the Dauphin's gaoler Simon paid with their heads, as did Camille Desmoulins, the prosecutor Fouquier-Tinville and Antoinette's judge Hermann. Philippe Egalité went to Lady Guillotine: so did Hébert, Chaumette, Danton, Saint-Just and Robespierre.

Those who escaped included two gentle people, the abbé Edgeworth and Madame Vigée Lebrun. Aunt Adélaïde and Aunt Victoire lived to a ripe age in Italy. Thomas Paine's door was chalk-marked as a signal for execution but a feverish illness made him unconscious, off and on, for a month, and to this he owed his life. The abbé de Véri survived, escaping the guillotine by a fortnight, so did Cardinal de Rohan, Jacques and Suzanne Necker, Adrien Duport, La Fayette, the brewer Santerre, and Sieyès, who was to bring Napoleon to power. Mercy left in October 1792 and ended his days in London, still rich, still with his mistress Rosalie Levasseur. Antoinette's dressmaker, Rose Bertin, set up shop in St James's.

At a material level also much was destroyed. Stone saints on the façades of locked cathedrals were decapitated and châteaux set on fire. Catherine of Russia remarked ironically that the Revolution was a blessing for the painter Hubert Robert, since it provided him with 'the most beautiful and freshest ruins in the world', and indeed Robert did paint the razing of the Bastille and the violation of the royal tombs. As farmers shot them, stags disappeared from the royal forests. Calonne's paintings were auctioned at Sotheby's; Louis's mythological dinner service, which he never had a chance to use, found its way to Windsor.

Meanwhile heads rolled, more than 3000 of them, until a catharsis was finally effected and with a sigh of relief Parisians learned of Robespierre's execution on 28 July 1794. The Assembly then tacitly agreed no longer to use the guillotine as a political weapon, and the Revolution that had begun in 1788 with the revolt of Parlements and nobility drew to a close. It provides a suitable moment to assess the lives of Louis and his Queen.

At the time of Louis's *sacre* the Comédie Française wished to perform a flattering play called *The Coronation of Telemachus*, but Louis forbade it. 'Praise during my lifetime is suspect,' he said. 'If I deserve it, I'll be praised after my death.'

What praise does Louis deserve? His reign as a whole faithfully reflects the character of the man: a hard worker devoted to the happiness of his people. In the fifteen years to 1789 Louis gave France six volumes of new laws, compared with only two volumes for the 59 years of Louis XV's reign. That is an impressive achievement. Many of the laws were designed to ease hardship or end injustice, just as Louis's foreign policy was designed to secure peace, and France under his reign was almost certainly a happier kingdom than the France of the Sun King.

Louis's administration was honest. The King kept a close watch on his Ministers, none of whom amassed a fortune as Louis XIV's

Ministers had done. There was a notable absence of graft and corruption. By and large Frenchmen's taxes went to benefit France, not to line the pockets of middle-men.

'For my people's happiness' – how often that phrase occurs in Louis's decrees, especially those curtailing Court expenditure. From the time of the first 'walkabout' at Reims the people knew that the King had their interests at heart and, seeing how much he did for them, they were encouraged to think that he would, and could, do even more. Only against the background of a benevolent, humanitarian reign is it possible to conceive such bold demands as those of 1789.

As for Louis's failures, the main one before 1789 lies in the economy. Shut away in Versailles, probably Louis did not know exactly how to get it moving. Instead of taking Turgot in 1774, he would have done better to choose a Minister who shared his interest in machinery and was prepared to modernize France's manufactories. Calonne came ten years too late.

In exoneration of Louis, it has to be said that he inherited a too classical education system that encouraged mathematics but did little for applied science. A legacy of uninventive technological education was to hamper France well into the Napoleonic period.

Louis's answer to the budgetary deficit was to cut royal spending to the bone: in so far as this alienated the Court nobles and weakened the police, thrift went before a fall. Louis also gave too little attention to the army: in 1786 a British envoy blamed the King for the fact that 'the Army of France appears to have been neglected.' This negligence cost Louis dear. One of the features of 1788, as later of Varennes, was the failure of army officers to carry out commands exactly. This in turn stems from a lack of moral fibre – reflected in the arts – and from a general tender-heartedness: together these undermined what discipline remained cementing the fortress of power.

Seventeen eighty-nine arrived and the universe finally did fall on Louis. The theatrical props and costumes of the Lesser Pleasures called for a king who would strut and stride, throw back his head, put his hand to his heart, utter highly charged speeches, and generally capture his audience. Louis was simply not that kind of man. Knowing this, he should have gone all out to win support behind the scenes, and his failure to do so deserves severe blame.

Could Louis have prevented the Revolution? The question needs qualifying, for Louis was himself a revolutionary, in that he abolished the *corvée*, established Provincial Assemblies and extended the franchise to six million Frenchmen. If by Revolution is meant the Third Estate's defiance of Louis and the insurrection in Paris, Louis, given his character and habits, could not have prevented it. France would have required a king of genius, able to provide a rising standard of living and simultaneously alter the social structure in such a way as to satisfy a developing class of professional men. Even a Louis XIV could not have achieved that.

Once it started, could Louis have controlled the Revolution? Young Napoleon Bonaparte, an eyewitness of the attack on the Tuileries, thought Louis could have won the day by getting on his horse and riding towards the people. Possibly; though in 1814, faced by a mob as violent as that outside the Tuileries, Napoleon deemed it prudent to hide behind an Allied uniform and an assumed name. To control the Revolution, sooner or later blood would have had to be shed, and it was not in Louis's character to shed it. So again the answer is no.

As a result of his failure before the States General, Louis had to accept the Revolutionaries' three main principles: end of class distinctions, more individual freedom, and a constitutional monarchy. This in itself would have been a good thing, and from the beginning of 1790 Louis tried conscientiously to make the new order work. But it never got going. Tensions within the Constitution and forces stronger than the merely political came into play; hatred obscured the reformers' generous feelings as Sade obscured love under eroticism and cruelty.

When the religious issue came to the fore Louis acted quite differently from Henri IV, to whom he had so often been compared. The earlier Bourbon, not overburdened with conscience, twice renounced his Protestant faith for the sake of national unity; in similar circumstances Louis remained loyal to the faith of his forebears. Yet in the two Kings' downfall a parallel does emerge. Henri was assassinated by Ravaillac for not forcibly converting Protestants; Louis was deposed for not forcibly persecuting Catholic priests.

It is tempting to say that Louis found himself in the wrong country at the wrong time. Modesty, reticence and quiet perseverance are qualities more admired by the English than by the French and this was particularly so in the second half of the eighteenth century. Louis, I think, would have made a good King of England.

Antoinette in many ways complemented her husband. Her

laughter covered his silences, her charm softened his bearishness. She was an exemplary mother to Louis's children; she co-operated in his economy drive and in his welfare schemes. At Versailles for the first time the Queen played a full role. She worked for friendship with Austria and her receptions at Trianon became an important factor in French foreign policy. Her character survives in the beautiful lines, the flowers and the innocent children of the Louis Seize style.

Antoinette in Versailles must have suffered from the hatred of those around her quite as much as any member of a depressed minority today. It is ironical that she came to be stigmatized as 'the Austrian woman', for some of Louis XIII's blood ran in her veins, while Louis XVI was, through his mother, one quarter Austrian.

It was not the French custom to depict the King and Queen together – the one double portrait known to exist was painted by an Austrian for Schoenbrunn – and this separation in paint typifies the attempt to separate Louis and Antoinette, first during the early years, then during the Revolution, when Louis's freedom of action was hindered by the suspicions engulfing his wife, and the wedding ring became the cunningest of manacles. Each was given the chance to leave the other, and if they had taken it they might have escaped with their lives, though considerably diminished in moral stature.

The way the King and Queen met death ensured that the monarchy would live. In 1815 Louis's clever brother, Monsieur, became King on the basis of the principles Louis had proclaimed in the royal sitting on 23 June 1789. His reign is generally accounted a success. He was followed by Artois, who as King Charles X ruled until 1830.

Under the Restoration the lime-burned bones of Louis and Antoinette were exhumed and given solemn burial in the basilica of Saint-Denis. Royal tombs having been desecrated under the Revolution, it is not Louis XIV or Louis XV who lie there now but the couple who paid for the earlier Kings' excesses.

Under the Restoration also writers began to interpret the lives of the King and Queen. The great intervening figure was Napoleon, and beside him Louis naturally seemed very pale. In 1815 Roederer, who hardly knew Louis but was a close friend of Napoleon, wrote this of the King: 'a weak character . . . his calm during danger was only patience, his courage in misfortune only resignation . . . The Queen's pride obliged him to maintain absolutism as a point of honour which, should he infringe it, would make him unworthy of her affection.'

This interpretation, which helped to absolve the Bourbons, was readily accepted and came to be endorsed by Memoirs, quite a few of them apocryphal, which catered also for the new mood of religion. Countless are the glasses of water handed to a thirsty Louis during his journey from Varennes, innumerable the packets of clean linen smuggled, with comforting notes, to imprisoned Antoinette. Before being created a baron and First Painter to Louis XVIII, Gérard painted out the chicken he had shown Louis XVI munching in *The Tenth of August 1792*, while the hen-house door at le Hameau was inscribed *Presbytère* and visitors were told that the Queen would often repair there to consult a saintly priest. 'Resignation' was lifted from Roederer and, preceded by the adjective 'holy', became the key to Louis's character. Edgeworth, at the foot of the steps to the guillotine, was credited with words he never spoke: 'Son of St Louis, ascend to heaven!' This kind of portrayal continued until 1870, when republican historians veered to the other extreme, to be followed by Marxists who saw the reign exclusively in terms of class struggle.

In recent years France seems to have rejected definitely any idea of a constitutional monarchy and, with it, a royal family which, as Walter Bagehot wrote, 'sweetens politics by the seasonable addition of nice and pretty events'. In today's France Louis and Antoinette resemble those exploded stars astronomers call black holes: invisible, yet exerting powerful gravitational waves. For the Left they are Reaction incarnate, while the Right honours in them mainly the *ancien régime*, and tries to get their trials reversed, as were those of Joan of Arc and Dreyfus. It is noteworthy that France has quite recently moved in the direction of two of the principles championed by Louis and his Queen. In 1958 under the Constitution of the Fifth Republic the President was granted freedom to act according to the interests of the country as a whole, while France has been drawing close to the Holy Roman Empire in the shape of Germany. She who coupled the double-headed eagle and the fleurs de lis on her seal would have welcomed the twinning of French and German towns.

Outside France Louis and Antoinette escape the glib political labelling which is still their fate in France, and this is surely a gain, since Left and Right in the political sense date only from the last couple of years of their reign. Against the looming mass of Versailles they stand, two isolated figures, last of a long line of kings and queens stretching back through the Dark Ages to Mérovée in the year 448; the old trees in the park have been felled; the winters are long and unusually severe; their children sicken and die; it is the winter of the monarchy; but with good will and energy they go about their scoffed-at tasks.

When little was known about Louis – and that mainly hearsay – the manner of his death assumed paramount importance. Now that the man, his intentions and his achievements are better known it is clear that his eventful reign is quite as significant as his last minutes. He brought to it the principle of justice that had characterized the French monarchy at its best, and also something of his own: a respect for other people's opinions, symbolized in his journey from Cherbourg, when the crowds shouted 'Long live the King!' and Louis called back 'Long live my people!'

He meant the people as a whole. He had no time for factions. And when intolerance suddenly became the mood of the age, Louis took his stand on tolerance. Antoinette chose to stand beside him. Both had their faults, but from an early age they had been obliged to struggle against clever enemies, and it was the will power and self-control learned in the gilded drawing-rooms of Versailles that carried them through in their prison and on the scaffold. They died for every man's right to freedom of conscience, and they died bravely. But it is their lives that matter quite as much as the manner of their death: the good they did, and the good they tried to do.

Obscene Writings against
the Queen

THE first printed work against Antoinette appeared on the occasion of her entry to Paris in 1773.· *Antoinette ou la nouvelle Pandore*, by one Mademoiselle Dionis, is a mildly xenophobic prediction that Antoinette of Austria will open a Pandora's box of troubles for France. It is not obscene, nor is the first song against the Queen, which originated like this. At the reception given after the death of Louis XV, at La Muette, one of Antoinette's ladies-in-waiting, the young Marquise de Clermont Tonnerre, tired with the long ceremony during which she was obliged to stand beside the Queen, sat down at last on the parquet and amused herself by peeping out between the panniers of Antoinette and her ladies and playing childish tricks to make them laugh. Antoinette could not repress a smile, which she quickly concealed behind her fan, and next day a song went round with the refrain:

> *Petite reine de vingt ans,*
> *Vous, qui traitez si mal les gens,*
> *Vous repasserez la barrière*
> *Laire, laire, aire, lanlaire, laire lanla.*

On 11 July 1774 the abbé Baudeau, an observer of the Paris scene, wrote in his diary: 'The Queen is said to sleep with the Duc de Chartres and M. de Lamballe: with the former after putting up stiff resistance, with the latter willingly; also with Madame de Lamballe, Madame de Pecquigny, etc., etc. The underhand cabal of the Chancellor [Maupeou] and the old bigoted aunts spread these stories, to try to ruin this poor princess, and retain sole control of the Court.'

As Antoinette saw more and more of the Princesse de Lamballe, the charge of Lesbianism came to the fore in the clandestine song of 1776 quoted in chapter 9.

On summer nights in 1778 the Queen used to walk in the garden of Versailles listening to music. According to Madame Campan, 'a few days before the Queen gave birth to her first child, a packet of manuscript songs about her and the leading Court ladies was thrown into the Œil de Bœuf. The packet was at once handed to the King, who was very angry. He said that he himself had attended the "promenade concerts" and seen nothing that was not quite innocent . . . that it was a crime deserving death to have dared slander the Queen, and that he wished the author to be sought, found and punished.'

One culprit was found, an eighteen-year-old ne'er-do-well duellist named Louis Edmond de Champcenetz, a son of one of the courtiers who played the prank on Louis XV's Persian cat. But he was only a hireling working for highly placed friends of Artois whom Louis could not prosecute without causing immense scandal. They wanted to insinuate that the child to which the Queen would soon give birth was a bastard, and that, after Monsieur, Artois still stood heir to the throne.

The following year saw the appearance of *Les Amours de Charlot et de Toinette*, which was seized and impounded in the Bastille; only a few copies of the original edition were to escape the looting of 14 July, but it was to be reprinted later, in 1789. This is one of the first writings to play up the King's supposed sexual incapacity. Antoinette finds '*son époux très auguste était mauvais fouteur*':

> *Attendu que son allumette*
> *N'est pas plus grosse qu'un féru;*
> *Que toujours molle et toujours croche,*
> *Il n'a de vit que dans la poche . . .*

At the end of the poem it is Charlot (the Comte d'Artois) who satisfies the young Queen.

The birth of the Dauphin produced the song quoted in chapter 13: an attempt to show that since the King was impotent the child must be a bastard and could not succeed to the throne.

With the Diamond Necklace affair the Queen made new enemies, notably Jeanne de La Motte, whose *Memoirs*, which appeared in a French edition of 5000 copies, introduce a new slander: the Queen has an abnormal sexual appetite. 'His Eminence found it strenuous to live up to the amatory standards of his royal paramour and made arch admission that he resorted to a variety of stimulants: first fortifying himself with a dose of Cagliostro's famous aphrodisiac, then stimulating himself further by a visit to the love-nest he maintained in Passy.' The model is evidently Louis XV.

When Louis and Antoinette learned that Madame de La Motte was preparing a revised, still more noxious edition of her *Memoirs*, they sent Gabrielle de Polignac to London to buy the manuscript. However, the author kept back a copy and from this, in October 1789, was printed the new edition.

Meanwhile, as more and more unnecessary officials had their jobs or pensions axed, Court slanders proliferated. In 1785 the author of the *Correspondance secrète* states: 'Clandestine writings, calumny and dirty songs that have been disseminated from the Court have completely changed French good nature.'

In 1789 appeared *Essais historiques sur la vie de Marie Antoinette d'Autriche*. Longer than earlier pamphlets – 79 pages – it brought together nearly all the earlier charges, even the fact that the Queen had ridiculed French etiquette in the person of Madame de Noailles. It has been attributed to Brissot, and if he did write it, it is the first Jacobin pamphlet against the Queen. It had a sensational success and before the end of 1789 went through fifteen editions.

Early 1791 saw, in Paris, the culmination of 'natural man'. In a dispatch dated 15 April 1791 Fernan Nunez writes: 'Some time ago a man claiming to be a savage exhibited himself at the Palais Royal, charging 24 sols. He spoke a language no one except his interpreter could understand and ate stones. Some months later the act was enlivened by a female savage. They showed themselves nude for 16 pesetas and, for 24 douros, publicly performed acts which certain animals never allow to be seen.'

Against such a background the Queen's sexual voracity became a dominant theme of pamphlets. *L'Autrichienne en goguette ou l'orgie royale*, by F. Marie Mayeur de Saint Paul, appeared in 1789, *Soirées amoureuses du général Mottier et de la belle Antoinette, par le petit épagneul de l'Autrichienne* in 1790, *Fureurs utérines de Marie Antoinette, femme de Louis XVI* in 1791, *Tentation d'Antoinette et de son cochon dans la tour du Temple* in 1792. But these and similar pamphlets are no longer products of the Court, written with a light and witty touch, they are crude attacks aimed at a working-class audience. In them appear dark and irrational forces – envy of supposedly superior sexual pleasure, a trampling of purity in the mud – forces that had been denied expression in the rosy literary forms of that day. Some of the pamphlets have illustrations of great obscenity, for example *Vie de Marie Antoinette d'Autriche . . . depuis la perte de son pucelage jusqu'au premier mai 1971, ornées de 26 figures.*

A résumé of one of these illustrated pamphlets will show the kind of attack to which the Queen was now subjected. The title-page reads: *La Journée Amoureuse ou les Derniers Plaisirs de M . . . Ant . . . Au premier de la République. Comèdie en trois actes, en prose, représentée pour la première fois au Temple le 20 août 1792.*

Antoinette begins the play with a monologue: 'J'ai été bien foutue et refoutue dans le cours de ma vie; mais je n'ai jamais eu tant de plaisir que cette nuit. Je l'ai passée toute entière dans les bras de Lafayette. Que le bougre est vigoureux! Hercule même ne m'aurait point procuré de plus vives sensations.'

The Princesse de Lamballe comes in, and the two women indulge in Lesbian practices. Antoinette: 'Enfonce ton doigt plus avant dans ma matrice. Je n'en puis plus . . . , mon amie, . . . je me meurs.' And later: 'Je veux que tes goûts soient les miens: ainsi dispose en souveraine de mon cul, de mon con, de toute ma personne. Pourvu que je décharge, tous les genres de foutre me coviennent.'

The Princess leaves, and Louis comes in. Antoinette gives him a glass of rum and unbuttons his trousers. 'Elle travaille son membre, fatigue son poignet de le faire dresser' – this is the subject of one illustration.

' "Décharge, mon homme, décharge." (De tems à autre elle glisse sa langue dans la bouche du roi.)' After a brief dialogue with his wife (he calls her Antoinette), Louis goes to sleep. When the Princess returns, Antoinette complains, 'Le bougre déchargea, mais ce fut à vit mollet et à force d'être patiné.' She then confides that Artois is the father of the Dauphin.

The Princess tells the Queen how Rohan has 'foutu à l'italienne en mémoire du chapeau qu'il recevait du pape,' and practises this on the Queen.

In the presence of the Princess Antoinette then copulates with one Dubois, the lover of her chambermaid, and talks about it afterwards. 'Je n'ai jamais été mieux foutue . . . A l'aspect de son monstrueux jean-chouart, j'ai été vraiment saisie de frayeur . . .'

The play ends with the Princess agreeing that this man of the people is immeasurably better endowed than their high-born lovers.

Once read and its staggeringly obscene illustrations once seen, such a pamphlet is not easily forgotten, and the effect of such propaganda on the populace of Paris can well be imagined. The Queen came to be seen as a loathsome, unnatural creature, sapping the strength of an impotent King, and prepared to indulge her sexual voracity at no matter what cost to the people.

It is a well known fact that obscene slanders are the most damaging of all forms of calumny. By denying a woman's virtue in the special sense they make it easy to attribute to her every kind of vice. This happened with the Queen. Because she was unchaste, she must also be thick-skinned and unfeeling. On the day after the Tuileries was sacked, Dr John Moore happened to be in the Riding School watching the Queen. 'A person near me,' he writes, 'remarked that her face indicated rage and the most provoking arrogance. I perceived nothing of that nature [but rather] dignified composure.'

Multiply that by ten thousand, and one has the mood of Paris during the Terror. It helps to explain how a juryman could consider the Queen as, quite literally, a *bête féroce*, and how Hébert could accuse her of incest with the Dauphin. Long before she came up for trial, the writers of obscene slanders had condemned Antoinette to death.

The King's Supposed Operation: Hearsay and Fact

A FAMILIAR version of the royal marriage runs like this. Louis XVI was malformed physically. He suffered from phimosis – abnormal smallness of the lip of the prepuce – and before he could perform the sexual act he required surgery. Louis feared an operation and kept delaying it. In 1777 Joseph came specially from Vienna to persuade him, for the sake of the alliance, to submit to the surgeon's knife. Louis yielded, the operation was successfully performed and in the following year Louis and Antoinette had their first child.

This version was put forward by Stefan Zweig in his biography of the Queen in 1932, and has been repeated by many subsequent writers about Louis, from Padover to Fejtö, though not by Faÿ.

Now Zweig began his work by having copies made of all Antoinette's letters to her mother in the Vienna State Archives – not just the truncated versions published in 1875 by Arneth. On the basis of these Zweig, a close friend of Freud, devised his famous Freudian interpretation of the Queen's life: frustrated sexually until 1777, she sought relief in a giddy but disastrous round of pleasure and spending.

Zweig's biography was a narrative without sources and notes. When he had finished it Zweig passed his copies of Antoinette's letters to a French friend, Georges Girard. In 1933 Girard published them as *Correspondance entre Marie Thérèse et Marie Antoinette*, explaining that 'This book, which owes everything to Stefan Zweig, should be considered the natural complement to his masterly biography.'

Both Zweig's biography and Girard's edition of the letters were very favourably received. The letters seemed to confirm the exactitude of Zweig's biography, particularly his all-important hypothesis that the marriage was consummated very late indeed, as a result of Joseph's visit.

There was however a flaw, unnoticed for forty years. The letters published by Girard are not quite complete. Two important passages dropped out – or were they suppressed? – and they are precisely the passages that invalidate Zweig's hypothesis. Photocopies of the two letters in question are in front of me as I write and the letters are published in their entirety at the end of this appendix.

The passages omitted by Zweig and Girard constitute strong evidence that the marriage was consummated as early as 1773. If this is true, what of the other evidence cited by Zweig in his version of the marriage?

First, the operation. Antoinette speaks of an operation in her letter of 15 Dec 1775. She does not specify what kind of operation, but says that her doctor and the King's doctor are divided on whether it would be useful. On 14 Jan 1776 she writes: 'Yesterday the King called in Moreau, surgeon of the Hôtel Dieu in Paris. He said more or less what the others said, that the operation was not necessary and that without one there was every hope [of a child] . . . He [the King] has promised me that, if there is nothing decided [by the doctors] a few months from now, he would himself decide to undergo the operation.' On 10 April 1776 she wrote: 'I am convinced the operation is no longer necessary.'

It sounds as though the purpose of the operation is not to make the sexual act possible, but to remedy some hindrance to fertility – but more of this presently.

Louis underwent a medical examination at the age of six, and another at the time of his marriage. The doctors would certainly have reported any malformation of the prepuce, since anything connected with succession to the throne was of vital political importance. But Louis got a clean bill of health. In 1771 George III of England copied in his own hand a report from Mr Ainslie: 'The King in speaking about a month ago in Me Du Barry's appartment said: "the Dauphin is well made and perfectly well formed yet has hitherto shewn no desire for women, nay rather seems to loath them." ' (Papers of George III, no. 10008.)

Mercy was worried that the Queen would be blamed for the sterile marriage and it was he who put out reports that Louis was perhaps physically malformed. The most explicit version of these is in a dispatch of the Spanish ambassador, d'Aranda, who we know from other evidence consistently retailed to Madrid second-hand reports from Mercy. D'Aranda wrote in summer 1774 that two hypotheses about Louis were being rumoured: one that the frenum tied down his prepuce so tightly as to make sexual relations very painful; the other that the lip of the prepuce was so small as to prevent a complete erection. In the first case, he says, the frenum might be broken during intercourse or else cut by a surgeon; the second would require circumcision, a serious operation for an adult.

D'Aranda writes of two quite different operations, and on hearsay only. Since there is no other evidence to support the story of physical malformation, it is probably no more than palace gossip. Of this, naturally, there was much, since Louis XIV and Louis XV – but not Louis XIII – had lost no time in producing children.

Six weeks later, on 23 September 1774, d'Aranda wrote a dispatch which seems to contradict his earlier hypotheses and to suggest that normal sexual relations were taking place. After noting the King's tenderness for his wife: *'Sus sirvientes interiores aseguran averle observado una perfecta y no escasa ereccion, con conocidas manchas en la camisa.'*

Professor Donald Bates, of the department of History of Medicine at McGill University, has kindly investigated the problem for me. He suggests that Louis *may* have suffered from hydrocoele, a collection of fluid around one testicle. Hydrocoele is now known to be a benign condition and never to be a cause of male infertility, but in the eighteenth century it was often suspected as the cause for failure to fecundate. It was fairly common in those days to operate on hydrocoele by making a small incision with a knife and drawing off the fluid with a hollow reed. This may well have been the proposed operation referred to by Antoinette in her letter to the Empress.

If Louis did suffer temporarily from hydrocoele, it is quite likely that the condition righted itself without surgery, for no record of an operation on the King has ever been found. Moreover, were a secret operation to have been performed, while the scar was healing Louis would have been unable to ride for at least a week. But his diary shows that the King took no such rest from hunting during the period under discussion.

In 1777 Joseph visited France. The visit had been planned years before, but for one reason or another delayed. Did Joseph give Louis advice about an operation? In his long letter to Leopold dated 9 June on the subject of the marriage, which I have quoted in the text, Joseph makes no claim to have given Louis such advice. Nor, as I have said, do we hear that Louis underwent an operation in 1777 – or in any other year.

In October 1777 Joseph wrote to Leopold, saying that the King and Queen had both written to thank him, 'attributing it [consummation of the marriage] to my advice. It is true that I discussed this thoroughly in my conversations with him and it was obvious to me that laziness, clumsiness and apathy were the only obstacles to it.'

No letters from Louis and Antoinette thanking Joseph for his valuable advice have ever been found. This is surprising, for Antoinette's other letters to her brother are in the Vienna archives, and Joseph would have had every reason to see that these particular letters were preserved.

Did the thank-you letters ever exist? The longer one studies Joseph's correspondence with Leopold about Louis the more it seems to be a prolonged boast by Joseph, who has cast himself as the know-all who sets everything to rights. The correspondence, to start with, is self-contradictory. In a letter to Leopold from Paris Joseph says that he has told Louis to have an operation, explaining that it is not dangerous, and Louis has agreed to undergo it. But in the letter of October quoted above Joseph says the only obstacles were 'laziness, clumsiness and apathy'. Joseph says not a word about an operation.

Moreover, in the Paris letter Joseph says, 'If I had asked him, he [Louis] would have shown me the most secret papers of state.' This claim, which contradicts everything we know of Louis, is implausible in the extreme. It does not presuppose one to believe the other boasts in the same series of letters.

One further aspect of the matter remains to be considered. On 30 August 1777 Antoinette wrote to her mother that, eight days earlier, her marriage had been *'parfaitement consommé'*, and that she was *'dans le bonheur le plus essentiel pour toute ma vie'*. In view of the letters of 1773 and the hopes she had expressed several times since then of being with child, Antoinette seems to be saying that she has for the first time enjoyed complete sexual pleasure: the word 'orgasm' in the sexual sense came into use only in the nineteenth century. Orgasm in the woman was well known to be conducive to conception.

Mercy knew that something had happened on 22 August, but not exactly what. He jumped to the conclusion most unfavourably to Louis: that the King had only now succeeded in having sexual relations with his wife. He passed on his story to d'Aranda. In his dispatch to Madrid dated 25 August 1777 d'Aranda wrote that Louis had told one of his aunts how pleased he was at 'the diversion', and how much he regretted not having experienced it earlier. But d'Aranda as usual is only Mercy's mouthpiece, and his report is of value only in telling us what Mercy *believed* had happened.

What is indisputable is that no record of an operation being performed or even needed has ever been found, and it is impossible to prove a person was operated on by saying that there is no proof he wasn't. Neither has any letter been found thanking Joseph for his 'advice'. All the evidence suggesting that Louis was malformed originates with Mercy, who naturally wanted to forestall charges that the Queen was barren.

I conclude that Louis consummated the marriage in summer 1773. In late 1775, worried at not having children, he considered the idea of an operation to relieve a possible cause of childlessness, such as hydrocoele, but his doctors decided it was unnecessary. From 1776 he and Antoinette had sexual relations more often than in the years 1774–5, and in the natural course of events, without the unneeded operation or any advice from Joseph, a child was conceived early in 1778.

TWO LETTERS FROM THE QUEEN TO HER MOTHER

ce 17 juillet 1773

Madame ma très chère Mère,

Votre satisfaction est tout ce qui pouvait ajouter à la joie et au sentiment que j'aurai toute ma vie pour l'accueil que j'ai reçu à Paris. J'avouerai à ma chère maman qu'en partant pour Compiègne j'ai eu quelque regret de m'éloigner de cette bonne ville; il est bien vrai que j'y ai été attendrie jusqu'aux larmes, surtout à la Comédie italienne, lorsque, le parterre ne faisant qu'une voix avec les acteurs, tout s'est écrié: 'Vive le roi!' Clerval, un des acteurs, ajoute: 'et ses chers enfants!' à quoi il a été fort applaudi. Je ne peux comparer cette grande journée qu'à celle où ma chère maman est venue au spectacle après la naissance de mon neveu de Florence. Quoique je fusse fort enfant, j'ai bien senti comme tous les coeurs étaient émus par la presence de ma tendre mère. M. le dauphin a été à merveille toutes les fois qu'il a été à Paris, et, si je l'ose dire, il a gagné dans l'esprit du peuple par l'air de bonne amitié qui était entre nous; c'est peut-être ce qui a fait dire qu'il m'a embrassée publiquement, quoique cela ne soit pas vrai; mais ma chère maman est bien trompée en croyant qu'il ne l'a pas fait depuis mon arrivée; au contraire depuis longtemps tout le monde remarque son empressement auprès de moi. Je puis bien dire à ma chère maman et à elle seule que depuis que nous sommes ici mes affaires sont fort avancées et je crois le mariage consommé, quoique pas encore dans le cas d'être grosse; c'est pour cela même que M. le dauphin ne veut pas qu'on le sache encore; quel bonheur si j'avais un enfant au mois de Mai. Pour mes règles je les ai toujours fort et bien, vous pouvez bien croire que je ne monte à cheval dans ce temps là.

Je suis fachée de l'état de la Weyrothen; sa résignation est la plus grande grâce que Dieu puisse lui accorder; je suis aussi bien fâchée de la de Pest.

Nous avons appris ici les couches de l'infante; l'infant, qui ne m'avait pas écrit depuis son mariage, m'a écrit cette fois-ci. Il est vrai qu'il a oublié que j'étais sa belle-soeur; il m'appelle sa cousine: c'est encore assez de parenté pour la conduite qu'il tient. Je souhaite qu'il en change: le roi n'a pas voulu que je lui réponds. Un des premiers officiers des mousquetaires revient de Naples et ne cesse de chanter les louanges de la reine. Vous ne sauriez croire, ma chère maman, quel plaisir cela me fait; j'espère que vous vous êtes trompée dans le temps de ses couches, vu la grosseur dont elle est; je désire fort que mes deux belles-soeurs accouchent heureusement.

Il me tarde fort que l'empereur revient; j'aimerais mieux qu'il ne vît pas le roi de Prusse. L'abbé se met à vos pieds; il a été également transporté et pour moi et pour ses compatriotes. Vous avez bien de la bonté, ma chère maman, de m'envoyer la liste de Luxembourg; n'espérant plus de revoir ma patrie, c'est une grande consolation pour moi de savoir ce qui s'y passe.

On a voulu depuis quelque temps nous faire des tracasseries; grâce à Dieu, le plus fort est passé, et nous n'avons plus de crainte. Le parti de M. le dauphin et le mien sont assez bien pris pour ne jamais manquer au roi et à nous. J'espère sur toute chose que ma chère maman sera toujours contente de moi, et me conservera toujours ses bontés et son amitié, qui me sont plus précieuses que tout.

ce 13 d'août 1773

Madame ma très chère Mère,

Deux jours après vous avoir écrit, nous avons cru Mr le dauphin et moi devoir dire au roi notre état. Il m'a embrassée avec bien de la tendresse en m'appelant sa chère fille. On a cru qu'il était bon de divulguer notre secret; tout le monde en a beaucoup de joie. Depuis ce temps-là il n'y a en rien de décisif pour la grossesse, mes règles sont venues le dernier du mois, comme à l'ordinaire avançant de quelques jours. Je ne désespère pas encore pour le mois de Mai. J'ai écrit à la reine de Naples pour son accouchement, je suis plus fâchée que je n'ai osé lui dire que ce soit encore une fille, mais j'espère bien qu'elle n'en restera pas là.

La presentation de la jeune Mme du Barry s'est très bien passée. Un moment avant qu'elle vint chez moi, on m'a dit que le roi n'avait dit mot ni à la tante ni à la nièce: j'en ai fait autant. Mais au reste je puis bien assurer à ma chère maman que je les ai reçues tres poliment: tout le monde qui était chez moi est convenu que je n'avais ni embarras ni empressement à les voir sortir, le roi sûrement n'a pas été mécontent, car il a été de très bonne humeur toute la soirée avec nous. Le voyage finira beaucoup mieux qu'il paraissait d'abord, nous n'entendons plus parler de mouvement ni d'intrique, entre nous il y a une parfaite union.

Nous avons eu trois petites fêtes chez la marquise Durfort; nous en avons encore une la semaine prochaine; je désire fort qu'il fasse moins chaud, surtout s'agissant de danse, car il fait aujourd'hui une chaleur excessive.

Je suis ravie que l'empereur n'ait pas son entrevue, mais je ne serai entièrement rassurée que lorsqu'il sera revenu de ses courses; je lui écris un mot par ce courrier.

Mercy m'a déjà parlé du prince Louis[1]; sa mauvaise conduite me fait peine de toutes manières. C'est un point encore plus fâcheux dans ce pays-ci, qu'il déshonore, que pour Vienne, qu'il scandalise; quand Mercy croira qu'il est temps, je ferai ce qu'il me dira, mais j'imagine qu'il voudra des ménagements, tant à cause de Mme Marsan que du credit de M. de Soubise.

J'attends Neny avec impatience. On me peint actuellement; il est bien vrai que les peintres n'ont pas encore attrapé ma ressemblance: je donnerais de bon cœur tout mon bien à celui qui pourrait exprimer dans mon portrait la joie que j'aurais à revoir ma chère maman; il est bien dur de ne pouvoir l'embrasser que par lettre.

Mon mari est touché de vos bontés; j'espère qu'il les méritera davantage.

[1]Rohan.

Sources and Notes

In a book where a mosaic of detail has been built up largely from primary sources it becomes impossible to give a reference for every statement or quotation. Works such as the *Recueil des anciennes lois françaises*, *Remontrances des Parlements* and *Dictionnaire des Institutions de la France* are the staple of any history of this period, and will already be familiar to students. So will certain secondary works such as Lavisse's History, the studies of Aulard, Flammermont and Lefebvre, and Professor Michael J. Sydenham's balanced account of the Revolution. I have limited myself to giving a source for new, unfamiliar or important quotations and for statements bearing on my main characters. I have also referred to recent works, unlikely to be found in standard bibliographies, which have proved especially useful.

Unless otherwise stated, the place of publication of French books is Paris, of English books London.

List of abbreviations:

AHRF	*Annales Historiques de la Révolution Française*
Arneth	Arneth & Geffroy, editors: *Correspondance secrète entre Marie Thérèse et le Comte de Mercy-Argenteau avec les lettres de Marie Thérèse et de Marie Antoinette* (1875)
Bachaumont	Bachaumont: *Mémoires secrets pour servir à l'Histoire de la République des Lettres en France depuis 1762* (London 1777–89)
Croy	Emmanuel de Croy: *Journal inédit 1718–84* (1906)
Découverte	*Découverte:* Bulletin du Comité pour l'Etude de Louis XVI et de son Procès. Published from 149 rue de Rennes, Paris VI (1973–)
Fersen	A. Söderhjelm: *Fersen et Marie Antoinette* (1930)
Fleury I	Comte Fleury: *Angélique de Mackau, Marquise de Bombelles* (1905)
Fleury II	Comte Fleury: *Les Dernières Années du Marquis et de la Marquise de Bombelles* (1906)
Girard	G. Girard editor: *Correspondance entre Marie Thérèse et Marie Antoinette* (1933)
La Rocheterie	M. de La Rocheterie et le Marquis de Beaufort, editors: *Lettres de Marie Antoinette* (1895)

Lescure	Lescure, editor: *Correspondance secrète inédite sur Louis XVI, Marie Antoinette, la Cour et la Ville* (1866)
Stormont	David Murray, Lord Stormont, ambassador to France 1772–78: dispatches in the Public Record Office, S.P. 78
Thrale	*The French Journals of Mrs Thrale and Doctor Johnson,* edited Tyson and Guppy (Manchester 1932)
Véri	Abbé de Véri: *Journal* (1928)
Walpole	*The Letters of Horace Walpole,* edited Toynbee (Oxford 1903–5)
Young	Arthur Young: *Travels in France in 1787, 1788 and 1789* (1794)

Preface

The example of Mercy's duplicity dates from November 1784, when Louis was mediating between Austria and Holland over navigation of the Scheldt. After telling Vermond what to do, Mercy explains: 'ce désir de ma part tient à mon goût pour les concordances . . . Je vous prie de brûler ma letter.' Hof- und Hausstaatsarchiv, Vienna, F. Varia 51 f. 233, and Vermond's reply f. 237. See *Découverte*, no. 2 (1973).

'I found no greater alteration . . .' P. Thicknesse, *A Year's Journey through France* (1789) II, 172. Thicknesse, author of *The Valetudinarian Bath Guide* and a treatise on writing in cipher, travelled France in a cabriolet, with a bass viol, a fiddle, two guitars and a kettle to make tea. Mrs Thicknesse sat beside him with a parrot on her shoulder, while their monkey, Jocko, in a pair of French jackboots, rode postilion. Because they had to spend carefully, Thicknesse's book is a good guide to prices.

Chapter 1: Versailles and its Master

The prank on Louis XV's cat: J. H. Dufort de Cheverny, *Mémoires* (1886) I, 124.

Marie Leczinska's fear of ghosts: Madame Campan, *Mémoires* (London 1833) I, 414–15.

Louis the Dauphin: E. de Broglie, *Le Fils de Louis XV* (1877).

The Dauphin's wedding ball: Luynes, *Mémoires* VIII (1862), 113–14.

Marie Josèphe de Saxe: C. Stryienski, *La Mère des trois derniers Bourbons* (1902).

Preparations in the nursery and nursery etiquette: S. Poignant, *Les Filles du Roi* (1970), using the Registres des Decisions du Roi (O[1]*) in the Archives Nationales.

'At four in the morning . . .' E. J. F. Barbier, *Journal* IV (1856), 33.

'The wet-nurse . . .' Luynes, *Mémoires* XIII (1863), 5 Sept. 1754 (Extraordinaire) cf 29 August 1754.

Berry's governor, Antoine de Quélen, Duc de La Vauguyon, born

1706, seems to have been a man of resource for at the battle of Fontenoy when ammunition ran out he ordered his cannon to fire powder only. His bluff helped to win the battle.

Berry's christening: *Mercure de France*, Nov. 1761.

Chapter 2: The Boy

Choiseul: G. Maugras, *Le Duc et la Duchesse de Choiseul* (1903).

'Repulsed, fettered, humiliated . . .' E. de Broglie, *op. cit.* 289.

The fundamental work on Louis's education is P. Girault de Coursac, *L'éducation d'un roi: Louis XVI* (1972).

Description de la Forêt de Compiègne telle qu'elle était en 1765, avec le guide de la Forêt par Louis Auguste Dauphin, was published in Paris in 1766. His map of the Environs of Versailles is in the Cabinet des Cartes et des Plans de la Bibliothèque Nationale.

Louis's character as revealed in his schoolboy exercises: Girault de Coursac, *op. cit.*, chapters 5–7.

As a matter of course, the King of France's children had their eyes examined by oculists. See Luynes, *Mémoires*, and S. Poignant, *Les Filles du Roi* (1970).

Louis's diary, which he was to continue until 31 July 1792, filled five small quarto notebooks, and was usually written up monthly from a daily rough draft. It is now in the Musée des Archives Nationales. Part of it has been published in L. Nicolardot, *Journal de Louis XVI* (1873).

Provence corrects Berry's French: Bachaumont, 25 March 1763.

The incident of the hat: Véri, 1 March 1775.

Hume's visit to Versailles: J. H. Burton, *Life and Correspondence of David Hume* (1846) II, 177 ff.

The death of Louis's father: Walpole, 20 Dec. 1765.

'The four Mesdames . . .' Walpole, 3 Oct. 1765.

Aunt Louise's departure: *Vie de la mère Térèse de St Augustin*, par une religieuse (1867); her nephews' letters I, 142–3.

Chapter 3: The Impossible Marriage

C. L. Morris, *Maria Theresa, The Last Conservative* (1938) and E. Crankshaw, *Maria Theresa* (1969).

'I insist on their eating everything . . .' Maria Theresa to Countess Lerchenfeld, quoted by Crankshaw, 250.

'You cannot possibly conceive . . .' Leopold Mozart to his landlord, 23 Jan. 1768. *The Letters of Mozart and his Family* (1938) I, 116–17.

Vermond's reports: Arneth, *Maria Theresia und Marie Antoinette* (1866) 354 ff.

'The only true happiness . . .' Arneth, 4 May 1770.

'Princess, I pray . . .' *Gazette de France* 1770, no. 42.

'I expected . . .' Duchess of Northumberland, *The Diaries of a Duchess* (1926), 111.

'The Dauphin appeared . . .' *idem* 113.

'Before his marriage M. de La Vauguyon . . .' Antoinette to Joseph, 22 Sept. 1784.

Mercy: the biography of Comte de Pimodan (1911).

'I have made sure of three persons . . .' Arneth, 16 Nov. 1770.

'A curious thing happened . . .' Arneth, 9 July 1770.

'Madame la Dauphine believes that none of her private papers are safe . . .' Arneth, 20 Oct. 1770.

Chapter 4: Husband and Wife

'On the first of [June] . . .' Duchess of Northumberland, *op. cit.* 134–5. Notices of Louis's prowess as a horseman: Girault de Coursac, *op. cit.* 256–7.

Louis's records of hunts fill a total of 507 pages. L. Nicolardot, *op. cit.*

'I love him with all my heart . . .' *Correspondance de Louis XV avec don Ferdinand infant duc de Parme* (1938), 156–7.

Hunting suppers: Girault de Coursac, *op. cit.* 258–60.

'Her eyes are of a lively blue . . .' Duchess of Northumberland, *op. cit.* 117–18.

Madame Du Barry's carriage: Bachaumont, 30 Oct. 1770.

'It is pitiable to see the weakness . . .' Arneth, 9 July 1770.

'A lecture on this excessive liking for the hunt . . .' Arneth, 1 July 1771.

'The prince had some days earlier brought on an attack of indigestion . . .' Arneth, 4 Aug. 1770.

Antoinette's dress bespattered with slops: Arneth, 18 May 1773.

Mercy went so far as to tell his fellow-ambassadors that Louis was impotent: dispatches of the Spanish ambassador, Fuentes, especially 26 Oct. 1771. Madrid, Estado Legajo 4129, no. 995.

'There was such a great crowd . . .' Arneth, 8 June 1772.

Plays at Compiègne; Arneth, 17 July 1773.

'I can tell my dear Maman, and her alone . . .' and 'Two days after writing . . .' Hof- und Hausstaatsarchiv, Vienna. Full text in Appendix B.

In approving Antoinette's refusal of the diamond ear-rings, Maria Theresa wrote: 'I do not know how to forgive the Empress of Russia for having accepted, and even displayed, her subject Orloff's gift of a superb diamond.' Arneth, 3 Feb. 1774.

Louis XV's death: Stormont, 1 May and 18 May 1774. 'The eruption is very copious and the small pox upon the face and breast of the confluent kind, though the physicians do not allow this, and have invented a new name and call it contiguous.'

Chapter 5: The Young King

'I feel the universe is going to fall on me . . .' Stormont, 11 May 1774.

'Whatever dreams the levity of the country may form . . .' Stormont, 22 June 1774.

'The power of the throne is absolute . . .': Louis XVI, *Réflexions sur mes Entretiens avec M. le Duc de La Vauguyon*, ed. Falloux (1851), 109–10, quoted Girault de Coursac, *op. cit.*, 149.

'You are not very respectful . . .' N. Mitford, *Madame de Pompadour* (1968), 147.

'I am the King . . .' Stormont, 18 May 1774.

'What is the best way of correcting the morals . . .' Stormont, 18 May 1774.

'Extremely agreeable and *sensible*.' Walpole, 5 Dec. 1765.

'A timid, irresolute mind . . .' Stormont, 21 April 1777.

Louis began his reign with a bêtise. On 12 May he signed an order obliging Sutton, the English inoculator, to leave France in two weeks, 'pressed thereto by a cabal of physicians'. Sutton had held himself ready, if required, to treat Louis XV during his fatal illness and, according to Stormont, had behaved 'quite honestly'. Louis quickly recognized the injustice of his order and withdrew it. Stormont, 25 May 1774.

Louis's letters to Vergennes: Archives Nationales K 164.

Louis's reply to Archbishop of Paris regarding inoculation: Baudeau, Chronique secrète, 15 June 1774, in *Revue rétrospective* III (1834).

Buonaparte on Véri: F. Masson, *Napoléon inconnu* (1895) I, 454. He was taking notes from *L'Espion Anglais* 1789.

Louis's dismissal of Boynes: Véri, 21 July 1774.

Louis's hesitation to dismiss Maupeou and Terray: Véri, 9 Aug. 1774.

'I am assured that the first time the King went a-hunting . . .' Stormont, 31 Aug. 1774.

Louis's rehearsal of his speech: Véri, 2 Nov. 1774.

'His Majesty spoke with great dignity . . .' Stormont, 14 Nov. 1774.

Antoinette as a Grey Sister: Métra, *Correspondance secrète* (1787), 7 July 1774.

Hardy on the Queen's 'revolution': S. P. Hardy, *Mes Loisirs* (1912), 8 Sept. 1773.

Opening of gates at La Muette: Bachaumont, 25 May 1774.

'I am worried by so much popular enthusiasm . . .' Arneth, 20 July 1774.

Chapter 6: The Reformer

'The waterworks are out of repair . . .' Franklin to Mary Stevenson, 14 Sept. 1767.

Louis's accounts: *Comptes de Louis XVI*, ed. Beauchamp (1909).

Louis and the Prince of Nassau: Baudeau, *op. cit.*, 16 July 1774.

Turgot: D. Dakin, *Turgot and the Ancien Régime in France* (1939) and E. Faure, *La Disgrâce de Turgot* (1961).

Louis and the grain riots: Véri, 26 May 1775.

'Versailles is attacked . . .': Faure, *op. cit.*, 256.

Véri's opinion of the grain riots: Véri, 26 May 1775.

Louis's coronation: Croy, III, 168–210; Arneth, 23 June 1775.

'It is astonishing . . .' Arneth, 22 June 1775.

'It has been tiring . . .' Arneth, 22 June 1775.

The appointment of Lamoignon de Malesherbes: B. Faÿ, *Louis XVI* (1968), 129, using Malesherbes's papers in the archives of the Tocqueville family.

For prisons: John Howard, *The State of the Prisons . . . and an account of some Foreign Prisons* (1777). Howard visited Paris in 1776.

Chapter 7: More Reforms and a Reverse

Louis's early legislation: *Recueil des anciennes lois françaises*, ed. Jourdan (1823–9), vol. 23.

Saint-Germain: Croy III, 222–78. Closing the Ecole Militaire would also save money. 'On croit qu'il y a un marché fait avec les Bénédictins pour prendre de jeunes élèves à 700 l. pièce dans les Ecoles militaires provinciales; ils coûtaient plus de 5000 l. à l'Ecole militaire de Paris, à cause du faste et des accessoires.' 20 Jan. 1777. L. de La Trémoille, *Mon Grand Père à la cour de Louis XV et celle de Louis XVI* (1904) 122.

The growing attacks on Turgot: Faure, *op. cit.* 457–79.

'Sire, I see here only two men . . .' Véri, 20 Feb. 1776.

The Guines affair: P. Girault de Coursac, *Marie Antoinette et le scandale de Guines* (1962). The British ambassador believed Guines to be innocent. Stormont, 8 Feb. 1775.

Malesherbes's resignation: Véri had described Malesherbes to Maurepas in these terms: 'If you want to know his weaknesses ask the man himself: no one is more eloquent or more ingenuous about his own failings.' It is remarkable how often Véri accuses Maurepas also of being weak; Turgot accuses Louis of being weak; Joseph accuses Antoinette of being weak; Dorset later will accuse Loménie de Brienne of being weak. Each thought the others had more freedom of action than they in fact possessed.

'One notices on the King's face . . .' Véri, 11 June 1777.

Louis meets Antoinette returning from the Opéra: Bachaumont, January 1776.

Turgot's letter to Louis: *Œuvres* V (1923) 448 ff. Holbach said to Turgot after his fall: 'You were a good coachman, and you drove your coach quite well; but you forgot the grease for the axles.'

'The King finds it difficult to refuse someone to his face . . .' Véri, 8 Dec. 1775.

'The Controller General, learning that the Queen hates . . .' Arneth, 16 May 1776.

Chapter 8: The King at Home

Louis's choice of suits: F. d'Hezecques, *Souvenirs d'un page* (1895).

Louis and his valets: Véri, 6 Feb. 1779.

'Louis XVI was perhaps the most punctual and exact man . . .' Séguret, *Mémoires* (Lyon 1875), 13.

Louis weighs the Duc de Croy: Croy, 16 April 1776.

Louis's library: G. Lamdin, 'Louis XVI Angliciste', in *Etudes Anglaises* xxii (1969).

Louis and a Minister's dying son: the Minister was Henry d'Ormesson, Controller General in 1783. Private communication from the late Comte Wladimir d'Ormesson.

Louis's humility at a ball: Véri, 1 Mar. 1775.

Louis XIV was ill thought of at this period. Véri writes: 'Aux dépens de qui fut-il magnifique et généreux? La réponse à cette question détruit toute l'admiration que produit une fausse magnificence . . . On croirait souvent qu'il oubliait d'être un homme.'

Two examples of the changed mood at Versailles under the new King: out of respect for servants' feelings, sedan chairs were rarely used; and Blaizot, the Court bookseller, now published not only the old *Almanach royal*, which listed high officers, but also an *Almanach de Versailles*, in which every servant was listed, down to the scullions.

Louis's sense of humour. Another example is given by Bachaumont, 26 Oct. 1778. Louis was at Marly. He had returned from a hunt and, half undressed but neither shaved nor powdered, he was tracing the hunt on a map. Young La Roche, premier valet de garde robe, evidently a son of the zoo-keeper, became impatient; hoping he would not be required, he left. Louis noticed, had him recalled and asked why he had left. ' "Sire, je m'en allais." "Je le vois bien, mais où alliez-vous?" "Sire, à la comédie." "Et votre service, qui le fera?" Sa Majesté prend des mains d'un officier son bâton d'exempt, le donne à La Roche, le poste en sentinelle à une porte, lui fait mettre sur l'épaule ce baton, en forme de fusil, lui place elle-même sur la tête son chapeau de chasse, en lui disant, "Restez là." Elle passe dans une piece voisine pour se raser et se poudrer; de temps en temps envoyait voir s'il était à son poste: revenue, le congédie et lui permet de se rendre au spectacle.'

Louis on the close-stool: F. d'Hezecques, *op. cit.*

The luxurious clothes of Provence and Artois: Lescure, May 1777.

'The Comte d'Artois, forgetting that his brother is King . . .' Walpole, 21 Jan. 1775.

Madame Elisabeth: Fleury I; and the Life by M. A. de Beauchesne (1869). She possessed Louis's sense of public service and she signed little notes to Angélique: 'De Votre Altesse, la très humble et très obéissante servante et sujette, Elisabeth de France dite la Folle.'

'They had a damask tablecloth . . .' Thrale, 19 Oct. 1775.

Maurepas urges Louis to stop Antoinette gambling: Véri, 11 June 1777.
Maurepas était impuissant: Métra, *Correspondance secrète* (1787) I, 4.

Miromesnil's judgment of Louis: Véri, 15 Oct. 1782, in *Revue de Paris*, November 1953.

Croy's opinion of Louis: Croy, 10 May 1783. In January 1782 he noticed that Louis took all his own decisions, IV, 239–4.

Chapter 9: The Queen's Happiness

Descriptions of the Queen: Stormont, 8 June 1774; Walpole, 23 Aug. 1775.

Antoinette tells Louis she loves him: Arneth, 12 Nov. 1773.

'The French . . . have stood still in music . . .' C. Burney, *The Present State of Music in France and Italy* (1775), 31.

Antoinette arranged that Mercy's mistress, Rosalie Levasseur, should also use her influence to get *Iphigénie* accepted. Rehearsing of *Iphigénie*: E. Newman, *Gluck and the Opera* (1895), 138–40. Rousseau attended the first night and wrote to Gluck complimenting him on 'une musique forte, touchante et sensible'.

Gluck's dedicatory letter to Antoinette: *Collected Correspondence and Papers of C. W. Gluck* (1962), 162–3.

Antoinette applauds Mademoiselle Heinel: Bachaumont, 16 June 1773.

Antoinette's dress at the races in 1777: letter of Countess Spencer, 13 Oct. 1777 in Chatsworth Family Papers 1st Series.

Maurepas's compliment: Métra, *Correspondance secrète* (1787), III, 14.

'Her hair since her illness has fallen almost all off . . .' Lady Clermont to Duchess Georgiana, 20 Oct. 1776, in *Georgiana*, ed. Earl of Bessborough (1955).

Request for English country dances: Lady Clermont to Duchess Georgiana, 26 Nov. 1775, Chatsworth Family Papers 1st Series.

'There were no diamonds . . .' Thrale, 19 Oct. 1775.

Antoinette's debts: in his diary, 15 Feb. 1777, La Ferté refers to 'Des gratifications que la Reine a demandées pour les musiciens qui ont été au sacre, gratifications qu'ils ont obtenues à force de persécuter S.M.' *Journal de Papillon de La Ferté* (1887). This is not the only instance of 'persecution'.

Jeering at the racecourse: Thrale, 4 Oct. 1775.

The Princesse de Lamballe: Dr Cabanès, *La Princesse de Lamballe Intime* (1922).

Gabrielle de Polignac and Homer: Madame Campan, *Mémoires* (1823) I, 134–5.

Madame de Polignac's advice to Duchess Georgiana: 9 June 1784. Chatsworth Family Papers 1st Series.

Lady Jersey on Antoinette's manner: letter of 13 Oct. 1784 to Duchess of Devonshire, Chatsworth Family Papers 1st Series.

Life at Trianon: Madame Campan, *op. cit.* I, 98–100, 214–19.

For Lauzun: G. Maugras, *Le Duc de Lauzun et la Cour de Marie Antoinette* (1909); Baronne d'Oberkirch, *Mémoires* (1835).

The change in Antoinette's handwriting: see reproductions of her letters in A. Geffroy, *Gustave III et la Cour de France* (1867).

Chapter 10: The Neckers

Suzanne Necker: M. G. Parry, *Madame Necker* (1913); Vicomte d'Haussonville, *The Salon of Madame Necker* (1882); C. Herold, *Mistress to an Age* (1959).

Antoine Thomas: Michaud, *Biographie Universelle* (1865) vol. 41.

'We have for King . . .' Lescure, February 1777.

Necker's appointment and reforms: Véri, and P. de Ségur, *Au Couchant de la Monarchie*, II (1913).

'Of all the King's Ministers . . .' Arneth, 27 April 1780.

'The King has just published . . .' Arneth, 15 Feb. 1780.

'I found some courage when with the King . . .' Necker, note on Louis XVI written in 1791.

Louis's abolition of the question préparatoire: Edict of 20 Aug. 1780.

'He acts now in one way, now in another.' Véri, 4 Sept. 1780.

Chapter 11: The First Child

Joseph II: S. K. Padover, *The Revolutionary Emperor* (1934); F. Fejtö, *Joseph II* (1953).

Joseph's visit to Versailles and Paris: Mercy's letter of 15 June 1777 to Maria Theresa in Arneth; Croy, 19 April to 30 May 1777.

Joseph wrote to Leopold, 11 May 1777, of his sister: 'Sa vertu est intacte; elle ese même austère par caractère plus que par raisonnement.'

'The people were enthusiastic about him . . .' Croy, 27 May 1777.

Antoinette's letters on the progress of her marriage: Girard, 14 Jan. 1776; 19 Aug. 1777.

According to Lady Elizabeth Foster, Joseph told Breteuil: 'Being conscious that a Man's passions may hurry him wrong, and that when he is much in love there are moments when his reason cannot resist the force of his feelings, I have never gone to see a Woman whose beauty I fear'd without having first gone to see a Woman of the Town.' Unpublished journal of Lady Elizabeth Foster, by permission of Lord Dormer.

'He is a little weak . . .' Joseph to Leopold, 9 June 1777.

'In the conjugal bed . . .' F. Fejtö, *op. cit.* 167. Suppressed by Arneth.

'I'm longing for it to be true . . .' Lescure, 20 April 1778.

The birth of Madame Royale: Croy, 19 Dec. 1778.

'The King finds it necessary . . .' Arneth, 25 Jan. 1779.

Joseph's pressure on Louis to support him over Bavaria: Arneth, letters from 18 Feb. 1778 to 14 Aug. 1778.

'She is tall and strong . . .' Arneth, 16 Mar. 1780.

Chapter 12: Help to the Insurgents

J. B. Perkins, *France in the American Revolution* (Cambridge, Mass. 1911); D. Echeverria, *Mirage in the West* (Princeton 1957); Stormont's dispatches from 1776 until his departure in 1778.

'I know your Majesty's aversion to war . . .' Archives Nationales K 164.

Beaumarchais's career in L. de Loménie, *Beaumarchais et son temps* (1856).

Franklin in France: C. A. Lopez, *Mon Cher Papa* (New Haven 1966).

La Fayette: L. Gottschalk, *Lafayette Comes to America* (Chicago 1935).

'The King is naturally steady . . .' Stormont, 23 July 1777.

'No advantage . . . of our present situation . . .' *The Diplomatic Correspondence of the American Revolution*, ed. J. Sparks (1829) I, 356.

'By various means the English Government . . .' Archives Nationales K 164.

'Perhaps Dr Forth is lying . . .' Véri, 22 Feb. 1778.

'From the River St Lawrence . . .' N. W. Wraxall, *Historical Memoirs* (1836) I, 114.

Louis's inability to stimulate men to serve him: Véri, 28 April 1778.

'Shall we dismiss Necker . . . ?' Véri, 2 Oct. 1780.

Intrigues surrounding Sartine's dismissal: Arneth, 18 Nov. 1780.

Maurepas's dying words: G. Selwyn, *His Letters and His Life* (1899), 174.

'I am sorry to be obliged to add . . .': Gérard to Vergennes in D. Echeverria, *op. cit.* 92.

In the last years of the war the French fared well only in Indian waters; the excellent officer in command there complained, however, of the lack of discipline of his officers. R. d'Unienville, *Hier Suffren* (Port Louis, Mauritius 1972).

In connection with the early orphaning of some Revolutionaries, it is interesting that Boswell, in 1764, interviewed Rousseau and criticized *Emile*: 'You say nothing in regard to a child's duties towards his parents. You tell us nothing of your Emile's father.' To which Rousseau answered, 'Oh, he hadn't any.'

Louis and the turkeys: F. M. de Grimm, *Correspondance littéraire* XI (1830), 212.

'May I beg the favour of you, Sir . . .' Franklin to Vergennes, 3 May 1785.

Chapter 13: Peace and Prosperity

J. Necker, *Compte Rendu présenté au Roi* (1781). Profits went to Suzanne Necker's poor fund. Of Necker's dismissal La Trémoille writes, 23 May

1781: 'Ses conditions étaient celles d'un dictateur: l'entrée au conseil, l'administration particulière des finances de chaque département des Secrétaires d'Etat [ministères]; la nomination de toutes les intendances; . . . un lit de justice pour l'enregistrement de l'Assemblée provinciale du Bourbonnais.' La Trémoille, *op. cit.* 193.

Calonne's career and reforms: R. Lacour Gayet, *Calonne* (1963).

Louis's visit to Cherbourg: J. M. Gaudillot, *Le Voyage de Louis XVI en Normandie* (Cherbourg 1967).

'A certain gentleman brought an action against the King . . .' Fleury I 166.

Louis quotes Metastasio: *Secret Memoirs . . . published from the journal . . . of the Princess Lamballe* (1895) I, 205.

Antoinette wears her hair in a cadogan: Bachaumont, 18 May 1783.

'Lately, the Duc de Normandie being taken suddenly ill . . .' H. Swinburne, *The Courts of Europe* (1895) II, 15–16.

Argument about culottes: *Secret Memoirs* (1895) I, 224–5.

Le Hameau and the fête for Gustavus III: G. Desjardins, *Le Petit Trianon* (Versailles 1885) 257–9, 287–91.

Axel de Fersen's career: Fersen, chapters 2 and 3. Baron Taube's letter to Gustavus III, 20 April 1780, says that Fersen was good at blind man's buff and other party games enjoyed by Louis and Antoinette. R. Sorg, 'Fersen et Marie Antoinette' in *Mercure de France* ccxlv (1933).

Fronsac: Madame Campan, *Mémoires* I, 217, and Swinburne, *op. cit*. II, 13–14.

Chapter 14: The Temper of the Age: Science and the Arts

Louis, Joseph and the map of Antarctica: Croy, 19 May 1777; a further discussion about Cook on 30 Jan. 1780.

Louis's expedition to the Pacific: P. Fleuriot de Langle, *La Tragique Expédition de Lapérouse et Langle* (1954). Dorset says La Pérouse had orders also to touch at New Zealand, 'with a design of examining into the nature of the timber there, which, according to M. de Suffrein's report, is of an excellent quality for repairing Ships, but more particularly for masts. I can now inform your Lordship, from good authority, that 60 criminals, from the prison of Bicêtre, were last Monday conveyed under a strong guard and with great secrecy to Brest, where they are to be embarked on board M. de la Peyrouse's ships, and it is imagined they are to be left to take possession of this lately discovered Country.' Dorset to Carmarthen, 9 June 1785, in O. Browning, *Despatches from Paris* (1909).

Parmentier: C. Delon, *Parmentier et la pomme de terre* (1881). French agriculture lagged behind England's. In the generality of Paris the turnip was unknown as late as 1784, and Lavoisier said that land in England produced two-fifths more than equivalent land in France. The French were behind in manuring, and used English terms to classify soils: loams, steel-marle, chalky lands, etc. They were amazed by superior English drills, threshing machines, harvesters and mowers. A. J. Bourde, *The Influence of England on the French Agronomes* 1750–1789 (Cambridge 1953).

Buffon: Louis erected a statue to the famous naturalist. The proposed inscription, *Naturam amplectitur omnem*, gave rise to the criticism, 'Qui trop embrasse mal étreint,' and was replaced by *Majestati naturae par ingenium*.

The backwardness of applied science in France lies at the root of her weak economy. Even after the war of American Independence, France could not capture American markets. To the list of products which England pioneered or made better than France could be added many more, such as Robert Barron's double action tumbler lock, Henry Cort's puddling process, Coxe's diving bell, and the very short light carriage gun of relatively large bore known as the carronade, which helped Rodney to win the Battle of the Saints. A further factor in the backward economy may have been that one day in three was a holy day. Braudel et Labrousse, *Histoire économique et sociale de la France*, II (1970).

Balloons: T. Cavallo, *The History and Practice of Aerostation* (1785). Croy, who describes the demonstration at Versailles (IV, 308–9), was tremendously excited by ballooning, although an elderly man.

Anton Mesmer: M. Goldsmith, *Franz Anton Mesmer* (1934) and R. C. Darnton, *Mesmerism and the end of the Enlightenment in France* (Cambridge Mass. 1968).

On 24 Aug. 1774 Louis appointed as his artistic adviser (Directeur des bâtiments du Roi) Charles Claude de La Billarderie, Comte d'Angiviller. Born 1730, honest and with excellent taste, Angiviller worked closely with the King. He gave his collection of minerals to the Cabinet d'histoire naturelle. There is a portrait of him by Duplessis at Versailles.

A curious feature of the reign is the large number of paintings about death shown at the Salon immediately before the Revolution:

1785   *Mort de la femme de Darius*, by Lagrénée l'aîné
        Cléopâtre au tombeau d'Antoine, by Menageot
        Mort d'Alceste, by Peyron
        Mort de Priam, by Regnault
1786   *Mort de Cyanippe*, by Perrin
1787   *Mort de Coligny*, by Suvée
1789   *Mort de Sénèque*, by Perrin
        Mort de Socrate, by Peyron

The dairy at Rambouillet: *Connaissance des Arts* (May 1958), 80–1. The statue of Amalthea is at Rambouillet; the bas-reliefs are in the Wildenstein collection, Paris.

Sèvres: G. Lechevallier-Chevignard, *La manufacture de porcelaine de Sèvres* (1908).

Royal furniture: P. Verlet, *Le Mobilier royal français* (1945–55); Gondouin's models for Antoinette: *Connaissance des Arts* (May 1958), 92–7.

The Trianon garden: G. Desjardins, *Le Petit Trianon* (Versailles 1885); Blaikie, *op. cit.*, 136, calls it 'one of the first Botanick gardens of Europe.'

A para-literary phenomenon at Versailles was the craze for puns. The master of the pun was Georges de Bièvre. His father was a surgeon named Maréchal, but Georges bought an estate, took a commission in the Musketeers and became henceforth the Marquis de Bièvre. This prompted a friend to say: 'Marquis is too lowly a title; you should call yourself Maréchal de Bièvre.' In 1784 Bièvre tried to get into the Académie Française, but was blackballed by the abbé Maury. This prompted the pun, '*Omnia vincit Amor, et nos cedamus Amori (à Maury).*'

Bièvre once asked the King: 'Does your Majesty know what sect the louse belongs to?' The King said he did not know. 'La secte d'Epictète (des pique-têtes).' Louis is later credited with scoring off Bièvre. 'What sect does the flea belong to?', the answer being 'La Secte d'Epicure (des piqûres).' G. M. de Bièvre, *Le Marquis de Bièvre* (1910).

Louis's edict reforming the King's Music (Archives Nationales, O^1 842) reveals the short terms of service required to qualify for a pension: only 20 years for singers, 15 for players of wind instruments. A lavish pension system in every department was one of the built-in features of Versailles and, given the climate of humanitarianism, probably could not have been cut back.

Royal improvements at the Opéra: N. Demuth, *French Opera* (Artemis Press, Sussex 1963) ch. 11–13.

Antoinette's deadline for shutters: P. Verlet, *Versailles* (1961), 687.

'My dear Sacchini . . .' *Grove's Dictionary of Music and Musicians* (1954) under Sacchini.

Louis's liking for parody: Bachaumont, 12 Oct. 1777.

Mercier's working-class plays are *La Brouette du vinaigrier* and *Le Déserteur*. Antoinette also secured a performance of young Lemercier's play, *Méléagre*, on 29 Feb. 1788. The last lines are:

> Périsse, comme moi, tout mortel téméraire
> Qui porte sur son Prince une main sanguinaire.

After the first performance Antoinette kissed the author.

'There is a place called the Morgue . . .' Thrale, 23 Oct. 1775.

Madame de Genlis, Philippe d'Orleans's mistress and herself a playwright, claimed to be horrified by the coarseness of the English theatre – adultery treated lightly or jokingly – compared with that of France!

Chapter 15: The Temper of the Age: Religion and Philosophy

Religion in France: Thrale, 24 Sept. 1775; 25 Sept. 1784. H. Daniel Rops, *L'Ere des Grands Craquements* (1968).

'They contain principles objectively false . . .' and Louis's reply: *Procez verbal de l'Assemblée générale du Clergé* (1775).

'The King my grandfather exiled you . . .' *Annual Register for 1774*, 33. D'Argenson had this to say about *billets de confession* as early as 1752: 'La perte de la religion ne doit pas être attribuée à la philosophie anglaise, qui n'a gagné à Paris qu'une centaine de philosophes, mais à la haine contre les prêtres, qui va au dernier excès . . .'

Philippe d'Orléans's supper party: Bachaumont, 3 Oct. 1783. His role as freemason: A. Britsch, *La Jeunesse de Philippe Egalité* (1926) ch. 7. J. M. Roberts, *The Mythology of the Secret Societies* (1972), ch. 6, shows that the idea of a Masonic plot controlling the Revolution is absurd.

Eléonore de Sabran's visit to a fortune-teller: *Correspondance inédite de la Comtesse de Sabran et du Chevalier de Boufflers* (1875).

The tendentious edition of *Robinson Crusoe* comprises volumes 1–3 of *Voyages Imaginaires, Songes, Visions et Romans Cabalistiques* (Amsterdam 1787–9).

Saint-Just's *Organt* in *Œuvres* (1908) I, 3–215.

Chapter 16: Diamonds

Rohan's career: J. Munier-Jolain, *Le Cardinal Collier et Marie Antoinette* (1927). According to one story current in Paris Rohan was hustled away to Vienna because he had given VD to Madame de Mailly. Archbishop Coxe's transcriptions of private French reports: B. M. Add MS 9380 (vol. 203).

The necklace affair: the documents cited by F. Funck-Brentano, *L'affaire du collier* (1901) and L. Hastier, *La Verité sur l'Affaire du Collier* (1955), who prints the relevant passages from the diaries of Castries and Véri. But I disagree with Hastier's conclusion that the Queen watched the Cardinal make an ass of himself in the Grove of Venus.

The significance of the rose handed to the Cardinal has not so far been remarked on. It is best understood in the light of a passage in Duchess Georgiana's letter of 29 Dec. 1783: 'Magnetism goes on at a great rate and *transporting* which is seeing any absent person by gathering a rose – quelles folies . . .' Chatsworth Family Papers 1st Series.

The arrest: I follow Castries's diary, closer to the event than Madame Campan or Georgel, and Antoinette's letter to Joseph, 22 Aug. 1785.

The trial: documents in F. Mossiker, *The Queen's Necklace* (1961).

The Queen's yacht: Véri, 10 Oct. 1785.

Three senior officers of the Bastille asked gratifications totalling 9000 livres because the Cardinal's large number of visitors had involved them in tiring extra work. Louis granted the gratifications.

The louis d'or showing the King with horns: C. Muller, 'Deux louis d'or satiriques de Strasbourg', in *Revue d'Alsace*, 1931.

Chapter 17: An Ace is Trumped

General: Véri, unpublished diary 1787–8; J. Egret, *La Pré-Révolution Française* (1962).

'It is amusing to hear courtiers say . . .' G. de Staël, *Lettres de Jeunesse* I (1962), 139.

My evidence for believing that Louis played a leading role in planning the reforms of 1787–8 is twofold: first, Calonne's notes and memoranda to the King, for example for the Cherbourg trip, show that Calonne is taking as his guiding principles the King's desire to help the poor and to achieve fairer taxation – the two threads running through Louis's reform programme ever since 1774; secondly, earlier reforms had been initiated, and carried through, by the King in collaboration with his Finance Ministers. Stormont's despatches bear this out for the Six Edicts, Necker's writings and Véri's diary for the provincial Assemblies (which proved so popular that the *cahiers de paroisses* expressly asked that they should be kept going according to the *ordonnance* of 1787). After his flight to London, Calonne claimed credit for the reforms, but he was writing with the intention of putting himself in a good light and in the hope of being recalled.

The assembly of Notables: J. Egret, 'La Fayette et les Notables', in *AHRF* Jan.–Mar. 1950; Comte de Brienne et Loménie de Brienne, *Journal de l'Assemblée des Notables* (1960).

Gilets aux Notables: Bachaumont, 26 Mar. 1787.

Calonne's pamphlet, entitled *Avertissement*: R. Lacour Gayet, *op. cit.* 233–4.

'Everyone's mouth is full of complaints . . .' Véri, 7 Sept. 1775. As Dauphin, Louis had written in one of his exercises: 'Les Français sont inquiets et murmurateurs . . . on dirait que la plainte et le murmure entrent dans l'essence de leur caractère.' Louis XVI, *Réflexions sur mes Entretiens avec M. le duc de La Vauguyon*, ed. Falloux (1851), 177–8, quoted in P. Girault de Coursac, *op. cit.* 169.

Brienne's memorandum and Louis's comments thereon: Comte de Brienne, *op. cit.* 79–83.

Louis's advice to Madame de Chabannes, Lescure, June 1787.

'Caricatures, placards, bons mots . . .' Jefferson to Adams, 30 Aug. 1787.

The royal sitting: Antoinette to Joseph, 23 Nov. 1787.

'From the moment of his exile . . .' Marquis de Ferrières, *Mémoires* (1822) I, 11–12.

'Mr and Mrs B [The King and Queen] are both a good deal tormented but if their ministers *are firm* it will all end well as the people as well as the King hate all the Parliaments.' Dorset to Duchess Georgiana, 22 May 1788. Chatsworth Family Papers 1st Series.

'He is always afraid of being mistaken . . .' Madame Elisabeth to Madame de Bombelles, 9 June 1788, in Fleury II.

The Day of Tiles: J. Egret, *Le Parlement de Dauphiné et les affaires publiques* (1942).

Louis and the 2000 angry Savoyards: Dorset to Carmarthen, 12 Jan. 1786, in O. Browning, *Despatches from Paris* (1909).

'The Queen does not like . . .' Véri, *Journal* 10 Jan. 1788. Archives de la Drôme.

The Queen continued to be maligned by courtiers, including her former rejected suitor, Lauzun, who in 1788 became Duc de Biron. 'The Duke of Biron had wanted a grant of the survivance of the Marshal de Biron's regiment and had applied to the Queen to sollicit it for him. She had told him that if he would apply himself to the King, she would support his application but did not choose to mention it first. Letters had passed between them on the subject, and one day, when she was getting on horseback, and Mr de Biron holding her stirrup, she was overheard to say, "Si vous ne demandez rien vous n'aurez rien." Afterwards, not obtaining the regiment, he quarrelled with the Queen, and having then an intrigue with Mme de Coigny he gave her the Queen's letters, which were perfectly innocent. But Mme de Coigny by selecting particular passages to which she gave unequivocal sense, and by getting hold of the expression above mentioned, and perverting it, contrived to make out a plausible story as if the Queen had been on the same footing with Biron as she herself was known to be, which story she circulated and made use of at political meetings, held at her house, in order to ruin the Queen.' *The Glenbervie Journals*, edited W. Sichel (1910), 74.

'I have just written three lines to M. Necker . . .' Antoinette to Mercy, 25 Aug. 1788, in La Rocheterie.

'Today the King received a packet of letters . . .' 26 Sept. 1788, Fleury II.

Malesherbes's advice to Louis: Véri, *Journal* 5 Oct. 1788. Archives de la Drôme.

'I regarded Louis XVI with admiration . . .' C. Desmoulins, *La France Libre*, in *Œuvres* (1874) I, 121.

Chapter 18: The States General

Shortly before the States General met Louis had a narrow escape from death. 'His Majesty was walking upon the leads of the Château which look upon a Marble Court, and was desirous of entering his Observatory, but not being able to pass the Stair-case on account of the Workmen who were repairing it, attempted to mount by means of a ladder which happened to have been placed there; when His Majesty had however ascended five or six of the rounds, the ladder, not being made fast, began to slip sideways at its top towards the Marble Court, into which he would in all probability have fallen the depth of at least 40 feet, had not one of the Workmen, who observed the King's situation, with great presence of mind seized the King in his arms and by that means saved Him from the danger to which he was exposed: His Majesty has settled out of his privy-purse an annuity of 1200 livres upon the Workman.' Dorset to the Duke of Leeds, 9 April 1789 in O. Browning, *Despatches from Paris* (1910).

Recueil de Documents relatifs aux Séances des Etats Generaux, ed. Lefebvre et Terraine (1953, 1962).

Sunday's procession of the three orders was watched by the King's younger children from the balcony of a private house. With typical thoroughness Gabrielle de Polignac had a surveyor examine the structure of the balcony to ensure that it was quite safe. *Recueil*, 119.

Louis's opening speech, *Recueil*, 201-2.

Etiquette as a barrier to Louis receiving members of the Third: Bailly, *Mémoires* (1821), 5 June 1789.

The Trianon encrusted with diamonds: Madame Campan, *Mémoires* (1823) II, 37.

'One hip is higher than the other . . .' Antoinette to Joseph, 22 Feb. 1788, in La Rocheterie. Already on 22 May 1788 Dorset had written to Duchess Georgiana: 'The Dauphin will certainly die.' Chatsworth Family Papers.

Talleyrand's letter to Louis: *Recueil*, part II (1962), 324-6.

Young's comment on Louis's plan: Young, 23 June 1789.

Mirabeau's speech: Duc de Castries, *Mirabeau* (1960), 328.

'The King went pale . . .' The testimony comes from Louis Philippe, an eyewitness. *Mémoires de Louis Philippe Duc d'Orléans*, I (1973).

'People are attacked in full daylight . . .' Letter of M. de La Bellangerais, 29 June 1789, in A. Le Muy, *Le XVIIIe siècle breton* (Rennes 1931).

Lady Elizabeth Foster's visit to Versailles in June–July 1789: D. M. Stuart, *Dearest Bess* (1955), 46-7.

Chapter 19: Captured

'If you want him to live, don't suffocate him . . .' Fleury I 246n. On crowds generally, G. Rudé, *The Crowd in the French Revolution* (1959).

Economic conditions in Paris: M. Reinhard, *La Chute de la Royauté* (1969). From Aug. 1788 to Nov. 1790 the Government spent about 74 m. livres on the importation of grain. S. T. McCloy, *Government Assistance in Eighteenth Century France* (Durham, N.C. 1946).

Desmoulins's description of the Palais Royal: letter to his father 1 July in *Œuvres* (1874) II, 322-5.

Besenval's softness emerges from the *journal de marche* of the Salis-Samade regiment, published by J. Godechot, *La Prise de la Bastille* (1965), 238-9. Besenval's *Mémoires* (1805) offer the predictable excuse that he had been given no clear orders.

Assault on the Bastille: J. Godechot, *op. cit.*, with full bibliography.

Launay's 'lenity and humanity': Dorset to the Duke of Leeds, 30 July 1789, in O. Browning, *Despatches from Paris* (1910).

Louis's activity on 14 July: J. Flammermont, *La journée du 14 juillet 1789* (1892).

'After Dinner walk a little under the Arcade . . .' Gouverneur Morris, *Diary of the French Revolution* (1939), 22 July 1789.

The Paris women's march on Versailles, and the procession back to Paris, as seen by the Saxon ambassador: J. Flammermont, *Les correspondances des Agents diplomatiques étrangers en France* (1896), 260–73.

'Let's soak her arms and hands . . .' *Correspondance inédite de la Comtesse de Sabran et du Chevalier de Boufflers* (1875).

'He was accustomed to throw his head very much back . . .' E. Rigby, *Letters from France in* 1789 (1880), 90.

'The people was all roaring out . . .' T. Blaikie, *op. cit.* 227.

Chapter 20: Diminishing Freedom

National guards following the King and Queen: Young, 4 Jan. 1790.

Louis's letter to Charles IV 12 Oct. 1789 in A. Mousset, *Un témoin ignoré de la Revolution: le comte Fernan Nunez* (1924).

The Dauphin's education: a document entitled 'Education du Prince royal' was submitted to Louis and annotated by him. Article 4 states that the Dauphin's gouverneur shall swear to bring up the boy 'dans les principles de justice, de liberté et d'égalité.' Louis crossed through 'et d'égalité', writing underneath 'mot à supprimer.' Archives Nationales C 184, dr. 113.

Mirabeau and the debate on the King's power to declare war: Castries, *op. cit.* 438–41.

Antoinette's message for Madame de Polignac: D. M. Stuart, *Dearest Bess* (1955), 2 July 1970. In September the Queen entrusted Emma Hamilton with a letter to Queen Maria Carolina of Naples, an unconscious kindness on Antoinette's part, for it opened the door to Emma's reception at the Neapolitan Court. B. Fothergill, *Sir William Hamilton* (1969), 254.

'We must inspire confidence in this unhappy people.' Antoinette to Leopold II, 29 May 1790.

'They cannot get away from the idea . . .' Joseph to Leopold, 8 Oct. 1789.

'How could Mirabeau . . .' Antoinette to Mercy, 15 Aug. 1790, in La Rocheterie.

'They are planning to legalize divorce . . .' Dispatch of Fernan Nunez, 12 Nov. 1790 in A. Mousset, *op. cit.*

La Fayette urges the Queen to divorce: *Correspondance entre le Comte de Mirabeau et le Comte de La Marck* (Brussels 1851) II, 57.

The Assembly's attitude to the Church: J. Leflon, *La crise révolutionnaire* (1949); A. Latreille, *L'église catholique et la Révolution française* (1946) and the mob's coercion of the Assembly: Fitz-Gerald to Leeds, 6 Nov. 1789 in O. Browning, *Despatches from Paris* (1910).

Louis's correspondence with Pius VI: A. Mathiez, *Rome et le clergé français sous la Constituante* (1911); J. Leflon, *op. cit.*

Ça ira played in St Sulpice: Dispatch of Fernan Nunez, 17 Jan. 1791 in A. Mousset, *op. cit.*

'O God, you see all the wounds . . .' B. Faÿ, *Louis XVI* (1968), 344.

Louis's coach stopped in the Tuileries courtyard: *The Despatches of Earl Gower* (Cambridge 1885), 22 April 1791.

Chapter 21: Flight

C. Aimond, *L'énigme de Varennes* (Verdun 1957); 'Deux relations de l'arrestation du roi à Varennes' *AHRF* July–Sept. 1972; S. Loomis, *The Fatal Friendship* (1972).

Pétion: *Mémoires inédits* (1866).

Louis's letter to Bouillé: F. C. de Bouillé, *Souvenirs et Fragments* I, 283.

Louis was obliged to pay 13,692 livres expenses in connection with his arrest and journey from Varennes to Paris: oats for horses, bread for the national guard, guns and ammunition, fitting up of rooms for the royal family, even 12 livres to the bell-ringers of St Etienne for ringing the bells for the *Te Deum* on his return to Paris. Archives Nationales C 184 dr. 113.

Chapter 22: The Choice

Louis's acceptance of the Constitution: 'He disputed every inch of the ground during eight hours,' wrote Madame de La Marck to Elzéar de Sabran, 'but the tears of the Queen, the imminent peril and that of his children decided him; they would all have been butchered if he had not written [the letter of acceptance].' P. de Croze, *Le Chevalier de Boufflers et la Comtesse de Sabran* (1894), 285.

In order to place Philippe Egalité in a more favourable light Louis Philippe, in his recently published *Mémoirs*, trots out the old Orleanist charge that Louis was secretly working against the Constitution; but the evidence cited is unconvincing. Louis's letter of December 1791 to the King of Spain is probably a forgery. *Découverte* no. 5 (1974).

The Civil Constitution in the diocese of Angers: J. McManners, *French Ecclesiastical Society under the Ancien Régime* (Manchester 1960).

'When everyone is taking the lead simultaneously . . .' Bailly, *Mémoires*, 20 July 1789.

Marat's career: A. Cabanès, *Marat inconnu* (1891).

Hébert's career: G. Walter, *Hébert et le Père Duchesne* (1946).

'The King believes that open force would be of incalculable danger . . .' Fersen 204–5.

'This winter [1791–2] submissively and with courage . . .' Bigot de Sainte-Croix to Louis, 18 July 1792. *Pièces imprimées*, tome III (1792) no. 264.

Antoinette's letters to Fersen and Mercy in 1791–2: Fersen 202–70; La Rocheterie II, 208–407.

Antoinette's visit to Blaikie: T. Blaikie, *op. cit.*, 230.

Fersen's visit to the Tuileries: Fersen 241–8.

Louis's energy in directing the war, hitherto almost unnoticed by historians, is attested by the Memoirs of Carnot, Mathieu Dumas and Cambon.

Dumouriez advises Louis to sanction the decrees: C. F. D. Dumouriez, *Mémoires* (London 1794).

Louis and the crowd on 20 June: *Découverte* no. 3 (1973).

The events of 10 October: Bigot de Sainte-Croix, *Histoire de la Conspiration du 10 août 1792* (1793); P. L. Roederer, *Chronique de Cinquante Jours* (1832); J. Moore, *A Journal during a Residence in France* (1793).

Louis in the stenographers' box: unpublished memoirs of T. Vauchelet, belonging to Monsieur Tarbé de Saint-Hardouin.

Chapter 23: The Assembly's Sentence

The royal family's imprisonment: J. B. Cléry, *Journal* (1823).

'It was about two o'clock when the butchers . . .' Maton de la Varenne, *Les Crimes de Marat* (1795).

The debate on whether to try Louis, and his trial, in Bouchez et Roux, *Histoire parlementaire de la Révolution Française* (1834–8), vols. 20–22.

J. Necker, *Réflexions présentées à la Nation Française* (1792).

'To a person less intimately acquainted than you are . . .' Gouverneur Morris to Jefferson, 21 Dec. 1792.

Robespierre: my characterization is based on his speeches and on the observations of those who knew him. Recent attempts to portray Robespierre as a champion of the 'little man' or of the people as a whole seem to me unconvincing, for they ignore the recurrent theme of his speeches: that a small 'pure' minority must control the 'impure' masses.

That Louis took his own decisions was emphasized by one of the speakers in the Assembly, Robert Lindet: 'Plus fort et plus affermi dans ses desseins que tout son conseil, il n'a jamais été influencé par ses ministres; il ne peut rejeter ses crimes sur eux, puisqu'il les a, au contraire, constamment dirigés ou renvoyés à son gré.'

'The bloodthirsty party of Robespierre . . .' *The Despatches of Earl Gower* (Cambridge 1885), 31 Dec. 1792.

Louis's will is in the Archives Nationales. It has been published in many editions and translations, including Arabic, and there is a facsimile of part of it in F. Furet et D. Richet, *La Révolution française* (1962).

Louis's last hours: Abbé Edgeworth, *Memoirs* (1815).

Louis's execution: Edgeworth, *op. cit.* and *The Wynne Diaries*, ed. Fremantle (1952), 186: in 1796 Cléry said: 'Louis XVI died with great courage and never showed a moment's weakness. His neck being so fat, his head did not fall at the first stroke and he was heard scream. The Queen had been kept in such piggishness during a great while that she was quite an eskalleton when she was killed. All her members trembled.' I am grateful to Mr Brian Fothergill for indicating this source to me.

The curtain dropped at a London playhouse: Grenville to Auckland, 24 Jan. 1793, in *Dropmore Papers* II, 373.

Chapter 24: The People's Sentence

Antoinette's captivity: documents in G. Lenôtre, *La Captivité et la Mort de Marie Antoinette* (1897) and E. Campardon, *Marie Antoinette à la Conciergerie* (1863).

Incident of the comb: L. F. Turgy, *Fragment historique sur la captivité de la famille royale* (1818). Another of the Temple guards, who was surly and taciturn and kept replying just by a nod of his head, the Queen referred to as 'The Pagoda'.

Antoinette's letter to Jarjayes in Baron de Goguelat, *Mémoires* (1823), 78.

Louis XVII's confession, Archives Nationales W297 dossier 261, is reproduced in A. de Beauchesne, *Louis XVII* (1853).

Antoinette's examination and trial: *Actes du Tribunal révolutionnaire*, ed. G. Walter (1968).

The Queen's correspondence with Barnave in 1791–2 was not treasonable or even two-faced: Gérard Walter, in an authoritative biography very hostile to the Queen (*Marie Antoinette* 1948), admits as much.

Trinchard's note: 'Je taprans mon frerre que jé été un des jurés qui ont jugé la bête féroche qui a dévoré une grande partie de la République, celle que lon califiait ci deven de Reine.' Bib. Nat. MSS. fr. 12759.

Antoinette's letter to Elisabeth: La Rocheterie II, 441–4.

Duchess Georgiana on the Queen's death: letter to her mother, 1 Nov. 1793 in *Georgiana*, ed. Earl of Bessborough (1955).

Fersen on the Queen's death: Fersen 310.

Chapter 25: Afterwards

Committee of Public Safety's plans for Madame Elisabeth and Madame Royale: *Dropmore Papers* II, 472.

There may have been another contributory factor in Louis XVII's fatal illness: 'Simon ne doute pas, quant à lui, que le Roi ne soit infecté du mal vénérien, quoique depuis la mort de la Reine on ne lui ait plus présenté de prostituées.' *Dropmore Papers* II, 529.

'Eléonore will never replace her in my heart . . .' Fersen 315.

'Praise during my lifetime is suspect . . .' Métra, *Correspondance secrète* 20 July 1775.

'A weak character . . . his courage in misfortune only resignation . . .' P. L. Roederer, *L'Esprit de la Révolution* (1815).

Among the most influential summaries of Louis's reign written under the Restoration is that of the Comte de La Marck, who was a close friend of Mercy and whose family came from the Austrian Netherlands. Resignation of course turns up: 'Il [Louis XVI] était parfaitement résigné sur ce que la révolution lui avait fait perdre du pouvoir et des droits de ses prédécesseurs. Je pourrais dire que, sous ce rapport, Mirabeau était moins résigné que lui.' Yet in the same book La Marck's own letters written during the Revolution depict Louis as active and far from resigned. *Correspondance entre le Comte de Mirabeau et le Comte de La Marck* (Brussels 1851) I, 107.

The hen-house at le Hameau inscribed '*Presbytère*': G. Desjardins, *Le Petit Trianon* (Versailles 1885) 202.

Index

Louis's family. *Above:* his father, Louis the Dauphin, in the uniform of a colonel of Dragoons, and his mother, Marie Josèphe, daughter of the Elector of Saxony. *Below,* Louis's brothers, the Comte de Provence ('Monsieur') and the Comte d'Artois.

Louis at the time of his marriage.

Antoinette at the time of her marriage. She had been taught the spinet by Gluck, whose operas she later championed.

Four of Louis's Ministers. *Above*: Maurepas taught Louis the
art of politics; Turgot ensured the freer movement of grain and
wine within France. *Below*: the Swiss banker, Necker, raised
loans to pay for the American war; Calonne encouraged manufacturing.

Louis in Court dress.
His jacket is of white velvet, with the insignia
of the Holy Spirit, France's highest order.

Antoinette, by her friend Elisabeth Vigée-Lebrun. The Queen wears
an inexpensive Creole-style dress, emphasizing her love of the natural;
her enemies criticized her for 'ruining' French manufactories by not
posing in a dress of elaborately worked Lyon silk.

Gabrielle de Polignac,
one of Antoinette's closest friends and later
governess of the royal children.

Axel de Fersen. After service in America he became Colonel of the
Royal Swedish Regiment in the French Army. At the Revolution he
remained in France as the King of Sweden's special emissary.

Antoinette's bedroom in the Petit Trianon. She chose the designs of the furniture herself.
Below: a table with steel and ormolu decorations made by Louis in his workshop on the top floor of Versailles and given by him to his Foreign Minister, Vergennes.

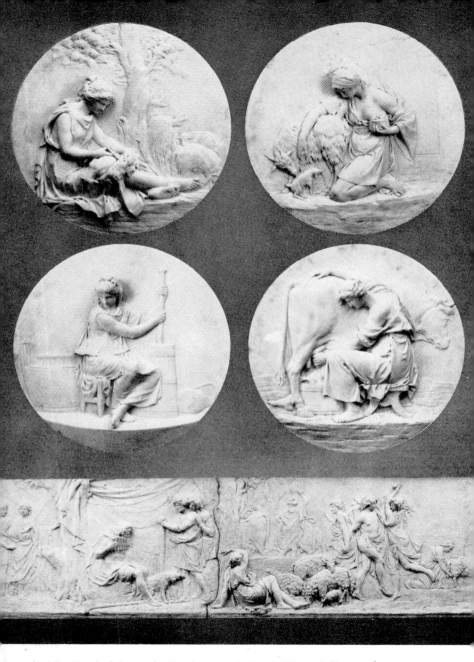

The Louis Seize style. Louis commissioned Pierre Julien to decorate Antoinette's dairy at Rambouillet with white marble sculptures. The medallions depict shearing, the provision of salt, butter-churning and milking; the frieze shows shepherds revelling, while, in the background, Mercury steals Admetus's cattle.

The Louis Seize style. Louis commissioned the Sèvres manufactory to make a State dinner service of blue and white porcelain. These plates, decorated by Dodin, show Meleager presenting the boar's head to Atalanta, and Andromeda being rescued by Perseus.

A gold coin portraying Louis with a cuckold's horns. After Louis had disgraced Cardinal de Rohan, friends of the Cardinal took their revenge by causing several such louis d'or to be issued by the Strasbourg mint.

Below: Louis aged thirty-two.

On 6 October 1789 2000 Parisian women broke into Versailles and forced the King and Queen to go to Paris. *Above:* a medal issued by the Parisian municipality idealizing the event: the Ville de Paris gently escorts Louis, Antoinette and the Dauphin towards their capital city; *Below:* a contemporary impression of the women.

Louis a few days before his execution, and Antoinette shortly
before the flight to Varennes. Both were under forty, but look older.
Below: the execution of the King.